I0609766

Japan's Orient

T90

Japan's Orient

Rendering Pasts into History

Stefan Tanaka

UNIVERSITY OF CALIFORNIA PRESS

Berkeley / Los Angeles / London

University of California Press
Berkeley and Los Angeles, California

University of California Press, Ltd.
London, England

© 1993 by
The Regents of the University of California

First Paperback Printing 1995

Library of Congress Cataloging-in-Publication Data

Tanaka, Stefan.
    Japan's Orient : rendering pasts into history / Stefan Tanaka.
        p.   cm.
    Includes bibliographical references and index.
    ISBN 0-520-20170-1
    1. China—Historiography.   2. China—Study and teaching—Japan.
    I. Title
    DS827.S3T36   1993
    951'.0072—dc20   92-20639
                                                                            CIP

Printed in the United States of America
9   8   7   6   5   4   3   2   1

*For my mother, Nancy Tanaka,
and in memory of my father,
Thomas Jiro Tanaka*

Contents

Acknowledgments

This project has developed over many years and has been influenced by many people. I would like to thank those whose help and influence appear both directly and indirectly—in a sense, this, like all books, is a collective project. Yet it is my voice that speaks throughout.

This narrative of my intellectual debts begins not with the inception of this research project, but with the realization that the histories of other people are rich and meaningful, even though they are often absent from or appear different in standard works. Stephen Dow Beckham introduced me to the importance and validity of constructing histories of the hidden, and Robert E. Burke nurtured that interest in a young graduate student who was being socialized into the profession of history through its margins. I am also thankful to Kenneth B. Pyle, who provided the basic historiography on modern Japan; it was his comment on a paper that spurred my interest in Japan and, now, other non-Western cultures. Although I do not remember the exact words, he responded to a poorly constructed sentence with the question, "Does any culture seek inferiority?" In retrospect, I see my error and his comment as a caricature of historiography at the time. We studied how non-Western cultures alter their societies in an effort to attain equality or superiority, but we used criteria and a framework that relegated them to an interpretive position as the perpetual inferior.

The vague discomfort I had with historical understanding was given greater precision by Tetsuo Najita and Harry Harootunian. It is to them that I owe the greatest debt for providing me with the stimulus and proper tools to pursue the study of history and cultural understanding. This book would be quite different, probably nonexistent, without their continuing attention to my ideas, research, and writing. I am also indebted to Akira Iriye, whose work to bring culture into the realm of diplomatic history—what today is often called intercultural relations—has also guided my work, and to William B. Sibley, who always seemed to make helpful comments when they were most needed.

For this study to be successful, it was crucial that I not go to either Tokyo or Kyoto University, where the legacy of scholars central to my project is still strong. The faculty and staff at Rikkyo University provided a congenial place for me to conduct my research. In particular, Gotō Ginpei introduced me to writings and scholars who facilitated and broadened my study, and Nomura Kōichi raised questions and points that have since become central components. Igarashi Akio, Kamishima Jirō, and Takabatake Michiō of the Faculty of Law gave abundantly of their time and provided valuable assistance. Goi Naohiro generously offered important advice, and Ogura Yoshihiko also made helpful comments.

The writing and rewriting of a manuscript is humbling; I have learned much from the careful comments and constructive criticisms of Talal Asad, J. Emiko Ohnuki-Tierney, Thomas Rimer, Robert J. Smith, Ronald Toby, and Frederic Wakeman. My colleagues at Clark, Paul Ropp, Michiko Aoki, Sally Deutsch, and Thomas Massey, commented on the manuscript at a later, but far-from-final, stage and pushed me to send it off. I am also thankful to those friends who have reminded me that this book is but a small part of life: Blair Ruble shared a common interest in life in the city and, intellectually, in ideas that transcend those discrete regions that now make up area studies; Akimoto Yasuhiro shared his knowledge of Tokyo along with good food and drink; and the now long-distance communication with Jim Fujii, Naoki Sakai, and Miriam Silverberg help sustain my curiosity in our field.

Financial support for this project spanned many years. I am thankful to the Trustees Fellowship of the University of Chicago for opening opportunities of which this book is but a part. Fellowships from the Japan Foundation generously supported one year each of language instruction at the Center for Inter-University Research in Tokyo and dissertation research. Yokota Kazuhiko, the person behind the Foundation, facilitated arrangements and represented the Foundation well. The Center for Far Eastern Studies of the University of Chicago provided support for the writing of the dissertation.

Finally, my deepest gratitude is for my parents, whose wisdom and spirit have guided my training, research, and writing; and for Kyoko, who has been most supportive and tolerant of the peculiar demands of my profession.

Introduction:
The Discovery of History

Nowhere has liberal philosophy failed so conspicuously as in its understanding of the problem of change.
Karl Polanyi, *The Great Transformation*

The various attempts of non-Western cultures to confront and adapt to modern (Western) civilization have been frequently recounted, almost always ending in incompletion or tragedy.[1] But these stories are usually situated within the same epistemology that guided the attempts in the first place—an epistemology that ignores the limitations and contradictions inherent in such change. These narratives, in other words, do not address the problematic of adaptation itself. Although the liberal and progressive ideals of nineteenth-century Western civilization may have opened new possibilities for some, it constricted, indeed repressed, opportunities for others.

In his search for the causes of the decline of nineteenth-century civilization, Karl Polanyi writes: "Scholars proclaimed in unison that a science had been discovered which put the laws governing man's world beyond any doubt. It was at the behest of these laws that compassion was removed from the hearts, and a stoic determination to renounce human solidarity in the name of the greatest happiness of

1. Curiously, today those who view Japan as a success story, whose beginning is traced to Commodore Matthew Perry's opening of Japan in 1853, consider Japan's Fifteen Year War (1931–45) as an aberration on this linear path.

JEDDO AND BELFAST; OR, A PUZZLE FOR JAPAN.—[SEE PAGE 758.]

Fig. 1. The Japanese ambassador confronts the arbitrariness of what constitutes civilization. He confidently asserts to the archbishop of Canter-
bury, "Then those People, your Grace, I suppose, are Heathen?" The
archbishop replies, "On the contrary, your Excellency: those are
among our most *Enthusiastic Religionists!*" *Harper's Weekly,* September 28, 1872, 756.

the greatest number gained the dignity of secular religion."[2] This statement describes both the problems of West–non-West confrontations
and our efforts to study them. We have tried to look at these phenomena using frameworks that seek the certainty of that secular religion,
forgetting that it, too, was a part of the historical problem. During
the late nineteenth and early twentieth centuries Japanese historians
had to confront the transformation of the various segments of the archipelago into a modern culture, but as a non-Western place, they also
reexamined whether a direct correlation existed between objects and
scientific knowledge and whether there is a Truth or a single correct
understanding.

An image from the London *Punch* (Fig. 1) illustrates well the complexity of this issue as seen across cultures.[3] Upon witnessing the violence of rioters in Belfast, Japanese elites question the categories of civilized and barbarian. Objective knowledge in this image is conveyed in
the attire: the Western gentlemen in modern fashions and the Japanese

2. Karl Polanyi, *The Great Transformation* (1944; Boston: Beacon Press, 1957), 102.
3. From *Harper's Weekly,* September 28, 1872, 756; explanatory text on 758.

visitors in their quaint and traditional samurai outfits. The picture embeds the epistemological distinctions between Occident/Orient, civilized/barbarian, modern/traditional, rational/nonrational, advanced/backward, knower/known, and so forth. The caption, in turn, raises the problematics of that objectivism. One fundamental problem is seen to emerge from industrial change: the dislocation of human society and loss of compassion in favor of an objectivistic measure—"the greatest happiness of the greatest number." A second lies in the Western definition of itself as the most civilized: the boisterous and violent become the "most *enthusiastic religionists*," while aristocratic Japanese remain heathen. A third problem has to do with the role of religiosity in constructing and maintaining belief in such self-representation. Fourth and finally, what is progressive and objective to one group might be restrictive and arbitrary to those who are objectified. In confronting these issues, Japanese faced the dilemma that is a main focus of this book; how to become modern while simultaneously shedding the objectivistic category of Oriental and yet not lose an identity.

The *Punch* image also displays the cultural specificity of history—the temporality implicit in images of a backward Orient and a modern West reaffirms the superiority of the West over its past, the Orient. Japanese intellectuals of the late nineteenth century recognized the historical nature of the relation between objects and knowledge as well as the centrality of religiosity. But as I will show in this book, this recognition led not to rejection and a different conception of knowledge, usually labeled as traditionalistic, but to an adjustment in which objects and knowledge were made to correspond with a Japanese perspective. The major Japanese historians, in short, accepted the possibility of Truth, objectivity, and progress—a belief in the scientific study of man generally and, more specifically, in Western Enlightenment and Romantic historiography—but not necessarily as set forth by Europeans. *Tōyō* (lit., eastern seas, normally translated as the Orient) became the archives—the pasts—from which history could be constructed. The leading object within that realm was *shina*.

Shina is the Japanese appellation for China most commonly used during the first half of the twentieth century. After World War II the name for China reverted to *chūgoku* (Middle Kingdom), a common name from before the Meiji Restoration (1868).[4] Throughout much of

---

4. A small number of people shifted to the name *chūgoku* during the 1930s, Takeuchi Yoshimi being one of them. However, to the extent that the major domestic newspapers are a guide, general usage did not change until after the war. See Takeuchi Yoshimi, *Chūgoku o shiru tame ni*, vol. 1 (Tokyo: Chikuma Shobō, 1967), 70–81.

Japan's modern period various groups used *shina* to emphasize differ-ence: nativist (*kokugaku*) scholars, for example, used *shina* to separate Japan from the barbarian/civilized or outer/inner implication of the term *chūgoku;* early-twentieth-century Chinese revolutionaries used it to distinguish themselves from the Manchus of the Ch'ing dynasty (1644–1912); and in early-twentieth-century Japan, *shina* emerged as a word that signified China as a troubled place mired in its past, in con-trast to Japan, a modern Asian nation.

While *shina* and *nippon* (the prewar and more nationalistic pronun-ciation of *nihon*—Japan) represent territorial constructions of nation-states, a broader geocultural notion of territoriality, *tōyō*, was formu-lated to encompass those parts. In a 1936 article, Tsuda Sōkichi (1873–1961), a historian at Waseda University, while recognizing sev-eral different uses of this word before the Bakumatsu period (1853–68), argued that the meaning of *tōyō* after the Meiji Restoration became simply "that which was not the Occident."[5] As a geocultural entity, *tōyō* is essentially a twentieth-century Japanese concept. In its earliest form, it was most likely used by Chinese merchants to refer to the body of wa-ter around Java (the waters to the west along the Indian coast being called *seiyō*, or western seas). The meaning in Japan began to change with growing awareness of Europe. Honda Toshiaki divided the Eur-asian continent into *seiyō* (West) and *tōyō* (East) in his *Seiiki monogatari* (1798) when comparing the trade of England and Japan, and by the mid–nineteenth century Sakuma Shōzan used *tōyō* to refer to Eastern values in his often quoted phrase "Eastern ethics as base, Western tech-niques as means" (*tōyō dōtoku, seiyō gei*). During the 1880s, *tōyō* appeared in a number of publications as an appellation for the culture of the East, and by the twentieth century the term, as used for example by Inoue Tetsujirō (1855–1944), Tokutomi Sohō (1863–1957), and Shiratori Kurakichi (1865–1942), signified the opposite of the Occi-dent, including especially those characteristics connected with Oriental civilization (*tōyō no bunmei*) and peace (*tōyō no heiwa*), but generally ex-cluding politics and conflict.[6]

In his criticism disputing the existence of *tōyō*, Tsuda pointed to the importance of the relation between history and language in the formu-lation of the twentieth-century meaning of *shina*. He wrote,

5. Tsuda Sōkichi, *Shina shisō to nihon* (Tokyo: Iwanami Shinsho, 1938), 112. Part two, "Tōyō to wa nanka?" was first published as "Bunka shijō ni okeru tōyō no toku-shokusei," *Tōyō shichō* (Tokyo: Iwanami shoten, 1936).
6. Katō Yūzō, *Kikō zuisō: tōyō no kindai* (Tokyo: Asahi Sensho, 1977), 149–64.

The odd proclamation that the culture of the Occident is materialist and that of the Orient is spiritual is a conspicuous example [of the continuation of Sakuma's "Eastern ethics as base, Western techniques as means"]. Those making such statements are, at the very least, half Sinophiles, and their so-called *tōyō* is primarily China [*shina*]. They use Chinese thought in opposition to Western thought, but because they are Japanese and the other is labeled Occidental [*seiyō*] thought, they call it oriental thought [*tōyō shisō*]. Therefore there is a latent belief here that Japanese thought developed from Chinese thought, particularly Confucian concepts. As a result, it is subservient [*jūzoku*].[7]

Shina, Tsuda has pointed out, was revived historically during the late nineteenth and twentieth centuries and transformed into an object within Japan's new ideological (broadly construed) space, represented by *tōyō*. In other words, *tōyō* provided the conceptual arena in which to make claims for an area as well as a cultural typology that encompassed and located both *shina* and other Asian entities.

In spite (or perhaps because) of the general acceptance of the term *chūgoku* for China since World War II, some contemporary observers, such as Enoki Kazuo, professor emeritus of Oriental history at the University of Tokyo and director of the Tōyō Bunko (Oriental Library) in Tokyo, remain dissatisfied. In the postscript to his book *Yōroppa to ajia* (Europe and Asia), published in 1983, Enoki discusses the different discursive fields represented in the names *chūgoku* and *shina*, though admittedly with intentions antithetical to this book. Nevertheless, he recognizes the fundamental importance of words in generating a certain understanding and in determining how people act. Enoki argues that the names *chūgoku* and *shina* do not portray neutrality in relations between peoples and nations—specifically, China and Japan. He asserts, moreover, that Japan should replace the current name for China, *chūgoku*, with *shina*, and offers four reasons. (1) *Chūgoku* is a name used by Chinese for their own nation; foreigners don't use it, and Japanese, too, are foreigners. (2) The term *shina* has historical roots in Japan extending far beyond the Meiji Restoration. The term probably entered Japan in the early ninth century in the sutras that Kōbō Taishi (Kūkai) brought back from China, sutras that Arai Hakuseki in turn used to select the characters for *shina* in reporting that Westerners called China *chiina*. *Shina* became popular during the Meiji period (1868–1912) as a name with a broader meaning than *shinkoku*, the name used for the Ch'ing empire (1644–1912). (3) The name *chūgoku* implies centrality. It represents a culturally chauvinistic attitude that China is the center of

7. Tsuda, *Shina shisō to nihon*, 112–13.

the world, is older, and is more civilized than other cultures. That the West does not call China the Middle Kingdom indicates the inappropriateness of that name in the twentieth century. (4) Because Japan uses Chinese ideographs and itself developed from Chinese culture, a distinction between *chūgoku* and *shina* "must be made."

For Enoki the need for this distinction derives from his belief in progress and a hierarchy of nations:

> Today, when we are expected to investigate the conditions and history of a country or region through a global perspective and to weigh how those conditions can be improved for the region and world, the belief that it [China] is a culture that is the center of the world is outrageous and anachronistic. A country befitting the former China [*chūgoku*] certainly does not exist today. No, on second thought, even the social structure of the former China was far from socialistic and democratic in its ideals.[8]

Enoki recognizes the implications of the term *chūgoku;* China is not entitled to a level which suggests that it is superior to any other country—especially modern nations—in the world. More specifically, it is "highly improper" for Japan to use *chūgoku*, a term that implicitly accepts China's superiority. *Shina*, he argues, is the more accurate and neutral appellation; it derives from the name China used by virtually all countries of the world and is merely a term that had been commonly and unquestioningly accepted since Meiji Japan. In other words, *chūgoku* represents a time when Japan was weak and imported the culture of China for its own development; *shina* should now be used because Japan is a modern nation. It has liberated itself from the antiquity of the Chinese world order.

A different interpretation of the meaning of *shina*, and one that is probably more consistent with modern Japanese views of China up through the Fifteen Year War (1931–1945), can be seen in the following soliloquy repeated in each scene of Satō Makoto's 1981 rock musical "Night and the Night of Nights" (*Yoru to yoru no yoru*):

Watashi wa shinajin	I am a Chinaman
shinajin de wa arimasen,	I am not a Chinaman,
de mo	nevertheless,
shinajin desu.	I am a Chinaman.

One can justifiably argue that the *shina* of this play is an allegory for the alienated Japanese. As a philological object, *shina* deflected the sense

8. Enoki Kazuo, *Yōroppa to ajia* (Tokyo: Daitō Shuppansha, 1983), 319–24; quote from 322–23.

that Japanese held any ideological position over the Chinese and served to indicate the victimization of Japanese, either by the United States or by government in general. The Japanese themselves have become the oppressed, the *shinajin*. Indeed, one scene that includes a figure resembling a victorious General MacArthur suggests the imposition of the American political system on a weak and hapless Japan.[9] At the same time, this soliloquy indicates that the word *shina* was—and in fact is— anything but neutral; whether Japanese or Chinese, the *shinajin* represents an oppressed and victimized group.

It would be difficult to resolve the discrepancy between Enoki's *shina* and that of Satō, but to argue that one is right and the other wrong necessitates a historical narrative that locates the first use of the term prior to its generally accepted locus. My purpose in raising this difference is not to find that first instance, from which I might devise a new narrative. Japan, of course, has a long history of trying to come to terms with its relation to the Asian continent, and there are a number of fine studies which describe different moments of this relationship.[10] But a quest for firsts or a hopeless debate on representativeness and typicality only conflates very different historical periods into one typology, with an undue amount of power thereby conceded to the narrator. A principal theme throughout this book is this power of the historical narrative; it was in the writing of and contestation over the meaning of history that twentieth-century Japanese historians "discovered" the beginnings of Japan's historical narrative in *tōyō*, thereby locating its origins and its relation to *shina*.

My assumption, which goes against the orthodox view of knowledge, is that there is no direct correlation between objects and knowledge and that understanding is constantly recreated. This work is thus part of a growing literature in the social sciences and humanities that questions the possibility of a singular truth. In his book *Women, Fire, and Dangerous Things: What Categories Reveal About the Mind*, George Lakoff, a cognitive psychologist, states: "The approach to prototype

9. For a recent book that discusses the success of the American Occupation, see Robert E. Ward and Sakamoto Yoshikazu, eds., *Democratizing Japan: The Allied Occupation* (Honolulu: University of Hawaii Press, 1987).

10. See, for example, David Pollack, *The Fracture of Meaning* (Princeton: Princeton University Press, 1986); H. D. Harootunian, "The Functions of China in Tokugawa Thought," in *The Chinese and the Japanese*, ed. Akira Iriye (Princeton: Princeton University Press, 1980), 9–36; Hashikawa Bunsō, "Japanese Perspectives on Asia: From Dissociation to Coprosperity," in ibid., 328–55; and Marius Jansen, *Japan and China: From War to Peace, 1894–1972* (Chicago: Rand McNally, 1975).

theory that we will be presenting here suggests that human categorization is essentially a matter of both human experience and imagination—of perception, motor activity, and culture on the one hand, and of metaphor, metonymy, and mental imagery on the other."[11] On a different spectrum Mikhail Bakhtin, who has become popular in recent years among anthropologists, literary critics, and historians for his concepts of polyphony, carnival, and heteroglossia, describes human mediation through the multiplicity of words:

> The word in language is half someone else's. It becomes "one's own" only when the speaker populates it with his own intention, his own accent, when he appropriates the word, adapting it to his own semantic and expressive intention. Prior to this moment of appropriation, the word does not exist in a neutral and impersonal language (it is not, after all, out of a dictionary that the speaker gets his words!), but rather it exists in other people's mouths, in other people's contexts, serving other people's intentions: it is from there that one must take the word, and make it one's own.[12]

The interpretations of Enoki and Satō agree—though not consciously—in this assumption that categories are constructed and constantly change; both argue that the word—that is, its meaning—was created. If one accepts Lakoff's argument that human categorization is a matter of human experience and imagination, then the exact configuration and meaning of *shina* and *tōyō* are also human constructions that locate, order, and circumscribe geocultural regions. Giving a territory specific meaning is far from a neutral act.[13] Enoki's claims to neutrality necessitate the acceptance of underlying concepts and facts that support his notion of truth. Although claiming objectivity, Enoki advocates the recreation of a *shina*—based on a narrative of the past—that indicates the superiority of a modern Japan over China. In fact, his attempt to rename China as *shina* can be seen as an effort to return this part of the Japanese language from that which serves "other people's intentions" to his—that is, Japan's (especially prewar Japan's)—own.

11. George Lakoff, *Women, Fire, and Dangerous Things: What Categories Reveal About the Mind* (Chicago: University of Chicago Press, 1987), 8.

12. Mikhail M. Bakhtin, *The Dialogical Imagination*, ed. Michael Holquist, trans. Caryl Emerson and Michael Holquist (Austin: University of Texas Press, 1981), 293–94.

13. For the notion of territoriality, see Robert David Sack, *Human Territoriality: Its Theory and History* (Cambridge: Cambridge University Press, 1986). Sack defines territoriality, which he describes as "a primary geographical expression of social power," as "the attempt by an individual or group to affect, influence, or control people, phenomena, and relationships, by delimiting and asserting control over a geographic area" (5, 19).

Satō, too, recognizes that the meaning of *shina* is historical, external, and restrictive. In the final soliloquy to his musical, the protagonist exclaims,

Mukashi kara	Since long ago
shinajin to yobarete imasu, ga	I have been called a Chinaman,
shinajin de wa arimasen;	but I am not a Chinaman;
de mo	nevertheless
shinajin desu.	I am a Chinaman.

A second similarity between Enoki and Satō's protagonist (who is portrayed by different actors using the same mask) involves the powerful ideological implications embedded in the name *shina*.[14] Enoki can claim the neutrality of *shina* only because he assumes a certain relationship—the superiority of a modern Japan over an unchanging China—which to him this word embodies. Neutrality requires the acceptance of this temporal hierarchy, which locates constantly changing worlds within fixed categories. The resistance of Satō's protagonist to being a Chinaman likewise indicates the powerful meaning of the word *shina*. It has been applied by an outsider—Japan—and defines the nature of China and the Chinese. Moreover, it denies the "Chinaman" a voice, who is therefore powerless to escape from its constraints except, at the end of the play, through death.

The scholars who inform the structure of this book are concerned in some way with this tendency of language to unify. A common theme running through the works of Mikhail Bakhtin, Michel de Certeau, Michel Foucault, and Emmanuel Levinas concerns the boundaries of a dominant ideology—what Levinas has called a totality—and the restrictions and possibilities for autonomy given that ideology.[15] My purpose in using these scholars is not to deify them as "correct" thinkers. Each concentrates on different aspects of knowledge: Bakhtin on the

14. This play depicts thirteen moments in the thirty-six-year life of a person in Tao City. A different actor or actress portrays the protagonist in each scene, using a mask when playing this role. The thirteen actors and actresses also take turns playing the narrator, the *shinajin*.

15. See, for example, Bakhtin, *Dialogical Imagination*; V. N. Vološinov, *Marxism and the Philosophy of Language*, trans. Ladislav Matejka and I. R. Titunik (New York: Seminar Press, 1973); Michel de Certeau, *Heterologies: Discourse on the Other*, trans. Michael Massumi (Minneapolis: University of Minnesota Press, 1986); Michel Foucault, *The Archeology of Knowledge*, trans. A. M. Sheridan Smith (New York: Pantheon Books, 1972); idem, *The Order of Things: An Archeology of the Human Sciences*, trans. Alan Sheridan (New York: Vintage Books, 1973); Emmanuel Levinas, *Totality and Infinity: An Essay on Exteriority*, trans. Alphonso Lingis (Pittsburgh: Duquesne University Press, 1969).

issues of finding and maintaining diversity in society; Foucault on the predominant systems of thought that underlie modern Europe; Certeau on those who act both within and beyond the discourse Foucault describes; and Levinas on the oppression of Truth. Neither does their presence in this work derive from a penchant for "abstract" theory; the goals of these intellectuals are strikingly similar to those of many early-twentieth-century Japanese intellectuals. Each seeks to uncover the fundamental system of thought in society, to analyze that thought through language, and to explore how people can function both as part of that system and as autonomous entities. Bakhtin, who went to the university during the Russian Revolution and was exiled to Siberia during the 1930s, succinctly describes the authority of language: "We are taking language not as a system of abstract grammatical categories, but rather language conceived as ideologically saturated, language as a world view, even as a concrete opinion, insuring a *maximum* of mutual understanding in all spheres of ideological life."[16] The early debates on the compatibility of the Japanese language to modern society, the drive to unify the Japanese language through education, and the obsession with the origin of the Japanese language are examples of this concern over the relation between language and culture in late-nineteenth-century Japan.[17]

Implicit in this view is the idea that language constantly changes; the meaning contained in words can change depending on the speaker, time, and space. In short, in the very appropriation of words and language, new meanings and contexts are created. Vološinov, a colleague of Bakhtin, states:

This social *multiaccentuality* of the ideological sign is a very crucial aspect. By and large, it is thanks to this intersecting of accents that a sign maintains its vitality and dynamism and the capacity for further development. A sign that has been withdrawn from the pressures of the social struggle ... inevitably loses force, degenerating into allegory and becoming the object not of live social intelligibility but of philological comprehension. The historical memory of mankind is full of such worn out ideological signs incapable of serving as arenas for the clash of live social accents. However, inasmuch as they are remembered by the philologist and the historian, they may be said to retain the last glimmers of life.

16. Bakhtin, *Dialogical Imagination*, 271; italics in the original.
17. See, for example, William Braisted, trans., *Meiroku zasshi* (Cambridge, Mass.: Harvard University Press, 1976); for questions related to the origins of the Japanese language, see, for example, Roy Andrew Miller, *Origins of the Japanese Language* (Seattle: University of Washington Press, 1980).

The very same thing that makes the ideological sign vital and mutable is also, however, that which makes it a refracting and distorting medium. The ruling class strives to impart a supraclass, eternal character to the ideological sign, to extinguish or drive inward the struggle between social value judgments which occurs in it, to make the sign uniaccentual.[18]

While Vološinov recognizes the temporality of words, he considers historians merely recorders of the past. Yet such social memory is not the same as the histories written by modern historians. Such histories—or History—are not as mutable as memory. By reviving certain "worn out ideological signs," historians play a crucial role in imparting a "supraclass, eternal character to the ideological sign." In this context the historian is not just a recorder, but one who creates or affirms a single truth through use of objective facts, a truth that eliminates the contention over meaning and gives the sign its uniaccentual character. In this way, Vološinov's statement can be seen as a summary of the emergence and acceptance of the discourse on *shina* in modern Japan.

The vitality and dynamism of the sign was most pronounced in the early twentieth century, when discussion of Japan's own sense of self in relation to Asia, Europe, and the United States was prevalent. As Tsuda has pointed out, the spatial locus of *shina* takes its meaning within Japan's formulation of a new geocultural entity, *tōyō*. My argument is that concepts embodied in the word *tōyō* served to unify the varied and disparate tendencies that existed in Japan during this period. The debate surrounding this term was not the first or only such discourse, nor was it farther reaching than others, but it did render a unitary language that gave Japan a new sense of itself and its relations with the outside. Through this concept, which contained and ordered the pasts of Japan and *tōyō*, the Japanese created their modern identity. As David Lowenthal states, "By changing relics and records of former times, we change ourselves as well; the revised past in turn alters our own identity. The nature of the impact depends on the purpose and power of those who instigate the changes."[19]

While *tōyō* was not created by academicians, this "new" entity received its historical and scientific authenticity in the academic field of *tōyōshi* (lit., Oriental history), which emerged at this time. Japanese scholars such as Shiratori Kurakichi, the principal architect of *tōyōshi* and professor of history at Tokyo Imperial University, used various

18. Vološinov, *Marxism and the Philosophy of Language*, 23.

19. David Lowenthal, *The Past Is a Foreign Country* (Cambridge: Cambridge University Press, 1985), 411.

pasts—those of Asia, Europe, and Japan—to "impart a supraclass, eternal character" to the concept of *tōyō*. In a rather self-congratulatory but largely accurate statement in the centennial history of the University of Tokyo, the author states, "One can say that Oriental history [*tōyōshi*] . . . established the historical perspective [*rekishikan*] of the Japanese, and the Department of Oriental History of the Faculty of Letters of the University of Tokyo has played virtually the decisive role."[20] *Tōyō* enabled the Japanese to fit the changes since the latter part of the Tokugawa period (1600–1868)—the decline of China, the arrival of the West with all its technical and cultural baggage, the new question of universality in human affairs, and the issue of cultural identity—into a comprehensive ideological system, the uniaccentual. The importance of this system was that it established—through a unitary, or monological, language—order and the ability for Japan to act autonomously. It defined their history.

The terms *tōyō* and *tōyōshi* present difficulties in translation, for they were a manifestation of the ambiguity of Japan's view of itself and position in the world. For the following reasons, therefore, I have chosen to leave these terms untranslated. On the one hand, *tōyōshi*, which developed to fill the void of the Enlightenment's "world histories" and supplement Western history (*seiyōshi*), can be seen simply as Japanese oriental studies (a contradictory appellation in itself).[21] Numerous Japanese historians turned to Japan's, China's, and even Asia's past to locate the artifacts that might narrate Japanese and Asian history—the progressive development of the mind—as defined by Enlightenment historians. By emphasizing the history of the East, as opposed to the West, these historians accepted and maintained a geocultural distinction between the two regions. But unlike the West's Orient, the term *tōyō* assumed merely cultural difference, not inherent backwardness.[22] The creation of *tōyōshi* thus authorized a particular Japanese view of Europe and Asia as well. It established modern Japan's equivalence—as the most advanced nation of Asia—with Europe, and also the distinction from and cultural, intellectual, and structural superiority over China. While Europe, as the West, became an other, that against which

20. *Tōkyō daigaku hyakunenshi, bukyokushi*, vol. 1 (Tokyo: Tōkyō Daigaku Shuppankai, 1986), 625.

21. For a fine study on the epistemological and ontological distinction between the Occident and Orient, see Edward Said, *Orientalism* (New York: Pantheon Books, 1978).

22. Where it is awkward to use a variant of *tōyō* to refer to Japan's orient, as opposed to the Western Orient, I have rendered the word in lower case: *orient, oriental*, and so forth.

Japan compared itself, *shina* became a different other: it was an object, an idealized space and time from which Japan developed.

The role of an idealized East in countering the negative aspects of Western (modern) society is quite evident in Okakura Tenshin's (1862–1911) *The Ideals of the East* (1904). The Asiatic culture that Okakura described possessed variations of science and liberalism but was free of the fragmentary, particularistic, and atomistic tendencies of Western societies. In many ways Okakura's Asiatic culture was a precursor to the notion of *tōyō:* it encompassed India, China, Japan, and the peoples in between; Asiatic culture was transmitted from India to China and finally to Japan; the Asiatic nature was characterized by its gentleness, moral ethics, harmony, and communalism; Japan's genius lay in its ability to adapt creatively only those Asiatic characteristics that were harmonious with its own nature; and Japan thus became the possessor of the best of Asia (it was a "museum of Asiatic civilization")—especially Buddhism, Confucianism, and art from ancient India and T'ang China. Moreover, it was Japan's destiny to revive Asia; Okakura proclaimed Japan to be "the new Asiatic Power. Not only to return to our past ideals, but also to feel and revivify the dormant life of the old Asiatic unity, becomes our mission."[23]

The broad outlines of Okakura's and Shiratori's notions of *tōyō* were quite similar. Certainly, there was no dispute that a *tōyō* existed: as Okakura's statement indicates, it was accepted as Truth. The question was how to revitalize that former state. But whereas Okakura's Asiatic culture involved a return to a past to regain a lost beauty of Asia and to counter negative and conflictual Western influences, the construction of the concept of *tōyō* was an attempt to extract from the past the datum for a positivistic history. In this regard, the notion of *tōyō* bears several key similarities to changes occurring in Europe during the eighteenth and nineteenth centuries, in particular the emergence of Romantic historiography and the European (especially German) "discovery of the Orient." In Europe, the neoclassical conception of historical time (chronologies and stories) was disturbed by the Enlightenment—the epistemological change from a finite world to a probable world. A history that amplified the finite world of states, major events, or persons was superseded by a new history that sought meaning. This it did in two ways: by separating the present from the immediate past and by searching for origins. As Lionel Gossman states, "The Enlightenment

23. Okakura Tenshin, *The Ideals of the East* (1904; Rutland, Vt.: Charles E. Tuttle, 1970), 223.

attack on tradition, the attempt to cut the present adrift from the past, was by no means incompatible with the idea that being cured of what was perceived as an alienated and weary traditional culture might involve a journey back to origins."[24] The student of modern Japan will recognize the parallel with Europe: the clear separation of the new Japan from its immediate past, the Tokugawa period; and the search in the ancient period for the "real" Japan (thus the Meiji "Restoration"). Whereas Romantic historians looked to the Orient for their origins, Japanese historians found them in *tōyō*.[25]

The formulation of *tōyōshi* and the development of the discourse on *shina* at this time should come as no surprise. By the Taishō period (1912–26) many of the domestic and international goals of the Meiji Restoration had been achieved. Yet all was not well. Tetsuo Najita describes the Japanese discomfort with turn-of-the-century changes:

A new discourse thus came into existence in post-industrial and post-constitutional Japan that in its basic character differed radically from the one articulated during the Restoration period, and that may be seen as the defining of a new system of action. Conflict was seen as a datum in everyday social and legal reality. At the micro level, expectation of achieving success and the fear of failure were viewed as constantly present in a new pluralized field of competition. At the macro level, dissension and consensus were seen as continually present along a broad range of organized conflicts. There was an awareness that the new constitutional arrangements had become a permanent fact; there was the recognition that through organized, legally sanctioned means legitimate political and social goals might be achieved; there was a general, albeit diffuse, sense of "failed expectation" about the course of modern development after the Restoration, and the belief that within the new order improvements were possible and overdue. In short, it was felt, all of society should be involved in reflection and action within the formal system of law in order to create legitimate and permanent spaces for justifiable goals, thereby interpreting the contours of the legal order in such a way as to make them less constraining and more encompassing of society's wishes and expectations.[26]

Internationally, Japan had nearly achieved the goals set out at the beginning of the Meiji period: the unequal treaties were renegotiated, the Sino-Japanese War (1894–95) gained Japan respect as a power in Asia,

24. Lionel Gossman, "History as Decipherment: Romantic Historiography of the Discovery of the Other," *New Literary History* 18 (Autumn 1986): 29.
25. See also Raymond Schwab, *The Oriental Renaissance*, trans. Gene Patterson-Black and Victor Reinking (New York: Columbia University Press, 1984).
26. Tetsuo Najita, "Introduction: A Synchronous Approach to the Study of Conflict in Modern Japanese History," in *Conflict in Modern Japanese History*, ed. Tetsuo Najita and J. Victor Koschmann (Princeton: Princeton University Press, 1983), 16.

while the Russo-Japanese War (1904–5) was seen to signal Japan's entry into the elite group of major world powers. Despite these gains, Japan had not achieved actual equality, nor had it alleviated conflict and differences with the European powers. Furthermore, these gains complicated its relations with the continent. Domestically as well, the promulgation of the constitution, the professionalization of the bureaucracy, and the broadening of the educational system did little to reduce political and intellectual conflict. Instead, conflict was construed as natural, but the arena in which it occurred had to be restricted. Najita states, "The problem, in other words, was no longer to eradicate conflict but to regulate it so that it would not be destructive to the national well-being, as might occur with an anarchic and mindless war of all against all."[27] This concern for regulation of conflict is apparent through what Carol Gluck has called the "Meiji ideology." The concern for morals, proper behavior, good citizenship, loyalty to the emperor, and so on were emphasized for fear of discord and disintegration.[28] *Tōyōshi*, too, was an integral part of this attempt to regulate conflict.

History here allowed the historian to "contemplate his origins—everything he has forgotten or repressed—without being destroyed by them." For the historian, the present was both the "child of the 'maternal' past and the architect of a 'paternal' future." As a child of the past, the historian was able to use history to avoid its pitfalls.

By making the past speak and restoring communication with it, it was believed, the historian could ward off potentially destructive conflicts produced by repression and exclusion; by revealing the continuity between remotest origins and the present, between the other and the self, he could ground the social and political order and demonstrate that the antagonisms and ruptures—notably the persistent social antagonisms—that seemed to threaten its legitimacy and stability were not absolute or beyond all mediation.[29]

But while the past could offer a sense of growth or progress, it also asserted a "paternalistic" mission to help the less fortunate. From this attempt to regulate conflict and bring a sense of order in a variety of realms—domestic, international, political, intellectual, and cultural—the centripetal tendencies led toward a unified language of *tōyō*.[30]

27. Ibid., 18.
28. Carol Gluck, *Japan's Modern Myths: Ideology in the Late Meiji Period* (Princeton: Princeton University Press, 1985).
29. Gossman, "History as Decipherment," 25, 24.
30. Bakhtin describes the ideological nature of this unified language thus: "A unitary language is not something given [*dan*] but is always in essence posited [*zadan*]—and

I have divided this study into two parts. Each is intended as an exploration of the relation between historical knowledge and contemporary issues, rather than a narrative of discovery, a last word, so to speak, on *tōyō*. Part One addresses the formulation of the notion of *tōyō* in Japan, especially in relation to the West (it is impossible to discuss the concept in isolation). Part Two focuses on the various attempts that were made to avoid a contradiction in *tōyō*. That is, while the concept was meant to give Japan a history as an Asiatic place, it also obscured Japan's distinctiveness vis-à-vis Asia, necessitated the construction of narratives that distinguished Japan from the continent, and, ultimately, became separated from its rapidly changing object of study.

In Chapter 1 I will discuss the changing conception of knowledge about Japan's pasts—from a recounting of notable events and people to a study of history as an objective and scientific discipline. This reappraisal took place within a vastly expanded intellectual realm, one not unlike that which found new importance in Neo-Confucianism during the early Tokugawa period.[31] The different frameworks for ordering time and space in the world histories of Europe offered early-Meiji intellectuals a new authority to reorder and explain their own history and culture. It is important to keep in mind, however, that Japanese were not attempting to adapt themselves to the new knowledge of the West, but rather to understand and incorporate that knowledge into their received knowledge and institutions. In his excellent discussion of the problem of nationalism in non-Western cultures, Partha Chatterjee describes this problematic: "The search therefore was for a regeneration of the national culture, adapted to the requirements of progress, but retaining at the same time its distinctiveness."[32]

Regeneration and adaptation reopen all a nation's different pasts, and spark contestation in selecting what is most appropriate to a new vision of the nation, the uniaccentual. Despite the diversity of explorations into Japan's past in the 1890s, a common feature was a movement

---

at every moment of its linguistic life it is opposed to the realities of heteroglossia. But at the same time it makes its real presence felt as a force for overcoming this heteroglossia, imposing specific limits to it, guaranteeing a certain maximum of mutual understanding and crystalizing into a real, although still relative, unity—the unity of the reigning conversational (everyday) and literary language, 'correct language' (*Dialogical Imagination*, 270).

31. Tetsuo Najita, "Intellectual Change in Early Eighteenth-Century Tokugawa Japan," *Journal of Asian Studies* 34 (August 1975): 931.

32. Partha Chatterjee, *Nationalist Thought and the Colonial World: A Derivative Discourse* (London: Zed Books, 1986), 2.

away from contemporary frameworks of enlightenment history and *kangaku*, the philological study of China. The rejection of both schools, I argue, resulted from the acceptance of the sweeping views of world development introduced from Europe. Having accepted a progressive and scientific conception of knowledge, Japanese historians, such as Yamaji Aizan (1865–1917), Naka Michiyo (1851–1908), and Miyake Yonekichi (1860–1929), faced the problematic of "de-objectifying" Japan—and Asia—from a unilinear concept of progress that confirmed Japan's place as a part of Europe's Orient. In other words, Japan was Europe's past and without history. It is through this recognition of difference that the writings of the historians of the 1890s should be seen as an attempt to establish a history for Japan. Yamaji turned to important figures in Japan's past; Miyake abandoned his comprehensive history of Japan for archeological studies; and Naka turned to China and Asia to unearth Japan's roots. In this sense, it is not "paradoxical," as other historians have argued, that these enlightenment historians turned to Japan's, or further to Asia's, past during the latter part of their careers.[33] But a contradiction does exist. For in the process of adaptation and regeneration, these historians were seeking to prove that they were not "Oriental," as defined by the West, by using the same epistemology of the West.

Just as these Meiji historians had rejected the objectification of Japan in enlightenment history, others disavowed the philological tradition of studying China. Several recent scholars have emphasized the legacy of *kangaku*, the academic field that *tōyōshi* replaced.[34] Yet this interpretation (which is challenged in detail in Chapter 3) is more a legacy of our—that is, Western society's—propensity to seek tradition in Asian thought, as well as the historian's emphasis on continuity. *Kangaku* stressed close textual reading of the classics and generally followed the style of the dynastic histories of Chinese historians. Yet even this conservative academic field was transformed during the Meiji period, when the decentering of China and the decline of Chinese learning and knowledge, begun during the Tokugawa period, finally rendered *kangaku* an anachronism.[35] Metaphorically, *kangaku* can be seen as the study of *chūgoku*; it was replaced by *tōyōshi*, the study of *shina*. Both

33. See Kenneth Pyle, *The New Generation in Meiji Japan* (Stanford: Stanford University Press, 1970), 88.

34. For the most recent exposition of this point, see Joshua Fogel, *Politics and Sinology: The Case of Naitō Kōnan (1866–1934)* (Cambridge, Mass.: Harvard University Press, 1984).

35. For a study on this decentering of China, see Harootunian, "Functions of China in Tokugawa Thought."

fields emphasized the close reading of texts, but it would be a mistake to extrapolate this similarity into a continuing tradition. The aim of *kangaku* was to determine the truth as defined by the classics; in *tōyōshi*, close reading was necessary to discern the true facts, which in turn explicate the progression and meaning of history.

In Chapter 2 I examine the contours of that new approach to history, which not only filled the void left by *kangaku* but also restored the centrality of China and Asia in Japanese thought. *Tōyō* provided the basis for a history (*tōyōshi*) by which Japanese, as Asians, could compare themselves against the West and at the same time, as Japanese, could measure their progress. As Tsuda's perceptive criticism quoted above suggests, *tōyō* was a perpetually changing entity that took numerous idealized forms, whether of a romanticized past or a troubled society. The pervasiveness in human interaction of this need for idealized others is succinctly described by Bakhtin: "In life, we do this at every moment: we appraise ourselves from the point of view of others, we attempt to understand the transgredient moments of our very consciousness and to take them into account through the other . . . ; in a word, constantly and intensely, we oversee and apprehend the reflections of our life in the plane of consciousness of other men."[36] Because the Orient was the origin for modern Western history, Japan, by turning to *tōyō* for its own past, made Asia the common ground and locus of comparison and contestation with regard to the West. In this way, Japanese were using the West and Asia as other(s) to construct their own sense of a Japanese nation as modern and oriental.

But as Japan's enlightenment historians were well aware, it is impossible to treat the Orient and Occident equally within the unilinear temporal framework of the European discourse on the Orient. To avoid this disparity, Shiratori and other historians sought a new basis—what Jürgen Habermas calls a prescientific philosophy of history—that would eliminate the unilinear notion of time fundamental to enlightenment history while still retaining Western scientific epistemology. In his criticism of positivism, Habermas points out that it rests upon a scientistic philosophy of history that serves as a concealed ideology behind claims of objectivism. He states, "Objectivism deludes the sci-

36. Quoted from Tzvetan Todorov, *Mikhail Bakhtin: The Dialogical Principle*, trans. Wlad Godzich (Minneapolis: University of Minnesota Press, 1984), 94; the transgredient designates elements of consciousness that are external to it but essential to its completion. For an analysis of the "other" as used in anthropology, see Johannes Fabian, *Time and the Other: How Anthropology Makes Its Object* (New York: Columbia University Press, 1983).

ences with the image of a self-subsistent world of facts structured in a lawlike manner; it thus conceals the a priori constitution of these facts."[37] The major difference between *tōyō* and the Western Orient was this a priori, atemporal framework within which different pasts were ordered into the uniaccentual.

Shiratori's prescientific philosophy of history was grounded in a North-South dualism, a dynamic process that governs all societies. He separated all peoples of Eurasia into the barbaric and nomadic tribes of the North, on the one hand, and the civilized and agrarian peoples of the South, on the other. The history that emerged painted Japan's external relations in terms of conflict—an inevitable and, when properly understood, productive result. This dualism (somewhat reminiscent of Herbert Spencer's division of societies into militaristic and civil) provided the general framework that explained the rise and fall of different national units, established *tōyō* as the mediating object between Japan and Europe, and located Japan's past in Asia. It also explained the individualistic, competitive, and alienating nature of Europe, whereas *tōyō* represented the hope that a peaceful and harmonious ideal would be reached through an oriental civilization that preserved loyalty, harmony, and communality.

But as this power to define one's own past suggests, the parts of *tōyō* were not equal; in Part Two I will show some of the contradictory uses Japan made of Asia. While *tōyō* enabled Japanese to construct a new past and to claim those characteristics which they argued were oriental, and thus timeless, the alienness of this new past made it imperative that they distinguish themselves from that same orient.[38] This separation of Japan from the alien continent was achieved by locating specific spatial and temporal units—such as *shina*—within *tōyō*. This process helped to objectify the geographic entity of China and establish it as belonging to Japan's past. The historical "facts" that were "structured in a lawlike manner" according to these redefined temporal and territorial categories confirmed, objectively, the truth that *shina* is Japan's past.

Chapter 3 focuses on the principal artifact that enabled Japanese intellectuals to claim both their orientalness and their distinctiveness: Confucianism. Confucian ideals, indeed, were pervasive enough to

37. Jürgen Habermas, *Knowledge and Human Interests*, trans. Jeremy J. Shapiro (Boston: Beacon Press, 1971), 67–88; quote from 69.

38. For a discussion on the problematic of the alien in national constructions, see Chatterjee, *Nationalist Thought and the Colonial World*, esp. 1–6.

support the notion of cultural transference within an Asiatic culture, as suggested by Okakura. This formulation thus showed development in *tōyō*, culminating with Japan's preeminence. But having been rehistoricized as Japan's past, *shina* was located as temporal inferior. Characteristics used to describe *shina*, such as atomization, bickering, and selfishness, distinguished it from Japan. Moreover, by using a metaphoric language of harmony, history proved the consequences of Japan's deviation from the proper historical path: it suggested what Japan should be—or at the very least, what it should not become.

As the separation of Confucianism from China suggests, the significance of *tōyōshi* lies in its creation of a Japanese self-understanding. By now it should be clear that this history is far from objective; these Japanese historians were formulating a unitary notion of a Japan that existed from the beginning of time. They were using artifacts—the pasts of China, Korea, Inner Asia, Japan itself—to create a history that, despite professions of objectivity, fostered a belief in the nation. In a discussion on the importance of historical signs to nationalism Peter Munz writes:

> Since the doctrine of nationalism required people to believe that every nation had existed for many centuries even when its existence was not socially and politically noticeable, the proof for its existence depended on the continuity of its linguistic and cultural coherence. Since not even that coherence was obvious to the naked eye, historians had . . . to demonstrate that the ruins and documents of the past . . . were part of the cultural heritage of each nation, monuments to the existence of cultural continuity.[39]

As Munz points out, credulity is crucial to the establishment of a nation. Knowledge must be impartial and frameworks universal; anything other might arouse doubt and uncertainty. To achieve these scientistic (and political) ideals, the human and natural sciences were merged, objectifying society and persons through fixed categories. People were not creators of texts from which history is produced; rather, history just happens. In fairness to these Japanese historians, their history did broaden the historical field from the dynastic histories of their predecessors, and the practice of their craft was as valid as that of their contemporaries in Europe or the United States.[40] Yet then as today, this practice deserves the following criticism: "The exact sciences are a monological form of knowledge: the intellect contemplates a *thing* and

---

39. Quoted in Lowenthal, *The Past Is a Foreign Country*, 393.
40. See Peter Novick, *That Noble Dream* (Cambridge: Cambridge University Press, 1988).

speaks of it. Here, there is only one subject, the subject that knows (contemplates) and speaks (utters). In front of him there is only a *voiceless thing*."[41] China—and Asia—became this "voiceless thing."

Despite the temporal separation of Japan and China, the transference of oriental characteristics, such as Confucianism, to Japan still implied that the Japanese were not really "Japanese," but rather oriental. The resolution of this problem—that is, the role of *tōyōshi* in defining Japan's essence, uniqueness, and destiny—is discussed in Chapters 4 and 5. To separate Japan from the Asian continent, these historians sought Japan's specific origins in protohistory. In fact, there was a revival of the question of the location of the ancient Japanese kingdom of Yamatai, reported in the ancient Chinese chronicles. This issue was important for two reasons: first, it established that Japanese were not linguistically, culturally, or genetically related to Malay-Polynesians, Koreans, or Chinese; and second, it authorized a history in which Japan and the imperial system were synonymous. The imperial system became that universalistic spiritual force that both placed Japanese within the history of mankind and made them unique. Like Leopold von Ranke's and Hegel's ideas on the combination of spirit and history, this Japanese variation allowed them to explain themselves as well as their connection to both China and the West.[42] And also like those German historians' propositions, it provided authoritative evidence of what Japanese should not become. As a result there was an eventual abandonment of the universal in favor of culturalism. In short, *tōyōshi* evolved from a discussion of Japan's position in the world to part of a larger discourse on Japan's *destiny* in the world, particularly in Asia.

The implication for power in this field of knowledge is clear. Knowledge here claims authority over its object. By rendering an external object comprehensible within one's own conceptual system, one has defined, limited, and authorized a certain view of that object, and it is within this field of knowledge that one acts. In his study *Orientalism*, Edward Said describes such a use of knowledge in the European discourse on the Orient, primarily the Middle East. Said shows how the French and British developed and defined a positional superiority; the Orient, as the past, was an object by which the progress of Europe could be measured. From this ontological and epistemological distinction, this field of knowledge developed into an institutional

41. Todorov, *Mikhail Bakhtin*, 18.
42. For a discussion of Ranke's spirit, see Chapter 1. For Hegel, see his *Philosophy of History*, trans J. Sibree (New York: Dover, 1956).

discipline that Europe used to create and manage the Orient: it described the Orient, authorized a particular view of it, taught it, and ruled it, all at once.[43]

What was not discussed in *Orientalism* is the dependence of the possessor, the subject, on its object. Japan, having defined itself in terms of the object, soon became captive to its own discourse. Its understanding of itself was fixed in the past, as oriental; *tōyō* was the source of Japan's orientalness as well as of the narrative of Japan's progressive development. But as the world changed—especially Asia—Japan faced a dilemma. Its understanding could change, but only at the risk of opening up questions of its own past; or it could continue to search for objective truth, as it defined it, and gradually be further separated from its object.

The final chapter of this volume examines how this separation between object and knowledge was possible. On one level, of course, this separation between Asia, the object, and the Orient is the problematic of the first five chapters. Although Said depicts the discourse on the Orient as a one-way relationship, the Occident over the Orient, the potential (or myth) of a reciprocal relation, the possibility of a dialogic exchange, provides a powerful motivating force to "be like the West" or to "modernize." One does not merely extract from the object, for that object might incorporate parts of the external discourse, or it might develop—or try to develop—a voice of its own. The attempt within *tōyōshi* to engage in a dialogue with the West by accepting many of the terms of Western scientific knowledge is an example of this reciprocity, what Bakhtin called an internally persuasive discourse: "In the everyday rounds of our consciousness, the internally persuasive word is half-ours and half-someone else's. Its creativity and productiveness consist precisely in the fact that such a word awakens new and independent words, that it organizes masses of our words from within, and does not remain in an isolated and static condition."[44] Power here can be based on consent. But because a culture incorporates the external object through indigenous channels and transforms that object, such a form of rule is difficult to maintain. Societies change, but the norms for determining objectivity in analyzing those societies do not change as readily or necessarily in the same direction. In *tōyōshi,* the creativity that was sparked became increasingly separated from and antagonistic toward the West, while still remaining modern. Both Japan and Europe had developed a discourse of self and of other, but each was rooted in

43. See Said, *Orientalism,* esp. 1–28, 201–84.
44. Bakhtin, *Dialogical Imagination,* 345–46.

different narratives based on a distanced, historical reality, one that ob-scured different viewpoints and realities.[45] From the Taishō period on, the value of the otherness of the West changed, serving increasingly as an example of what the Japanese should not become. The outcome of this clash of different, monologic conceptual systems resulted eventu-ally in the Pacific War, which Akira Iriye has characterized as one be-tween two competing cultural systems.[46]

The relation between power and this discourse on *shina* was equally compelling. In the years leading up to the Fifteen-Year War, Japan de-veloped a rather elaborate and sophisticated research structure focusing on China. But this research contributed to an increasing separation of Japan from the continent, not the reverse. Historical and contemporary studies on China and Asia merely confirmed what Japanese had sus-pected: change—especially protest—in China now came to be seen not as criticism of Japan's vision, but as ignorance. But this discourse was not restricted to what some have characterized as a historical discipline detached from reality; by definition, *tōyōshi* was an integral part of so-ciety—that is, Japanese society. This was true also of private and semi-private research institutions such as the Tōyō Bunko and the Research Bureau of the South Manchurian Railway Company. Here, the pre-scientific philosophy of history became submerged and was no longer questioned. As Said asserts of the discourse on the Orient, this dis-course objectified *shina*, defined it, authorized a particular view of it, taught it, and managed it.

The Chinese, too, attempted to engage in a dialogue with Japan, uti-lizing the same terms of Japan's discourse. Numerous students came to Japan to study, a seemingly positive response that no doubt confirmed to the Japanese the correctness of their view. Tai Chi-t'ao, a Kuo-mintang leader, marveled at the wealth of research on China that Japan had accumulated by the beginning of the Shōwa period (1926–90) and lamented that Chinese students in Japan did not study Japan itself; they saw little in Japanese history, literature, or culture that was worth studying and opted instead for English (which brought them greater monetary reward). The political implications of Japan's knowledge were not missed by Tai: "They [Japanese] have placed it [*shina*] on a cutting board and dissected it thousands of times. It has also been in

---

45. Bakhtin states, "The authoritative word is located in a distanced zone, organi-cally connected with a past that is felt to be hierarchically higher. . . . Its authority was already *acknowledged* in the past" (ibid., 342).

46. See Akira Iriye, *Power and Culture: The Japanese-American War, 1941–1945* (Cambridge: Harvard University Press, 1981).

serted into test tubes and experimented on ad infinitum."[47] To counter this objectification, Tai argued that Chinese must develop a field, *nihonron* (Japan studies), that would research Japan's national and social foundation: its character, thought, customs, and traditions. Such learning, he argued, was necessary to counter that of the Japanese. Yet just as the West had failed to listen to Japan, Japan failed to listen to China. When the Chinese rose up and transgressed the accepted tenets of this discourse, they were chastised. Naitō Kōnan (1866–1934), a contemporary of Shiratori and a Sinologist at Kyoto Imperial University, whom biographers consider sympathetic to Chinese culture, accused those Chinese who participated in the anti-Japanese riots after the Paris Peace Conference, and the Chinese youth in general, of being utterly ignorant of their own country's history and current affairs.[48] Naitō knew what was best for China; the Chinese youth did not.

The monologism of this discourse returns us to the soliloquy quoted above: the dilemma of the "Chinaman" was not in the name, but in the embedded meaning that accompanied and restricted him. The tragedy here, too, was that the failure to effect a dialogue with China led increasingly to a dominant position, one that entailed force and eventually war.

The central figure in this study is Shiratori Kurakichi, professor at Tokyo Imperial University from 1904 to 1925. I must emphasize, however, that this is not a biography, and those who seek one will be disappointed by the following outline.

Although not the "first," Shiratori is considered to be the scholar primarily responsible for the formation and formulation of *tōyōshi* as an academic and scientific field of history. Many consider *tōyōshi* of the prewar era and Shiratori's career as synonymous. Tsuda, a former student of Shiratori, best summarized Shiratori's contribution: "Throughout his lifetime he has made considerable contributions, directly, to the development of oriental studies and, indirectly, to the general development of history and other related academic fields. Also, his work has

47. Tai Chi-t'ao, "Chūgokujin ga nihon mondai o kenkyū suru hitsuyōsei," in *Nihonron*, trans. Ichikawa Hiroshi (Tokyo: Shakai Shisōsha, 1970), 6. This work was first published in 1928 in Shanghai. Tai obviously did not address this theme as *shina*, preferring the name *chūgoku*, but the field he was describing and its authority is this same discourse on *shina*. Paradoxically, although his book is a criticism of this prewar antecedent to what is now called *nihonjinron*, it is still to be found in the *ninhonjinron* sections of bookstores in Tokyo.

48. Fogel, *Politics and Sinology*, 235, 262–64.

transcended academics by contributing to our country's prestige; he has given our oriental studies a special place in world academia, and his academic achievements have also played a leading role in parts of Chinese academia."[49]

Shiratori was born on February 4, 1865, in Nagara-gun, Hasemura (near present-day Mobara), in the prefecture of Chiba to the east of Tokyo. He attended elementary school near his home, and beginning in March 1879 he attended the Chiba Middle School, where he met Naka, who is often considered the founder of *tōyōshi*, and Miyake Yonekichi, an enlightenment historian. In 1883 he entered the Tokyo University Preparatory School and upon the reform of the school system (1886) was admitted to the First Higher School in Tokyo. In 1887 he entered the newly formed History Department of the Faculty of Letters at Tokyo Imperial University. After his graduation in 1890 he took a position as professor of history and geography at Gakushūin (Peers' College), and in 1904, following two years of study in Europe, he became professor of history at Tokyo Imperial University.[50]

As a student, Shiratori was one of the first students of Ludwig Riess (1861–1928), who at twenty-six was hired to teach history and historical methods in this new department at the Imperial University. The creation of this department and the employment of Riess, a student of Leopold von Ranke, had a major effect on Japanese historiography, for at about this time enlightenment history was seen to have run its course and its proponents and critics were searching for new methods and broadening the field of inquiry. Riess provided a scientific, rationalistic methodology that corresponded to the needs of the new national university and training ground for bureaucratic elites.[51] According to

49. Tsuda Sōkichi, "Shiratori hakushi shōden," *Tōyōgakuhō* 29 (January 1944): 326.

50. I have relied primarily on Tsuda's biography (ibid.) for biographical information. But see also Goi Naohiro, *Kindai nihon to tōyōshigaku* (Tokyo: Aoki Shoten, 1976); and, for biographical and anecdotal information, Yoshikawa Kōjirō, ed., *Tōyōgaku no sōshishatachi* (Tokyo: Kōdansha, 1976), 15–70.

51. See Bernard Silberman, "The Bureaucratic State in Japan: The Problem of Authority and Legitimacy," in Najita and Koschmann (eds.), *Conflict in Modern Japanese History*, 226–57, esp. 234–38. Also see Byron K. Marshall, "Professors and Politics: The Meiji Academic Elite," *Journal of Japanese Studies* 3 (Winter 1977): 71–97; and idem, "Growth and Conflict in Japanese Higher Education, 1905–1930," in Najita and Koschmann (eds.), *Conflict in Modern Japanese History*, 276–94. For an essay that traces the genealogy of researchers on Japan's early modern foreign relations to Riess, see Leonard Blussé, "Japanese Historiography and European Sources," in *Reappraisals in Overseas History*, ed. P. C. Emmer and H. L. Wesseling (Leiden, Neth.: Leiden University Press, 1979), 193–222.

Tsuda, Riess emphasized the "objective" methodology of Ranke's history, though it is unclear whether he conveyed the religiosity that was integral to Ranke's theory of history.[52] Little is known of Shiratori's student days at the University of Tokyo, yet despite (or perhaps because of) the truncated view of Ranke that Riess conveyed to Japan, Shiratori's biographers agree that Ranke had a lasting impact on the young student, who closely read the works of that famous German historian. Tsuda, for example, emphasized Shiratori's objective methodology, inductive reasoning, and short, highly detailed monographs—the same qualities that are commonly attributed to Ranke. Hatada Takashi, a third-generation student of *tōyōshi*, has gone so far as to claim that because of its origins in such a positivistic methodology, *tōyōshi* was a study of history devoid of theory (*mushisō*).[53]

This emphasis on methodology is a principal reason why, despite a position on par with Naitō, his more celebrated colleague at Kyoto Imperial University, Shiratori has been considered a relatively minor figure in Japanese historiography. To be sure, Shiratori was not a major "intellectual" on the level of a Nishida Kitarō or Yoshino Sakuzō (1878–1933). Yet an emphasis on methodology certainly has some merit, and Shiratori worked hard to build a solid academic structure for this nascent field. His detailed monographs established a model for others to follow. In his twenty-two years at the University of Tokyo he taught and trained a considerable number of students and historians. He also worked to establish the institutional stature of *tōyōshi* as an interdisciplinary study. He broadened the area of historical inquiry to include language, mythology, and ethnology, and he actively participated in and founded numerous institutions dedicated to the development of this field: he was a charter member of the Shigakkai (Japan Historical Association) and became director in 1929; he became chairman of the Nihon Minzokugakkai (Japan Anthropology Association) in 1934; and he founded the Ajia Kyōkai (Asiatic Society) in 1905, which merged with the Tōyō Kyōkai (Oriental Society), publisher of the *Tōyō gakuhō*, in 1907. He was also among the first to work for the Research Bureau of the South Manchurian Railway Company, formed in 1907, and served as the initial research director (1923) of the Tōyō Bunko, Japan's premier independent research library specializing in Asia.

52. Tsuda, "Shiratori hakushi shōden," 339–40.
53. Ibid., 22–23; Goi, *Kindai nihon to tōyōshigaku*, 79–80; and Hatada Takashi, "Nihon ni okeru tōyōshigaku no dentō," *Rekishigaku kenkyū* 270 (November 1962): 28–35. See also Ienaga Saburō, *Nihon no kindai shigaku* (Tokyo: Nihon Hyōron Shinsha, 1957), 80–85; and for an account in English, see Fogel, *Politics and Sinology*, 119–20.

The image of *tōyōshi* as a methodological (positivistic) field has also been reinforced by recent historians, especially those who were trained in this field. After World War II, and especially during the early 1960s, when grants from the Asia and Ford Foundations spurred debates on the relation between academic research, funding, and policy, many scholars criticized the prewar study of China as overly positivistic, its studies too divorced from reality. For example, Hatada Takashi and Noma Kiyoshi, historians in the Research Bureau, argue that the methods they used, with their focus on objectivity, purity, and accuracy, distanced them from reality and obscured their view of the field's modernistic framework, which placed Japan between China and Europe. This methodology, they continue, facilitated their complicity with such colonialist institutions as the Research Bureau by obscuring political connections between their actions and imperialistic policy.[54] They locate the blame not in themselves, but in a modernist methodology in which the theoretical framework was hidden from their view. These scholars recognize that the positivist method privileged facts and hid a pre-scientific philosophy of history, but they fail to identify properly what that philosophy of history was, merely attributing it to "Western modernism." Ironically, the West here is still an "other"—no longer evil, but still the cause of many of Japan's prewar dilemmas.

A slightly later generation has been more critical. Goi Naohiro, for example, expanded the argument to suggest that *tōyōshi* scholars did not possess a sense of subjectivity or any class consciousness. Ogura Yoshihiko built on the same criticism but approached the issue by arguing that the problem resided in the "bureaucratic arrogance" of these scholars, and suggested that their narrow perspective prevented any broader view.[55] But like the earlier generation, these historians, too, stopped short of analyzing the broad ideological underpinnings of *tōyōshi*. Such limited criticism of Shiratori and *tōyōshi* in many ways indicates the successful creation of an ideology acceptable to Japanese thought, but it also points ultimately to failure. This success is in the transparency of Shiratori's fundamental theory, which his objective studies overshadowed. Indeed, his theory has reached the level of common sense—as Enoki's inability to recognize the discourse incorporated in the word *shina* suggests. The failure, despite the heroic efforts

54. Hatada, "Nihon ni okeru tōyōshigaku no dentō," 28–35; Noma Kiyoshi, "Chūgoku nōson kankō chōsa no kikaku to jisseki," *Rekishi hyōron* 170 (October 1964): 1–15; and Goi, *Kindai nihon to tōyōshigaku*, 70–71.

55. Goi, *Kindai nihon to tōyōshigaku*; Ogura Yoshihiko, "Nihon ni okeru tōyōshigaku no hattatsu," in *Ware ryūmon ni ari* (Tokyo: Rōkei Shoten, 1974), 35–59.

of a few, such as Tsuda, lies in the inability of Japanese intellectuals of the Shōwa era to escape from the hermeneutics that Shiratori helped to create.

Although most critics have emphasized the methodological dimension of Shiratori's work, a few scholars have reached deeper into Shiratori's complex historical philosophy. Even though Tsuda argued that Shiratori prioritized facts and opted for brief, objective, and detailed studies over broad sweeping histories, he also recognized Shiratori's awareness of historical trends. Enoki, too, recalled a statement by Shiratori that indicated how important he considered a conscious philosophy of history to be: "Because I write positivistic articles, many people believe that that is history; but such articles form the skeleton of history and are not true history [*hontō no rekishi*]."[56] Shiratori's project was more than a mere competition with Western Orientalists to uncover new information and areas of study.[57] If it is to be characterized as a competition at all, it should be seen as one to define the nature of Asia.

The goal of this book is not to write an "intellectual biography" of Shiratori, but to uncover this project of defining Asia. For it was in the effort to establish Japan as the authority on Asia, and thereby to engage in a dialogue with the West, that *tōyōshi* and the discourse on *shina* came together. The principal problematic faced by Shiratori and his peers was the conciliation of culture with civilization, or difference with sameness.

    56. Tsuda, "Shiratori hakushi shōden," 346; Enoki Kazuo, *Tōyō Bunko no rokujūnen* (Tokyo: Tōyō Bunko, 1977), 272. Yue-him Tam also recognizes a similar historical perspective; see his "In Search of the Oriental Past: The Life and Thought of Naitō Kōnan (1866–1934)" (Ph.D. diss., Princeton University, 1975), 215–23.
    57. For an interpretation that emphasizes such competition, see Goi, *Kindai nihon to tōyōshigaku*, 43–44.

PART ONE

Finding Equivalence

History as a professional discipline based on archival study and rigorous methodological training began in the nineteenth century. Whether in the work of Michelet, Ranke, Macaulay, or the university scholars influenced by them, historical writing was primarily concerned with the nation states in the West, their political administrative development, and their military and cultural expansion. A small number of historians also studied the ideas of elite thinkers, from Plato to Durkheim, that provided the intellectual fuel for the civilization of the West. Other civilizations were ignored, and indeed in each country most research and teaching was concerned with its own national history.

Lawrence Stone, Review of
The New History and the Old,
by Gertrude Himmelfarb

Narrative history always claims to relate "things just as they really happened." ... *In fact, though, in its own covert way, narrative history consists of an interpretation, an authentic philosophy of history.* ... *And when they [narrative historians] speak of "general history," what they are really speaking of is the intercrossing of such exceptional destinies, for obviously each hero must be matched against another. A delusive fallacy, as we all know.*

Fernand Braudel, quoted by Hayden White,
The Content of the Form

CHAPTER ONE

From *Kangaku* to *Tōyōshi:*
The Search for History

The impact of the West and the reaction against the West are common clichés in the history of Meiji Japan. Certainly, Europe and its culture played a major role in Japan's development, but too often that impact has been described as an "either-or" proposition, with those who were partial to Western ideas being extolled. Such a predisposition blurs an important problem of this period; that is, how could Japan regenerate society by adapting from the alien West while still retaining its own distinctiveness? The difficulty of this process is discussed in Peter Dale's provocative book *The Myth of Japanese Uniqueness.* Using Toynbee's characterization of the Herodian and the zealot to describe Japan's encounter with the West, Dale states, "The Herodian discovers that his adoption of foreign material culture to defend indigenous autonomy subtly alters and subverts the very values he strives to protect. He quickly learns that the imported infrastructure has a logic all its own, and that the 'mechanically propelled Trojan horse' of alien civilisation drastically disrupts and reorganises the social fabric upon which the ideology of his traditional outlook rests."[1]

Clearly, this process of encounter and adaptation was not new to Japan. David Pollack describes the place in Japan of a figurative and real China from the eighth through the eighteenth centuries in terms of a dialectical relationship between China, the alien form, and Japan, the native content. He uses the analogy of "a frog [at] the bottom of its

---

1. Peter Dale, *The Myth of Japanese Uniqueness* (London: St. Martin's Press, 1986), 47.

well, who would define its world almost exclusively in terms of its walls: the sky and world outside the well, the shape of the water in which it lived, its notions of security and danger, the proper dimensions and proportions of things, would all be most meaningfully expressed in terms of 'walls.' "[2] Regardless whether one agrees that there was only one alien and one native (which I do not), this relationship can be extended to include an alien West. In Pollack's metaphor, China constitutes Japan's walls, which changed during the nineteenth century.[3] The categories that were used to understand the complex events and processes of a previous age were no longer appropriate; the domestic discontinuities and the appearance of a technologically superior West could not be bounded by preexisting categories.[4] In the nineteenth century, therefore, new categories had to be created that would "render otherwise incomprehensible social situations meaningful [and] so construe them as to make it possible to act purposefully within them."[5] The bricks that were used to construct China were now seen differently; they were crooked, decaying, and even tumbling down.

This shift did not entail the simple replacement of China by the West. Using a different design but many of the same bricks, Japanese constructed a different wall, one that altered everything: the shape of the water, its security, and, in the end, Japan itself. The difference between the use of China and the use of the West was that the previous world was one in which all life was construed as being part of a fixed realm. To be sure, some intellectuals of the Tokugawa period sought to expand and even dismantle this age-old thought system, but they were very much in the minority. Even the radical Mito solution in many ways proposed a return to a purity from before the corruption of time, suggesting that the solution lay not in some new future system, but in a system that had already been tested and proven.[6] The West brought

2. Pollack, *Fracture of Meaning*, 4.
3. For the role and "decentering" of China during the late Tokugawa period, see Harootunian, "Functions of China in Tokugawa Thought."
4. For a discussion of these issues, see Tetsuo Najita and Irwin Scheiner, eds., *Japanese Thought in the Tokugawa Period* (Chicago: University of Chicago Press, 1978); and Najita and Koschmann (eds.), *Conflict in Modern Japanese History.*
5. Clifford Geertz, *The Interpretation of Cultures* (New York: Basic Books, 1973), 5.
6. Mito was a collateral domain to the ruling house during the Tokugawa period. During the early nineteenth century a number of intellectuals proposed reforms that addressed the growing disjuncture between the fixed ideal and changing society. These proposals proved to signal the decline of the existing government, the *bakufu*, rather than to reform it. For further information, see J. Victor Koschmann, *The Mito Ideology: Discourse,*

a different perspective, the probable future; knowledge was infinite, but to understand and harness it one had to understand the underlying historical laws that would indicate what was to come. The key to understanding was history.

Japan's earlier studies of the past had been used largely to affirm the status quo or to "discover" the errors of the immediate past; the notion of progress, however, transformed Japan's very history and world vision.[7] As a sociological study, history was no longer merely a strategy to describe what ought to have been; the focus now was what in fact is, what will be, and what ought to be. History, then, became not only the way by which Japan would know itself, but also its tool for relating, in the present and in the future, to a broad and uncertain geocultural world.

As Dale's Herodian figure suggests, it would be a mistake to assume that all Western ideas were accepted intact. Moreover, although reference was and is made to a singular West, this geocultural construction represented simply all those people, ideas, organizations, institutions, structures, and so forth that were over there in Europe; in short, they were not Japanese. The willing and even eager acceptance of selected Western things during the early Meiji period should be seen as Japan's attempt to participate with the West as an essentially equivalent—though not always equal—entity. Seemingly "Western" aspects might have been adopted, but the purpose was to effect Japan's regeneration; constitutionalism, modernity, rationality, and capitalism were merely tools for that regeneration. In this very process of adoption, the ideas accepted by Japan were altered. In the end, a new understanding of Japan, Asia, and Europe was created, one very different than that which had existed previously.

In this chapter I look at the process of change in the formulation of a history of Japan and how it led to the discovery of Japan's Asiatic past. This turn to an Asian past emerged from two problems that Japanese intellectuals encountered in their very acceptance of Western progressive historiography. First was the realization that the notion of universal progress, which implies comprehensiveness—a totality and

---

Reform, and Insurrection in Late Tokugawa Japan, 1790–1864 (Berkeley and Los Angeles: University of California Press, 1987).

7. For a recent study on progress as a nineteenth-century Western notion, see Peter J. Bowler, *The Invention of Progress* (London: Basil Blackwell, 1989).

generality—is not neutral. The geographic area privileged by this totality, rather, was Europe; non-Europe was separated and distanced by the same hierarchical generality—the sequence and order—that explained the progress of the West.[8]

The second problem is a more fundamental contradiction within history itself. For history to be relevant, it must be usable; it must correspond to contemporary needs of society (however defined). Yet to maintain its authenticity, it must also be objective. (Lawrence Stone alludes to this issue in one of the epigraphs to Part One.) The modern historical profession is built on a scientific epistemology that pretends to be objective and universal. Yet the history that was written, especially during the late nineteenth and early twentieth centuries, is that of Western nation-states, international and domestic politics, and a male elite. Despite paeans to universality, these histories were about the writer's own nation. In other words, they were objective because they fit the universe of national ideals. Importantly, Japanese did not reject the progress or modernity underlying such history. Instead they created a historical narrative that was similarly universalistic, objective, and useful to Japan.[9]

The realm for this new past was *tōyō*, which was at once contiguous with Western histories and antithetical to them. Geographically, *tōyō* expanded the area of the Western universal; it added the "Far East" to the Western Orient, thereby reinforcing the Western split between the Orient and Occident. But it also reflected an awareness that such territorial categories, especially those defined by Europe, are not neutral or objective. By elevating *tōyō* to an equivalent half of the whole, this history offered a competing totality—a new sequence and order—to the universal of the West.

The extent to which intellectuals actually created a dialogue acceptable to both Europe and Asia is evident in *tōyōshi*'s synthesis of the major historical methodologies prevalent during the late-Meiji period. In 1928 Sugimoto Naojirō, a recent graduate of the University of Kyoto's Department of History, described this synthesis by using the metaphor of the family: "Western historiography was the older brother to *tōyōshi*, which was born from the womb of Chinese historiography and raised

8. Fabian, *Time and the Other*, 2–4. For other accounts on alterity, see Said, *Orientalism*; Tzevetan Todorov, *The Conquest of America*, trans. Richard Howard (New York: Harper Colophon, 1984); and Chatterjee, *Nationalist Thought and the Colonial World*.
9. Lawrence Stone, Review of *The New History and the Old*, by Gertrude Himmelfarb, *New York Review of Books*, December 17, 1987, 59–62; also see Novick, *That Noble Dream*.

in the cradle of Meiji civilization." This syncretism, Sugitomo stated, was the product of corrections to the limitations and faults of Western "world" history as well as that of *kangaku*.[10] It was from the effort to establish equality in difference that historians consciously located the study of the history of Japan and Asia in the context of world history; here, *tōyōshi* transcended the old and new.[11]

The Quest for History

At the time of the Meiji Restoration, historical studies in Japan were quite unlike those of today. In general, history up to the Tokugawa period consisted of chronologies and compendia of leaders and events related to political power. These philological studies of the Chinese and Japanese classic texts established a moral and ethical imperative that either affirmed or condemned the contemporary world. For example, the monumental *Dai nihon shi* (Great History of Japan) was written to establish a historical basis for the *bakufu*, the government established by Tokugawa Ieyasu in the seventeenth century. In contrast, Motoori Norinaga's (1730–1801) classic study of the *Kojiki* (712) emphasized the inappropriateness of Chinese culture and Neo-Confucianism for Japan. Each of these works was restricted to a finite world that reached back to either ancient Japan or a forgotten China. By the nineteenth century, however, the limitations of such philological studies had become increasingly apparent; the idealized past as the model for an ethical and moral society could no longer account for domestic and international change.

The intellectual and social changes that followed the Meiji Restoration were in many ways similar to those surrounding the Enlightenment and the French Revolution in Europe, where the advent of "probable knowledge" rendered the finite world of earlier thinkers anachronistic as a new, but unknown, social order came to the fore. The changes in Japan were equally cataclysmic. Although the social order had been in decline for many decades, the Restoration signaled a new,

10. Sugimoto Naojirō, "Honpō ni okeru tōyōshigaku no seiritsu ni tsuite," *Rekishi to chiri* 21 (April 1928): 439.

11. In his essay on *tōyōshi*, Hatada stated that although the field was critical of the past, its major defect was its inability to synthesize the old and new into a different ideology; see "Nihon ni okeru tōyōshigaku no dentō," 34.

if uncertain, beginning. Those elites leading the regeneration of society found the notions of rationality and progress, rooted in science, particularly attractive. Science presented an aura of objectivity and efficiency, while the idea of progress explained how societies have (or have not) changed and held out hope that less advanced cultures could also evolve into that future, ideal society. History was necessary to explain social change (progress) in an orderly fashion according to universal standards.

Although numerous historical schools emerged in Japan during this period to order the various pasts into a comprehensible whole, the two most important were enlightenment (*bunmei*) history and "national" history. Both, like their European counterparts, were conservative.[12]

PROBABLE KNOWLEDGE WITHIN AN ORGANIC COMMUNITY

Intellectuals of the early-Meiji period eagerly adopted the "world histories" of Europe so as to develop a history in which Japan, too, could be part of the universal order. The fact that enlightenment historians, such as Fukuzawa Yukichi (1835–1901), Taguchi Ukichi (1855–1905), Miyake Yonekichi, and Naka, looked to the West does not mean that their ideas were liberal. In their quest to establish a new historical understanding of Japan, they sought a scientific methodology that prioritized the study of human activity as a regulated and historical object. Through their reading of the histories of Western civilization, they came to believe that universal laws existed that govern all societies, including Japan, and they attempted to place Japan into that universalistic framework.[13] In this sense the West, a geographical and idealized entity that represented progress and modernity, replaced China as Japan's ideal.

Taguchi was one of the first to apply this new notion of progress, in his *Nihon kaika shōshi* (Brief History of Civilization in Japan). His historical conception was based on the notion that the study of human society can ultimately be reduced to a single, all-encompassing law, one

12. For studies of these different schools, see Numata Jirō, "Shigeno Yasutsugu and the Modern Tokyo Tradition," in *Historians of China and Japan*, ed. W. G. Beasley and E. G. Pulleyblank (London: Oxford University Press, 1961), 264–87; Peter Duus, "Whig History, Japanese Style: The Min'yūsha Historians and the Meiji Restoration," *Journal of Asian Studies* 33 (May 1974): 415–36; and Carol Gluck, "The People in History: Recent Trends in Japanese Historiography," *Journal of Asian Studies* 38 (November 1978): 25–50.

13. Kuwabara Takeo, ed., *Nihon no meicho* (Tokyo: Chūkō Shinsho, 1962), 12–13.

that included Japan. "The enlightenment [*kaika*] of human society," he stated, "is governed by a fixed principle [*ittei no ri*]. . . . We must recognize that the path of this force [*seiryoku*] is quite narrow."[14] According to Taguchi, placing Japan on this path required the elision of over a millennium of Japan's past. Its deviation from this universal had begun in the sixth century, when the imperial court came under strong influence from the continent, especially T'ang China (618–907); Buddhism delimited Japanese imagination with its concept of reincarnation; and the importation of T'ang grandeur directed valuable resources toward the embellishment of the court and away from the people. Putting Japan back on a universal course thus meant the disavowal of the corrupting influences of Buddhism, Confucianism, and materialism. Although Taguchi suggested a return to ancient Japan, the point was not so much to regain a lost purity as to return to the early stages of Japan's proper course of development. Taguchi's history was devastating in its implications for a society seeking to reconstruct itself, for it required the forgetting of Japan's aristocratic, militaristic, and feudal ages—in other words, of virtually its whole recorded past.[15]

Perhaps more than at any other time in history, the West was, for Japanese intellectuals, the manifestation of an ideal toward which Japan had to strive if it was to be successful or even survive. Taguchi did not accept the notion that India, China, and Japan shared a common heritage, arguing instead that Western countries had understood the universal order and properly utilized that knowledge to advance to their present superior level. His criticism of Buddhism and Confucianism sharply contrasts with later historical narratives, which have extracted aspects of both systems of thought as fundamental elements of Japanese ideas. It is important to remember that Taguchi's purpose was not specifically to imitate or be like the West. He and his contemporaries did not consider the West inherently superior, only historically more advanced. He stated, "We study physics, psychology, economics, and other sciences not because the West discovered them, but because they are the universal truth."[16] Fukuzawa's famous article "Datsu-A ron"

14. Quoted in Ienaga, *Nihon no kindai shigaku*, 72.
15. There is an interesting parallel with Rammohun Roy's search to a pre-Muslim golden age to reconstruct a history of India. Like Taguchi, he eliminated most of the recorded past; his three periods were the age of god (Upanishads), 900–600 B.C., the age of darkness, 600 B.C.–A.D. 1800, and the age of future expectations.
16. Quoted in Pyle, *New Generation*, 90. Fukuzawa Yukichi similarly argued that Japan should study and follow the universal laws that he believed encompassed all societies; see, for example, *An Outline of a Theory of Civilization*, trans. David A. Dilworth and G. Cameron Hurst (Tokyo: Sophia University, 1973).

(Dissociation from Asia) indicates similar caution. While this essay was no doubt a plea for Japan to distance itself from Asia in order to gain equivalence with (or at least diminish the separation from) Europe, Fukuzawa's likening of Western civilization with the measles, a disease that relentlessly spreads to all corners of the globe, reflects his ambivalence on the value of enlightenment.[17] For both Taguchi and Fukuzawa, Japan's achievement of Western knowledge would put it on a par with the West. The universal, then, was a concept that explained different levels; difference was placed solely on a temporal, not an ontological, plane.[18]

The conditions in which these Meiji intellectuals lived bore several similarities with those facing European writers, including Saint-Simon (1675–1755) and Auguste Comte (1798–1857), the two men most instrumental in formulating positivistic sociology. Both were concerned with the perceived disintegration of society. Frank Manuel points out that "Saint-Simon by his own testimony was communicating the same urgent longing of men for a society in which they could feel themselves integral parts, an organic society, as contrasted with a state in which isolated units competed and fought with one another."[19] Comte, who sought to prevent the breakdown of the idealized social fabric of postrevolutionary France, also prioritized the group: "The scientific spirit makes it impossible to view human society as being really composed of individuals. The true social unit certainly consists in the family alone."[20] Science, thus, precluded the study of the individual and emphasized the social unit. The notion of the progress of civilization was tied to an ideal organic society in which the members, each different and with diverse abilities, combined into a harmonious organic whole. The key to Comte's sociology was a scientistic philosophy of history, defined by three social stages—theologism, metaphysics, and positivism—that allowed the study of human existence as a science.

17. Fukuzawa Yukichi, "Datsu-A ron," in *Fukuzawa Yukichi zenshū* (Tokyo: Iwanami Shoten, 1960), 10:238–40.

18. For a discussion of liberal and conservative applications of progress to the non-West, see Chatterjee, *Nationalist Thought and the Colonial World*, 10–17.

19. Frank E. Manuel, "From Equality to Organicism," *Journal of the History of Ideas* 17 (January 1956): 69. See also Robert A. Nisbet, "Conservatism and Sociology," *American Journal of Sociology* 58 (1952): 167–75; idem, "The French Revolution and the Rise of Sociology in France," *American Journal of Sociology* 49 (1943): 156–64; and Eric R. Wolf, *Europe and the People Without History* (Berkeley and Los Angeles: University of California Press, 1982), 7–9.

20. Quoted in Keith Michael Baker, *Condorcet: From Natural Philosophy to Social Mathematics* (Chicago: University of Chicago Press, 1975), 480.

According to Comte, the development of man can be traced through the progress of his mental faculties: from theologism—the attribution of events to supernatural forces—to positivism—the use of reason and observation to unearth truth.

The European historians who had the most direct influence on Japan followed similar lines of thought. François Guizot (1787–1874), whose *History of Civilization* was widely read by Japanese intellectuals, defined civilization as both the progress of society and the progress of individuals. But while both were necessary, they were not of equal importance. Guizot feared the excesses of power—both of government and of the people—and believed that society determines what is best and that change, though desirable, must be gradual: "We trust that the time now approaches when man's condition shall be progressively improved by the force of reason and truth, when the brute part of nature shall be crushed, that the godlike spirit may unfold. In the meantime let us be cautious that no vague desires, that no extravagant theories, the time for which may not yet be come, carry us beyond the bounds of prudence, or beget in us a discontent with our present state."[21]

Henry Thomas Buckle (1821–62) also subordinated the individual to nature in his *History of Civilization in England*, another historical text widely read in Meiji Japan. He stated:

I hope to accomplish for the history of man something equivalent, or at all events analogous, to what has been effected by other inquirers for the different branches of natural science. In regard to nature, events apparently the most irregular and capricious have been explained, and have been shown to be in accordance with certain fixed and universal laws. This has been done because men of ability, and, above all, men of patient, untiring thought, have studied natural events with the views of discovering their regularity: and if human events were subjected to similar treatment, we have every right to expect similar results.[22]

Buckle, too, affirmed progress and order, but unlike Guizot, his universal was more restrictive. "Man" was not an individual, but represented the social or collective unit whose acquisition of knowledge (progress) brought about civilization.[23] Buckle's philosophy of history grounded progress in two basic natural conditions: "Climate," which controlled the accumulation and distribution of wealth, and "Aspects of Nature,"

21. F. Guizot, *The History of Civilization from the Fall of the Roman Empire to the French Revolution*, trans. William Hazitt, 3d U.S. ed., vol. 1 (New York: D. Appleton, 1874), 29, 34.
22. Henry Thomas Buckle, *History of Civilization in England* (London: Longmans, Green, 1908), 6.
23. For his discussion on the relation between nature and history, see ibid., 65–148.

which determined knowledge. By emphasizing the group or whole and the "natural," or scientific, conditions, he virtually eliminated the possibility for action outside of this norm, and confined the possibility of progress—that is, the attainment of knowledge—to Europe.

This notion of progress rooted in an organic society was well suited to the needs of early Meiji elites for a concept that could render order out of a seemingly chaotic situation. They saw positivistic history as the way by which the new nation-state, Japan, could become a part of "world" civilization, eradicate arbitrary (archaic) social hierarchy or relations, determine what was best for society, and establish a sense of order and sequence. History could be formulated to describe Japan's past, present, and even future in comparison with Europe. Like Neo-Confucianism at the beginning of the Tokugawa period, this new conceptual order was an optimistic one. The optimism, however, was rooted not in an elitist ideal that all men could achieve sagehood, but in an assumption of change toward an ideal order, an order that existed only in the context of an organic society. Moreover, as a forward-looking yet at the same time conservative ideology, it was effectively mobilized to counter popular movements such as the *jiyū minken undō* (freedom and popular rights movement).[24] Acceptable change had to be gradual and could only be validated through the scientific investigation of the past; caution, prudence, and, above all, objective knowledge were essential.

OBJECTIVE HISTORY AND THE NATION

The other major historical school of the time was the "national" school, or school of textual analysis (*kōshōgaku*).[25] Current scholarship has emphasized the differences between this school and that of enlightenment history, based chiefly on institutional affiliation and methodology. While I do not refute these distinctions, such an interpretation, I argue, overlooks important similarities.[26] Both enlightenment and national historians believed that history should be rational and progressive; both considered society to be the primary unit of analysis; and both emphasized gradual change.

24. For two studies that describe this movement as a populist alternative to the system established by the ruling clique, see Irokawa Daikichi, *The Culture of Meiji* (Princeton: Princeton University Press, 1985); and Roger Bowen, *Rebellion and Democracy in Meiji Japan* (Berkeley and Los Angeles: University of California Press, 1980).

25. For two studies that describe the historiography of this period, see Duus, "Whig History, Japanese Style," 415–36; and Gluck, "The People in History," 25–50.

26. For a description of these schools, see Ienaga, *Nihon no kindai shigaku*, 71–90.

Present-day historiography, in exploring the development of the national school, has emphasized continuity and change; the presence of elements of *kokugaku* (nativist learning), especially careful textual analysis (*kōshō*); and German (Rankean) historical methods. Above all, the approach was scientific, objective, and lacking an explicit theoretical framework. Peter Duus states this common view succinctly, and politely:

These academic historians were as much in revolt against the praise-and-blame approach of traditional historiography as men like Fukuzawa and Taguchi, but they fought not by seeking out general laws of civilization, but by careful verification of historical facts. . . . They devoted themselves to gathering facts, compiling chronologies, and subjecting classic works of historiography (such as Rai Sanyō's *Nihon gaishi*) to rigorous textual criticism. They were capable, critical, and dedicated scholars, but basically uninspiring, without an axe to grind or the passion of political commitment.[27]

Institutional affiliation was an important characteristic of this school; as faculty of the Imperial University in Tokyo, the preeminent university in Japan, these historians worked for the state. Indeed, article one of the Imperial Ordinance outlining the organization and function of this university stated, "It shall be the purpose of the [Tokyo] Imperial University to teach the sciences and the arts and to probe their mysteries in accordance with the needs of the state."[28] This connection was manifested in numerous ways. From 1887, for example, Tokyo Imperial University graduates were exempted from civil service exams. The professors of this school, particularly during the Meiji period, likewise enjoyed considerable prestige within the bureaucratic hierarchy: their salaries were in the top 8 percent of the bureaucratic pay scale, and they also carried considerable weight in the formulation of social policy.[29]

27. Duus, "Whig History, Japanese Style," 419–20; Ienaga Saburō argued, "These positivistic national historians were solely preoccupied with collecting materials and verifying historical facts; however, they overlooked the fundamental spirit of historical consciousness" (*Nihon no kindai shigaku*, 85). Numata, though downplaying the role of Riess and emphasizing the indigenous historical tradition, comes to essentially the same conclusion; see "Shigeno Yasutsugu and the Modern Tokyo Tradition," 264–87.
28. Quoted in Frank O. Miller, *Minobe Tatsukichi: Interpreter of Constitutionalism in Japan* (Berkeley and Los Angeles: University of California Press, 1965), 15.
29. One of the best-known examples of the connection between knowledge and national policy was that linking the Faculty of Law of Tokyo Imperial University, the constitution, and the bureaucracy; see F. Miller, *Minobe Tatsukichi*. For the relation between Tokyo Imperial University and the bureaucracy, see Marshall, "Professors and Politics"; idem, "Growth and Conflict," 276–94; and James R. Bartholomew, "Science, Bureaucracy, and Freedom in Meiji and Taishō Japan," in Najita and Koschmann (eds.), *Conflict in Modern Japanese History*, 295–341.

Nevertheless, affiliation as a major criterion for categorization accepts objectivism as an unquestioned mode of history, with methodology hiding larger ideological issues. The parallels with the American historical profession are not coincidental.[30]

The history department of the Faculty of Letters at Tokyo Imperial University was organized in 1887. To shape this new discipline, a young student of Leopold von Ranke, Ludwig Riess, was hired to teach "modern" history. In his teachings, Riess emphasized Ranke's methodological side, not his religious tendencies.[31] Riess also fostered the collection of material, the establishment of archives, the objective evaluation of historical data, the publication of empirical articles, and professional cooperation through an academic society.[32] In his fourth year in Japan, Riess celebrated these accomplishments in the inaugural issue of the journal of the newly established Historical Association (Shigakkai), in which he reflected on the state of historical studies: "Japanese scholars have already established a historical association and a monthly publication, and are working to renovate their former ways, elevate the level of historical research, and make history purely scientific. I hope that my colleagues believe in and remember the enormity of this project and impress all scholars with its importance."[33]

The notion of objectivity, however, obscures a critical assumption that contradicts the presentation of history as neutral: someone (or some body) must decide which past should be highlighted for the good of each social unit. *Kōshōgaku* historians were not merely applying a new methodology to the study of the past. In Riess's use of the word "renovation" (*isshin*), or as Duus puts it, "revolt," an underlying ideology is implied that informs such change. A value-laden choice is necessarily entailed. Take the goal of progress, for example. Partha Chatterjee states, "The rational knowledge of human society comes to be organized around concepts such as wealth, productive efficiency,

30. See Novick, *That Noble Dream.*

31. Because this biography of Shiratori was written in 1944, one wonders whether Tsuda felt restrained from describing a similar religiosity in his mentor's work; see Tsuda, "Shiratori hakushi shōden," 339.

32. Two major collections compiled during the Meiji period, the *Dai nihon shiryō* (Chronogical Source Books of Japanese History) and *Dai nihon komonjo* (Old Documents of Japan), emerged from the *Hanawa shiryō* (Chronological Source Books of Japanese History), a collection of documents on ancient Japan begun in the Tokugawa period by Hanawa Hokiichi (1746–1821). See Ienaga, *Nihon no kindai shigaku,* 80–82. See also Numata, "Shigeno Yasutsugu and the Modern Tokyo Tradition," 266, 283–85.

33. Rudōhi Riisu, "*Shigakkai zasshi* ni tsuite iken," trans. by Ogawa Kinjirō, *Shigakkai zasshi* 1 (April 1890): 1.

progress, etc. all of which are defined in terms of the promotion of some social 'interests'. Yet 'interests' in society are necessarily diverse; indeed, they are stratified in terms of the relations of power."[34] While the notion of objectivity gave knowledge authority as an impartial judge, knowledge and expertise endowed the new state with objectivistic criteria for determining what was to be and for whom.[35]

These suggestions of an underlying ideology raise a fascinating (and troubling) issue that confronts historians today: the relation between the goal of objectivity and authorial position. Regardless whether one looks on either of these historical schools positively or negatively, there is little doubt that both were attempting to create a new field of history based on scientific methodology. Scholars of both schools believed that their methods would elevate the history of Japan—the nation (*kokumin*) here being the primary unit of investigation—to the level of Western history. Enlightenment historians emphasized the imperative of the universal law that would lead toward an understanding of Japan's progress and would eventually guarantee its equality with and independence from the West. *Kōshōgaku* historians, like scholars of the enlightenment school, did have "an axe to grind" and "political commitment," only in their case their commitment was to "renovate" the concept of history so that the Japanese nation could be understood in terms of Western history. The difference between the two groups was one of emphasis. Enlightenment historians believed that it was first necessary to identify the universal laws and place Japan into that mold. *Kōshōgaku* scholars, while also speculating on a general conception of history, prioritized the collection of materials.

By the late 1880s the young historians of both schools had confronted the problematics of objectivity and authorship, of progress and the non-West, and probably understood better than Riess what the creation of a new historical field in Japan meant. For Riess, "renovation" meant objective and scientific studies in which the Western narrative of progress was already accepted. But the Japanese, who constantly debated the nature of history, were less sanguine. The combination of progress, as a universal law, and nationhood are, after all, potentially contradictory. While the notion of progress may explain the rise of most Western nations, it also authorizes a hierarchy of cultures with Europe at the top and all others representing various imperfect stages

34. Chatterjee, *Nationalist Thought and the Colonial World*, 14.
35. For a study on the relation between authority, legitimacy, and knowledge as used by the Meiji state, see Silberman, "Bureaucratic State in Japan."

of Europe's past.[36] The placement of non-Western countries in pre-existing categories denies their own nationhood beyond that which is already defined. The impact is evident in Guizot's description of the Orient: "In other states, say, for example, in India and Egypt, where again only one principle of civilization prevailed, the result was different. Society here became stationary; simplicity produced monotony; the country was not destroyed; society continued to exist; but there was no progression; it remained torpid and inactive."[37] In other words, the Orient has no history. While Guizot at least left some possibility for progress, Buckle's notion of progress was based strictly on "objective" geoclimatic standards—Climate and Aspects of Nature—which only Europe possessed. He concluded, "Hence it is that, looking at the history of the world as a whole, the tendency has been, in Europe, to subordinate nature to man; out of Europe, to subordinate man to nature.... The great division, therefore, between European civilization and non-European civilization is the basis of the philosophy of history."[38]

These Japanese historians realized that the writing of history required the alteration of both the norms and the conditions that give rise to progress. This fact is suggested in Riess's self-congratulatory inaugural-issue article, in which he also complained that, "because the books that have lasting value are those with a clear thesis and an academic theory [*gakusetsu*] agreed upon by all major historians, *today's abstract debates on methodology should not be handed down to future generations.* Certain people say that because Japanese have an affinity for abstract discussions, we must first turn to such issues to awaken the interests of the reader and gain a following; but again, I cannot condone this."[39] It is one of the ironies of history that the Japanese, who today are reputed to be weak in creativity and abstract reasoning, were once accused of being overly concerned with such abstract and theoretical ideas. Even those historians closest to the rigorous methodology preached by Riess exhibited a discomfort with the restrictions and uniformity it imposed. Their discussions, which centered on enlightenment ideology itself, indicate that the theory "agreed upon by all major historians" was in fact different from that of Reiss.

36. This distinction between Europe and the other existed long before the development of social science; see, for example, Said, *Orientalism*.
37. Guizot, *History of Civilization*, 37.
38. Buckle, *History of Civilization in England*, 152–53.
39. Riisu, "*Shigakkai zasshi* ni tsuite," 4–5; italics in the original.

The totality and generality of that universalistic law proved to be the mechanically propelled Trojan horse mentioned by Dale.

Limitations of Enlightenment

By the Meiji twenties (1887–96), Japanese historians' initial enthusiasm for a philosophy of history that implicitly imposed a uniformity based in European progress had waned, and they began to turn toward a Japanese and Asian past.[40] Yet as I mentioned above, these enlightenment intellectuals, although they did espouse Western ideas, could not be considered liberal. Moreover, it is misleading to cast the issues in terms of a struggle between liberalism and nationalism, for these frameworks are not antithetical.[41] The issues studied by enlightenment historians, such as the extent to which Western civilization should be adopted and Japanese culture preserved, were merely parts of a much broader issue: the political, cultural, and intellectual autonomy of Japan.

The shift away from enlightenment history toward Japan's roots was due in large part both to Japan's very acceptance of enlightenment history and to the ultimate failure of that history to accommodate Japan as an equal. In their initial eagerness to find Japan's progressive path, enlightenment historians overlooked the ideological implications of the spatial and temporal categories that ensured Europe's preeminence. Territoriality, as an "attempt by an individual or group to affect, influence, or control people, phenomena, and relationships, by delimiting and asserting control over a geographic area," by definition made for hierarchical ordering.[42] Control was facilitated by a unilinear concept of time that ranked territories based on certain types of development or learning. The Orient, as a geocultural territory commonly described as backward, stagnant, or primitive, is located in a realm of perpetual inferiority to the West.[43] The prescribed course consigned Japan to be a perpetually incomplete version of the West.

40. Ienaga, *Nihon no kindai shigaku*, 72, 74–80; and Pyle, *New Generation*.
41. See, for example, Chatterjee, *Nationalist Thought and the Colonial World*, 1–35. For a study that has characterized the change as a shift away from Western liberal thought to a more nationalistic stance, see Pyle, *New Generation*.
42. Sack, *Human Territoriality*, 19.
43. See Said, *Orientalism*; and Todorov, *Conquest of America*.

The extraction of Japan—and any non-Western society—from this temporal inferiority is not easily accomplished. While accepting the Western concept of progress, many of the same enlightenment and national historians sought to alter and expand the parameters. Both Naka and Miyake attempted to eliminate the Eurocentric bias in Buckle's *History of Civilization in England* (Naka was one of its translators). Naka, for example, added race and imperial succession to geography as basic factors affecting historical development;[44] and Miyake turned to Japan's ancient culture in order to discover an ontological equivalence with Europe and the causes for their different levels of cultural development.

Other scholars discovered difference in the sociology of Herbert Spencer, another widely read European scholar. On the one hand, Spencer's writings promulgate a notion of progress. In his *Principles of Sociology*, Spencer argued that while the two types of society, militaristic and industrial, can coexist, virtually all societies evolve from the militant type to the democratic and industrial type. He stated, "Where the industrial activities and structures evolve, this branch of the regulating system, no longer as in the militant type a rigid hierarchy, little by little loses strength, while there grows up one of a different kind: sentiments and institutions both relaxing. . . . Military conformity coercively maintained gives place to a varied non-conformity maintained by willing union."[45]

On the other hand, Spencerian social evolution also readily explained the international behavior of the European nations—especially their imperialistic forays into Asia—and emphasized what the Japanese had known for quite some time: they must strengthen themselves to survive in the international arena. The application of Spencer's "survival of the fittest" notion to Asian affairs proved an important breakthrough by emphasizing the possibility of difference *within* a framework of progress. This concept provided an alternative to the fixed path already blazed by Europe, for here progress was seen to depend on successful adaptation to one's own environment. Katō Hiroyuki, for exam-

44. In his proposed seven-volume *Shina tsūshi* (A General History of China, 1888–90), which was never completed, Naka divided Chinese history into three periods: ancient, pre-Ch'in; medieval, Ch'in to Sung; and feudal, Yuan to present.

45. Quoted in J.D.Y. Peel, ed., *Herbert Spencer: On Social Evolution* (Chicago: University of Chicago Press, 1972), 157, 158–59. For a different interpretation, see Duus, "Whig History, Japanese Style," 421–22, who argues that these typologies are polarities separate from Spencer's evolutionary model of social change. See also Bowler, *Invention of Progress*, esp. 37–39.

ple, used this idea to recenter cultures in their particular surroundings. Each nation, he argued, is slightly different, with its survival relying on its ability to adjust and compete, both against nature and against other cultures. Nakae Chōmin's (1847–1901) *Discourse of Three Drunkards on Government*, too, is eloquent testimony to the dilemma facing Japan in this period.[46] Here, the Gentleman believing in universal laws advocates jumping ahead of Europe toward the democratic and peaceful ideal; the Champion, while accepting progress, stresses the "reality" of power politics and imperialism; and Professor Nankai (lit., South Seas) offers a middle road that deemphasizes concerns about Europe. This essay, in my view, indicates the rejection by all three "drunkards" of the West as the manifestation of an ideal to be strived for and, instead, a concern for progress—though keeping Western ideas and Europe in mind—within the particular context of Japan's history and capacity. The West, in other words, becomes merely another culture (though in some aspects still a superior one), a fellow competitor on this rocky path toward progress.

This realization encouraged historians to give Japan a "history" that was contiguous and equal with that of Europe, as a way to open up a dialogic relation with the West. Intercourse between Japan and Europe was to take place on an equivalent basis but, importantly, with difference fully recognized. To define Japan through a historical narrative similar to that of Europe, many Japanese, including such enlightenment historians as Naka and Miyake as well as such national historians as Kume Kunitake (1839–1931) and Shigeno Yasutsugu (1827–1910), turned to Japan's past. Other Japanese reached into the history of Asia to achieve the same purpose. For each the past provided the archives with which to affirm cultural or historical equivalence, historical change (as opposed to stagnation), and Japan's potential and capacity as a modern nation.

Search for Equality in Difference

Tōyōshi emerged in the 1890s out of this recognition that European world history was merely *seiyōshi*, a history of the West that

46. Nakae Chōmin, *A Discourse by Three Drunkards on Government*, trans. Nobuko Tsukui (New York: Weatherhill, 1984).

privileged European culture as superior to all other cultures. In the preface to a 1906 reference book by Takakuwa Komakichi on the history of Asia, Shiratori wrote:

In retrospect, during the early years of Meiji, our country earnestly imitated Western countries and rapidly imported their culture [*bunbutsu*] without sufficient time for assimilation. Even history courses directly used the textbooks written in those countries. Although such books bear the titles of world or global history [*sekaishi, bankokushi*], in actuality they are no more than the record of the rise and fall of European countries. The affairs of East Asia are virtually neglected. At one time some books that were well received in our schools, such as [William] Swinton's *Outlines of the World's History*, asserted that non-Caucasian peoples do not have true history. Without doubt this seriously misrepresents our countrymen.[47]

Tōyōshi, the history of the East, was established as one half of the whole, in opposition to *seiyōshi*, but it was much more than mere description of the events and people of Asia. As Shiratori's dissatisfaction suggests, *tōyōshi*'s importance was also ideological: it involved the representation and understanding of Japan. It was needed to show that Japan also has a "true history."

Most accounts date the beginning of *tōyōshi* to 1894, when Naka proposed that the middle school curriculum separate world history into Occidental and Oriental history. The Ministry of Education accepted this division two years later. Until then, foreign history had been equivalent to "world history," with Chinese history taught separately following the *kangaku* emphasis on language and ethical training. Naka argued that in the teaching of foreign history, the history of Asia should be presented just as that of Europe was. On one level, Naka was attempting to move the study of China away from chronologies of political figures and events to a positivistic view of history in which the same laws govern all human societies. As a counterpart to European history, thus, *tōyōshi* served to expand the limited geographic area of the Western universal. On another level, however, Naka was seeking to establish the very boundaries of *tōyō*, in terms of the connection between the Occident and Orient: *tōyō* was defined as the vast region to the east of Europe; it expanded the Orient—Middle East, India, and Inner Asia—eastward to include China and Japan. It did not, however, include Southeast Asia.

47. Shiratori Kurakichi, "Jo" [Preface] to *Tōyō dairekishi*, by Takakuwa Komakichi (1906), in *Shiratori Kurakichi zenshū* (Tokyo: Iwanami Shoten, 1969–71), 10:445 (hereafter cited as *SKZ*).

Naka's ideas also reflect a converging view among Japanese intellectuals that *tōyō* could provide the beginnings for a narrative of Japanese history. The explanation for reforming the middle school curriculum included the following statement: "By investing in the history of *tōyō*, we can pay attention to the mutual influences between our country and all oriental countries since ancient times, and furthermore probably explain the interaction between all oriental and Occidental countries."[48] Japanese historians generally agreed that not only did Asia house the artifacts that would unlock Japan's history, but it also provided the beginnings of Western history. Thus, an accurate depiction of *tōyō* would take Japan out of the shadow of the West. In his preface to Takakuwa's book, Shiratori argued that such a historical understanding of Asia was crucial to a coherent Japanese view of history. He stated, "If a school's curriculum lacks classes on oriental history [*tōyōshi*], the students' historical awareness, without any path to measure the interaction between Japanese and Western history, will end in incoherence and disunity."[49] As both the beginnings of an autonomous history and the medium that tied Japanese and Western histories together, *tōyō* was the realm that would provide coherence and unity.

Although by the early 1890s *tōyōshi* had been institutionalized as a distinct subject at the middle school level, and although consensus on the importance of a *tōyō* to counter the Occident was rapidly emerging, there were nevertheless several competing notions of how *tōyō* should be constituted. Just as Taguchi was able to develop a historical narrative that denied characteristics which today are considered inherently Japanese, other historians took advantage of the fact that the exact relation of Japan and Asia had not yet been canonized. Several historians, such as Miyake, turned to ancient Japanese and Chinese history for the objective data that would fit Japan into the universal laws of enlightenment; the conservative philosopher and Confucian scholar Inoue Tetsujirō sought to deny the mediating structures of Western histories, emphasizing instead the specificity of each culture; and Shiratori, a student of Naka and Riess, synthesized several perspectives to establish the intellectual structure of the field that has become known as *tōyōshi*.[50]

48. Quoted in Nakayama Kyūshirō, *Shigaku oyobi tōyōshi no kenkyū* (Tokyo: Kenbunkan, 1935), 98–99; see also Miyake Yonekichi, "Bungaku hakushi Naka Michiyokun den," in *Naka Michiyo isho* (Tokyo: Dai Nihon Tosho, 1915), 31–33.

49. Shiratori, "Jo" to Takakuwa, *Tōyō dairekishi*, in *SKZ*, 10:447.

50. This convergence on Asia's past was not limited to these three men. Intellectuals such as Miyake Setsurei and Okakura Tenshin attempted to establish a different universal through "Truth, Beauty, and Goodness" or art. These universals were to be neutral, or at the very least non-Western, and ones that eliminated positivistic time.

BEYOND ENLIGHTENMENT

The career of Miyake Yonekichi reflects the ambivalence that enlightenment, as a historical idea, fostered when applied to Japan— or any non-Western nation.[51] Miyake was born in 1860 in Wakayama and briefly attended Fukuzawa's Keio Gijuku, later Keio University. (He did not graduate, and left school for academic reasons.) There is little doubt that Miyake was influenced by enlightenment historians, such as Fukuzawa and Taguchi, for the vestiges of this background are clear in his *Nihon shigaku teiyō* (A General History of Japan). This survey, an ambitious work that, had it been completed, would have filled twenty-five volumes, was one of the first attempts to write a multivolume history of Japan according to the new historical framework. It also reveals the problems encountered in constructing a non-Western history along the lines of Western Enlightenment. Miyake complained:

Today those who carry the title of historian, being gray-haired old men, cannot face the brilliance of Western academic methods. Alone, they open the warehouse of curios and dawdle. . . . [Yet] those who study Western methods and understand contemporary social issues are completely ignorant of our country's history. Even the occasional person who discusses our history using Western scholarship has limited knowledge because he spends little time investigating actual historical materials.[52]

By 1887, the year the first and only volume was published, Miyake was well aware of the need for a new history. "Actually," he said, "this is an era when we are trying to produce a major change in the research methods of history."[53] He was skeptical of Enlightenment philosophy for its Eurocentrism and critical of *kangaku* because it was too closely allied with China. Miyake's new historical discipline was outlined in his manuscript for the second volume of *Nihon shigaku teiyō*, which was probably written around 1890–91.[54] In a section entitled "The True Meaning of History" (*rekishi no hongi*), Miyake described history in the following way: first, "history is the academic field of knowing the vestiges of the past." It is specific to a locale, group, or nation; it entails change and includes language, customs, folk traditions, art, religion, as well as politics. The people (*kokumin*) must know these pasts to under-

---

51. See Ozawa Eiichi, "Meiji keimōshugi rekishi to Miyake Yonekichi," *Shichō* 70 (November 1959): 1–28; and idem, *Kindai nihon shigakushi no kenkyū: Meiji hen* (Tokyo: Yoshikawa Kōbunkan, 1968), 350–55. Also see Ienaga, *Nihon no kindai shigaku*, 71–73.
52. Ozawa, "Meiji keimōshugi rekishi," 8.
53. Ozawa, *Kindai nihon shigakushi*, 463.
54. This unpublished manuscript was discovered in 1959. Ozawa estimated the date of completion; see "Meiji keimōshugi rekishi," 24.

stand Japan's relation to the general trends of world history. Second, "history is strongly related to literature." Early scholars used poetry (before written language) and prose (such as the *Heike monogatari*) to depict their world, making these important resources. Third, "history is a scientific, academic field." History must critically examine data to create an accurate record of the past and to understand the interrelation among the various parts. In this way, history will "illuminate the progress of the nation" and "become a mirror to the future."[55]

There is little doubt that Miyake accepted the notion that human society can be studied scientifically and that such knowledge is crucial to Japan's progress. But he sought to use Western history to generate a scientific history of Japan; he was not interested in molding Japan to Western world histories. Thus, while he believed in progress, he did not endorse the underlying philosophy of history that privileged Europe. Specifically, he denied Buckle's geographic determinism. He wrote, "If one looks at the past through [Buckle's Climate and Aspects of Nature], when the countries of Europe, which are now called the center of civilization, were wriggling in hideouts of thieves [*shurui no sōkutsu*], we had already achieved a high level of civilization. The reason that we are now a bit behind in the race for enlightenment does not lie in the obstruction of nature, but in social activity."[56] Here Miyake was closer to Spencer, for without rejecting progress, he argued that each culture progresses or recedes according to its own ability to adjust to its surroundings. Although nature is important, it does not determine the mental abilities of different peoples. The answers to Japan's slower development were to be found in social factors. An understanding of these factors could be reconstructed from the ancient myths and legends, but only by using critical methods.

Here is a new academic field called anthropology [*jinruigaku*]; in the overall evolution [*keihatsu*] of races, this field [original illegible] researches the development of order from customs and traditions to law, of weapons from wooden clubs and stones to cannons, and of society from hamlets to a nation [*kokumin*]. Data include everything from all civilized people to the hordes of ignorant barbarians. A comparative study will clearly bring out the developmental order of these systems. This study, along with the study of ancient texts [*kyūji*] will allow us to excavate the progress of peoples from barbarian and uncivilized to enlightened.[57]

55. Ibid., 53–55.
56. Ozawa, *Kindai nihon shigakushi*, 355.
57. Ozawa, "Meiji keimōshugi rekishi," 26.

Miyake's conception of a historical field that explains Japan's past was much broader than that defined by Riess. His quest to describe the totality of Japan's past is evident in his openness to evidence from such diverse fields such as archeology, art, and language. Among these, he singled out language as the particular source of intellectual development. He called the study of the past through language *kyūjigaku* (lit., study of ancient texts), stating: "Furthermore, *kyūji* emerged from language. Because the development of language accompanied that of thought, at the beginning language was inadequate and incomplete. The poetic genre has long preserved the ancient tales [*kyūji*]; depiction [*keiyō*], simile [*reikai*], and metaphor [*hiyu*] were abundant. Thus, gradual progress evolved from linguistic analogies. . . . Language expressed thought, but at the same time, thought produced language."[58] Because ancient man's understanding of his world is embedded in the ancient texts, language, not geography, was the key to understanding the development of knowledge.

The study of ancient tales served two purposes. First, language was the common denominator, the universal, that removed progress from specific geoclimatic regions. All ancient cultures, Western and Asian alike, attempted to understand their world through representation; songs, poetry, myths, folklore, and art were the media for recording and understanding the environment. In order to extract historical data from these ancient texts, Miyake argued (in a vein reminiscent of Ogyū Sorai [1666–1728], the eminent Confucian scholar) that one must immerse oneself completely in the contemporary culture and context: "I believe that the many miraculous and outrageous deeds in ancient history were not direct reports, but are folk tales in the ancient language, in other words, popular accounts in the contemporary dialect. . . . However, those who repeated these [tales] believed them; but because their intellect was still undeveloped and knowledge was incomplete, that which appears irrational was rational and what is now mysterious was not."[59] For Miyake, *kyūjigaku* was a nonbiased field whose practitioners could describe the development of society without using the labels of irrationality and mysteriousness so frequently attributed to non-Western cultures.

Miyake's quest for evidence also led him beyond the archipelago to the continent. In his biography of Naka he contrasted himself to his

58. Ibid., 44. Miyake first explored the importance of myths and legends in a series of articles that appeared in the journal *Mon* during 1889.
59. Ibid., 32–33.

colleague, who, he argued, sought simply to understand Chinese history, whereas his own interest in China and Inner Asia was to discover the roots of Japanese culture.[60] Indeed, this assertion certainly has merit. In 1888 Miyake participated on a project with Ernest Fenollosa and Okakura Tenshin to study, preserve, and catalog Japanese art. After investigating ancient art and sculpture principally in Nara and Wakayama, the region where he was born and raised, Miyake began a series of articles in which he used ancient art to speculate on Japan's roots and its ancient connection with the continent. For example, Miyake concluded that the lion-hunt pattern on the Banner of the Four Devaraja found at the Hōryūji Temple in Nara originated in Assyria.[61] By tying Nara to Assyria, Miyake was suggesting Japan's connection to an ancient Asian civilization that predated European civilization.[62] Asia, Miyake implied, was not merely contiguous with both Japan and Europe, it was a part of Japan's past.

The other role of this new field is contradictory: to preserve these myths and legends in the face of the onslaught of scientific knowledge. This desire to preserve ancient stories is in fact part of the fundamental problematic of this chapter—how to write a progressive history while maintaining national distinctiveness. Although Miyake was in the end not very successful, his history does indicate a revived interest in Japanese religiosity. Miyake turned to the *Kojiki*, a key source of Japan's historical as well as mythological past, to contrast his history with earlier views, especially that of Motoori Norinaga (1730–1801).[63] The main difference, Miyake pointed out, is that Motoori tried to revive an idealized past, whereas he, Miyake, sought to preserve these ancient texts as essential resources for the understanding of progress and Japan's identity. "In today's world predominated by empiricism, one cannot believe anything that is neither empirical nor positivistic, nor can one believe old books. We live in a skeptical world, and we are destroying our ancient customs and beliefs. Nevertheless, we are not without a religious spirit [*shinkō no kokoro*]; the clamor for a critique of empiricism is actually a desire for belief. Religious spirit must not be

60. Ozawa, *Kindai nihon shigakushi*, 353–55; and idem, "Meiji keimōshugi rekishi," 18–19.

61. Ozawa, *Kindai nihon shigakushi*, 456–57.

62. This quest for roots in ancient cultures was probably informed by histories of Western civilization. Assyria and Babylon are often included in narratives that go back to the "cradle of Western civilization." Today the same geographical area is the Middle East.

63. Though critical, Miyake had considerable praise for Motoori's classic study on the *Kojiki*.

destroyed."[64] Miyake was certainly ambivalent on the value of modernity, perceiving its alienating potential. History, while necessary to understand Japan's relation with the West, was also important for understanding and preserving Japan's cultural heritage. For Miyake, the West was far from an ideal; the West was merely part of the whole, one with both positive and negative qualities.

Regardless whether one prefers to describe Miyake's history as a continuation of or reaction against the problematic presented by enlightenment history, there is little doubt that enlightenment thought led to a greater interest in Japan's and Asia's pasts. Miyake strongly believed that scientific knowledge would bring about a better understanding of the world; his identification of language as that basic characteristic that is common across humankind indicates his acceptance of progress, but a progress that would not be subsumed by the Western histories popular during the early Meiji period. Significantly, volume two of *Nihon shigaku teiyō* was not published, and none of the subsequent twenty-three planned volumes were even written.

MAPPING A NATIONAL PAST

Around the same time that Miyake was working on the second volume of his history, Inoue Tetsujirō, professor of philosophy at Tokyo Imperial University, gave a speech to the recently founded Historical Association on the need for more studies on Asia. This speech, "Tōyōshigaku no kachi" (The Value of Oriental Studies), clearly outlined his rationale and program for a new field of oriental studies.[65] Inoue in many ways represented *kangaku*, the school that Miyake criticized as anachronistic, and this article was an indirect rejoinder to such criticisms. But despite these differences, numerous similarities can be identified as well. For Inoue, too, the continent was the means by which Asians could inform Westerners about Japan and Asia, understand Japan, and account for differences among nations.

Inoue's conception of this new field centered on China and was directed toward a reformation of *kangaku*. His reason for this focus was simply that the study of *tōyō* had greater value for Japan than other academic fields. It would lead toward a better understanding of Asia, and Japanese research on Asian history would correct European miscon-

64. Ozawa, "Meiji keimōshugi rekishi," 28.
    65. Inoue Tetsujirō, "Tōyōshigaku no kachi," *Shigakkai zasshi* 2 (November 1891): 704–17; (December 1891): 788–98; and (January 1892): 1–14.

ceptions of Japan. "I believe," he said, "that a pressing issue for Japanese is [how] to use historical research to inform those [Western] nations about Japan and clarify Japan's progress. When they understand both the historical facts and this level of progress [*shinpo*], their contemptuous expressions will undoubtedly disappear. Here, the value of oriental studies to Japanese is truly enormous."[66] Inoue attributed Europe's lack of understanding of Asia to the difficulty of Asian languages. He argued that just as it would be difficult for Japanese to learn hieroglyphics to study Babylonian history, the handful of Western scholars who specialized in Japan encountered the same problem. For this reason, he argued, studies by European scholars on Japan are "like that of a child"—boring and frequently containing mistakes and strange interpretations. Thus, he continued, because of the nascent stage of Oriental studies in Europe, it would be to Japan's advantage to develop this field itself and then report the findings to Europe; "The duty [*gimu*] of Japanese is to see that orientals are thorough in conducting their own historical research in those areas overlooked by Western scholars, that we properly inform Westerners, and that academic society evaluate the overall benefits." In other words, through academia, the Japanese had to define the orient and then inform the West.[67]

Inoue believed that the roots of the problem were ignorance and misunderstanding, not epistemology or ontology. By researching and reporting a "correct" account of Japan's higher level of progress than that of other Asian countries, Japanese scholars could teach Europeans to distinguish Japanese from others. Such encounters as when Inoue was mistakenly—and, he believed, condescendingly—called a Chinese or Ceylonese while in Europe would be eliminated. This argument is similar to that of Fukuzawa in "Datsu-A ron," for both sought to show Europe that Japan was much more advanced than Asia. But while Fukuzawa described Japanese history in Western terms, Inoue sought equivalence through cultural relativism. He argued that *tōyō* had developed differently from the Occident, which gave it a different political system, literature, religion, and culture. But despite this emphasis on the historical specificity of each culture, he believed that a Japanese description of Asia's past would show that Japanese history bore many similarities to that of Europe and that the level of sophistication in each was rather similar.[68]

66. Ibid., November 1891, 717.
67. Ibid., 709–17 (quote at 716); and December 1891, 797–98.
68. Ibid., December 1891, 788–98.

This solution may seem simplistic, but Inoue was well aware of the epistemological dilemmas that confront those who attempt to write a progressive and scientific history. Inoue perceptively argued that science situates all things according to fixed principles, with no room for variation. Science, he argued, is ahistorical, for there is no distinction between time and place; events occur anywhere and anytime, making science synchronic. History, in contrast, always changes and never repeats itself; it is successive (*sokusesushon*) and continuous (*keizoku*). The philosophy of history and embedded temporal and territorial categories, he argued, are creations of particular people and events; they are not universal. Inoue's history was diachronic and culturally specific; it eliminated any implication that Japan must be like the West—or even like Asia.[69]

This new historical field, he contended, could be built within *kangaku*, which, however, would have to be considerably altered. First, he emphasized that the historian must have breadth, with knowledge of an expanded body of material. He must be able to select and utilize materials judiciously, for "among events, unrelated factors do not exist."[70] Inoue's expanded archives included works on all of Asia, as well as on politics, law, religion, literature, military studies, commerce, and so forth. Second, Inoue recognized the crucial role of methodology in determining the outcome of historical research. "The value of a history is extremely different depending on methodology; the difference is like night and day [lit., heaven and earth—*shōjō*]."[71] Inoue did not offer a specific methodology, but argued that awareness was necessary to see through different authorial positions. He believed that this recognition of subjectivity, especially as molded by national perspectives, would allow scholars to separate the means of analysis from the conclusions. Thus, despite his dim view of European research on Japan, he urged Japanese historians to read Western writings in order to gain insight into aspects that they themselves might not notice. And for an accurate reading, he insisted on the use of the original texts of European historians rather than interpretations or translations. (Westerners might have difficulty learning Japanese, but Inoue foresaw little problem in Japanese learning European languages.) Finally, he emphasized the importance of understanding historical trends and events to bring out the "hidden spirit" of history. This spirit was not a universal law, but sim-

69. Ibid., January 1892, 1–14.
70. Ibid., 1–3.
71. Ibid., 4.

ilar to Ranke's particularistic side where he connected this spirit to the nation: "Each nation has a particular spirit, breathed in by God, through which it is what is and which its duty is to develop in accordance with . . . the ideal."[72] Both Inoue and Ranke, in this regard, highlighted a religious ideal that privileged the cultural uniqueness of his own country. Inoue cited Shintō around the Meiji Restoration as an example of this "hidden spirit."[73]

Inoue's last two points are refractions of other attempts to construct a historical field in a non-Western society. Where Miyake used *kyūji* to extend the realm that could be included within a progressive history, Inoue accepted the idea of historical development, but not one of progress. His discussion of methodology recognized the Eurocentrism and restrictiveness of science, but rather than creating a new, broader objectivity, he simply claimed that his proximal perspective as a Japanese and Asian was valid as well. For Inoue history by its very nature was local, not scientific. Because history is continuous and cumulative, he wrote, "one can justifiably say that history is reason [*riizon*]." Reason for Inoue could be likened to a raison d'être: "when one completely forgets one's past, awareness disappears, in other words, reasoning [*risei*] disappears. One's understanding of oneself disappears."[74] In the same way that an individual must know his past, "in a nation [*kokumin*], history becomes the reason for the nation." From this understanding of history, he believed, the *kokutai* (national essence), an awareness of the nation, inevitably arises.[75] Inoue brought history's national purpose—as the basis of a nation's identity—to the surface.

In his effort to define an oriental history Inoue was very perceptive of some of the contradictions in history as well as of difficulties involved in reconciling the human sciences with an autonomous Japan. But his rejection of a scientific universal in history ran counter to trends then prevalent in historical studies in Japan, and even his writings moved in the direction that he criticized. Although he saw his program as a way to revive *kangaku*, the methodology he emphasized virtually precluded any continuity; aside from his skepticism of the possibility of

72. Leonard Krieger, *Ranke: The Meaning of History* (Chicago: University of Chicago Press, 1977), 162.
73. For Inoue's awareness of Ranke, see "Tōyōshigaku no kachi," January 1892, 4. For a discussion of Rankean historiography in Japan, see below. In support of his effort to elevate Shintō, Inoue cited the slogan *sonnō jōi* (Revere the emperor, expel the barbarian).
74. Ibid., 13.
75. Ibid., 14.

a scientific explication of cultures, his outline of oriental history bore more similarity to Miyake's ideas than to the exegetical studies that predominated in *kangaku*. But by trying to extend *kangaku*, a different academic heritage, in this way, he reinforced an emerging category, *tōyō*. Lest readers think that Inoue was anachronistic, some of his ideas—the rejection of unilinear time, the priority of cultural diversity over universalism, and the denial of a prescientific philosophy of history—were revived in the 1930s.

SYNTHESIS: A FALSE START

Even though Shiratori was relatively young at this time and his training was different from that of Miyake and Inoue, his early writings reflected similar concerns. There is no doubt that Shiratori was a positivistic historian; his highly detailed and narrowly conceived monographs certainly support this interpretation.[76] As one of the first students of Riess, Shiratori, too, argued that the study of history must be scientific; an objective understanding of the past was possible only through thorough investigation of a manageable area, the gathering and analysis of all related information, and critical verification of old documents. It is generally because of this rigorous critical and textual methodology that Ranke's much repeated and often misunderstood quote, "wie es eigentlich gewesen" (as it actually was), has also been identified with Shiratori.[77] Shiratori worked doggedly to build the historical study of *tōyō* into a scientific and objective academic field, and *tōyōshi*'s reputation even today as a methodologically oriented field that emphasizes only scientific objectivity reflects his success in this endeavor.[78] This preoccupation with methodology, however, has by far overshadowed the concept of history that Shiratori also developed. For Shiratori, methodology was but the tool to understand the complexity of an event and the laws or tendencies hidden within. He was quite

76. Ironically, Shiratori has been described as "casual" regarding his use of sources; improper citations were apparently not uncommon in his drafts. See Yoshikawa (ed.), *Tōyōgaku no sōshishatachi*, 45–46.
77. Krieger, *Ranke*, esp. 1–20. For studies that emphasize Shiratori's objectivity, see Tsuda, "Shiratori hakushi shōden," 346–47; Goi, *Kindai nihon to tōyōshigaku*, 79–80; and Hatada, "Nihon ni okeru tōyōshigaku no dentō." For an account in English, see Fogel, *Politics and Sinology*, 119–20.
78. For this interpretation, see Hatada, "Nihon ni okeru tōyōshigaku no dentō"; and Tsuda, "Shiratori hakushi shōden," 346–47. For a summary in English, see Fogel, *Politics and Sinology*, 119–20.

aware that a framework, a prescientific philosophy of history, establishes the criteria that determine what is accurate, objective, correct, and true.

Shiratori should perhaps be best known as a synthesizer of mid-Meiji ideas. Even though at least one biographer has discounted any connection between his early writings and his later career, that early work is highly reminiscent of Miyake and Inoue.[79] As early as 1890, Shiratori experimented with various ideas to center the study of history on a unilinear notion of progress. As he put it, "Everything within society is from this inevitable mechanism [progress]. The variations that exist struggle against one long continuous thread; in a similar way, when events that appear to be accidental and independent are thoroughly investigated, one will find that they belong to the underlying trend and are connected to the previous era." The role of history is to understand that mechanism: "The persons from the past who became famous and are called heroes are merely those who understood the direction of this social power and grasped the opportunity. In other words, heroes are the children and tools of society."[80] This conviction that history contains the secrets to understanding human society—the collective group—was a consistent feature of all his writing. Thirty-eight years later, near the end of his career, Shiratori credited Guizot with pointing the way for the historical profession in Japan: "True history is not placing emphasis on facts; but, based on a theoretical methodology, it is possessing a thorough knowledge of cause and effect."[81] For Shiratori, facts were essential to fill the gaps of a broader historical narrative. Nevertheless, the use of the metaphor of children raises the question of human agency in enlightenment history: if one must always obey the law, an inevitable mechanism, does the child (or nation) ever gains its own subjectivity?

Identifying the exact nature of this inevitable mechanism, the "authentic philosophy of history" that would combine the subjective needs of Japan with demands for universalistic and objective knowledge, proved difficult for the young Shiratori. Like Inoue and Miyake, he

79. Goi argues that there is little connection between Shiratori's writings and later studies; see *Kindai nihon to tōyōshigaku*, 23. Others would probably agree with Goi, for they, too, do not consider his first two articles—"Rekishi to chishi no kankei," *Shigakkai zasshi* 1 (December 1889): 56–64; and "Rekishi to jinketsu," *Shigakkai zasshi* 2 (January 1890): 5–9—which were not included in his collected works.

80. Shiratori, "Rekishi to jinketsu," 8, 9.

81. Shiratori, "Gakushūin ni okeru shigakka no enkaku," *Gakushūin hōninkai zasshi* 134 (October 1928), in *SKZ* 10:379.

found it easier to write history in negative terms; for Shiratori, scientific historical methods became the authority that would diminish the stature of *kangaku*. His 1890 article "Rekishi to jinketsu" (History and Heroes), for example, confronted the exegetical study of the Chinese classics directly.[82] He stated that the history of Asia has been that of great men and heroes—a bias, he noted parenthetically, that was not unique. But these exemplary men, he continued, were often elevated or created by later generations to authorize tradition and norms of behavior. The restraints imposed by such chronologies, he pointed out, impeded the Japanese abilities of inquiry and synthesis. This attack equated *kangaku* with *shina*, the once-great culture that, though still proud and self-centered, was now backward and decaying. Positivistic history freed the present from the confines of an ideal that was fabricated to perpetuate respect for the authority of the past; the heroes of the past, like *shina*, the culture Japan had so revered, had been dethroned from their unassailable position.

This use of science to reject *kangaku*, however, does not signify full acceptance of a Western theory of history. "Occidentals," Shiratori complained, "are apt to fall into self-indulgent arrogance and conceit. They believe that the discovery and invention of world culture [*bunbutsu*] occurred among their race, and consider yellow and black people inherently inferior races with no creative abilities."[83] In an abridged translation of James Bryce's "The Relations of History and Geography," Shiratori made a subtle change that eliminated its cultural specificity. In a passage where Bryce wrote that man is "largely determined and influenced by the environment of Nature," Shiratori gave mankind a far more active role. The translation reads, "Although man struggles against nature and regulates [*seigyō*] nature, . . . man, as one part of nature, is controlled by climate [*fūdo kikō*], which bounds progress and decline."[84] Although one might dismiss this change as an error in translation, the difference between Bryce's statement and Shiratori's translation suggests new meanings created by the appropriation of someone else's words. The change from nature over man in Bryce to

82. Shiratori, "Rekishi to jinketsu," 5–9. Shiratori's ideas bear a similarity to Hegel's discussion of great men and history; see Hegel, *Philosophy of History*, 29–35.

83. Shiratori, "Shina jōdaishi," in *SKZ* 8:545–77 (quote at 549).

84. Shiratori, "Rekishi to chishi no kankei," 57. The original reads, "In other words, he is in history the creature of his environment, not altogether its creature, but working out also those inner forces that he possesses as a rational and moral being; but on one side, at all events, he is largely determined and influenced by the environment of Nature" (James Bryce, "The Relations of History and Geography," *Contemporary Review* 49 [March 1886]: 426–27).

man over nature in Shiratori parallels Miyake's criticism of Buckle's geographic determinism. While Shiratori, like Buckle, described Climate as the "scientific" determinant for the accumulation of wealth, now man, not Nature, determines knowledge. Yet despite his attempt to give Japan the potential for historical development by giving man power over nature, Shiratori accepted most current scientific concepts: the role of climate in societal development, the priority of the group, and a belief in progress. It is not surprising, then, that he was unable to explain difference.

Shiratori directly (and unsuccessfully) confronted this failure in an unpublished article on ancient China from circa 1904. He based his argument on the data of several prominent European Orientalists, including James Legge, Pierre Laffitte, and Terrien de Lacouperie, while working within a progressive framework similar to that of Comte, with movement from fetishism, the interpretation of all objects and affairs of the external world in terms of animate life; theology, the voluntary use of abstract conceptions to distinguish objects within one's own consciousness; and positivism, the combination of phenomenal experience with spiritual experience.[85] China, he argued, was still within the first stage; the utterly accurate and minute descriptions of the phenomenal world were evidence that it had reached the most advanced level of fetishism. Japan, with its polysyllabic language, had reached the metaphysical stage.

The use of the Comtean framework and the work of European Orientalists signals Shiratori's attempt to place his work within the same scholarly dialogues of these Europeans. But although he was working within the same framework, his purpose was different; by reassigning Japan to a more advanced stage of development than China, he separated the two nations and tried, unsuccessfully, to extract Japan from the limitations imposed by the categorical norms for determining progress. He could not, however, overcome the Western positivist tenet that difference—in other words, the non-West—translates to inequality, indeed, inferiority. It is significant that this article—his only work that applied Comte to Asian history—was not published, for surely he realized that by placing China (fetishism) and Japan (metaphysics) within this Comtean scheme, Asian history was still being defined in terms of Western hierarchy.

85. Shiratori disavowed any connection to Comtean positivism, but went on to describe progress as a three-tiered unilinear progression; see "Shina jōdaishi," in *SKZ* 8:558–59. For Shiratori's engagement with these Orientalists, see 545, 550–58, and 573–76.

Although each of these Japanese intellectuals received very different training—Miyake was largely self-taught, Inoue was schooled in philosophy, and Shiratori was trained in positivistic history—by the 1890s their interests converged on a single issue: alterity, which brought forcefully to Japan's attention with the Western expansion into Asia. For Japan, then, the West became another other, in addition to a China that was rapidly losing its preeminent position. Yet the question of universality forced Japan to dig deeper into Asia's past. A dialectic that separated self and other, Japan and China, or Japan and the West could not be so facilely perpetuated when Japan was in the process of modernizing.

By the 1890s, however, this inquiry was still cast in terms defined by the West. Thus Miyake, Inoue, and Shiratori each attempted to reject the part of Western thought that, he believed, forced Japan to be like the West: Miyake and Shiratori renounced geographical determinism, while Inoue disavowed mediating categories of science to describe a national past. They did not, however, resolve the issue. Miyake and Shiratori's adherence to a unilinear concept of progress precluded difference, while Inoue's rejection of science eliminated the potential for dialogue with Europe. Miyake virtually stopped writing history after 1890, and Inoue would become well known (indeed, infamous) for his work on national ethics and spirit. Shiratori would discover an escape from this predicament in Ranke's spirit.

Formulation of an Idea

In the five years following his appointment to Gakushūin in 1890, Shiratori did not publish, ostensibly because he was busy preparing for his courses on oriental history. His first article in five years displayed a considerable difference from earlier work. After 1895 he wrote rather detailed studies, first on the ancient culture of Korea and the Ural-Altaic peoples, later on China, and then on Japan. But while the content and scope of these articles themselves were different, the thrust remained consistent with his general historical project. History was still the means to tie Japan, Europe, and Asia together into a conceptual order that accounted for both difference and equality. After his appointment to Tokyo Imperial University in 1904, the importance of these studies to the formulation of an overall philosophy of history became more apparent.

In 1908 Shiratori began to give greater definition to *tōyōshi* and the field of history in general. Indeed, this seems to be the decade when history as a positivistic science gained preeminence over other historical visions. In one of his few articles devoted exclusively to historical methodology, "Shihitsu no kyokuchi" (The Ideal of Historical Writing), Shiratori called his methodology *kōshō*, textual analysis. Although today he has, understandably, been categorized within this positivistic school, his version of *kōshō* differed considerably from the earlier historical compendia and textual studies that he condescendingly criticized as being something that anyone could do.

Shiratori used the metaphor of a carpenter building a house to describe the ideal historian.[86] He likened *kōshō* to a scaffolding—the means for acquiring the necessary materials, which in the case of history had two dimensions. First, just as a wide variety of materials is necessary to build a house, a vast array of events, peoples, ideas, and so forth exists in the past, which must be sought out from a wide range of fields, including those not normally considered part of the historian's realm. Shiratori's writings on mythology, ethnology, and comparative linguistics among Koreans, Hsiung-nu, Manchus, and Mongols during this period reflect his belief that "nonhistorical" fields, such as the human sciences, philosophy, natural sciences, geography, and astronomy, facilitate construction of a historical understanding. In other words, the whole culture of a nation is crucial for an accurate history. Second, material must be carefully evaluated for accuracy. The historian must eliminate errors and falsifications from frequently embellished historical records and must also immerse himself in the period to understand those facts in their own context. This part of Shiratori's methodology, which he called the scientific half—the technique—has overshadowed his overall vision, as was similarly the case with Ranke. But just as the scaffolding facilitates the placement of materials and is then removed, he considered such detailed studies as preparatory to understanding the whole: "Textual analysis [*kōshō*] does not appear in history, it is merely the preparation and preliminary inquiry."[87]

The other half of history is the artistic side; Shiratori criticized those who wrote dry factual narratives (a comment that is common in the historical profession today as well): "The only point is that there are no mistakes. . . . Facts [*jijitsu*] are indeed accurate, but they are not at all interesting to read. It has reached the point that only the specialist

86. Shiratori, "Shihitsu no kyokuchi," *Bunshō sekai* 3 (January 1908): 64–69.
87. Ibid., 66.

has the perseverance to read [history]."[88] He asserted that like the poet who has the "power of synthesis and imagination," the historian must be able to synthesize masses of data. Those who concentrate on minutiae too often are unable to discern the general trends and the spirit of the age. These trends and spirit form the structure—the reason for history—that will allow the facts to remain without the methodological scaffold.

The model for Shiratori's ideal historian was Ranke, not so much the positivist Ranke, but a historian whose dominant historical trends offered a framework for synthesizing objective inquiry.[89] For example, in one of his first meetings as a young student with his mentor, Hashimoto Masukichi approached Shiratori for detailed information on ancient China. Shiratori's advice, he recalled, was that he read Ranke's *History of the Popes.*[90] Shiratori's regard for Ranke as a well-rounded historian perhaps comes through better in this lavish praise: "His prose is outstanding, concise, and elegant, and at the same time he satisfies both the intellect [*risei*] and emotions with his sophisticated ideas and revealing descriptions of the spiritual world."[91] Shiratori saw in Ranke the ability not only to uncover facts, but also to use those facts to write an elegant history (a goal that one can easily argue Shiratori himself did not achieve) that synthesized a considerable range of evidence and uncovered general trends (*taisei*).

The religiosity alluded to above provided an avenue for Shiratori to resolve the dilemma that plagued him during his early career. He uncovered the possibility of writing such spirit into history in Ranke's emphasis on "dominant tendencies," a suitably vague concept that facilitated a union of the universal—that which all societies have—and the particular—the description of that idea through a society:

Each age is immediate to God, and its value depends not on what comes out of it but in its own existence, in its very self. Therewith the consideration of history, and especially of individual life in history, gets its entirely distinctive charm, since by it every epoch must be viewed as something valuable in itself and as entirely worthy of consideration. The historian has thus to direct his main attention in the first instance to how men have thought and lived in a certain period, and then he will find that apart from the certain unchangeable and eternal main ideas—for example the moral—every epoch has its particular ten-

88. Ibid., 65.
89. For a reappraisal of Ranke, see Krieger, *Ranke.*
90. Enoki, *Tōyō Bunko no rokujūnen,* 272.
91. Shiratori, "Shihitsu no kyokuchi," 68.

dency and its own ideal. . . . All generations of mankind appear equally justified before God, and so too must the historian regard the matter.[92]

The *History of the Popes* was the first work in which Ranke employed the theme of Christianity, not only as the universal spirit essential for bringing out the particular, but also as a history in its own right, one that embodied the ideal he was seeking.[93] Thus, because the appearance of the universal spirit is specific to time and place, individuals (and particularly the nation) developed differently, often to correct the past: the reformation of Catholic corruption was "one of the most characteristic and successful tendencies of the human spirit, . . . opening it to the freedom of a new and different progress."[94] This new freedom and progress were specific to Protestants, especially Germans. The main theme in the *History of the Popes* was the distinction between increasing political considerations among the Catholics and the priority of religious conviction among the Protestants. In other words, the dominant tendency, Protestant progressivism, combined the priority of spirit over the secular world with Germany's rise.

This theme was used by Shiratori as well, who saw in this religious spirit the unifying theme for the Japanese nation-state, one that opened Japan to "the freedom of a new and different progress." In contrast to an earlier article, "Shina jōdaishi," where he posited the spiritual world as part of the final stage of development, he now called religiosity Japan's basis for progress. Since this spirit was prior to and much more vague (that is, closer to the origin of man) than the universal of positivism, Shiratori could point out that the cultures of Japan, Asia, and Europe were essentially equivalent: they all possessed spirit. But because that tendency developed differently according to specific geographic conditions, it also allowed for different essences and origins. Hence, although Shiratori's history was informed largely by Western historiography, through adaptation it was altered into a theory with a similar structure but quite different context, and one with far-reaching implications. The Japanese political system, he argued, was a religious government (*shūkyōteki seiji*) called *matsurigoto*, meaning that all the affairs of the nation are determined by the gods.[95]

92. Quoted in Krieger, *Ranke*, 229.
93. Ibid., 151–52.
94. Ibid., 138, 154.
95. See, for example, Shiratori, "Nihon ni okeru jukyō no junnōsei," in *SKZ* 10:236. The character *sei* can be read *matsurigoto*. The political implications of this interpretation will be discussed in Chapter 4.

Hayden White's comments on Ranke's unifying concept are especially relevant:

The "idea of the nation" was for Ranke not only a datum but also a value; ... Ranke revealed as much when he characterized the "idea of the nation" as eternal, changeless, a thought of God. He admitted that peoples may come and go, churches may form and disappear, and states may arise and perish; and that it is the historian's task to chronicle their passage or, in later times, to reconstruct them in their individuality and uniqueness. But to grasp their essence, to perceive their individuality and uniqueness, is to seize the "idea" which informed them, which gave them their being as specific historical existents, and to find the unitary principle which made them a something rather than an anything. And this is possible only because the "idea" of a nation is timeless and eternal.[96]

Shiratori, too, was seeking that unifying principle, the essence of culture through which he might unearth Japan's "individuality and uniqueness" and give it "being as specific historical existents." But he differed from Ranke in that the contestation for difference in Ranke's formula occurred within a common understanding of Europe, and problems raised by the distancing of non-Europe from Europe were not an issue.[97] Unlike Ranke, Shiratori had not only to account for the difference of the nation, but also to place East and West on a level of equivalence. His "idea of the nation," therefore, was not a "thought" of God, but a historical concept, rooted deep in the protohistoric age. By basing Japan's "idea of the nation" on a historical idea—a manifestation of the concept of heaven or, in other words, the imperial institution—Shiratori found a way to identify the uniqueness of Japan and thus give it an identity. But despite being historical, as the manifestation of a universal spirit, the imperial institution was also removed from history and became timeless. It was a common denominator of all human societies and could be studied scientifically to understand how cultures develop. While Ranke's "idea of the nation" functioned to discourage the social scientific search for universal laws, Shiratori's use of Ranke's "idea" co-opted such laws. Science was necessary to uncover, objectively, that progressive "idea." As White points out, the search for a universal questions the idea of nation as an absolute value and reveals the *"purely historical nature* of national characteristics."[98] But while for

---

96. Hayden White, *Metahistory: The Historical Imagination in Nineteenth-Century Europe* (Baltimore: Johns Hopkins University Press, 1973), 172.
97. See Chatterjee, *Nationalist Thought and the Colonial World*, 1–35.
98. White, *Metahistory*, 174; italics in the original.

Ranke this revelation might have been undesirable, in that it would have called into question the objectivity of his studies, for Shiratori it was necessary to explain Japan's difference. The particularistic potential for such a theory is clear. One merely has to drop the assumption that this universalistic spirit, though manifested differently, is rooted in all cultures; it then becomes possible to affirm Japan's unique heritage, even while retaining the belief in modernity and science.

The elevation of spirit to a timeless norm allowed Shiratori to solve many of the issues that had confronted Meiji intellectuals. He was able to shed the odious parts of both *kangaku* and enlightenment history and instead create a history that was similar to that of the West, specifically, Germany. Much as the West had used the Western Orient and the "world of Islam" in its self-construction, Shiratori used religiosity to construct a new historical narrative useful to Japan.[99] This idea was no more arbitrary than Comte's positivism or Ranke's spirit, and served a similar role: it organized the concepts of change, progress, and the social unit. Progress was no longer tied to a unilinear scheme of development, but to something timeless, the idea of the nation. Moreover, historical study, as the mediation between the study of man and of science, remained scientific and objective. To mix two metaphors used earlier, having laid the foundation, the Japanese were now able to begin construction on their own Trojan horse. It was now necessary to gather the proper materials, the historical facts that would support the "idea."

99. For an excellent paper that examines the importance of Islam to the distinction between East and West, see Talal Asad, *The Idea of an Anthropology of Islam*, Occasional Paper Series, Center for Contemporary Arab Studies, Georgetown University (Washington, D.C., 1987). Asad states, "It is too often forgotten that 'the world of Islam' is a concept for organizing historical narratives, not the name for a self-contained collective agent" (11).

CHAPTER TWO

Tōyōshi: The Convergence of East and West

The question of universality and cultural integrity inevitably confronts non-Western cultures in their effort to understand the relationship between themselves and modernity, usually equated with the West. In fact, during the Meiji period this issue defined the debate on history in general and Japan's history more specifically. The pretense that Western history explains the history of all cultures by relegating cultures like Japan to the perpetually inferior category of the Orient perhaps makes this issue inevitable. The comprehensiveness of history is succinctly described by Emmanuel Levinas:

> Totalization is accomplished only in history—in the history of the historiographers, that is, among the survivors. It rests on the affirmation and the conviction that the chronological order of the history of the historians outlines the plot of being in itself, analogous to nature. The time of universal history remains as the ontological ground in which particular existences are lost, are computed, and in which at least their essences are recapitulated. Birth and death as punctual moments, and the interval that separates them, are lodged in this universal time of the historian, who is a survivor.[1]

In the modern world, one wonders whether difference on equivalent terms that do not define and thus objectify an object, person, or society is possible. In a fascinating book critical of the eclectic and traditionalist approaches of Arab intellectuals, Abdallah Laroui also locates the problem in history. He writes, "So that it could not be used exclusively

1. Levinas, *Totality and Infinity,* 55.

by any one group, the historical narrative had to be as universal and as neutral as possible; thus it could play a vital role in the formation of that ideology which was gradually to win the allegiance of the majority and which consequently was to be called 'orthodoxy.' "[2] The dilemma is that a universal cannot be neutral if it becomes an orthodoxy that wins the allegiance of the majority. By the very fact that a majority and minorities exist and allegiance is won suggests conflict, possession, and a hierarchy between knower and known, orthodox and heterodox, and right and wrong. The power of history derives in large part both from its potential to define the categories and content of narratives and from the transparency of these frameworks. Even if the allegiance of a large body of people—a nation or a region—is won, this makes history universal only for those who accept it. Those exterior to it must either be won over—suggesting that something will be lost—or formulate a new universal. Since Japanese historians were not won over, they had to become the survivors or majority that defined their own past and made history transparent again.

Although Shiratori discovered an idea in Ranke's religiosity that would allow him to create a history that emphasized Japan's own subjectivity, the restrictions of Western categories remained. To be fully autonomous, he still had to redefine those categories by altering Japan's oriental past. This chapter will examine his efforts to deny existing categories, to redraw parameters and boundaries, and to rewrite that past. Such actions—denial, redrawing, and rewriting—imply that the new history must be constructed from a greater variety of events, objects, places, and peoples than had previously "existed."[3] Temporal and spatial categories must be established, as well as subcategories that order, categorize, and give value to certain fragments of those discovered pasts. Just as the Orient provided the past for the creation of a Western history, *tōyō* became the authority and precedence for a Japanese history that explained issues such as political development, social ideals, military and cultural expansion, and cultural values. Thus, even as these historians were extracting from the past to determine Japan's origins and relation to Asia, they were also constructing *tōyō*.

2. Abdallah Laroui, *The Crisis of the Arab Intellectual: Traditionalism or Historicism*, trans. Diarmid Cammell (Berkeley and Los Angeles: University of California Press, 1976), 18.

3. For fascinating works on the use of the past in memory and history, see Lowenthal, *The Past Is a Foreign Country*; Benedict Anderson, *Imagined Communities* (London: Verso, 1983); and Eric Hobsbawm and Terence Ranger, eds., *The Invention of Tradition* (Cambridge: Cambridge University Press, 1983).

This search for history evolved from a dialogue with Western Orientalists into a competition with them over the content of that history. Asia became the contested region that provided the origin and evidence for their respective narratives. Dialogue existed during the 1890s and into the 1900s as Japanese intellectuals drew on competing theories of Western Orientalists to debate Japan's beginnings in relation to Asia. As Taguchi's historical narrative indicates, Japan's "oriental heritage," that is, its cultural affinity to India and China, was not widely accepted. Other intellectuals debated whether Japanese perhaps originated from the Malay-Polynesian race, whether they derived from the same people as Koreans, or whether the original Japan was an early thalassocracy comprising present-day Japan, Korea, and southeastern China. But as the concept of *tōyō* gained weight, and because it—and the Western Orient—represented the origins of both East and West, historical scholarship evolved into a competition with the West over ideology. Each side accumulated the historical evidence that filled in the narrative gaps, proved their past, and affirmed their ideological position in the contemporary world.

The framework that Shiratori used to order Japan's history was called a North-South dualism. Like the stages of progress, the typologies of this dualism, though based on an assumption of conflict as opposed to intellectual growth, were rendered transparent by the historical facts that supported it. In the end, rather than accounting for alterity, the Japanese established their own totality.

The Search for Origins

In the inaugural issue of the newly founded Historical Association's journal, *Shigakkai zasshi*, Shigeno Yasutsugu, the interim president, stated: "In opening this association today we hope to assist the nation-state [*kokka*]. By using materials collected by the Historical Bureau [Shikyoku] and referring to historical research methods of the West, we will investigate and compile the facts of our country's history."[4] In the following decade, the articles in this journal focused primarily on ancient Japan and its relation to the Asian continent. Substantial debate existed over what that past contained—that is, who

4. Shigeno Yasutsugu, "Shigaku ni jūji suru mono wa sono kokoro shikō shihei narazarubekarazu," *Shigakkai zasshi* 1 (December 1889): 5.

and what events were to be included (the immediate past, the Tokugawa period, for example, was virtually eliminated) and how those different components were to interact. The issue of which past best conforms to Japan's larger geocultural world was a driving force behind this inquiry, and questions that had been considered "settled" now reemerged. In 1891, for example, articles on Japan's protohistoric society reopened a debate that Motoori Norinaga had put to rest when he confirmed Kyushu as the location of Yamatai, the ancient kingdom mentioned in the *Wei chih*. Research on the ancient history of Korea also became popular; many felt that the period of Korea's three kingdoms held the key to answering the questions of Japan's origins.[5]

JAPAN AS A THALASSOCRACY

Two scholars whose writings suggest the diversity of interpretations are Kume Kunitake and Inoue Tetsujirō. Indeed, one article in this inaugural issue, the first of a series of three by Kume, played an important role in raising several issues about Japan's origins and ancient relations with the continent. Despite being categorized as a positivist scholar, Kume believed that Japan's history should be explained within the framework of general historical laws: "Just as the ocean waves are rarely still, the hundreds and thousands of years of a country's expansionary and contracting tendencies are not fixed. When prosperous, we annex others; when weakened, we are invaded by others, form alliances, or are divided. Neither can mountains or rivers constrain, nor can oceans separate. Because it is obvious that this [law] shines on the history of all countries, Japan, too, should be included."[6] This view shares much with those of the historians discussed in Chapter 1: the belief that history has value, that it is dynamic, and that certain laws govern peoples. Moreover, Kume did not accept the implications of enlightenment, that Japan's past was stagnant or, at best, lacked progress. Yet Kume differed from his predecessors and contemporaries in his attempt to present an interpretation of the begin-

5. The three kingdoms were Koguryŏ (37 B.C.–A.D. 668), Paekche (18 B.C.–A.D. 660), and Silla (57 B.C.–A.D. 935). On the debate of Japan's origins, see John Young, *The Location of Yamatai: A Case Study in Japanese Historiography, 720–1945* (Baltimore: Johns Hopkins University Press, 1958), 86–104; Hatada Takashi, "Nihon ni okeru chōsenshi kenkyū no dentō," in *Nihonjin no chōsenkan* (Tokyo: Chikuma Shobō, 1969), 235.

6. Kume Kunitake, "Nihon fukuin no enkaku," *Shigakkai zasshi* 1 (December 1889): 15.

nings of the history of a Japan that extended beyond its contemporary geopolitical borders—a familiar strategy in the histories of Western civilization.

Kume argued that Japan before Jinmu (the mythical first emperor) was a sort of thalassocracy encompassing Kyushu, Korea, and southeastern China. As historians of protohistoric Japan know today, such arguments only open a Pandora's box, for they raise direct questions of origins and the nature of Japanese culture. At this time, the Japanese passion for uniqueness and resistance to any suggestion of derivation from Korea had not yet become dogma. Thus, while Kume's article may not have initiated the debate on Japan's origins, it was certainly one of the earliest modern attempts to define Japan's origins, and it was a precursor to the debate that followed over whether Japanese were related to Malay Polynesians or Ural Altai (Tungus, such as Koreans, Mongols, and Turks).[7]

Kume's article served as a virtual challenge to historians, for he not only accused them of having tunnel vision, but he also questioned long-standing facts or "traditions" and provided an interpretation at odds with many cherished beliefs. For example, he criticized the notion of Japan as an island nation that had not changed in thousands of years. He complained, "At present, hardly anyone has inquired into the history [*enkaku*] of Japan's geographical expanse [*fukuin*]; it is considered trivial. Because the ancient Ōyashima has been designated as the archipelago—Tōyōakitsu-shima [Honshu], Iyo [Shikoku], Tsukushi [Kyushu], Sado, Iki, Tsushima, etc.—everyone believes that Japan— the five home provinces and seven roads [*gokishichidō*]—was defined from the beginning. This is a premature conclusion."[8] Few predecessors or peers would have denied relations between Japan and the continent, but Kume went beyond them in arguing that racial and cultural affinity served as the basis for a dynamic historical narrative.

Kume divided Japanese history into three periods that coincided with geopolitical changes: (1) a thalassocratic period, when Japan was located along the southern part of the Japanese archipelago (including Kyushu), Korea to the north, and southeastern China (Fukien) to the south; (2) the era in which relations with southeastern China ended

---

7. See Hatada Takashi, "Nihonjin no chōsenkan," in *Nihonjin no chōsenkan*, 3–50 (first published in *Ajia, afurika kōza* 3 [1964]).
8. Kume, "Nihon fukuin no enkaku," December 1889, 15.

and Japan was tied with Kaya (Mimana), an ancient kingdom on the Korean peninsula, from the time of Emperor Sujin (ca. the third century A.D.) to Empress Saimei (r. ca. 655–61); and (3) the current period, in which Japan's borders became defined by the archipelago.[9]

To fill this periodization, Kume used passages from the *Nihon shoki* and *Kojiki,* not as actual facts, but as allegorical data that describe historical events.[10] For example, to prove Japan's connection with southeastern China, Kume located *tokoyo* (lit., land of darkness)—the mythical land that appeared in the legend of Mike-nu no mikoto, the brother of Jinmu, and to which Emperor Suinin sent Tadima mori to acquire the "seasonless fruit tree" (*tachibana*)—in Fukien.[11] Kume also pointed to the locations of the early Japanese capitals as further evidence of a maritime connection. The early capital at Pimuka (southeastern Kyushu), for example, was ideal for ruling Kyushu, but as Japanese political power extended to Korea, new settlements that faced Korea—Kashii (Fukuoka) and Kikki (Izumo)—were also established.[12]

There is little doubt today that the chronology of Japan's ancient histories, especially the *Nihon shoki,* is largely myth, but during the 1890s the value and validity of these texts were important issues. Kume used these legends and found corroborating evidence in the *Hou Han shu* and the *Liang shu* to construct his cyclical theory of Asian development. This cycle took its essential form from a system of hereditary rule based on benevolence and wisdom, with a cycle lasting typically about ten generations, or two hundred to three hundred years.[13] Using this "fact" and calculating backward from Emperor Sushun (r. 587–92), with the average reign deemed to be twenty-five to thirty years, Kume

9. The tenth emperor, Sujin is now considered a legendary emperor. This approximate date is taken from Kume's own periodization; the legendary reign is 97–30 B.C.

10. Although he was vehemently attacked for his article, "Shintō wa saiten no kozoku," he sought not to destroy *shintō,* but to establish grounds so that it could weather the skepticism of his day. A similar situation will be described in the following chapter on Shiratori's murder theory of Yao, Shun, and Yü.

11. Kume, "Nihon fukuin no enkaku," December 1889, 16–17. For the legend of Mike-nu no mikoto, see Donald L. Philippi, trans., *Kojiki* (Tokyo: University of Tokyo Press, 1968), 159–69; and W. G. Aston, trans. *Nihongi,* new ed. (Tokyo: Charles E. Tuttle, 1972), 108, 114. For the legend of Tadima mori, see Philippi (trans.), *Kojiki,* 226–27; and Aston (trans.), *Nihongi,* 186–87, esp. n. 1.

12. Kume, "Nihon fukuin no enkaku," December 1889, 18–19.

13. Ibid., January 1890, 11–16; he cited numerous examples, such as the T'ang and Ming dynasties in China and the Ashikaga and Tokugawa periods in Japan.

established the beginning of Japanese history: according to his scheme, Jinmu reigned sometime between 69 B.C. and A.D. 42.[14]

This thalassocracy, Kume further asserted, came to an end around the reign of the eleventh emperor, Suinin, as internal dissension within each region caused a decline in the benevolence of the rulers. Legends in the *Nihon shoki* (he cited the abdication of Ama no hi hoko in favor of his younger brother, Chiko, and the return of the jewels that had belonged to Ina-pi no mikoto) depicted the end of the thalassocracy and conflict within Korea that led to its division into three states.[15] In Japan, a corresponding situation existed in the rebellion of Kumaso in Kyushu—recorded in the *Hou Han shu*—and Ezo (Ainu) in the north. Japan, however, was able to avoid the division that beset Korea thanks to the wise policies of Keikō, the twelfth emperor, who gave priority to restoring domestic tranquillity and reversed Sujin's and Suinin's policies of domestic suppression and adventurism abroad. Foreign contact was not completely abandoned, for Japan maintained some of its ties, especially with Kaya. Thus Kume argued that even though Japan's continental presence was now not as strong as in the past, Jingū's expedition to Korea around the first half of the fourth century, which many see as Japan's first invasion of Korea, was not for the sake of plunder or aggrandizement, because Korea was indebted (*ongi*) to Japan.[16] This second period ended around the reign of Empress Saimei; the geographical area of Japan now contracted further, becoming restricted to those islands of the archipelago that still defined Japan's territory at the outset of the Meiji period.

The problem with this narrative (indeed, with all such narratives) is that it did not solve questions of Japanese origins but only raised new ones. Rather than directly addressing the issue of Japanese origins, Kume assumed that the Japanese people were an indigenous race that simply expanded into other regions. The people of this thalassocracy, he stated, most likely originated from a "southern island" of the Japanese archipelago, which he implied was Kyushu, for he accepted com-

14. Kume pointed out that this period corresponds to one of rebellion in southeastern China during the reign of emperor Yuan-ti (48–32 B.C.), which he interpreted as conflict between an independent Min yüeh and Chinese, and to that of the founding of Silla, the ancient Korean kingdom, around 57 B.C.

15. Kume, "Nihon fukuin no enkaku," January 1890, 16; and ibid., February 1890, 9–10. Because Ina-pi no mikoto is the brother of Jinmu, this legend is tied to the founding of Japan and Korea. It is a Japanese myth; Aston mentioned that he did not find Chiko or a counterpart in Korean legends, thus casting doubt on this figure's existence.

16. Ibid., February 1890, 14.

mon knowledge of the time, that the capital of Japan before Jinmu was Pimuka.[17] These primitive people, he claimed, gradually developed a rudimentary understanding of navigation and began to travel, especially to Korea; eventually they migrated to the southwest, settling in southeastern China around Canton. Kume found some similarities between the Min yüeh, Koreans, and Japanese, but this consanguinity did not necessarily mean equivalence: the Min yüeh and Koreans, he argued, originated from the Japanese.

Despite (or because of) Kume's positivist claims, the parallels of his narrative to events in contemporary Asia are readily apparent. According to his cycle, difficult periods (which he would probably liken to the Bakumatsu period) were always followed by two hundred years of just and prosperous rule. But such prosperity, he suggested, was possible only if one was properly vigilant and one's foreign policy was not overly ambitious; one must first rule well at home and refrain from adopting heavy-handed measures to venture abroad. Nevertheless, his belief that Korea and Japan were related and that the former bore an obligation to Japan of course provided precedence for closer relations, with Japan preeminent. Eventually, arguments like Kume's would serve as a historical justification for the annexation of Korea.[18]

MALAY-POLYNESIAN ROOTS

On May 30, 1890, several months after the publication of Kume's article, Inoue took up his colleague's challenge and presented his version of the origins of the Japanese people in a speech to the Historical Association entitled "Proof of the Origins of the Japanese People." In contrast to Kume, Inoue argued that Japanese and Koreans had very little in common. Instead, Japan's ancestors were related to the Malay-Polynesian peoples, who, he found, physiologically resembled the common, not elite, Japanese.[19] He cited as proof of his

17. Ibid., December 1889, 18.
18. Hatada, "Nihonjin no chōsenkan," in *Nihonjin no chōsenkan*, 36–41.
19. Using craniofacial and odontometric evidence, C. Loring Brace has recently suggested a South Pacific lineage of early Japanese. Brace argues that craniofacial features among remains from Yayoi and modern Japanese bear a great similarity to Koreans, Chinese, and Southeast Asians, whereas Jōmon, Ainu, and South Pacific peoples have different characteristics. Furthermore, the latter group also made a recognizable contribution to the makeup of the warrior class in the Kamakura period. See Brace, "Reflections on the Face of Japan: A Multivariate Craniofacial and Odontometric Perspective," *American Journal of Physical Anthropology* 78 (1989): 93–113.

theory passages in the *Nihon shoki* and the *Kojiki* that mentioned animals like the crocodile and multiheaded snakes common to Southeast Asia; the worship of yin and yang, which he likened to the phallic worship of Borneo; cognate words, such as "I" (Japanese *aga* or *ago*, Malaysian and Javan *aku*, Sanskrit *aham*, and Latin *ego*) and "fire" (Japanese *pi* or *po*, Malay *api*, and Javan *abi*); the preponderance of the number eight in the *Kojiki;* the quarrel between Hiko hoho demi no mikoto and his brother Ho-susori no mikoto (who wore a loincloth—warm-weather attire) over the latter's fish hook, which he claimed was strikingly similar to legends in Borneo; and the presence of a sun mythology in Java but not among northern Asian peoples.[20]

Inoue did not deny that nomads from the north passed through Korea and settled in Japan, but these people were not nearly as important to his narrative as the Malays. His primary purpose was to refute the idea that the Japanese and Koreans originated from the same people: "Simply, that is an absurd [*ranbō*] concept. It is truly the idea of a layman."[21] Instead he countered with an interpretation that the Japanese are a mixed race composed primarily of Malay stock, but also of some northern people (whom he did not specify), a few Chinese, and even Ainu (whom he admitted grudgingly). He agreed that there are similarities with Koreans but only because they, too, are from a mixed stock. But, he emphasized, the nature of that mix and the two people's subsequent development—customs, habits, personality, physique, and language—differ.[22]

The target of Inoue's refutation went beyond domestic scholars such as Kume; he was also criticizing the predominant interpretation among Western Orientalists that the Japanese belong to the Ural-Altaic linguistic group.[23] In another article on the racial origins of Japanese, Inoue traced the myriad Western interpretations of Japan's origins and concluded that virtually all were "absurd hypotheses." In particular, he contended that the thesis of similarity between Japanese and Mongols (Ural Altai) was an erroneous notion initially set forth by Western scholars to suggest Japanese inferiority to the West.[24] Inoue called on

20. Inoue Tetsujirō, "Nihon minzoku no kigen ni kansuru kōshō," in *Tetsugaku to shūkyō* (Tokyo: Kōdōkan, 1915), 732–63.

21. Inoue, "Kinji no nihon jinshuron," in *Tetsugaku to shūkyō,* 793.

22. Ibid., 793–94.

23. For Shiratori's criticism of Inoue, see *"Nihon shoki* ni mietaru kango no kaishaku," *Shigaku zasshi* 8 (April, June, July 1897), in *SKZ* 3:115–54, esp. 150–51.

24. Inoue Tetsujirō, "Jinshu, gengo oyobi shūkyō nado no hikaku ni yori, nihonjin no ichi o ronsu," *Tōhō kyōkai hōkoku* 20 (December 1892): 27–37.

physiological evidence (that should strike us as humorous today) to show otherwise. For example, he declared that the Mongolian blue spot (a small bluish area, like a birthmark, that disappears after infancy), common among Japanese and other Asian babies, does not indicate physical inferiority to Caucasians, largely because it is also not found among Ainu babies, whom he considered definitely inferior to Japanese. He also used historical artifacts to show equivalence; for example, he found that both the ancient Western civilizations, such as ancient Greece and Phoenicia, and the ancient Asian civilizations, such as Persia and India, had a similar system of worship centered on the yin and yang or phallic culture.[25]

These historical debates indicate the difficulty of finding difference within predefined categories. Both Kume and, as I shall describe shortly, Shiratori attempted to work within the framework of Western historical methodology. Both, moreover, are examples of historians who turned increasingly to Asia to relocate Japan's origin as the beginning of a progressive history. Inoue, in contrast, proposed a Malay-Polynesian tie to counter the more popular (and, he believed, European) interpretation of Japan's Ural-Altaic roots. To extract Japan from the categories imposed by Europe, he used a different origin and narrative that described Japan in contiguous, equivalent, and distinct terms vis-à-vis the West.

Despite differences among these scholars, an overriding commonality marks them: Asia was becoming the spatial and temporal object through which Japanese defined themselves. Yet it is also evident that Japanese self-perception was directly related to their acceptance or rejection of the Western totality. The shift in this role of the West as "other" would figure significantly in the subsequent development of tōyōshi.

Dialogue with European Orientalists

Shiratori began his career within this climate of debate concerning Japan's origins, and most of his research during the first two decades of his career was engaged with these issues. In a 1905 speech he stated, "For many years I have conducted research in various

---

25. Inoue, "Nihon minzoku no kigen," in Tetsugaku to shūkyō, 739, 775.

fields to learn the origin of the Japanese. At first I investigated the history of Korea, which is related to Japan, then that of the peoples of Manchuria, who are related to Koreans, and I gradually looked into other ties. Finally, realizing that I could not learn [Japan's origins] unless I went to Central Asia, I followed the vestiges of the peoples related to us and ended up as far west as Hungary."[26] Shiratori's early studies on ancient Korea and Manchuria provided evidence to show that ancient Japan was related to the Ural-Altaic peoples (including the people of Korea). They directly refuted Inoue's interpretation of a Malay-Polynesian root; and they also challenged Kume's findings, such as the identification of Himiko (as leader of Kumaso), the location of *tokoyo* and the "weak waters" (*jakusui*), and the nature of early Korean history.

In his analysis of Japan's historical studies on Korea, Hatada Takashi has argued that Kume and Shiratori represent two contrasting views, with Shiratori asserting that there was no connection between Japan and Korea.[27] Hatada, however, was comparing late-nineteenth-century "national" historians, like Kume and Shigeno, with Shiratori during his later career. During the 1890s, though, and throughout much of the Meiji period, Shiratori, too, argued that Japanese as well as Koreans belonged to the Ural-Altaic family. It was not until after the Russo-Japanese War that he concluded there was little ancient relation between Japanese and Koreans outside of trade and intercourse.

Shiratori's early acceptance of a Japanese-Korean affinity probably derived from his receptiveness of studies by Western Orientalists, such as Julius Heinrich Klaproth and Friedrich Hirth, which at the time provided the general framework for his quest for Japan's origins and history. When he found their proof to be scanty, he looked for evidence that would fill those gaps.[28] But their research also provided an authoritative voice that he could use in domestic debates. In an 1897 article on the Hsiung-nu, a people on China's northern border during the Han dynasties (206 B.C.–A.D. 220), Shiratori placed Inoue's suggestion that

26. Shiratori, "Gengogakujō yori mitaru 'aino' jinshu" (speech presented in 1905), in *SKZ* 2:349. In 1928, Shiratori recalled that his career as a specialist on Asia began by accident. As one of two historians (Ichimura Sanjirō taught Chinese history), he was responsible for teaching the history of Asia outside of China; he claimed that he began with Korea and Manchuria because they were the two countries closest to Japan. See "Gakushūin ni okeru shigakka no enkaku," in *SKZ* 10:378–83.

27. Hatada, "Nihon ni okeru chōsenshi kenkyū no dentō," 226–48.

28. Shiratori, "Chōsengo to 'Ural Altai'go to no hikaku kenkyū," *Tōyō gakuhō* 4–6 (1914–16), in *SKZ* 3:1–2; and idem, "*Nihon shoki* ni mietaru kango no kaishaku," in *SKZ* 3:150–54.

the Hsiung-nu were related to Indo-Germans within the Western historiographical debate on Asia to reveal the problems with that view as well as to support his proposal that instead these people were related to the Turks (he would later change this identification, singling out the Mongols).[29]

The principal similarity between Shiratori and Western Orientalists involved the use of linguistic evidence. Comparative linguistics was attractive in that it served as a common and "objective" methodology for understanding ancient Asian culture. Language, Shiratori believed, was the key to uncovering the prehistoric past: "When asked how one can know the true origins [*hongen*] of humans where history does not exist, one method is through language. Language tells [*kataru*] that history."[30] In the introduction to his compendium of Korean and Ural-Altaic words, he wrote, "One senses that knowledge of language is the most essential [element] in Western scholars' research on matters of the Orient. To scientists, for whom the object of inquiry should be natural phenomena, language is certainly not a critical requisite. But actually, language is both foundation and stepping stones for those who, to the slightest degree, study culture."[31]

While Shiratori perhaps believed it necessary to justify the use of comparative linguistics to Japanese social scientists, in Europe philological methods dominated the field of Oriental studies up through the mid–nineteenth century. European scholars—missionaries in particular—produced numerous grammatical and lexicographical studies and dictionaries as well as translations. Much of this work was directed toward the identification and, hence, classification of ancient tribes who lived in the vast plains between Europe and China.[32] Such linguistic research viewed language as a system of normatively identical forms. Language was static; it became an object of study in itself, removed from the context of its existence.[33]

29. Shiratori, "Kyōdo wa ikanaru shuzoku ni zokusuru ka?" *Shigaku zasshi* 8 (August 1897), in *SKZ* 4:1–8.

30. Shiratori, "Gengogakujō yori mitaru 'aino' jinshu," in *SKZ* 2:350.

31. Shiratori, "Chōsengo to 'Ural-Altai'go to no hikaku kenkyū," in *SKZ*, 3:1.

32. For a brief introduction to early European Oriental studies, see Nathaniel Schmidt, "Early Oriental Studies in Europe and the Work of the American Oriental Society, 1842–1922," *Journal of the American Oriental Society* 43 (1922): 1–14.

33. Vološinov describes this methodology in *Marxism and the Philosophy of Language*, 71: "European linguistic thought formed and matured over concern with the cadavers of written languages; almost all its basic categories, its basic approaches and techniques were worked out in the process of reviving these cadavers."

The scarcity and limited nature of ancient sources hinder interpretation—or, more kindly, they allow the philologist a broad range of interpretive possibilities—for in the end they offer only glimpses and hints of the origins and early history of people who lived (or roamed) between Europe and China. Two frequently used sources are the standard histories of the early Chinese empire, the *Han shu* and the *Shih chi*, especially the chapters dealing with Han expansion, which reached as far west as Central Asia.[34] Other data must be gleaned from a wide—and often contradictory and unreliable—variety of sources, such as subsequent Chinese histories, Korean mythologies such as the *Samguk sagi* and *Samguk yusa*, and Japan's *Kojiki* and *Nihon shoki*. But rather than serving as a means to a greater understanding of the tension and interaction that is a part of language—what Vološinov calls its multiaccentuality—philological analysis viewed the text as something self-evident and assumed that everything of past cultures could be gleaned from these few sources.[35]

The connection between the Orient and this study of language is no accident. Many believed that language, by allowing the decipherment of alien and mysterious writings, would unlock the secrets to the origin of man. The emergence of Oriental studies in the West, certainly, was connected to the search for the universal primordial religion, and it is no surprise that the first philologists were priests. But philology also served a different group of scholars, ones who were largely responsible for the "renaissance" of the Orient. These scholars believed that the secret to mankind, the "hyperantique," lay hidden in the anonymous Vedas of India and other obscure reaches of the Orient.[36] For these scholars, discoveries of the obscure and hidden past served as the beginning of a new philosophy of history. Vološinov states,

This grandiose organizing role of the alien word, which always either entered upon the scene with alien force of arms and organization or was found on the scene by the young conqueror-nation of an old and once mighty culture and captivated, from its grave, so to speak, the ideological consciousness of the newcomer-nation—this role of the alien word led to its coalescence in the

34. A.F.P. Hulsewé, *China in Central Asia: The Early Stage—125 b.c.–a.d. 23* (Leiden, Neth.: E. J. Brill, 1979), 1–3. Trade goods have even been found in India and parts of the Roman Empire; see Ying-shih Yü, *Trade and Expansion in Han China* (Berkeley and Los Angeles: University of California Press, 1967).
    35. Vološinov, *Marxism and the Philosophy of Language*, 23.
    36. Schwab, *Oriental Renaissance*, 70–81, 203–21.

depths of the historical consciousness of nations with the idea of authority, the idea of power, the idea of holiness, the idea of truth, and dictated that notions about the word be preeminently oriented toward the alien word.[37]

At least since its renaissance in the eighteenth century, the Orient has held deep ideological significance. In general, the interest of Western Orientalists was to describe—overtly or covertly—the past of the Western world, and their studies of Sanskrit and the Semitic languages tended to emphasize the people of Asia (India) only in terms of the development of Western civilization. As research on the Ural-Altaic peoples followed in the early nineteenth century, a similar classificatory system was established by Klaproth and Remusat that likewise gave to Asia a certain position on Europe's periphery.[38] A key issue that would develop from this classificatory system concerned the *Han shu* and *Shih chi* report that the Hsiung-nu were different from the Yüeh-chih and the Wu-huan. If the Hsiung-nu were Turks, then the latter tribes could be identified as Indo-German; if, however, the Hsiung-nu were Mongols, then the latter might be Turks. In other words, one interpretation emphasized Caucasian roots, the other, Asian.[39]

For Shiratori, and *tōyōshi* as well, language was the means by which the prehistoric past and culture of Asia could be historicized. But the difference between the *tōyōshi* scholars and the Western Orientalists was that the former saw Asia as *Japan's* past, whereas the latter saw it as that from which Europe had—literally and figuratively—developed. Asia, then was the common denominator that connected East and West with a shared and equal origin, but at the same time, because of the different emphases, which were "scientifically" and "objectively" determined, it

37. Vološinov, *Marxism and the Philosophy of Language*, 75.

38. According to Tsuda, Shiratori's interest in Oriental studies began after his reading of Klaproth's *Tableaux historiques de l'Asie*. Miyake Yonekichi probably brought this book back to Japan in 1888 and introduced it to Shiratori. Goi agrees with Tsuda but also emphasizes the importance of this research to the domestic interest in uncovering Japan's roots; see *Kindai nihon ni okeru tōyōshigaku*, 46–47.

39. The commonly accepted system was first set forth by Klaproth in his *Asia Polyglotta*. Among the major ancient tribes, he classified the Hsiung-nu, Ting-ling, T'ieh-le, T'u-chüeh, Chien-k'un, and Uighur as Turk; the Tung-hu, Wu-huan, Hsien-pei, T'o-pa, Juan-juan, Khitan, Shih-wei, Jürchen, and Manchu as Tungus; and only the Mo-gen (thirteenth-century Mongols) and Tatars as Mongol; see Shiratori, "Mōko minzoku no kigen," in *SKZ* 4:26. For a more recent account, see E. G. Pulleyblank, "The Chinese and Their Neighbors in Prehistoric and Early Historic Times," in *The Origins of Chinese Civilization*, ed. David N. Keightley (Berkeley and Los Angeles: University of California Press, 1983), 413–66.

led toward very different—though equally modern—world visions. Each side was struggling to be the "decipherer of alien, 'secret' scripts and words, and a teacher, a disseminator, of that which has been deciphered and handed down by tradition."[40] Both the various European and Japanese scholars sought to capture the alien word as part of their own national history.

Shiratori entered the debate on Japan's ancient ties to the continent in December 1894 with his article on Tan'gun, the mythical founder of ancient Korea. This article, in which he argued that Tan'gun was in fact merely the creation of later writers, was the first of the highly detailed and positivistic studies for which he has been generally remembered and misunderstood. Shiratori, however, was not the first to argue that Tan'gun was merely a mythical figure; Naka offered a similar interpretation. Yet unlike Naka, who was content to show simply that the legend was a fabrication, Shiratori went further: he argued that despite its fictive nature, the story still bore historical significance. The historical meaning of such a legend was embedded in the text, and it was the job of the historian to separate fiction from fact.[41]

This effort not only to criticize past errors but also to recreate history belies the utility of such positivistic methods to the nation. Such a use of artifacts—in fact, the creation of historical data proper—also extended to Shiratori's well-known questioning of the legends of Yao, Shun, and Yü and his debate with Naitō Kōnan over the location of Yamatai.[42] In each exercise his detailed arguments, though ostensibly positivistic (in the methodological sense), served as solid, factual components for a new perspective that "corrected" what he considered to be inaccurate views of Asian history and culture. Linguistic methods served merely as one medium that "objectively" proved his interpretation of the legends, helped to identify Japan's origins, and traced the migration patterns of the Asian peoples. All in all, by reidentifying legends, events, and people, Shiratori sought to reclassify these peoples as belonging to a *tōyō* free—but not isolated—from the constraints of Western ideology.

40. Vološinov, *Marxism and the Philosophy of Language*, 74.
41. Shiratori, "Dankun kō," *Gakushūin hōninkai zasshi* 28 (January 1894), in *SKZ* 3:1–14; and idem, "Chōsen no kodensetsu kō," *Shigaku zasshi* 5 (December 1894), in *SKZ* 3:16–17.
42. For a discussion of his interpretation of these Chinese sage-kings, see Chapter 3. The debate between Naitō and Shiratori on the location of Yamatai will be covered in Chapter 4.

Although his view on the relation of Korea to Asia would change considerably in the following years, his conviction that that relation had been crucial to the formulation of Japan's culture and identity remained constant throughout his career. Shiratori's argument on the legend of Tan'gun can be summarized as follows: he first noted that the legend could be found only in the *Samguk yusa* and not in any early Chinese historical texts. Had Tan'gun been a contemporary of Yü, the Chinese sage-king, he would certainly have received at least a passing mention in the Chinese classics. Instead, using the Korean texts *Tongsa* (Eastern History) and *Koryŏ sa* (History of the Kingdom of Koryŏ), he argued that the Tan'gun legend was started by Buddhist priests who entered Korea from 372.[43] Tan'gun, Shiratori argued, was not the founder of Chosŏn (Korea), as alleged in the *Samguk yusa;* in his view, Chosŏn did not exist until approximately the fifth century. If one carefully read these legends, Shiratori pointed out, one could learn that Tan'gun was the great-grandfather by adoption of Chumong, the mythical founder of the kingdom of Koguryŏ.[44]

The identification of Tan'gun as a legendary figure based on Buddhist scripture had several implications far beyond exposing this Korean legend as myth. First, Shiratori disputed the interpretation of some Western Orientalists that Korean culture (and hence Japanese culture, since some people in both Europe and Japan insisted on the similarity of Japan and Korea) derived from India. By connecting this legend to Buddhist scripture Shiratori separated ancient Korean history into two eras: that before the influence of Buddhism, and that after. More important, by locating the arrival of Sanskrit and Buddhism relatively late in the area's development, Shiratori argued, in essence, that Koreans were not racially related to the people of India or southern Asia. Thus, while he did not deny the influence of India, he did claim that that influence came late.[45]

43. For a discussion of this legend, see Ilyon, *Samguk Yusa: Legends and History of the Three Kingdoms of Ancient Korea,* trans. Tae-Hung Ha and Grafton K. Mintz (Seoul: Yonsei University Press, 1972), 9–20; Shiratori, "Dankun kō," in *SKZ* 3:3–6; and idem, "Chōsen no kodensetsu kō," in *SKZ* 3:18.

44. As additional evidence that this legend was tied to Koguryŏ, he argued that both the Tae-baek mountains, where Tan'gun landed, and the capitals he allegedly founded, Pyongyang and Asadal, were in Koguryŏ; see Shiratori, "Dankun kō," in *SKZ* 3:13; and idem, "Chōsen no kodensetsu kō," *SKZ* 3:19.

45. In an article in which Shiratori traced the genealogy of the Korean Hangul writing system, he agreed with Western Orientalists on that system's Sanskrit origins, but he also argued that it did not arrive in Korea until the Mongol invasion; see "Ridō, on-mon," *Shigaku zasshi* 8 (January 1897), in *SKZ* 3:107–13.

This exercise reveals how Shiratori interacted with Western Orientalists, for whom he held much respect, at this stage of his career. For example, he questioned Wilhelm Schott's assertion that the Korean language had an affinity with Sanskrit, based on the similarity of the word for heaven (Turkish *tangri*, Korean *tongmyŏng*, and Japanese *takamagahara*). Shiratori agreed that the terms are cognates, but where Schott concluded that they derived from Sanskrit, Shiratori argued that the Japanese *ama* (heaven) is in fact closer to the Manchurian word for heaven, *abka* or *amka*.[46] Here, Shiratori took up the interpretation first offered by Klaproth in his *Asia Polyglotta* and expanded upon by other scholars such as F. Müller and W. G. Aston: that Japanese and Koreans were members of the Ural-Altaic linguistic group.[47]

The dialogue with these Orientalists also gave Shiratori an authoritative voice with which to argue against Japanese scholars such as Inoue. For example, Shiratori attacked Inoue's genealogy of Japan's Malay-Polynesian roots in a series of articles in which he compared words in the *Nihon shoki* with Korean and Ural-Altaic words.[48] Shiratori singled out Inoue in his conclusion—which included a point-by-point refutation of Inoue's assertion regarding the Japanese/Malay-Sanskrit links between the words for I and fire—and accused him of employing a tautological argument. Here, the categorization of linguistic data determined which narrative of Japan's roots and history would prevail. Evidence that did not fit that narrative was deflected or elided.[49] Shiratori's linguistic studies helped shift the search for Japan's origins away from Southeast to Northeast Asia.

Second, by dating the creation of the Tan'gun legend after 372, Shiratori disputed Kume's hypothesis that Ina-pi no mikoto was the founder of a unified Korea that later separated into several states.[50]

46. Shiratori, *"Nihon shoki* ni mietaru kango no kaishaku," in *SKZ* 3:150–54.

47. Shiratori, "Chōsengo to 'Ural Altai'go to no hikaku kenkyū," in *SKZ* 3:1–2; and idem, *"Nihon shoki* ni mietaru kango no kaishaku," in *SKZ* 3:150–54. Shiratori did not change his interpretation that Koreans are members of the Ural Altai throughout his career. See, for example, his 1915 speech to the Japanese Anthropological Association, "Gengo jō yori mitaru chōsen jinshu," *Jinruigaku zasshi* 30 (August 1915), in *SKZ* 3:374–75; and his catalog of Korean words bearing similarity to Ural Altai, "Chōsengo to 'Ural-Altai'go to no hikaku kenkyū," in *SKZ* 3:1–280.

48. Shiratori, *"Nihon shoki* ni mietaru kango no kaishaku," in *SKZ* 3:150–54.

49. Shiratori frequently used etymology to identify origins and cultural genealogy. A good example is his discussion on the ancient kings of Silla; the names Hyŏkkŏse, Kŏsŏgan, and Nisagŭm, he concluded, bear a resemblance to the titles for king, *khan* and *kaghan*, used by the Tung-hu. See his "Chōsen kodai ōgo kō," *Shigaku zasshi* 7 (February 1896), in *SKZ* 3:69–80.

50. See Shiratori, "Jakusui kō," *Shigaku zasshi* 7 (November–December 1896), in *SKZ* 5:1–22, where he attacked Kume's argument that *tokoyo* and the *jakusui* listed in the

Shiratori argued that the legend most likely arose around the reign of King Changsu (r. 413–91) of Koguryŏ, after the introduction of Buddhism but before 551 when the story was recorded in the *Wei shu*. Its purpose was political: to marshal the growing popularity of Buddhism in Koguryŏ's campaign to unify Korea and to provide a historical basis— contemporary to the Chinese sage-king Yü—for Koguryŏ's primacy.[51] By identifying Tan'gun and the unification of Korea with the reign of King Changsu, Shiratori showed that Korea as a unified country developed relatively late in the history of Asia, and later than Japan.

Third, periodization is not neutral; the placement of Korean unification after that of Japan indicates that Shiratori, like Kume and Inoue, studied Korea to understand Japan. All three of these Japanese scholars privileged Japan over Korea: Inoue separated the two, placing Japan in a more preeminent position; Kume believed that Korea was established by the ancient Japanese; and Shiratori, though more ambiguous in his overall assessment, also sought to maintain Japan's distance from Korea. As early as 1896 he was careful to point out that even though Japanese and Koreans might have the same racial origins, they were not therefore necessarily the same; rather, they had developed independently.[52] He argued, for example, that there is no connection between the Japanese phonetic alphabet and Hangul and that Japanese and Koreans represent different branches of the Ural-Altaic family, Koreans belonging to the Tungusic branch and Japanese to the Mongol branch.[53] Again linguistic identification provided the objective data for distinguishing culture: the Japanese reverence for the left as honesty and the right as crookedness, for instance, recalled the custom of the Hsiungnu (in the Mongol branch), who were the only other Ural-Altaic people to favor the left. Other members of the Ural Altai, including the Koreans, as well as all Indo-Germans were partial to the right.[54]

Nihon shoki were in southwestern China. Shiratori argued that although this term can be identified in four different areas throughout history, each is in the northeastern region of Asia.

51. Shiratori, "Dankun kō," in *SKZ* 3:7–8, 13–14; and idem, "Chōsen no kodensetsu kō," in *SKZ* 3:19–24. For a similar interpretation on King Tongmyŏng, the founder of Puyŏ, see "Chōsen kodai chimei kō," *Shigaku zasshi* 6–7 (October 1895–January 1896), in *SKZ* 3:52–54; and "The Legend of the King Tung-ming, the founder of Fu-yu-kuo," *Memoirs of the Research Department of the Tōyō Bunko* 10 (1938): 31–39.

52. Shiratori, "Chōsen kodai kanmei kō," *Shigaku zasshi* 7 (April 1896), in *SKZ* 3:97.

53. Shiratori, "Ridō, onmon," in *SKZ* 3:107–13; and idem, "Chōsen kodai ōgo kō," in *SKZ* 3:75–76.

54. Shiratori, "Kokugo to gaikokugo to no hikaku kenkyū," *Shigaku zasshi* 16 (February–December 1905), in *SKZ* 2:334–47. The purpose of this comparison of Japanese

According to Shiratori, although Japanese may have belonged to the Ural-Altaic family, they differed from and, as I will show below, were in many ways superior to other members of this group, especially the Koreans. More than any other time during his career, these years (he visited Europe between 1901 and 1903) marked the period of greatest exchange of ideas between Shiratori and the Western Orientalists. Certainly, he did not agree completely, but he usually fell in line with the Westerners' interpretations. In other words, his participation was well within the bounds set by the existing debates. But he would soon discover that participation required the acceptance of too many of the categories that were used to subordinate Japan and Asia within the Western totality. As a result, rather than leading to a convergence of views and greater understanding, this early attempt to engage in dialogue with European Orientalists had the opposite effect.

The Emergence of a Monologue

In 1901 Shiratori stated, "If we stop to reflect, the affairs of the orient have again become insufferable; even though research [on Asia] by the people of the orient is felicitous and proper as well, contrary to expectations Western scholars have seized the initiative, and, as in the political world, the domain of oriental studies has been invaded and violated."[55] After a decade of study, Shiratori's view of Western knowledge of the Orient gradually converged with that of Inoue: Oriental studies was a field that Western Orientalists temporarily controlled, though they were not entitled to that possession. But it would be a mistake to consider Shiratori's conflict with his European colleagues as conservative and anti-Western. No doubt Shiratori was sincere in emphasizing the merits of and reasons for respecting these scholars. His positivistic studies, which both affirmed and revised various of their interpretations, assumed a strong familiarity with that ac-

---

with other languages was to "clarify the roots of the Yamato people."
    55. Shiratori, "Juteki wa kanminzoku no ue ni oyoboshita eikyō," *Tōyō tetsugaku* 8 (January 1901), in *SKZ* 8:3. See also his criticism of Klaproth in "Taisei no gakusha ga indo jimanshu de aru to shōsuru hokuteki seii no shurui ni tsuite," *Shigaku zasshi* 11 (December 1900): 117–21.

ademic discourse. The two papers he presented in Europe between 1901 and 1903 worked in two directions, affirming some Orientalists' interpretations but also reclassifying certain tribes as Asiatic rather than Caucasian.[56]

His research, however, increasingly challenged the taxonomy of Western Orientalists and offered a classificatory system that shifted the Asiatic past from the Orient of the West to Japan's *tōyō*. Shiratori was well aware that the Western classificatory system was not neutral. Western scholars, he believed, were creating and establishing a field of knowledge with which Europe determined how the Orient was to interact with Europe. Metaphors of war and conquest emphasized his sense of urgency to redefine the Asiatic past. In 1907, after the Russo-Japanese War, he exclaimed,

The public has said that upon the conclusion of this war, our nation [*kokumin*] should declare peace and relax. This is a grave misperception! After surveying circumstances, our nation [*kokumin*] has to pass through two levels of war before we are truly accepted as a great power. It is a war of arms and a war of peace. In other words, along with the denouement of this war, we must expect the beginning of fierce competition in the enterprise of peace.[57]

Yet despite these dire warnings that Asia might lose its freedom to define itself, he felt confident enough to brag that the Japanese criticism of European theories "is clearly a major achievement of our academic society. Just as our countrymen, like those in the practical world—government and industry—are now independent of the West, in academe as well, our scholars are now able to research matters independently without guidance from the West."[58] Such independence, of course, meant that Japanese scholars alone were sufficiently capable of defining the history of Asia with any accuracy. (Significantly, despite his abun-

---

56. These two articles, "Über die Sprache des Hiung-nu Stammes und der Tung-hu Stämme" and "Über den Wu-sun Stamm in Centralasiens," are examples of early dialogue with Western Orientalists. Shiratori offered more evidence to support the commonly held view that the Hsiung-nu were Turkish; using linguistics, he contested the virtually unanimous opinion that the Tung-hu tribes were Tungus and proposed a Mongol ancestry (he later concluded that they were a combination of Mongol and Tungus); and he argued that the Wu-huan were not Caucasian (Indo-German) but a Turkish tribe that lived in the plateaus to the north of Tien Shan. See his "Mōko minzoku no kigen," in *SKZ* 4:27–29; for a later discussion on the Tung Hu, see his "Tōko minzoku kō," *Shigaku zasshi* 21–24 (April 1910–July 1913), in *SKZ* 4:63–320.

57. Shiratori, "Ajia kenkyū wa sengo no ichidai jigyō nari," *Gakushūin hōninkai zasshi* (March 1907), in *SKZ* 10:51.

58. Ibid., 57.

dant research on the Ural-Altaic peoples, Shiratori did not publish another article in Europe until 1923, twenty years later.)

Shiratori's historical maturation is evident in the way he criticized Western Orientalists. Unlike earlier criticism in which he sought to fill lacunae and thereby revise knowledge of the Orient, Shiratori now began to question the very methodology and data of his European colleagues. He accused them of employing crude philological methods, using utterly obscure passages, and drawing premature conclusions. When studying the ancient Ural-Altaic groups, he argued, it is not sufficient simply to identify the names recorded in the ancient histories and tie them to contemporary ethnic groups. Klaproth's assertion, for example, that the Wu-huan were Goths was based merely on a passage in Yen Shih-ku's *Wu sun chuan* that these people had blue eyes and red beards. Such an interpretation, Shiratori asserted, was based more on wishful thinking than fact.[59]

Shiratori's textual criticism, however, did not seek merely to negate European historical writings. Like his articles on ancient Korea, Shiratori's analyses of Ural-Altaic languages served as the basis for a new historical framework. During the last decade of the Meiji era—the same period that saw him moving from the universalism of Comte to Ranke's spirit—Shiratori discovered in the Ural Altai the material that allowed him to formulate a new philosophy of history, one that served as his prescientific norm for what Laroui criticized as a neutral and universal history. While Ranke's dominant tendencies provided the idea, the Mongols provided the data to order such a revision.

The first step toward a revival of the Mongols can be found in Shiratori's disagreement with the Ural-Altaic classificatory system of Western Orientalists, which focused on the Caucasian peoples and virtually ignored the Mongols. If Western Orientalists are correct, he complained, one would have to limit the Mongols to their spectacular but fleeting appearance in the thirteenth century.[60] He believed otherwise: "There is no mistake that in various areas there is value in researching these [northern barbarians], who were a major force in Chinese, no, in oriental, history." One year later, in 1901, he expanded the Mongols' role, envisioning them as the key to the unfolding of world history; they became the major force affecting the history of both the orient

59. Shiratori, "Mōko minzoku no kigen," in *SKZ* 4:26; and idem, "Taisei no gakusha ga indo jimanshu de aru," 119–20.

60. Shiratori, "Mōko minzoku no kigen," in *SKZ* 4:26–27, 56–57.

and Europe.[61] By reclassifying the Hsiung-nu, Tung-hu, Juan-juan, and other peoples as members of the Mongol subgroup, Shiratori created a genealogy that elevated the Mongol influence in Eurasian history. In one article he argued, by means of a highly detailed study of seventeen Hsiung-nu words found in Chinese texts, that the Hsiung-nu, a powerful barbarian nation of the early Han period, was completely misidentified by Western scholars. He acknowledged that the Hsiung-nu possessed characteristics of each Ural-Altaic subgroup— Turk, Mongol, and Tungus—but rather than considering the Hsiung-nu as Turks (Klaproth) or as a political unit made up equally of the three subgroups (Lacouperie), he maintained that they were Mongols influenced only somewhat by the other two subgroups.[62]

Shiratori's map of the approximate locations of the three principal subgroups differed considerably from that which Western Orientalists commonly accepted. Like Klaproth, he, too, assigned the Tungus to the east, the Turks to the west, and the Mongols in between. But by assigning the Hsiung-nu and Juan-juan (the powerful northern tribe of the third and fourth centuries which unified the region north of China) to the Mongol subgroup, he created a genealogy of the Mongols dating back to the third century B.C. that comprised the most powerful tribes of Inner Asia. By locating the source of the great population movements in Central Asia, Shiratori showed that the origins of Europe and the Far East lay in Asia, not Europe. Furthermore, many of the barbarians who entered and even settled Europe were not Indo-Germanic tribes, as argued by Western scholars, but Asian.

Two examples of the link between his positivism and his philosophy of history may be found in his study of the queue and his analysis of the concept of heaven among Ural-Altaic peoples. In 1925, Shiratori presented a paper examining the queue among the people of northern Asia, which, significantly, was published in English four years later by the Tōyō Bunko.[63] Ostensibly this is an ordinary historical essay, tracing the custom of wearing a queue from the Hsiung-nu to the thirteenth-century Mongols. But after identifying the origin of the queue, Shiratori supported his genealogy with evidence showing to

61. Shiratori, "Shina no hokubu ni yotta kominzoku no shurui ni tsuite," *Shigaku zasshi* 11 (April 1900), in *SKZ* 4:10; idem, "Jūteki ga kan minzoku no ue ni oyoboshita eikyō," *Tōyō tetsugaku* 8 (January 1901), in *SKZ* 8:3–15.

62. Shiratori, "Mōko minzoku no kigen," in *SKZ* 4:54–58.

63. Shiratori, "Ajia hokuzoku no benpatsu ni tsuite," *Shigaku zasshi* 37 (January– April 1926), in *SKZ* 5:231–301; and idem, "The Queue Among the Peoples of North Asia," *Memoirs of the Research Department of the Tōyō Bunko* 4 (1929): 1–69.

whom, where, and when it spread. At times his argument is tautological. His resolution of conflicting data in the *Wei shu*, which identified the Juan-juan as Hsien-pei (Tungus), and in the *Sung shu* and *Liang shu*, which identified them as Hsiung-nu, is simple: both the Juan-juan and the Hsien-pei are a mixture of Mongol and Tungus, which influenced each tribe differently. The Juan-juan are known to have worn queues. Therefore they are closer to the Hsiung-nu, who also wore queues, than to the Hsien-pei, who shaved their heads.[64] He also alluded to corroborating evidence—that Juan-juan words in the *Wei shu* are similar to Mongol—but in effect he concluded that early tribes that exhibited cultural traits such as the wearing of a queue, a custom commonly attributed to thirteenth-century Mongols, had either to be ancestors of the Mongols or to have been subjugated by a Mongol tribe.

This genealogy, by implication, demonstrated that the culture of Asia moved from Central Asia toward the west. For example, Shiratori stated that it was "remarkable" that the only Turkish peoples identified in Chinese histories as wearers of the queue, the T'ieh-le (fourth century A.D.) and the T'u-chüeh (sixth century), "had close relations with the Juan-juan." The T'u-chüeh, formerly slaves of the Juan-juan, probably adopted this custom from their Mongol captors, later spreading it among the western Turks and several Ural peoples. The Magyars, too, took to wearing the queue at one time; in fact, said Shiratori, the Hungarian word for queue, *bürt*, derived from the Turkish, *bürkcek*.[65]

Such a narrative directly opposes Lacouperie's argument that Chinese culture originated in the West. According to Lacouperie, the first infusion of culture into China, from the Chaldo-Elamites, occurred around the reigns of Yao and Shun, the mythical sage-kings; the second infusion, during the Chou dynasty (1122–221 B.C.), was traced to Bactria and Khorasmia.[66] When viewed against Lacouperie's interpretation that Asian civilization originated in the West—and implicitly, that Asians were incapable of developing their own culture—Shiratori's attempt to elevate the Mongols and show their influence on both the West and East is certainly no less reasonable (and perhaps more so) than that of Lacouperie. These differences—regardless of right or wrong, rational or irrational—do highlight the different ideological positions held by Orientalists and *tōyōshi* scholars.

64. Ibid., 12–18.
65. Ibid., 64–66.
66. Terrien de Lacouperie, *Western Origin of the Early Chinese Civilization: From 2300 B.C. to 200 A.D.* (1894; repr. Osnabrück: Otto Zeller, 1966), 376–84.

Shiratori's study of the word for heaven among Ural-Altaic people supported this elevation of the Mongols. In addition, the concept of heaven that he extracted in this study became that dominant tendency of *tōyō* that is ontologically equivalent to Western spirituality. Shiratori began this research as early as 1896 as part of his study of Tongmyŏng, the founder of the ancient Korean kingdom Puyŏ.[67] But by the last decade of the Meiji era, Shiratori had extended this work to suggest the commonality of heaven as a religious belief in *tōyō*.

In his 1907 article in which he traced the genealogy of the Mongols, Shiratori argued that the Ural-Altaic peoples worshiped heaven as the supreme spirit. The Mongol and Turkish word for heaven, *tangri* (lit., high place), signified "both the expansive actuality of heaven and a divine spirit that resides there." In addition, he continued, the Chinese word for heaven, *t'ien*, bears the same meaning as this Ural-Altaic word, and is perhaps etymologically related to the Tibetan word for high, *teng*. By using a fascinating tactic in which he carefully distinguished between the Chinese *t'ien* and the Tibetan word for heaven, *nam*—which several Western scholars (he cited Schott specifically) mistakenly identified as deriving from the Sanskrit word *nab'as* (air)—he elevated heaven to a religious belief that was common to all people, even superseding the West's God. He pointed out that the Tibetan words *nyima* and *nam* mean sun, and *namca, namch'wa,* and *namde* mean light. Therefore, he continued, "the *nam* of heaven might be the word that emerged from the meaning 'to shine brilliantly,' just like *deva* and *deus* of the Indo-German linguistic family."[68]

This etymology supported Shiratori's categorization of the peoples of Eurasia. In the above discussion, he shifted from a linguistic analysis—indeed, he even discounted evidence that contradicted his interpretation—to a search for cultural similarities through the concept of heaven. These techniques allowed him to distinguish Ural Altai and Chinese—the peoples of *tōyō*—from those of the West.[69] The Ural Al-

67. This article fell within his earlier classificatory work that sought to prove that Korean was a Ural-Altaic language rather than being derived from Sanskrit, as argued by Schott. See Shiratori, "Chōsen kodai ōgo kō," in *SKZ* 3:79–80; also idem, "Chōsen kodai chimei kō," in *SKZ* 3:50.

68. Shiratori, "Mōko minzoku no kigen," in *SKZ* 4:30–33 (quote at 32). Another reason for such an argument was to counter Inoue's assertion that the Ural-Altaic people did not worship the sun.

69. He made a similar analysis of the phrase "son of heaven" (*ch'eng-li ku-t'u*), found in such Chinese texts as the *Han shu*. He cited several examples to show that the phrase was indigenous to the Ural-Altaic people, especially the Hsiung-nu, the ancient Korean

tai and Chinese worshiped a heaven that was an expansive sky in which dwelled divine spirit(s) (including the sun); the Indo-Germans, in contrast, worshiped the sun as the source of light. Here he was able to define more precisely the difference between the two peoples while simultaneously showing that they had a common basis in their spiritual worship, which was similar enough that Western scholars mistakenly argued for their affinity. By placing the spirit of *tōyō* on the same ontological level as the "spirit of" the West, Western religions become merely one manifestation of this spirit. The preeminent Western God, the ontological given, was now questioned and relegated to a status no different from that of other religions.

Shiratori also made an important distinction between China and the Ural Altai. All cultures, he stated, with the exception of China, have a vertical cosmology (*uchūkan*), which divides the universe into heaven, hell, and the phenomenal world—or *takamagahara* (high plain of heaven), *yomi* (underworld), and Japan.[70] By identifying the same spirit among the Ural Altai and the Japanese, Shiratori aligned Japanese with the Ural Altai, separated Japanese spirit and essence from China, and showed that the Japanese have a spirit equivalent to that of Europe. The implications were summarized by Shiratori: "When [the Japanese vertical worldview is] seen in this way, one can understand that Japanese are not satisfied with only the phenomenal world; they also possess a creed [*shinnen*] that seeks an even higher level. Thus, the Japanese nation [*kokumin*] has a deep reverence for the gods."[71] By placing Japan in *tōyō* he also set up the possibility for a form of probable knowledge. Japanese make up a progressive nation, one that, steadied by this religiosity, continuously grows and moves forward. Religion became the mediating idea that enabled Shiratori to introduce developmental time into his study of culture.

When asked what is our religion, it is rooted in the imperial household. . . . Our Japaneseness [*yamato damashi*] and our national spirit [*kokuminteki seishin*] are nurtured through this [belief]. . . . Thus, the foundation of the Japanese national spirit is immovable. Because it is immutable, when Confucianism entered from China, we accepted Chinese thought and systems [*seido*] to the ex-

---

kingdom of Puyŏ, the Mongols, and the ancient Japanese. He then used the title, Deval Putra, of the leader of the Ta Yüeh-shi, who lived around Sinkiang, to draw the boundary. Even though these words are Sanskrit, Shiratori argues, the concept was picked up from the Hsiung-nu, for the "spirit of this appellation" was not used in cultures to the south such as India, Persia, and Bactria. See ibid., 33–37.
    70. Shiratori, "Kokutai to jukyō," in *SKZ* 10:282–83, 287.
    71. Ibid., 288.

tent suitable to this fundamental spirit. And when Buddhism came from India, we accepted only the complementary parts of those teachings. For this reason, the spiritual world of our country has become rich [*hōfu*], for the fundamental spirit of the Japanese people has not been lost from the introduction of foreign ideas and systems. This unique belief stands like the central pillar.[72]

Shiratori's research on the peoples of northern Asia, then, countered the philological evidence marshaled by Western Orientalists, and sought to turn *tōyō* into, to paraphrase Vološinov, the depths of the historical consciousness of Japan.[73] These peoples became the objects which showed that the peoples of the Eurasian continent had similar origins: no one people or race was inherently inferior or superior. In other words, this research painstakingly unearthed facts that eliminated the meaning embedded in the epistemological and ontological distinction between Occident and Orient, or West and East. But rather than settling for a concept of history that accounted for differences among all cultures, Shiratori and his peers developed a history which paralleled that of the West. A common expression during the Meiji period was "the general trends" or "trends of the times" (*taisei*), the continuous process that had developed from and is based on the past. As Shiratori put it, "In affairs of the world, nothing occurs accidentally. The present is a continuation of the past, and to know accurately the present, one must certainly know the past. To know the future, one must investigate both the past and the present."[74] Having discarded what he considered to be the problems of history, he used his studies on Asia to create a different prescientific philosophy of history that set norms and definitions of objectivity and factuality agreeable to the new Japanese nation-state. To better understand how these positivistic studies helped to shape his philosophy of history, we must now turn to his notion of North-South dualism.

The North-South Dualism

Shiratori organized his research on the peoples of Asia into a dynamic framework that combined various theories and concepts prevalent during the Meiji period—ideas of progress, the scien-

---

72. Shiratori, "Nihon ni okeru jukyō no junnōsei," in *SKZ* 10:236.
73. Vološinov, *Marxism and the Philosophy of Language*, 75.
74. Shiratori, "Manshū mondai to shina no shōrai," *Chūōkōron* 27 (June 1912), in *SKZ* 10:147.

tific study of man, positivistic methodologies, the notion of geoclimatic influences on culture, and the assumption of the inevitability of international conflict. This framework divided peoples and cultures according to geographical area, explained their development (or lack thereof), and described their basic characteristics. Despite (or perhaps because of) the breadth of this framework, it was also transparent. Objective historical studies, such as Shiratori's on the queue and heaven, while they did not specifically mention the overarching structure, nevertheless supported and defined it by filling in the gaps. This transparency is apparent even today. Two well-known theories presented by students of Shiratori and *tōyōshigaku*, Egami Namio's on the horserider and Nakane Chie's on vertical society, both fall within this framework.[75] I do not mean to suggest that more recent scholars have not made important contributions; they have. My point here is that a number of important theories about Japan fall within an intellectual genealogy that was constructed in the early twentieth century.

The general contours of Shiratori's North-South dualism had taken form by the Russo-Japanese War (1904–5) and, despite some fine tuning, remained virtually the same throughout his career.[76] In this scheme, world (Eurasian) history is divisible into two basic cultural types: the North (militaristic, *bu*) and the South (cultured, *bun*). These typologies resemble Herbert Spencer's description of the development of world history as a gradual movement from militarism to civilization, but in contrast to Spencer's ideal types, Shiratori did not impose values of good or bad, primitive or advanced. Instead, his types were timeless: neither militarism nor industrialism was superior to the other; both were necessary. Because contact and conflict between these types were inevitable, the ideal culture was one that adopted the strengths of both, thus improving and strengthening themselves relative to their neighbors. East and West now became mere regions, and according to Shira-

75. See for example, Egami Namio, *Kiba minzoku kokka: nihon kodaishi e no apurochi* (Tokyo: Chūō Kōronsha, 1967). For an English study based on this idea, see Gary Ledyard, "Galloping Along with the Horseriders: Looking for the Founders of Japan," *Journal of Japanese Studies* 1 (1975): 217–54. Nakane Chie's best-known work in English is *Japanese Society* (Berkeley and Los Angeles: University of California Press, 1970).

76. Many today will find this theory a bit farfetched. Nevertheless, various central elements—for example, the centrality of the Ural and Altaic language groups and the division of peoples into pastoral nomads and villagers—have appeared in the English. There are, for example, a number of similarities to Owen Lattimore's study, *Inner Asian Frontiers of China* (New York: American Geographical Society, 1940); and Eric R. Wolf has used the distinction between nomads and villagers—though in a manner far more differentiated than Shiratori's dualism—in his *Europe and the People without History*.

tori's framework, each lost the ontological distinction of Orient and Occident that was so deeply ingrained in Western thought. Europe, then, was not superior to Asia because of innate racial superiority, unique geoclimatic conditions, or mere historical priority; its development followed the same historical forces as did China and Japan. Unlike the optimistic Comtean positivism, this philosophy of history considered international relations as necessarily conflictual. Indeed, this is hardly surprising, for this dualism is certainly a product of the age of imperialism. In a world in which expansion, conflict, and war seemed to authenticate and reinforce the slogan "survival of the fittest," Shiratori eliminated the optimism of Spencer and instead posited that survival (and implicitly, in the twentieth century, civilization) depended on a nation's ability to respond properly to this conflictual relationship. He stated, "When one becomes powerful, . . . the other side counteracts that rise by increasing its strength." The history of *tōyō*, then, was a long narrative of conflict—adaptation or stagnation, survival or subjugation. Conflict accounted for Asia's unsurpassed ancient civilizations, their fall, and their eventual reemergence, none of which a unilinear theory could accommodate. Thus when a society declined or fragmented, it would eventually rebuild and reunite; "This process," Shiratori stated, "is a transformation [*hentai*], not a state [*jōtai*]."[77] In other words, because change was constant, inferiority was a temporary, not a permanent or immanent, condition.

To give credence and authority to this dualism, Shiratori first used geography to establish a scientific grounding. "Geography," he stated in an early volume of the findings of the Research Bureau of the South Manchurian Railway, "is the foundation of history."[78] Using a similar interpretation as Buckle, he argued that geographical conditions mold fundamental cultural characteristics. But while Buckle used geography as a "condition," a fact that determined the progressive spirit of Europe and various levels of incompleteness among non-European cultures, Shiratori used these geographically determined types as two poles (North and South) whose interaction and conflict created and destroyed societies. They were not cultural traits, but the very keys to the transformation of history.

Shiratori divided the Eurasian continent, geographically and culturally, by the mountain ranges that ran from eastern Europe, along the

77. Shiratori, "Tōyōshi ni okeru nanboku tairitsu," *Tōyōshi kōza* 16 (July 1930), in *SKZ* 8:69, 70.
78. "Jo," *Manshū rekishi chiri* (Tokyo, 1913), in *SKZ* 10:451.

Himalayas, to the Liaotung peninsula. The vast land to the north, the desert and steppes from Manchuria to the north shore of the Black Sea in southern Russia, was inhospitable, the cold climate and infertile ground inhibiting the natural development of high culture. The people of this region, whom he called *kiba minzoku* (horse-riding people), were basically hunters and gatherers; they were nomadic, simple, skilled horsemen and fierce fighters, and their leaders were autocratic. Because of this military prowess and a lack of resources, they often invaded and plundered others, especially civilizations to the south.[79]

In contrast, Shiratori identified the warm, fertile lands south of the mountains as the birthplace of world civilization. In an article discussing both regions, he stated at the outset, "Asia is where civilization originated. Even though the condition of present-day European culture is truly dazzling, when one looks into the past, historical facts clearly place the origin of civilization in Asia—Assyria and Babylon to the west and China and India to the east. After all, in terms of geography and civilization [*bunmei*] as well, Europe is no more than a peninsula of Asia."[80] Originally, the Southern people were also nomads like those of the North, but because of the favorable climate, fertile land, and ready transportation, they developed a sedentary, agricultural society that allowed for leisure time and the emergence of art and education.

The North and South typologies eliminated many of the contradictions between universality and difference that had plagued earlier historians. By establishing the common origins of Europe and Asia, Shiratori tied the two regions together, equalized them, and developed new norms in which a unilinear concept of progress was no longer a prerequisite to civilization. The North-South dualism offered a compelling philosophy of history, was dynamic, assumed conflict among nations, emphasized culture rather than technology, and valued progress. In this philosophy of history, culture determined politics: those societies that did not properly study, understand, and follow the underlying tensions that always existed between the two types were doomed to extinction—or, in the case of modern nation-states, to be swallowed by

79. Egami Namio, a student of Shiratori's, would later transform this notion of horseriders in the north to suggest the migration of a Ural-Altaic group to Japan. See Egami, *Kiba minzoku kokka;* Ledyard, "Galloping Along with the Horseriders"; and Gina Barnes, *Protohistoric Yamato: Archeology of the First Japanese State* (Ann Arbor: University of Michigan Center for Japanese Studies, 1988), esp. 16–24.

80. Shiratori, "Shijō yori mitaru ōa no taisei," *Yamato shimbun,* February 24–26, 1915, in *SKZ* 8:33.

stronger, expansionistic ones. Because, according to this argument, affairs could be understood only in terms of the interrelation of these typologies, the "trends of the times" became dependent on this highly subjective, though no less scientific, understanding of the world.

Even though Shiratori provided a general outline to substantiate this recentered history of the Eurasian continent, his interest was in the eastern part of that landmass. According to his narrative, while Assyria, Babylon, India, and China all represented the South, the first three civilizations fell into decay, leaving China as the most representative Southern society. The role of Shiratori's detailed studies unearthing the genealogy of the Mongols is apparent here: Shiratori was using the same authority of history that Western Orientalists used to authorize themselves as the originators of civilization. But whereas in Western histories civilization gradually moved westward and progressed from primitive to advanced, for Shiratori the North-South tension was most evident in the conflict between China and Inner Asian peoples, the Ural-Altai. Like the Western histories, however, it too explained the constant rise and fall of cultures in both Europe and Asia: "Long ago, the power of the Asian continental culture [North] overwhelmed the world, and those not afflicted were rare; one can find those areas only outside of its sphere of power: England on the west and Japan on the east."[81]

Shiratori did not ridicule these militaristic cultures as, he claimed, most Western scholars did, but neither did he limit himself to extolling the glories of the past. More important, he sought to identify the essence of each culture and, by placing them in the context of historical process, to understand the forces that led to their steady decline. Yet he did not stop there, for he also built a pendulum into his theory: even though one force might be defeated, it eventually returns and overcomes its suppressors. In Asia this natural force was reinforced by a tendency toward unification: "One must mention that throughout East Asian [tōa] history, there are periods of dissolution among these two forces, but the overall flow that sews it together and gives coherence is a tendency toward 'unification, unification.'"[82] Shiratori left little doubt that a trend of the twentieth century would be the recovery of Asia. It was the task of rigorously trained historians who understood these processes to suggest ways in which the revival of tōyō might be facilitated.

81. Shiratori, "Shijō yori mitaru ōa no taisei," in SKZ 8:33.
82. Shiratori, "Tōyōshi ni okeru nanboku tairitsu," in SKZ 8:70.

Shiratori began his narrative of this North-South conflict around the Spring and Autumn period (770–403 B.C.), when the Hsiung-nu crossed the western borders of China virtually at will; by the Ch'in and early Han periods, this tension between the North and South was fully manifested. This conflict established one of the fundamental characteristics of Chinese history: the perpetual threat posed by the northern barbarians. But this threat was not constant, and the actors in this conflict, while always belonging to one typology, constantly changed. As an example of this process, Shiratori argued that an important reason for the unification of China following the Spring and Autumn period was to protect its borders; but to compensate for such increased power, the Hsiung-nu unified the area from Liaotung to Tien Shan under their king, Mo-tun (209–174 B.C.), and again invaded China.[83] Near the end of the Later Han dynasty (A.D. 25–220), both powers had become so weakened that the Hsien-pei and Wu-huan, who lived on the periphery near Liaotung and had remained neutral, were able to take advantage of their enfeebled neighbors. Here was another component of this dualism: a third, weaker power on the east or west was always waiting either to form an alliance that tipped the balance, to rush in and conquer, or to assume the position of North or South. Shiratori found evidence for this pattern at the end of the early Han period when the Hsien-pei attacked the Hsiung-nu, and also around the fourth century, when the Juan-juan formed the second great Northern kingdom unifying the same region from Liaotung to the Tien Shan and from Lake Baikal to the Great Wall.[84]

During the late T'ang, Shiratori did point out, the T'u-chüeh and Uighur, both members of the Turkic subgroup, unified the Northern region after the fall of the Juan-juan—one of the few times he allowed the Turks this privilege of serving as the major representative of the North. But despite the size of their kingdom, which spread from Jehol in the east to the Black Sea in the west, it was merely an aberration, being superseded by an even greater empire, that of the thirteenth-century Mongols. According to Shiratori's narrative, the T'u-chüeh were sandwiched between major Mongol kingdoms, and as former slaves of the Juan-juan they were also influenced by that Mongol

83. For a description of relations during this period and of tribute paid to the Hsiung-nu, see Yü, *Trade and Expansion in Han China*.
84. Shiratori, "Manshū no kako oyobi shōrai," *Sekai* 8 (January 1905), in *SKZ* 8:19–20.

subgroup.[85] Here the importance of his philological studies to this ideological construct is evident. The Mongols came in direct contact with China and other Asian cultures, except Japan, and also set off waves of migrations that left the legacy of the Northern culture in Europe. The Turks were forced to migrate west to the Caspian and Aral seas, and they in turn forced the Iranian peoples to migrate to Assyria in the south and to the northern coast of the Black Sea.[86]

This dualism also explained the emergence of cultural characteristics. Even though fluidity and nonlinearity eliminated the congruence of territory and a fixed notion of development (that is, West as developed, rational, and modern and the non-West as the opposite), Shiratori used the dualism to explain how existing nation-states developed the characteristics for which they are today known—in the case of China, for example, its conservatism and lack of progress. From the turmoil of the Warring States period (403–221 B.C.), Confucianism emerged and presented an idealistic alternative to the conflict and regionalism fostered by the states. It was from this communal ideal that China gradually developed into a "horizontal" society, which both prevented the emergence of a central unifying belief structure and led to the loss of any sense of nation or of interest in political affairs. Although traces of China's imminent decline could be found during the Han dynasty, Shiratori identified the period as the high point of Chinese culture, for it combined both Southern characteristics with strong martial skills. China's cultural superiority lasted through the T'ang, serendipitously coinciding with the period of Japan's greatest borrowing from China. But this strength also led to China's eventual decline: the Chinese, recognizing their cultural superiority, assimilated the successive waves of conquerors from the North, but in so doing developed an arrogance that caused them to reify their own culture.[87] This conservatism, Shiratori argued, was the root of the Chinese national essence (*kokutai*).

85. Ibid., 18–20; idem, "Mōko minzoku no kako o ronjite genzai no jōtai ni oyobu" (unpublished manuscript, mid Taishō), in *SKZ* 8:44–45; and idem, "Sekaishi ni okeru mōko no chii," *Mōkogaku* 1 (1937), in *SKZ* 8:86–89.

86. He used the name for the new nation-state when referring to Persians. He cited Cimmerians, Scythians, Sarmatians, and Massagetae as examples of those forced to migrate. See ibid., 88–89.

87. See, for example, Shiratori, "Waga kuni no kyōsei to narishi shiteki genin ni tsuite," in *SKZ* 9:161–64; and idem, "Shina rekidai no jinshu mondai o ronjite konkai no daikakumei no shinin ni oyobu," *Chūō kōron* 26 (December 1911), in *SKZ* 10:136–42.

The process of assimilation also fostered a decline in the vitality of the successive Northern peoples. Until the Sung period (960–1127), virtually all tribes who ventured south of the Great Wall, such as the Juan-juan and T'u-chüeh, became assimilated into Chinese society. Thereafter, the Khitans, Mongols, and even Manchus tried to preserve their own culture after entering China, but without success. Shiratori lamented that the once mighty and fierce Northern people had lost much of their early vigor and courage.[88]

Just as this North-South dualism was the key to understanding the history of Asia, it also, Shiratori argued, applied to the formation of Europe, the "peninsula of Asia" as he once called it. Here, Shiratori resolved the dilemma of Japan both being emplotted as the past of the West (the Orient) and having a future. Even though the West was superior in the nineteenth and early twentieth centuries, this superiority was historical and, like that of China, subject to decline; just like a child advancing ahead of its parent, Japan had surpassed China and could also surpass the West.

In contrast to the constant tension between the North and South in eastern Asia, conflict in Europe was infrequent, a difference that Shiratori's narrative reflected. The extent and nature of belligerent contact in fact explained the unique national characteristics of each country of Europe. A major European characteristic was the quality of independence, a legacy largely of Greek culture. The lack of invasions by the North, Shiratori argued, allowed the early Greeks to develop an independent and democratic spirit, which was epitomized in their city-states. The concept of people's rights evolved in Europe from this Greek spirit as the principal means for limiting the power of the ruler.[89] With subsequent invasions by the North, which varied in terms of length and severity, this characteristic was eliminated or became diluted throughout Europe.

The country most affected by both of the basic types was Russia. Because Russians shared a border with the Mongols, like the Chinese they were heavily pressured by these barbarians. Until 1236 the Mongols freely roamed the plateaus to their south, imparting some of their cultural traits—which explains the Cossacks' military skill. But it was

88. Shiratori, "Mōko minzoku no kako o ronjite," in *SKZ* 8:45–46; and idem, "Sekai ni okeru mōko no chii," in *SKZ* 8:85–89.

89. "Tōzai kōshōshi gairon" (unpublished speech presented at the 49th lecture on oriental studies at the Tōyō Bunko, November 10–20, 1938), in *SKZ* 8:122–25.

mainly during the two-hundred-year occupation after their invasion that they actively imposed the Northern characteristics on Russians. Shiratori concluded that autocracy and militarism were the two most conspicuous legacies of the Mongols' conquest.[90] The autocratic form of government was a direct adaptation of the system the Mongols used to control Russia, one that Russian rulers kept intact in order to control their newly acquired territories, Poland and Finland to the west and Turkey and the Black Sea region to the south. Shiratori concluded, "In other words, the autocracy of Russia is a result of being ruled by the Asian people, and its perpetuation is a result of Russia's control of the Asian people."[91] Shiratori's opinion of the Russians was clear in his assessment of the "Yellow Peril": because the Russians, though Caucasians, possess more Asian (that is, Northern) characteristics, they, not the Japanese, should be considered the Yellow Peril![92]

Even though Russia prevented the Mongols from dominating most of Europe, vestiges of their occupation affected virtually all areas of Europe. The farther west, the less was their influence. Germany was "tormented" by the Magyars, descendants of the Huns (Hsiung-nu), for centuries, and Italy and France were subdued by Attila the Hun. In addition, the westward movement forced many to migrate into areas not actually occupied by the conquering forces. To the south, the Ottoman Turks entered the Balkans; and Spain and Portugal were occupied by the Kingdom of Cordoba.[93]

Shiratori's conception of this interaction as determining the character of different nations was evident in his description of Germany and England. Through the Hungarians, the Germans were forced to confront and adopt various Northern characteristics, especially militarism and authoritarianism. But being European, they retained some essential European traits as well—the concepts of freedom, rights, and duties. The tension between the two forces, however, reduced both sets of characteristics. England, in contrast, was untouched by Northern forces and remained the only nation to preserve the "purity" of European characteristics. In fact, Shiratori opined, England "probably did

90. Shiratori, "Shijō yori mitaru ōa no taisei," in *SKZ* 8:34.
91. Shiratori, "Rokokumin to ajia minzoku to no kankei," *Kokka gakkai zasshi* 18 (August 1905), in *SKZ* 10:22–26 (quote at 26).
92. Shiratori, "Waga kuni no kyōsei to narishi," in *SKZ* 9:171.
93. Shiratori, "Shijō yori mitaru ōa no taisei," in *SKZ* 8:35.

more to develop these ideas," as evidenced by the fact that it is the only country of Europe to have developed true constitutional law.[94]

In 1938, near the end of his career, Shiratori introduced a subtle shift to this North-South dualism, which indicates the failure of *tōyōshi* to engage Western Orientalists in any dialogue. In a retrospective speech he stated that the Eastern and Western forces in the dualism were the "warp," while the North and South were the "woof." Neither could be understood without the other. Unlike in the earlier versions of his dualism, where North and South were the principal powers that determined how nations developed, thus blurring the fundamental distinctions between the Orient and Occident, Shiratori now chose to emphasize the differences between East and West as well. North and South still influenced East and West, but his elevation of East-West differences, so long submerged, perhaps reflects his frustration at the lack of dialogue with European Orientalists, a failure of communications that paralleled Japan's increasing alienation from the international community. Still, despite this adjustment, the dualism, as a philosophy that used Eurasian history to explain Japan's past, present, and future, remained. It had, after all, over forty years of positivistic studies supporting its authority.

By the time of this retrospective, Shiratori's thinking had matured significantly compared to his writings of the early 1890s. This fact is most apparent in his level of confidence. After almost fifty years of scholarly research, he was no doubt secure in his role as an expert on Asia and East-West relations. His positivistic research had confirmed the veracity of a history that was useful to Japan and at odds with that of the West, and *tōyōshi* had exposed a major shortcoming of Western thought—the labeling of non-Western cultures as incomplete variations of Western ones.[95] Shiratori responded to such a Eurocentric history as follows:

What we had called world history is predominantly the history of Europe with a part of Asian history appended. But this became the norm when our academic world followed the history used in the West during the Meiji period. It is utterly impossible to explain world history by focusing on only European or so-called Western history. In particular, in this history the cultures of distant China and India have been disregarded; how can this be called world history?

94. Ibid.
95. For two fine studies that discuss this problem of the Occident in history, see Said, *Orientalism;* and Laroui, *Crisis of the Arab Intellectual.*

Moreover, another defect has been virtually to overlook the nomadic peoples who live in the northern regions of Asia; it is difficult to comprehend the truth about Asian history without investigating those who make up the main part of the Eurasian continent. Hereafter, therefore, when we investigate sincerely [i.e., objectively] the trends of world history, we can be confident that by cleanly abandoning this bias and accurately investigating the power [*seiryoku*] of these Northern peoples, Asian history will become a constituent part of world history.[96]

The North-South dualism did eliminate many Western biases. It established common origins, was rooted in what might be termed a geocultural science, and provided a dynamic force through which the trends of history might be studied. Metaphors of conflict and war prevailed, being congruent both with the imperialism prevalent in East Asia and with Western theories, such as Spencer's sociology. The theory of dualism thus created a more neutral concept (to the Japanese), one with the potential for acceptance—if a universal can ever be accepted by diverse cultures—by both West and East. It retained, moreover, many of the historical methods and concepts of the West, enough so that Shiratori's history and *tōyōshi* are still seen as Western-style history and rooted in "modernism."[97] For Japan, this universalistic vision freed it from Western hierarchization and the implicit inferiority of Asia to Europe.

In the end, however, neither Europe nor Asia accepted this vision of the world. Rather than being universal, the North-South dualism facilitated a history of *tōyō* that merely elevated Japan to the same level as a few countries of Europe. (One might argue that this is true of any history that claims universality.) This history endowed Japan with a pure progressive spirit like that of England, and, like Ranke's privileging of German Protestantism, it explained Japan's spiritual source of that progress—that is, the worship of the imperial institution.

The tragedy is that the combination of a positivistic methodology with this philosophy of history prevented any possibility of *tōyōshi*—like Orientalism—from comprehending difference. In this quest for objectivity, neutrality, and utility—a contradictory enterprise of modern history as a whole—Japanese, too, created a monologue that was defined in terms of the outside. The dualism set the norms and categories for

96. Shiratori, "Tōzai kōshōshi gairon," in *SKZ* 8:115.

97. See, for example, many of the criticisms written during the Asia–Ford Foundation debates: Hatada, "Nihon ni okeru tōyōshigaku no dentō"; and Andō Hikotarō and Yamada Gōichi, "Kindai chūgoku kenkyū to mantetsu chōsabu," *Rekishigaku kenkyū* 270 (November 1962): 28–35.

later monographs, but these monographs merely substantiated the trends and categories already posited in this philosophy of history. Thus, despite (or because of) their common origin and parallel framework, the so-called universal trends of Europe and Japan merely diverged. Europe retained its world vision, which had served the West well (and still does) and, more important, is authorized by objective research. *Tōyōshi* worked within a different framework and, while speaking in the same scientific terms as Western Orientalists, steadily proceeded in a different direction, also authorized by scientific objectivity. In other words, both, although professing science, objectivity, and universality, were merely conducting monologues and failed to share any understanding.

Asia, rendered by both sides as an orient, of course, was caught in the middle of this intellectual battle to define the world. Neither alternative was acceptable. Certainly *tōyōshi* provided some Asians with a small opening by pulling them out of the Western hierarchy and imperialism, but they merely ended up within a new totality led by Japan. Within *tōyō*, the other regions became incomplete variations of Japan; their option was either to follow the historical trends as defined by Japan, or resist.

PART TWO

Creating Difference

---

*I have seen in Japan the voluntary submission of the whole
people to the trimming of their minds and clipping of their
freedom by their government, which through various
educational agencies regulates their thoughts, manufactures
their feelings, becomes suspiciously watchful when they show
signs of inclining toward the spiritual, leading them
through a narrow path not toward what is true but what
is necessary for the complete welding of them into one
uniform mass according to its own recipe. The people accept
this all-pervading mental slavery with cheerfulness and
pride because of their nervous desire to turn themselves into
a machine of power, called the Nation, and emulate other
machines in their collective worldliness.*

Rabindranath Tagore, *Nationalism*

Interlude:
Difference and Tradition

It is perhaps one of the ironies of this field of history that, while recognizing the need for difference from and dialogue with the West, it employed the very methodology that precludes such recognition. There are similarities between *tōyō* and the Western Orient, but each possesses a different meaning. Like popular knowledge about other cultures, which is often half-true at best, these orients are but rooted in a deeper representation of self and others. The different sides were not even discussing the same orient. The core geographic area of the Western Orient was the current-day Middle East and India; that of *tōyō* was China and Inner Asia.[1] To be sure, it was recognized that other areas existed, but they were merely appendages—geographically adjacent and for identification purposes bearing similar characteristics as the Orient or *tōyō*—to these principal locations. The similarity was in the acceptance of a progressive concept of history, which required a past that was prior and primitive, thus simple and pure. For the creators of both narratives, their orient served as the locus of their past.

My discussion in the next four chapters explores how this formulation of *tōyō* led to a monologue that, although using similar terms and a similar framework, became fully independent of a Western universal. For the Japanese, *tōyō* established the historical narrative, that homoge-

1. According to the definition of *tōyōshigaku* in the *Ajia rekishi jiten* 7:95, the Orient and *tōyō* encompass different geographical areas, western Asia on the one hand, and eastern Asia on the other. This suggests, then, that Eastern history would be a more appropriate translation for *tōyōshi* than oriental studies or history.

neity of language which specified their nature and the points or "paths" of contact with other cultures. For both Japanese Sinologists and Western Orientalists, their respective orients provided for the continuity of history; in them was to be found the antiquity from which they could begin a narrative of their civilization.[2] China, or more accurately *shina,* was the center of *tōyō.* Here, *tōyō* played a dual role: like the Western Orient, it was the respected antiquity, but for Japan it was also one that was older than the beginnings of Europe. In this way Japan was able to place itself on the same level as the Occident and incorporate the figurative future—the West—into its world. However, contemporary *shina* was a disorderly place—not a nation—from which Japan could both separate itself and express its paternal compassion and guidance.

This utility of history is, of course, not unique to Japan. As Raymond Schwab indicates, the historical debate among the European Orientalists was to a certain degree a competition for originality: to be the discoverer of a culture's beginnings. Such discoveries often lead to exaggerated claims of importance and historical significance; Schwab quotes Benjamin Constant's recollection of a conversation with Friedrich Schlegel:

It is worth noting that whenever a man believes he has made a discovery, in whatever realm of science, he is fond of attributing everything to this discovery. The English, the masters of India, maintain that everything comes from there. Schlegel, who has devoted four years of his life to learning the Indic language, says the same thing. The French, since their return from Egypt, see the origin of everything there. Levesque, who wrote a history of Russia, locates the source of all religion in Russian Tartary. Each would have what he knows best be the source of what others know. One must be wary of adopting such a hypothesis, but it is essential to be aware of precisely what is known about a subject before beginning to write about it.[3]

Being "the source of" establishes one's own view as historically prior to others and enables one to create a narrative that distinguishes one's own culture from another. Attribution and possession suggest that much more is involved than academic recognition. The victor in the debate over origins and subsequent narratives may establish the boundaries of inclusion, the relations of those within, and the explanations for exclusion (and simultaneously what one must do to cross those boundaries). One aspect of this debate was discussed in the previous chapter: the attempt to counter the Western narrative of the Orient.

2. See Schwab, *The Oriental Renaissance.*
3. Ibid., 70.

The other aspect, which will be the focus of the following chapters, was the enterprise among Japanese historians to establish the Truth—that is, a usable past explicating Japan's emergence.

One thing that made this narrative so compelling was the use of different voices to effect self-authorization. To establish "what others know" historians used existing knowledge, both to give authority as well as to elicit agreement. The modern, scientific framework in combination with certain parts of *tōyō*—the historical "facts"—provided both a commonality for scholars and an authoritative, objectivistic language that proved the validity of the discourse. Yet such history is believable from its congruence with contemporary events. The early historical project, up to the Russo-Japanese War, led to a search in the Orient for the answers to such questions as how or whether Western pasts (i.e., culture) might be combined with a native tradition. *Tōyō*, by contrast, was part of an effort to look inward into Japan's own past and write a different narrative.

It is not a contradiction to say that as Japan was becoming more modern and "Western," both socially and politically, its leaders were becoming more concerned with Japan itself. This, indeed, is a universal problem of nation-state construction. If leaders were to be successful in unifying the nation-state, they had to expand social and political networks to the whole population and to all parts of the archipelago, yet in so doing participants became increasingly diverse. The so-called liberals and conservatives identified the problems that emerged—social dislocation and a sense of malaise—as Western. The modern historian Oka Yoshitake cited Tokutomi Sohō's despair at the changes among the youth; while Tokutomi found much to praise about pre-Restoration youth at the outbreak of the war—"Their willingness to sacrifice themselves for the state differed not in the least from the sacrifice of a martyr for his religion"—contemporary youth had lost "all, or at least a major portion of the national awareness." To Tokutomi, the rise of individualism (he, of course, had earlier extolled a variation on such a concept) led to this decline of loyalty to the state, and indeed, to the very decline of belief in the nation-state.[4] Moreover, this perception of a waning national spirit was reinforced by the rise of political prob-

4. Oka Yoshitake, "Generational Conflict After the Russo-Japanese War," in Najita and Koschmann (eds.), *Conflict in Modern Japanese History*, 200–201. See also Harry D. Harootunian, "Introduction: A Sense of an Ending and the Problem of Taishō," in *Japan in Crisis*, ed. Bernard S. Silberman and H. D. Harootunian (Princeton: Princeton University Press, 1974), 3–28.

lems—for example, the Great Treason Trial, the textbook controversy over the legitimacy of the Northern and Southern courts in fourteenth-century Japan, the rise of socialism, and the Taishō political crisis—in which questions about the very center of that belief, the imperial institution itself, were raised. During this same period, the turmoil in China intensified as the Ch'ing dynasty was overthrown and a republican government was established in China—though briefly. This change also affected Japan, not only because of the cultural and geographical propinquity of China, but also because of the historical and cultural connections that were then being drawn between Japan and China.[5]

But the same variety that gave this narrative its authority also filled it with contradictions. To establish "what others know," it was necessary not only to discover an origin, but also to fill in the narrative gaps that give meaning to the origin. Here historians ran into another problem; the more one digs into the past in search of one's identity, the more one finds evidence that there is no origin, that "it was fabricated in a piecemeal fashion from alien forms."[6] The fear in Japanese society at this time was that the society that they romantically supposed to have existed in the past—a rather idealized picture indeed—was disintegrating and fragmenting from the changes wrought over the preceding forty years.

Japan's continuity with an Asiatic past also comprehended alien forms that bore certain meanings not necessarily in line with the ideal Japan. While *tōyōshi* scholars were trying to create a narrative of Japan's early emergence by showing its connections, tenuous though these might be, to the continent, they were also opening the way for a narrative stating that the Japanese were not, in fact, unique. On the one hand, the history that they produced suggested that the Japanese developed from the same race and culture as other Asians; they, too, were Oriental, the opposite of Western, modern society. On the other hand, the progressive notion of change suggested that they were becoming

---

5. According to Masaru Ikei ("Japan's Response to the Chinese Revolution of 1911," *Journal of Asian Studies* 25 [February 1966]: 213–27), the revolution of 1911 "came as a shock to the Japanese." Public opinion generally supported the revolutionaries, while the *genrō* opposed the formation of a republican government in favor of a constitutional monarchy. In any event, the revolution certainly stirred up political debate on the suitability of republican government in Asia.

6. Michel Foucault, "Nietzsche, Genealogy, History," in *Language, Counter-Memory, Practice*, ed. Donald F. Bouchard (Ithaca, N.Y.: Cornell University Press, 1977), 142.

like the West. Not only were they acquiring all the accoutrements of modern society, but they were also discovering its ills.

This ambiguity, while a source of much discomfort, can be productive. In a critique of Foucault, Michel de Certeau states:

Contrary to the original intentions behind the invention of a given formula . . . continuity is ruled by the ambiguous. . . . The issue is not the relation of illusion to truth (as the mythology of progress would have us believe), because the deception is mutual. It is the relation of other to other. The ambiguity proper to the exchanges between cultures, or related to their succession, does not nullify the reality of the connections, but rather specifies their nature. Ambiguity of communication is related to an "anxiety" that intertwines the continuity of history and the discontinuity of its systems: difference.

It is in fact difference which carves the isolating gaps into the homogeneity of language and which, conversely, opens in each system the paths to another. The internal instability of cycles and the ambiguity of their connections do not constitute two problems. Rather, it is in these two forms—the relation to other and the relation to self—that a single unending confrontation agitates history; it can be read in the ruptures that topple systems, and in the modes of coherence that tend to repress internal changes.[7]

In Japan's case, this combination of historical ambiguity and social change—Certeau's "ruptures that topple systems"—was resolved through a history that described a world of conflict. That world—which, of course, existed outside Japan—was depicted by metaphors of war. Yet that confrontation also led the Japanese back to their past, to tradition, where metaphors of harmony could be used to assert "coherence" and "repress internal changes." In his analysis of the strategies Japanese used to address such conflict, Oka writes: "Under the repeated shock of such events, the Japanese ruling elite became hypersensitive to the point of morbidity concerning Japan's national origins and 'national essence' [*kokutai*]." The relation between these events and this rearticulation of the past was well expressed in the Boshin Edict of 1908:

Only a short while has passed since the war, and governmental administration is increasingly in need of new vigor and discipline.

We desire that all classes should be united in mind and spirit, devoted to their callings, diligent and frugal in their work, faithful, and dutiful. They should cultivate courtesy and warmheartedness, avoid ostentation and adhere to simple realities, guard against laxity and self-indulgence while undertaking arduous toil.

7. Certeau, *Heterologies*, 180–81.

The heritage of our divine ancestors and the illustrious history of our nation shine like the sun and stars. If our subjects cleave to tradition and sincerely strive for its perfection, the foundation for national development will largely have been secured.[8]

Tradition in this case was not a timeless behavior or cultural characteristic that had always existed among Japanese. To be sure, there are antecedents for the elements that compose tradition, but the very need for the government to emphasize the traits listed above as "traditional" indicate, at the very least, that the values which Japanese are supposed to hold were tenuous. In the case of the Boshin Edict, the selection of these qualities as embodying Japan's "tradition" was made in reaction to the West; the increasing heterogeneity evident in Japan since the Restoration was attributed to the negative influence of European values, especially individualism and materialism. The pious wish for the preservation of tradition was the conscious choice of leaders to idealize certain aspects of Japan's past in order to arrest the disintegration of society, perceived or actual. Laroui describes a similar tendency in Arab societies: "Tradition will appear above all in the guise of a traditionalization effected by an elite at different stages of its history. Tradition *qua* structure is always inferred as the theoretical basis of what is formulated."[9] Laroui argues, correctly I believe, that tradition as traditionalization, as a creation in reaction to a threat, is itself unstable and constantly changing. The result of this ideological undertaking is "a greater cohesion, but in such a framework that this cohesion is in itself a goal and a value; all social life is oriented toward the interior. At all levels, therefore, we observe a process of retrospection."[10] It cannot be emphasized enough, however, that this retrospection was not limited to so-called conservatives, or *kokusuisha;* modern politicians, cosmopolitan Western-educated intellectuals, and industrialists all participated in this turn to the past.

Thus, after creating an understanding that emphasized the similarities and sameness of Japan with the West and *tōyō,* these historians had to distinguish again Japan from Asia and the West. To do so they needed to create a Japanese origin that, ontologically on the same plane as these entities, also set Japan apart. On the importance of this origin, Foucault writes:

    8. Oka, "Generational Conflict," 204; passage from the Boshin Edict quoted from 217.
    9. Laroui, *Crisis of the Arab Intellectual,* 41–42.
    10. Ibid., 37.

It is no longer origin that gives rise to historicity; it is historicity that, in its very fabric, makes possible the necessity of an origin which must be both internal and foreign to it: like the virtual tip of a cone in which all differences, all dispersions, all discontinuities would be knitted together so as to form no more than a single point of identity, the impalpable figure of the Same, yet possessing the power, nevertheless, to burst open upon itself and become Other.[11]

The origin became the imperial system. As the mythological beginning, it was metaphysical, thus foreign; it was a part of *tōyō*, a timeless entity that was similar to the Ural-Altaic peoples' belief in heaven. It was also a manifestation of the universal spirit, a religious belief similar to the European belief in God (i.e., the Protestant God) that both equalized East and West on an ontological level and served as the source for progress. The result was a blurring of the geopolitical boundaries of Asia, or perhaps of the world (though race of course redefined those boundaries). Japan's possession of *bun* (culture, South) and *bu* (military, North) connected it with the continent.

But time was also historical; in Japan, North and South interacted differently, and Japan's religiosity was manifested differently through the imperial system. Historical time separated Japan from *tōyō*. By defining the imperial system as Japan's origin, it also became historical; it was both the "Same" and "Other." But while enabling historical time, the spirit and dualism were overshadowed by the objective facts of the historical narrative. The job of historians thus became the description of Japan's emergence from this point of origin. According to this narrative: Japanese learned from other cultures, taking in the best characteristics but only if they harmonized with this creed. Here, *tōyōshi* allowed the alien and all discontinuities to be knitted together into the mythology of the imperial system, the principal reason for Japan's uniqueness. The difference that was created set Japan apart from the West and from Asia, especially *shina*. Within Japan, however, the possibility for difference and variation diminished increasingly in favor of unity of the nation.

In the following three chapters I will show how *tōyō* figured in the creation of a history of Japan. In Chapter 3 I discuss the role of China as the source of those traditions which the Japanese turned into their own—as a source, in short, of their cohesion. *Shina* was turned into Japan's past, and through these narratives it was separated from Japan by means of developmental time. Chapter 4 explores the debate over

11. Foucault, *Order of Things*, 329–30.

the historical origin of Japan, the attempt to create a historical—as opposed to mythological—narrative of Japan's imperial system, which was to serve as the origin and center for all of Japan's progress. While thus far I have limited my discussion to a few historians, participation in what I have called a discourse on *shina* was in fact not limited to a few scholars, but was joined by a number of publicists and intellectuals. This broader arena will be the focus of Chapter 5. The final chapter explores the institutionalization of this discourse on *shina* in various research organs connected to Japan's imperialist structure. But even though (or perhaps because) the object of study was China, research generally adhered to the main historical framework and failed to see China (and by extension Korea and Manchuria) as anything but Japan's past.

CHAPTER THREE

Shina: The Separation of Japan from China

Shiratori's studies on Confucianism, which first began to appear in 1909, added definition to *tōyōshi*. These studies were both a continuation of his construction of *tōyōshi* and a tactic to eliminate the alienness of that history. His questioning of the veracity of the legends of Yao, Shun, and Yü, the three Chinese sage-kings, and the ensuing debate with *kangaku* scholars indicate that his Confucianism was a part of both China's and Japan's past. In the introduction to his discussion of Yao, Shun, and Yü, for example, he used the first person-possessive, referring to the Chinese classics as "our ancient texts" (*waga koten*).[1] Ostensibly, like his research on the legend of Tan'gun, this project was a positivistic exercise in reconstituting a part of China's past. These Chinese classics are not, of course, Japanese; but in his discussion of Confucianism and statements of the importance of Confucianism to Japan's development and *kokutai* (national essence), the acquisition of these classics as Japanese becomes more apparent. In other words, his research on Confucianism specified how those quintessential—that is, timeless—*tōyō* characteristics became a part of Japan's past.

This tactic raises a vexing problem of historical narrativity, for at the same time that Confucianism was being absorbed, it was alien and included elements inappropriate to Japan's national goals. Shiratori resolved this conflict by depicting the historical separation of Confucianism in China and Japan. In the former, Confucianism changed from a

---

1. Shiratori, "Shina kodensetsu no kenkyū," *Tōyō jihō* 131 (August 1909), in *SKZ* 8:382.

universalistic ideal to a historical structure, while in the latter that ideal became a value that facilitated historical change. This shift was delineated through his North-South dualism. In a sense, the historical process led to an ahistorical description of China. Because Chinese society was constantly threatened by Northern peoples, he argued, the Chinese turned to Confucianism as a system of values that might provide social cohesion, and they relied on their superior cultural system—which he distinguished from nation—to defend themselves. Yet as the values of Confucianism became institutionalized over the centuries, a conservative structure emerged in which the form became more important than those values that gave it meaning. This conservatism led to China's decline—or more accurately, its failure to change.

In Japan, the values and ideals of Confucianism combined with different historical circumstances to facilitate a different history from that of China. While possessing many of the same Confucian values, Shiratori argued, Japan had not been confronted with the constant threat of barbarians (the benefit of being an island country) and instead developed a progressive ideal, one that accepted ideas and objects from other cultures. Thus, although it had many of the timeless qualities of *tōyō*, it was also historically distinct from Asia. In contrast to the stoppage of history in *shina*, Japan's history was processual, one of constant advancement.

Again, this reinterpretation of the past is fully congruent with Shiratori's awareness of contemporary events. Because of claims for the scientific veracity of his history, he believed that this work was applicable to the present, especially the perceived atomization of Japanese society and revolution in China. In his view, Confucianism could play an important role in Taishō Japan—that is, it could help prevent social disintegration, counter the ills introduced by the alien West, and explain the decay of a historically alien *shina*. By isolating the causes of the Chinese decline and, especially, selectively creating a new Confucianism for Japan, he described the interaction of Japan's progressive spirit, a national ethic of social cohesion, and the country's obligations as leader of *tōyō*.

But as other scholars began to emphasize the organic whole at the expense of progress, the conservatism that Shiratori identified as China's major problem easily took root in Japan. Whereas he sought comparability within a processual framework, other intellectuals who held different conceptions of the West and its influence further limited

Shiratori's view of Confucianism to the extent that, as Laroui points out, the hoped-for cohesion itself became a "goal and a value."[2] Others who modified his history went to the same extreme he identified as the problem of *shina*. Japan's new Confucian heritage became a goal; the structure became more important than the values. In this solidification of historical truth, the traditionalization of Confucianism in Japan was completed.

The Debunking of Yao, Shun, and Yü

Shiratori's 1909 lecture to the Oriental Association (Tōyō Kyōkai) shocked Japanese specialists in ancient Chinese history and invited the severe criticism of *kangaku* scholars, the philological specialists on China. In this presentation, Shiratori argued that Yao, Shun, and Yü were not actual historical figures but anthropomorphic manifestations of ancient ideals. *Kangaku* scholars labeled this theory the "Murder of Yao, Shun, and Yü" because this hypothesis undermined the base on which Confucianism and existing Chinese historiography rested. Shiratori, that is, cast doubt on the very existence of the Hsia (2205?–1766? B.C.) and Shang (1766?–1122 B.C.) dynasties and exposed the three sage-kings as mythological rulers. Although the subsequent debate with Hayashi Taisuke (1854–1923), who assumed the burden of defending Confucianism and *kangaku,* was relatively short lived, it is nevertheless significant, for it illustrates just how Japanese scholars represented *shina* and thus constructed Japan's own identity.[3]

Shiratori's attack focused on the *Book of Documents* (*Shu ching*), the earliest of the Chinese classics to cover the deeds of these sage-kings. He argued that when these records are examined carefully and ob-

2. Laroui, *Crisis of the Arab Intellectual,* 37.

3. Shiratori, "Shina kodensetsu no kenkyū," in *SKZ* 8:381–91. Hayashi's criticisms are found in "Gyō, Shun, Wu no massatsuron ni tsuite," pt. 1: *Kangaku* 2 (1911): 863–74; pt. 2: *Tōa kenkyū* 1 (January 1911): 20–25; pt. 3: *Tōa kenkyū* 2 (January 1912): 30–34 (*Kangaku* was renamed *Tōa kenkyū* in 1911). Shiratori's rebuttal to Hayashi's first series of criticisms was " 'Shōsho' no kōtō hihan (toku ni Gyō, Shun, Wu ni tsuite)," *Tōa kenkyū* 2 (April 1912), in *SKZ* 8:393–98. Hayashi's reply to this rebuttal was "Futatabi Gyō, Shun, Wu no massatsuron ni tsuite," *Tōa kenkyū* 2 (September 1912): 22–26. For a summary of this debate see Goi, *Kindai nihon to tōyōshigaku,* 97–104.

jectively—that is, outside the framework of Confucianism—their unbelievability as accounts of historical events is clear. He pointed in particular to an imbalance and unnaturalness in the deeds of each of the sage-kings: Yao was known for his astronomical observations, which resulted in the creation of a calendar, and for the ideal of succession by ability rather than lineage, in that he chose Shun to succeed him instead of his own son; Shun was known for his filiality and sterling conduct despite his scheming stepmother, father, and younger brother; and Yü was known for his diligent work to rid the land of the floods that had been plaguing China. To prove the artificiality of these sage-kings, Shiratori argued that the characters used for the names of Yao, Shun, and Yü were connected to their appointed deeds. The character for Yao, who represents the ancient Chinese ideal of a ruler with heavenly virtues, suggests supreme and heavenly matters; Shun is a homonym of *shun* (follow), and both are related to the Chinese ideal of filial piety (*hsiao shun*); and the character for Yü, through a rather tenuous line of homonyms and relationships, is related to a certain geographical area (thus signaling the establishment of the territory of China).[4] Shiratori provided additional evidence, such as textual analyses of the astrological relationship to geographical names, and concluded: "The creator of the legends of Yao, Shun, and Yü probably took into consideration the concept of the trinity of heaven, earth, and man [*tenchijin sansai setsu*] to compose this legend. In this way the legends of Yao, Shun, and Yü were not successively created but were coexistent."[5] In other words, rather than being the records of actual rulers, they were created simultaneously.

Whereas the legendary nature of these sage-kings is common knowledge today, Shiratori's interpretation took Japanese China specialists by surprise.[6] In the postscript to volume eight of Shiratori's *Collected Works*, Kurihara Masuo stated that the significance of this theory was to remove the study of ancient China from the domain of exegetical studies and employ modern historical methods instead.[7] Indeed, Shira-

---

4. Shiratori, "Shina kodensetsu no kenkyū," in *SKZ* 8:387–89.
5. Shiratori inserted the furigana (*sakusesshīvu*) and (*kōekijisutento*) for the compounds *danzokuteki* and *heiritsuteki; ibid., 387.
6. During the nineteenth and twentieth centuries, the *chin-wen* [*kung-yang*] school of Confucianism in China also disputed the authenticity of some ancient texts—though in a different way. As early as 1900 Naitō criticized Japanese *kangaku* scholars for being some one hundred years behind their Chinese counterparts; see Fogel, *Politics and Sinology*, 108.
7. Kurihara Masuo, "Henshū kōki," in *SKZ* 8:595.

tori's study on the mythical sage-kings which "was considered to be *tōyōshigaku*'s 'declaration of independence' from *kangaku*," marked the end of *kangaku* and the emergence of *tōyōshi* as the premier field of study on Asia.[8]

Certainly one of Shiratori's intentions was to use what he considered to be modern, scientific historical methods to distinguish myth from fact. Yet although the debate with Hayashi gave the impression that Shiratori took an anti-Confucian position, he was not really trying to render Confucian legends obsolete by pointing out their flaws. As we will see in Hayashi's criticisms, Shiratori's selective use of information was questionable and scientistic at best. Science provided the rationale and objective authority for reevaluating the merits and value of Confucianism as well as purging it of aspects inappropriate to twentieth-century Japan. But Shiratori was definitely not attempting to destroy the value of these sage-kings, and it is questionable whether he was even attempting to eliminate Confucianism. He complained of extreme interpretations: earlier studies in which legends and historical facts were undifferentiated, and modern research that virtually discarded all legends as fictitious. Shiratori believed that although the protagonists of legends might be fictitious and that legends themselves are not valid sources for factual data, all legends are historical artifacts. As media for transmitting true affairs (*shinsō*), he found such stories to be a window to people's ideals: "For this reason, when one seeks to research the history of a people [*kokumin*] and to describe their spirit [*seishin*], one must investigate the legends unique to them and offer a proper interpretation."[9] For Shiratori, an accurate interpretation required that he separate Confucianism from its metaphysical foundation, thereby altering it to fit his modern philosophy of history. The result was the historicization of Confucianism, giving it a place in the development of the culture of *tōyō*.[10]

Two points were crucial to Shiratori's overall argument: first, that the trinity of heaven, earth, and man was older than the Confucian classic, the *Book of Documents;* and second, that the existence of a form of heaven worship—he called it "shamanism"—in China was no

---

8. *Tōkyō daigaku hyakunenshi,* 627.

9. Although he was criticizing recent scholarly trends in Japan, there is little doubt that he also believed Chinese scholarship merged legends with facts as well; see "Shina kodensetsu no kenkyū," in *SKZ* 8:381–82 (quote at 382).

10. See, for example, his article comparing Confucianism in Japan and China, "Nihon ni okeru jukyō no junnōsei," in *SKZ* 10:234–48, esp. 240–41.

accident.[11] By showing that the legend of the sage-kings was created
after the spread of a metaphysical way of thinking based on the trinity,
Shiratori separated Confucianism from China's origin. In his 1912 article rebutting Hayashi, he emphasized, "We should realize . . . that the
Canon of Yao is not based on actual astronomical observation; [rather,]
based on both knowledge of the twelve astrological signs and the
twenty-eight constellations, and the concept of yin and yang, it was
produced from astrology."[12] He supported this statement by pointing
to the symmetrical alignment of the constellations in the story of the
creation of the seasons and calendar in the Canon of Yao. Each of the
four areas to which Yao sent the brothers of Hsi and Ho represented a
constellation: east and south were from the twelve signs of the zodiac,
and west and north were related to the twenty-eight constellations.[13]
By removing the classics from the Confucian universe, Shiratori was attempting to show that Confucianism was based on a metaphysical outlook that entered China around the beginning of the Chou period.

The way of thinking that existed well before the creation of Yao and
Shun, he argued, was remarkably similar to that of the Aryan and
Semitic races.[14] These similarities, he continued, were not accidental,
but had a common origin. Despite his acknowledgment of numerous
conflicting studies by Westerners, Shiratori believed that such thought
probably arose among the Semitic people and gradually diffused to the
west and east. He offered evidence that the yin and yang dualism and
the trinity of heaven, earth, and man also existed in Chaldea and Assyria and was a part of India's Vedic religion. Variations on the yin-
yang dualism were evident as well in the god of good (yang) and god
of dark (yin) of Zoroastrianism and in the Buddhist concepts of absolute truth (shinnyo) and darkness (mumyo). He later argued that this dualism was common among ancient civilizations that were surrounded
by deserts and barbarians—the latter, of course, representing the

11. The word "shamanism" was spelled out in roman letters in Shiratori's text; see
"Shina kodensetsu no kenkyū," in SKZ 8:390.
12. " 'Shōsho' no kōtō hihan," in SKZ 8:395, is Shiratori's response to Hayashi's critique, "Gyō, Shun, Wu no massatsuron ni tsuite." The Canons of Yao, Shun, and Yü are
the separate sections of the Book of Documents that discuss these sage-kings.
13. Shiratori also discovered the same astrological evidence in the Canon of Yü; he
argued that the names of four of the nine Shang dynasty states correspond to the points
of the compass: Chi = north, Ching = east, Yang = south, and Liang = west. The names of
these states, he continued, derive from different parts of the astrological constellations;
ibid. See also his "Jukyō no genryū," Tōa no hikari 7 (September 1912), in SKZ 9:56–58.
14. In the 1909 article he favorably compared the trinity to the worship of heaven
among the Turks, Mongols, and Manchurians; see "Shina kodensetsu no kenkyū," in
SKZ 8:390.

"dark" contrast.[15] He found further evidence in early intercourse; citing the significant amount of trade between China and Inner Asia, especially around Sinkiang, he extrapolated from an argument by Christian Lassen, who wrote that the concept of the twenty-eight constellations probably entered India around 1150 B.C., to suggest that the same thought also probably entered China around this time.[16] Asia and Europe, in short, shared the same ontology: the religious spirit.

The existence of a shamanistic belief was necessary to show that China—as well as all of Asia, including Japan—had history, not mere chronology. Although he did not detail China's pre-Chou culture, Shiratori disavowed the existence of the Shang dynasty and replaced it with a more primitive society. He asserted that before true metaphysical concepts were introduced, China's intellectual world was limited to a form of shamanism similar to the heaven worship of the Northern barbarians—a relationship with the North that reinforced China's Asianness. More important, Shiratori gave China a history framed in terms of progress and development. In other words, having removed Confucianism from its fixed metaphysical realm, he could argue that China, like the West, had spirit as well as historical development during the early stages of its history.

It was only with the Chou dynasty (1122–221 B.C.), Shiratori maintained, that Chinese civilization as we have come to know it began. When the new metaphysical concept—the five elements—entered and combined with the indigenous animism, the religious aspect among the Chinese people, especially the worship of heaven, was strengthened. This basic religious spirit expanded during the turmoil of the Chou dynasty. Reacting to the oppression of the Chou feudal lords, the common people created the legend of Yao, Shun, and Yü, based on their worship of heaven, as an expression of their ideal political system. Confucius later used these legends in his writings, but because he was concerned not with religion but with the order of society and conduct of government, he secularized this religious concept into an ideology that emphasized moral governance and ethical social relations.[17] To

---

15. Shiratori, "Tōzai kōshōshi gairon," in *SKZ* 8:116. He also found similarities in early descriptions of the constellations: the number of constellations was similar to India's twenty-seven (originally twenty-eight) and Arabia's twenty-eight constellations; and the concept of the five stars, which probably originated in Assyria, was, for example, the basis of the concept of five elements and connected to the Five (mythical) Emperors, Fu-hsi, Shen-nung, Huang-ti, Yao, and Shun. See " 'Shōsho' no kōtō hihan," in *SKZ* 8:396–97.

16. Ibid., 397; Lassen's study is *Indische Alterthumskunde*, vol. 2 (Leipzig, 1873).

17. Shiratori, " 'Shōsho' no kōtō hihan," in *SKZ* 8:396–98; and idem, "Jukyō no genryū," in *SKZ* 9:60.

Shiratori, then, Confucianism was clearly distinct from the earlier thought of the people, as well as separated from prior Chinese history. Through this ideology, Confucius turned an ideal notion of government into an ethical theory that addressed the turmoil of the Spring and Autumn period.

In a recent analysis of the debate between Shiratori and Hayashi, Goi Naohiro pointed out that Shiratori was clearly trying to place ancient China into a broader historical framework and to provide an example of what Goi called his inductive research method—the reading of the past through the contemporary situation.[18] While Goi's statement may be extreme—the same criticism can be made of any positivistic study whose assumptions are not accepted—Shiratori was totally consistent with his North-South dualism, and he firmly believed that he was describing the origin of Chinese civilization. Origin, for Shiratori, was not the beginning of culture, but the formation of what he considered to be the unique characteristics of a civilization. The essence of Chinese civilization lay in this combination of metaphysical thought, which entered China around the beginning of the Chou period, with indigenous animistic beliefs. The location of China's origin accomplished two things. First, by "discovering" the common roots of the Aryan race and people of *tōyō*, Shiratori used China's past to show that *tōyō* was not inherently inferior to Occidental cultures.[19] Difference resided in history, not race or climate. Second, the separation of Confucianism from China's beginnings gave China the possibility for a history on the level of the West. But to write that history, the parts of *shina* became data, objects for the historian to interpret as he saw fit.

The Distancing of
Confucianism from China

As Shiratori had expected (in the introduction to his "*massatsu*"—murder—theory he cautioned his audience to respond with "cool heads"), traditional scholars of Chinese history, especially Confucianists and Taoists, countered with severe criticism. Even

18. Goi, *Kindai nihon to tōyōshigaku*, 98–99.
19. Unlike most Western Orientalists who went to great pains to distinguish between the two, Shiratori tended to conflate the Aryans with the Semites; see "'Shōsho' no kōtō hihan," in *SKZ* 8:396.

though the debate with Hayashi was relatively brief, it was far from dispassionate. In a short article in which he first voiced his disagreement, Hayashi bluntly criticized Shiratori for his inductive methods, for using evidence from the late Chou to make inferences about the late Shang and early Chou cultures.[20] Rather than bolstering traditional Confucian thought, however, this debate only showed up the failure of Confucianism, as a universalistic system of thought, to survive the claims of a new scientific ideology and demonstrated the extent to which the history of ancient China had become objectified.

Hayashi's attack on Shiratori, published in 1911 in a series of three articles, focused on two major themes: first, he questioned Shiratori's assertion that the *Book of Documents,* especially the sections on the three sage-kings, was created by later generations rather than by contemporaries of the sages; and second, he argued that the level of Shang culture was more advanced than Shiratori depicted.[21] Hayashi began his critique by attempting to unravel the basis of Shiratori's theory—the prior existence of a metaphysical way of thinking. He argued that Yao, Shun, and Yü should not be grouped together; ancient Chinese texts clearly differentiated the sage-kings Yao and Shun from Yü, the founder of the Hsia dynasty. Also, even though the trinity of heaven, earth, and man appears in the *Book of Changes* and is evident in the cosmographic homologies within the Chou bureaucracy, it did not exist as such before the Chou: the three elements of the trinity were not equal, and even during the Chou period, heaven (*t'ien*) alone was worshiped as a broad and all-encompassing deity.[22] In his second article, he used archeological evidence from the recent discovery of what was believed to be Yin (near present-day Anyang), the last ancient capital of the Shang dynasty, and this proved to be the most damaging aspect of his attack. Oracle bones found at that site seemed to verify that a civilization—that is, a Chinese civilization—existed before the Chou, for they contained the names of seventeen pre-Chou emperors, many of whom were listed in the *Book of Documents.*[23] Moreover, because the style of

20. Hayashi Taisuke, "Tōyōgaku ni okeru kinji no shinsetsu ni tsuite," *Tōyō tetsugaku* 17 (January 1910): 28–35, esp. 34–35.

21. Hayashi's criticisms are found in "Gyō, Shun, Wu no massatsuron ni tsuite" (3 pts.).

22. Ibid. (pt. 1).

23. The oracle bones, inscriptions on turtle shells and ox bones, were used in divination by Shang priests and were discovered at a cite near Anyang in 1899. This evidence was introduced to Japan in 1909. Hayashi played an important role in reporting these findings to Japan, and in 1916 he received the Imperial Award of the Japanese Academy

the characters was well beyond a primitive stage, Hayashi contended that the characters were inscribed (before 1000 B.C.) at least one thousand years after they were conceived, thus pushing the existence of a Chinese civilization back to at least 2000 B.C.[24] Hayashi's last article, in which he tried by means of astronomical evidence to prove the existence of the Hsia dynasty, was his weakest.[25]

The debate ended inconclusively with Hayashi attempting to dispute evidence marshalled by Shiratori: he questioned ancient knowledge of the zodiac, discarded the significance of the numbers nine and five, and suggested that a Spring and Autumn–period state by the name of Ch'u might have existed earlier. As before, he did not attempt to oppose Shiratori's contention that much of early Chinese thought was from other civilizations, except to state:

In general, Shiratori's research method is to consider only what is suitable to his argument. In this haphazard method of accumulating and patching together materials, he skillfully attaches an explanation and hurriedly forms a conclusion. The disregard of other information is reprehensible. If this is so-called higher criticism [kōtō hihan], then I can only regret that it is woefully inadequate. The development of civilization [bunmei] certainly has antecedents and sequence; civilization is not something that suddenly gushes forth in one dynasty.[26]

Hayashi's rebuttal cast doubt on numerous points of Shiratori's hypothesis and was certainly correct in exposing his selective use of materials. As Hayashi pointed out, Shiratori's analysis of names was occasionally strained; moreover, neither the equality of heaven and earth nor the cosmological construct of the trinity of heaven, earth, and man existed before the Chou period.[27] Shiratori himself emphasized the

---

for his book *Shūko to sono jidai*. For a recent study on Shang China and the use of oracle bones, see David N. Keightley, *Sources of Shang History* (Berkeley and Los Angeles: University of California Press, 1978).

24. Hayashi, "Gyō, Shun, Wu" (pt. 2).

25. He argued that the Han revision of the calendar was a reversion to that used during the Hsia dynasty. Moreover, according to a 1909 article in the *Tenmon geppo* (Astronomy Monthly), the location of the constellations Hydrae, Aquarii, Scorpii, and Pleiades was different from that recorded in the book of Yao, a difference that is to be expected after four thousand years. See Hayashi, "Gyō, Shun, Wu" (pt. 3).

26. Hayashi, "Futatabi, Gyō, Shun, Wu," 25. Shiratori used the phrase "higher criticism" (kōtō hihan), an expression reminiscent of Hegel's critique of philology (*Philosophy of History*, 7), in the title of his rebuttal to Hayashi.

27. The trinity of heaven, earth, and man was created during the Ch'in and Han periods as a comprehensive system of thought that would unify the divine, natural, and hu-

worship of heaven alone, rather than the three parts of the trinity, in later articles. The archeological finds in Honan—which Shiratori ignored throughout his career—provided the most damaging criticism. But the oracle bones also produced evidence of the practice of divination, as well as of the shamanistic beliefs posited by Shiratori.[28] Also, present-day historiography has not yet determined the connection between Shang and Chou cultures: evidence suggests both difference, supporting to some degree Shiratori's argument of the importation of culture, and continuity.[29] In any case, neither Shiratori nor Hayashi finally succeeded in presenting a convincing argument. The problem centered ostensibly on the validity of the Confucian texts; in fact, however, the two men were not engaged in a historical debate over the existence of Yao, Shun, and Yü, but instead, each was defending his respective ideology.

It is an irony of this debate that the scholar who argued for the need to determine the true nature of Chinese origins so that the flow of history could be understood did not investigate—in fact ignored— history before the Chou period. Instead the search for a beginning was conducted by his opponent, whose goal was to maintain the Confucian universe. But Hayashi was bound to fail because he could no longer depend on those presuppositions that served as the very foundation of Confucianism. To defend the Confucian tradition Hayashi turned to a premise of the positivistic historical studies of the late Meiji period: the necessity of a clear beginning, a linear narrative, and "scientific" evidence. Yet by assuming the continuous development of ancient Chinese civilization and by attempting to prove the existence of the Hsia dynasty, Hayashi could rely only on tradition to carry his argument. His tactic was to stretch Shiratori's hypothesis to its limit, where the weight of the large body of Confucian exegetical studies might suffice to place

man worlds. See Wm. Theodore de Bary, Wing-tsit Chan, and Chester Tan, *Sources of Chinese Tradition* (New York: Columbia University Press, 1960), 222–23.

28. This tendency to ignore archeological evidence persisted until at least 1950. Wada Sei, a student of Shiratori, for example, questioned in his *Chūgokushi gaisetsu*, vol. 1 (1950), whether the archeological finds at An-yang are actually the ruins of Yin, the capital of the Shang dynasty; see Goi, *Kindai nihon to tōyōshigaku*, 106. See also Miyazaki Ichisada, "Chūgoku jōdai no toshikokka to sono bochi," *Tōyōshi kenkyū* 28 (December 1969): 265–82; and 29 (December 1970): 147–52. For a brief discussion of divination in early China, see Joseph R. Levenson and Franz Schurmann, *China: An Interpretive History* (Berkeley and Los Angeles: University of California Press, 1967), 20, 21.

29. See David N. Keightley, "The Late Shang State: When, Where, What?" in Keightley (ed.), *The Origins of Chinese Civilization*, 523–64.

the burden of proof on Shiratori. Yet although he criticized Shiratori for deducing the past from more recent evidence, Hayashi, too, in extrapolating from the late Shang back to the Hsia, relied on the same flawed method. Hayashi stated that if one recognized the existence of civilization in the late Shang and early Chou, then "it is natural that one must also recognize that it was the result of the previous thousand years, the Hsia and Shang dynasties."[30] Hayashi, in other words, was trying to reaffirm a past as the "opening of great human wisdom"; Shiratori, conversely, sought to reconstruct a past in order to understand the present and future.

Hayashi, in his attempt to defend the existence of a past that had gone unquestioned for centuries, was fighting a losing battle; for in the face of a new scientific epistemology, the "unity of the book," as Foucault puts it, was destroyed.[31] It is apparent in this debate that the unity of Confucianism was broken, with even Hayashi now falling outside that original discourse. What was at one time common knowledge, the temporal and spatial coevality of China and Confucianism, now had to be proven. By reconstituting the Asiatic space from China to tōyō and by showing that shina developed from a primitive culture that in its formative years was influenced by Northern tribes, Shiratori broke the unity in which China and Confucianism had the same beginning. Hayashi, too, failed to maintain that unity. No longer able to apply the most powerful weapon of Confucianism, the weight of its longevity, he had to turn instead to a realm outside Confucianism. Yet by seeking his evidence in archeology and astronomy and resorting to a positivistic methodology, he, perhaps inadvertently, showed the limits of Confucianism. At the outset of this debate he stated, "If Yao, Shun, and Yü did not actually exist, then one has to admit that Confucius lied. It is inconceivable that such a sage would do this. However, Professor Shiratori has presented the above 'murder theory' attacking a widely accepted view among Confucianists. Therefore, I will investigate this [issue] from a completely different perspective than usual among Confucianists."[32] Still, Hayashi could do no better than to show that a Shang society had existed and that Shiratori's theory, in not taking into

30. Hayashi, "Gyō, Shun, Wu" (pt. 1), 865.

31. Michel Foucault states, "The book is not simply the object that one holds in one's hands; and it cannot remain within the little parallelepiped that contains it: its unity is variable and relative. As soon as one questions that unity, it loses its self-evidence; it indicates itself, constructs itself, only on the basis of a complex field of discourse" (*Archeology of Knowledge*, 23).

32. Hayashi, "Gyō, Shun, Wu" (pt. 1), 864–65.

account the new archeological evidence, was also flawed. More than anything else, this debate confirmed Shiratori's historicization of Confucianism: Confucianism had not existed since the founding of China; it was merely an ideology created in response to problems in ancient China. Shiratori's general thesis was soon accepted by virtually all China scholars, even those of the *kangaku* school.

The failure of Confucianism, an age-old discourse, to survive the challenges of scientific methodology was evident in comments of other scholars. In a lecture at Hiroshima in August 1911, Naitō Kōnan criticized both historians, but particularly Shiratori, for not keeping abreast with the various schools of Confucianism in China.[33] He accused both *kangaku* and *tōyōshi* specialists of being at least seventy, and probably one hundred, years behind the scholarship of China. He found Japanese scholars woefully inadequate: older professors rose to their positions because of their age and knowledge of Chinese writing (*kambun*), despite their ignorance of ancient Chinese history; as for younger scholars, they often create twisted hypotheses because they do not read all the fundamental texts. He complained, "Claiming to know history, they have made a huge mistake by connecting the three names of Yao, Shun, and Yü to heaven, earth, and man."[34] Instead of formulating specious hypotheses, he continued, Japanese scholars should pay more attention to the debate among Chinese schools, particularly between the *ku-wen* traditionalists and the revisionist *chin-wen* (*kung-yang*) school. Naitō praised such scholars as Chang Pin-lin, the *ku-wen* revolutionary, and K'ang Yu-wei, the *chin-wen* theorist and politician, and he particularly commended the latest syncretic trends by scholars such as Wang K'ai-yun.[35] In a later article he lauded the critical inter-

33. This lecture was presented in Hiroshima on August 8, 1911, before the full series of Hayashi's criticisms appeared; see Naitō Kōnan, "Shina gakumon no kinjō," in *Naitō Kōnan zenshū* (Tokyo: Chikuma Shobō, 1969–76), 6:48–66 (hereafter cited as *NKZ*). Masubuchi Tatsuo argued that Naitō's critique was aimed at the low level of Japanese *kangaku* scholarship compared to that of China; see "Nihon no kindaishi ni okeru chūgoku to nihon" (pt. 2), *Shisō* 468 (1963): 869–70. In his biography of Naitō, Joshua Fogel (*Politics and Sinology,* 157) cited this article as evidence of Naitō's support for Ch'ing scholarship but did not examine its relation to the debate on Confucianism in Japan.

34. Naitō, "Shina gakumon no kinjō," in *NKZ* 6:49.

35. The debate between these two Confucian schools was especially heated during the late nineteenth and early twentieth centuries as China was grappling with Western imperialism and its own cultural traditions. In general, the *ku-wen* scholars emphasized the authority of the classic texts, while the *chin-wen* scholars reinterpreted Confucianism

pretations of the *chin-wen* school as a first step toward the study of ancient China using a scientific methodology. The next step, he asserted, was to combine such textual research with archeology, especially the evidence from the ruins of Yin. In the final analysis, though, the position of the *chin-wen* school was little different from that of Shiratori, whom Naitō criticized for his failure to use "objective" archeological evidence—in fact, both failed in this regard. The difference was that whereas Naitō looked on Chinese scholars paternalistically, Shiratori was his academic rival. But Naitō himself is confirmation that change had occurred; he, too, asserted that ancient China, including Confucianism, must be studied scientifically and objectively.[36]

This separation of Naitō's scholarship from China and his similarity to Shiratori was evident in a 1922 article on the Canon of Yü. Naitō stated in the opening sentence, "There is no doubt that the Canon of Yü in the *Book of Documents* provides important historical data for research on economic conditions in ancient China."[37] Here, the Canon of Yü was no longer significant for its relation to Confucianism, but as a source for understanding China's past. In this article, Naitō compared the section on Yü with the *Erh-ya*, an early lexicon that was then believed to have been compiled during the Shang, and the *Chou-li* (Chou Rituals), a description of governmental organization during the early Chou dynasty. Using textual analysis to compare such information as the names of the nine states, knowledge about canals, and taxation procedures, Naitō concluded that the Canon of Yü was not compiled before the Warring States period (403–221 B.C.).[38] His overall argument, moreover, though critical of Shiratori's methodology and differing in detail, bore a striking similarity to that of his scholarly ad-

---

as progressive thought. For an analysis of the nature of this debate during the late Ch'ing, see Joseph R. Levenson, *Confucian China and Its Modern Fate: A Trilogy* (Berkeley and Los Angeles: University of California Press, 1958), 79–94. Naitō's evaluation of these scholars, however, was not determined by their "progressive" or "traditional" thought, but by whether they examined the texts critically. Thus while he was generally sympathetic to the *chin-wen* school, he could also praise Chang Pin-lin without contradiction; see "Shina kotengaku no kenkyū ni tsuite," *Tōhō jiron* 2 (February 1917), in *NKZ* 7:159–64.

36. See also Fogel, *Politics and Sinology*, 19. For a 1970 article by a protégé of Naitō that continues this belief in the veracity of Japanese objectivity over biased Chinese studies, see Miyazaki, "Chūgoku jōdai no toshikokka."

37. Naitō, "Wukō seisaku no jidai," *Tōa keizai kenkyū* 6 (February 1922), in *NKZ* 7:165.

38. Ibid., 167, 168, 171.

versary. He, too, argued that Confucianism was not a timeless norm but had changed according to the different needs facing ancient China. Naitō suggested that Confucius's teachings formed a political ideology to restore the Chou system, with the ideal of Yao and Shun developing later.[39] The difference with Shiratori is evident: the legendary figures of Yao, Shun, and Yü were established after Confucius, not created by the people and canonized by Confucius. Only ten years after the Shiratori-Hayashi debate, therefore, the question was not whether the sage-kings existed, but when and under what conditions in the Chou dynasty they were created.

In his criticism, Naitō indirectly raised an important point about the study of Confucianism in Japan and even China: its separation from China, the context of its early development. China was now an object of study from which Japan had become removed, politically, ontologically, and academically. Shiratori, Hayashi, and now Naitō used Confucian texts as data from which to glean information on China's past. Neither Hayashi nor Shiratori cited any contemporary Chinese scholars; yet in all his articles, Shiratori maintained his position as an authority on China. The absence of Chinese scholars was not, I believe, an oversight, but reflected Shiratori's conviction that he was presenting a new interpretation based on scientific methodologies that took into account the unique characteristics of Asia as well as recent trends.

This debate indicates that all three scholars were part of the growing separation of Japanese scholars from China and Chinese Confucianism. Their ties and affinity to China were through the texts that contained the past which Japan had lost and should recover. Naitō's biographers have generally argued that he was much more sympathetic to China than Shiratori, praising its culture and maintaining many friendships with Chinese scholars. These claims, particularly the latter, are no doubt true, but his praise for China was reserved for a culture that had peaked during the Sung dynasty. He did not necessarily assert, as did others, that China since the Sung had utterly stagnated, but he did acknowledge that it had not advanced. Shiratori, too, found reason to praise parts of Chinese culture. In an article on the Japanese national essence and Confucianism, Shiratori recognized the *Analects* as a masterpiece without peer and also emphasized that Confucianism was still applicable to the present.

39. Naitō, "Shōsho keigi," in *NKZ* 7:20.

When looking at the Chinese and pondering China's present condition, it is a major mistake to believe that Confucianism itself is insignificant and worthless because they created it. Countries rise and fall. Even ones that are now declining were prosperous in the past, and even today's great countries were weak in the past. Three thousand years ago China's culture was highly developed. Because China today is destitute, some question [the value of] Confucianism, which is the crystallization and maturation of Chinese thought and spirit that was nurtured between those moments. Is [Confucianism] worthless or to be regarded with contempt?[40]

The answer was obvious, but the Confucianism that Shiratori advocated be preserved was considerably different from that of China's past.

Confucianism as History: The Decline of China

Among both *tōyōshi* and *kangaku* specialists of China, this debate marked the end of Confucianism as the universalistic thought of China and its unfolding as merely another—albeit predominant—"ism" in the history of *tōyō*. Recent accounts suggest that this debate came to a premature end because of Shiratori's inability to reply adequately to criticism.[41] Shiratori, however, suggested that he did not continue the debate because it had veered away from his original intention. He responded angrily at being labeled the "murderer" of the sage-kings, stating that the issue was the relevance of Confucianism in the twentieth century, not whether the sage-kings actually existed: "When we research [this subject] coolly and calmly, contrary to expectations the true, priceless aspects emerge from the background and the value of Confucianism is demonstrated. Then for the first time the spirit of Confucianism comes to life."[42] The purpose of his theory, he asserted, was to preserve Confucianism:

According to my theory, Yao, Shun, and Yü were not actual historical figures. But because the thought that produced them as ideals actually existed among ancient Chinese, I gave them an even firmer foundation. . . . Until recently, peo-

---

40. Shiratori, "Kokutai to jukyō," *Kokugakuin zasshi* 23 (January 1917), in *SKZ* 10:280.

41. Kurihara Masuo mentioned in the postscript to Shiratori's *Zenshū* (7:595) that the archeological evidence brought up by Hayashi was believed to be an important factor in bringing this debate to a premature end.

42. Shiratori, "Nihon ni okeru jukyō no junnōsei," in *SKZ* 10:241.

ple have called Yao, Shun, and Yü emperors who lived more than four thousand years ago. My theory posits that the Chinese produced them as ideal emperors (though in a more recent period than had been thought), and they continue to have an exalted position in the minds of later generations of Chinese. In other words, I explained that these three figures are the manifestation of the spirit of Confucianism, and as long as Confucianism remains, they are alive. Thus, the foundation of Confucianism did not crumble, but contrarily, it gained a solid foundation. Therefore, I am not an enemy of Confucianism; I am its defender.[43]

Shiratori's defense of Confucianism was, of course, selective at best; he was correct in stating that he had helped to preserve Confucianism, but only as a Japanese ideal. This debate signaled the beginning of a revitalization of Confucianism in Taishō Japan, and ironically it opened the way for *kangaku* and *tōyōshi* scholars alike, while retaining their differences, to come to remarkably similar conclusions regarding Confucianism in China and Japan. This revitalization, however, was not tied to any academic breakthrough, but to increasing political and international problems.

During the nineteenth century, the fortunes of Confucianism in Japan had been tied to certain perceptions of the moral order and social cohesion. Confucianism was part of that past from which morals and ethics were extracted to act as an antidote to the individualism and competition fostered by capitalism. The Imperial Rescript of Education of 1890, the centerpiece of the Confucian revival, highlighted the morals and ethics—not the system of thought—necessary to unify Japan. Motoda Eifu, the major Confucian scholar of the Meiji period and tutor to the Meiji emperor, was the central figure in this early alteration of Confucianism in Japan into an ethical doctrine. By equating the Japanese emperor with the Chinese monarch, he tied Confucian virtues of loyalty and filial piety to the imperial system.[44] This reassertion of Confucianism in Japan was an outgrowth of the *kokutairon* (national essence-ism) professed by Mito scholars during the waning years of the Tokugawa period. Like the Mito interpretation, it was an eclectic selection of elements lacking full consideration of the implications of Confucianism to modern Japan. The problems with this adaptation of Confucianism became evident after the promulgation of the Imperial

43. Ibid., 240–41.
44. For a discussion on the Rescript of Education as "the structural principles of a moral nation," see Fujita Shōzō, *Tennōsei kokka no shihai genri*, 2d ed. (Tokyo: Miraisha, 1983), 7–34.

Rescript and the death of Motoda.[45] After 1890, organizational activity on Confucianism declined.

The conflict between positivistic knowledge and the Confucian universe, and the very success of Motoda in ensuring a place for Confucianism in Japan, are two possible reasons for the waning of organizational activity. But two further reasons can be cited, ones more pertinent to the present discussion: first, the paradox of relying on a Chinese system of ethics to reinforce loyalty to the Japanese emperor while denouncing China for its backwardness; and second, the omission or oversight of the Mandate of Heaven, the revolutionary potential in Confucianism which allows the people to overthrow a ruler who does not abide by his charge to rule benevolently.

DIFFERENTIATION THROUGH
HISTORICAL STRUCTURES

The dilemma created by drawing on *tōyō* while also distinguishing Japan from the rest of Asia was evident in a September 1911 article by Inoue Tetsujirō, whom many consider the successor to Motoda. To establish emperor worship as the Japanese national ethic, Inoue distinguished between two types of family systems: the nuclear (*kobetsu*) family and the national (*sōgō*) family system. This distinction of social structures enabled him to merge loyalty (*chū*)—which implied the object of that loyalty, the head of a moral family (*kazoku dōtoku no kunshu*)—with the Confucian concept of filial piety (*kō*), a combination that facilitated the connection between Confucianism and the emperor, head of the family-state of Japan.[46] But Inoue's interpretation also separated China from Japan. Japan alone, he argued, possessed both national and nuclear family systems; China had only nuclear families. Thus, while Chinese possessed the virtue of filial piety, its moral system did not encompass loyalty to their emperor.[47]

45. Nomura Kōichi, "Kindai nihon ni okeru jukyō shisō no hensen ni tsuite no oboegaki," in *Kindai chūgoku kenkyū*, ed. Kindai chūgoku kenkyū iinkai (Tokyo: Tōkyō Daigaku Shuppansha, 1958), 3:233–70; and Warren W. Smith, *Confucianism in Modern Japan* (Tokyo: Hokuseido Press, 1959). Smith argued that Confucian activities shifted to the research of Chinese texts and ancient history.
46. Nomura, "Kindai nihon ni okeru jukyō no shisō no hensen," 250–52; for the contradiction between loyalty to the emperor and ethical ideals within Confucianism, see Levenson, *Confucian China*, bk. II, 27–30, 61–62.
47. Inoue Tetsujirō, "Waga kokutai to kazoku no seido," *Tōa no hikari* 6 (1911): 1–19.

Clearly Inoue, too, was part of the changing discourse that rehistoricized *shina*—separating China from its idealized past—and repositioned some elements as belonging to Japan's legacy. By emphasizing the importance of ancestor worship in a family system—in the case of the national family, the continuous imperial line—Inoue attempted to elevate the Japanese emperor to the pinnacle of a cohesive Japan, as compared to the Chinese monarch, the leader of a culture. His identification of ethical virtues as inhering in both the national and the nuclear family enabled him to count loyalty to the emperor as the most fundamental value of the Japanese nation-state. Although Confucian concepts were clearly important, he mentioned neither Confucianism per se nor recent revolutionary events in China (the Wuchang uprising, which led to the 1911 Revolution, broke out in October). By ignoring both the Chinese past and present, he suggested that loyalty and filial piety to the nation were uniquely Japanese qualities.

Inoue also used this analysis of the family system to assert Japan's superiority over Europe. Family-centered ethics, he emphasized, are broader and stronger than law. Invoking Spencer's statement that nomadic people do not worship their ancestors, Inoue asserted that Europeans forfeited their worship of ancestors because they, too, were nomadic; emigration to America was proof that they lacked rich farmland and a stable rice culture. To Inoue, this mobility led to the rise of contradictory ideologies: individualism and socialism. Individualism emphasized the will of the person at the expense of social unity, whereas under socialism all individuals were equalized for the sake of the group. The family system, he suggested, is superior: although it privileges the group, it does not force everyone to the same level but allows for personal development.[48]

Here, the concepts of family, morality, and filiality functioned as fundamental beliefs that might arrest the perceived atomization of Japanese society. Inoue's individual and national family systems provided a strategy for establishing the virtues of loyalty and filial piety as part of a Japanese individualism that was superior to—that is, allowing for greater social harmony—and freer of contradictions than that of the West. In other words, the family became the central value, more important than other social customs and institutions.

The weakness of Inoue's manipulation of this ethical ideal into a Japanese tradition lay in his inability to distinguish Japan's past from that

48. Ibid., 12–17.

of China. He succeeded only in extracting parts of Confucianism from China, describing a different family system, and ignoring those aspects that were unpalatable. By the 1910s, however, this *kangaku* strategy for preserving Confucianism in Japan in the face of new Western ideas and historical methods was no longer sufficient to manage changing conditions, domestically or internationally. A more careful delineation of the historical moments at which Japan and China diverged was necessary.

DIFFERENTIATION THROUGH HISTORY

By the beginning of the Taishō period, Japanese elites were still debating, both constitutionally and ideologically, the nature of the imperial institution, on which *kangaku* scholars had based their survival in Japan. As is evident in Hayashi's argument as well as Motoda's analogy, the distinction between the Chinese and Japanese emperor—that the former derived his legitimacy from adherence to the examples of the sage-kings, whereas the latter gained his by virtue of his divine lineage—was not yet an issue for those *kangaku* scholars who were attempting to preserve Confucianism as the ethical thought of modern Japan.[49] Nevertheless, this issue could no longer be ignored. Domestic and international events—such as the textbook controversy over the legitimacy of the Northern and Southern dynasties, the influx of socialism, the Taishō political crisis, and, in China, the 1911 Revolution—all threatened (or seemed to threaten) the imperial institution. Concern over reverberations of these issues to the imperial system would lead to a more far-reaching interpretation of Confucianism in Japan.[50]

Shiratori focused on the same problem as Inoue: how to preserve certain aspects of Confucianism in Japan while at the same time separating Japan from China. The main distinction between the two men's

49. For the distinction between the Chinese and Japanese emperors, see Levenson, *Confucian China*, bk. II, 119–20.

50. See, for example, Takada Shinji, *Nihon jukyōshi* (Tokyo: Chijin Shokan, 1941), 274, who argued that this revolution was the major factor in the reappraisal of the Confucian concepts of revolution and *wang-tao* (the way of kings). For a biography of Kōtoku Shūsui, a socialist who was accused by the government of plotting to assassinate the emperor, see Frederick G. Notehelfer, *Kōtoku Shūsui: Portrait of a Japanese Radical* (Cambridge: Cambridge University Press, 1971); and for a discussion of the debate on the legitimacy of the fourteenth-century Southern court, see Shuzo Uyenaka, "The Textbook Controversy of 1911: National Needs and Historical Truth," in *History in the Service of the Japanese Nation*, ed. John S. Brownlee (Toronto: Joint Centre on Modern East Asia, 1983), 94–120.

approaches was that Shiratori relied on history rather than structure to show difference. In several articles on Confucianism that followed his debate with Hayashi, Shiratori clarified his strategy for separating Confucianism from Chinese history; it is here that Shiratori's concern for culture converged with politics. By historicizing Confucianism, Shiratori explained China's decline, Japan's ascendancy, and the sanctity of Japan's imperial system.[51]

Shiratori distinguished the Japanese imperial system from the Chinese emperorship by extending the separation of the spiritual and the historical to the universalistic spirit that informed Confucius and the institutionalization of Confucianism. Confucius, he argued, recorded his doctrine during the Spring and Autumn period as ethical ideals that might protect Chinese from the abusive power of the many princes who ruled over small kingdoms. Confucianism was a manifestation of the universalistic spirit that was a part of Southern cultures; it was, "in a word, *minshushugi*—no rather, it is *heiminshugi.*"[52] Shiratori had some difficulty naming this concept, which is usually translated as democracy; in his early articles he called it a form of *minshushugi*, but by 1918 he had settled on *minponshugi.*[53] His definition that the leader worked for the people and their welfare, however, did not change. Shiratori described the spirit manifested in the Chinese Will of Heaven as follows: The ruler exists for the sake of the people, and the one who governs according to the will of the people receives an appointment from heaven as emperor. As long as he governs according to the will of the people, he retains his appointment. The proper, ethical ruler should care for the people, reduce taxes, lighten military service, not impose corvée taxes, and show humility and self-sacrifice. Moreover, as indicated in the abdication of Yao in favor of Shun, and Shun for Yü, the Son of Heaven is not a hereditary ruler, but the most capable person who represents the Will of Heaven and that of the people. Still, even though Shiratori struggled to find a proper term, it is clear that he saw *minponshugi* as unconnected to any Western form of democracy. He

51. Shiratori, "Jukyō no genryū," in *SKZ* 9:53–69; idem, "Nihon ni okeru jukyō no junnōsei," in *SKZ* 10:234–48; and idem, "Kokutai to jukyō," in *SKZ* 10:276–89.
    52. "Jukyō no genryū," in *SKZ* 9:54.
    53. These terms are usually translated as "democracy," though the nuances are quite different. The characters for *minshu* suggest people as leaders; for *minpon*, based on people; and for *heimin*, common people. For his use of the term *minshuteki*, see "Manshū mondai to shina no shōrai," in *SKZ* 10:156, 157; and his distinction between *minponshugi* and *minshushugi* is in "Shina ni okeru gendai no kakumei ni tsuite," *Tōyō jihō* 237 (June 1918), in *SKZ* 10:292–94.

stated this difference succinctly: "It is not, as is often true today, a theoretical [*rikutsuppoi*] and conceptual [*chishiteki*] relationship to the modern state; it is a relation that seeks an ethical and compassionate attitude."[54]

This distinction between Confucian *minponshugi* and Western democracy provided a historical basis for describing both the similarities in the political ideals of East and West and their differences. According to Shiratori, the legends of Yao, Shun, and Yü expressed an ideal deriving from the same universal spirit that existed among the Ural-Altaic peoples and those of Europe. Yao's selflessness, Shun's filial piety and benevolence, and Yü's diligence and devotion to work, in addition to the abdication of Yao and Shun, were legendary representations of an ideal government centered on the worship of a supreme force in heaven.

This ideal political system, according to Shiratori, never existed in China proper, but was formulated to address specific conditions in the Chou dynasty. As he put it, "The *Book of Documents*, which expresses this thought [Will of Heaven], is not one in which idealistic rulers, like Yao and Shun, wrote about actual government and its values. One can only see these ideal leaders as a pretext for a conception that confronted the threat to the welfare of the people and shattering of peace among states. In other words, the *Book of Documents* is not history [i.e., recorded past], but scripture."[55] He continued that Confucius's writings were based on these ideals but used only those parts that addressed contemporary problems; Confucius employed the sage-kings as ethical models to create an ideology that would end the chaos, warfare, and excessive taxation of the Spring and Autumn period. But while Confucius emphasized ethics and morality, he omitted religious concepts, especially the worship of heaven. Shiratori explained, "Because Confucius's teachings cultivate our feelings and lives, and these reach the states as well as the realm, they are purely moral and ethical and do not include a tinge of religion. Therefore these [teachings] are not consistent with those ideals that appear in the *Book of Documents*."[56] The in-

54. Shiratori, "Manshū mondai to shina no shōrai," in *SKZ* 10:156–57; and idem, "Jukyō no genryū," in *SKZ* 9:54–55, 62. Even though Yü had designated a successor in the same tradition as Yao and Shun, the people turned to his son for guidance. Quote is from "Shina ni okeru gendai no kakumei," in *SKZ* 10:292–94.
55. Shiratori, "Jukyō no genryū," in *SKZ* 9:55. Shiratori explicitly stated later in this article (64) that the *Book of Documents* was not written by Confucius but attributed to him by later generations.
56. Ibid., 63.

consistency was between the spirit and the historical; elsewhere he stated, "In their wisdom as individuals and rulers, Yao, Shun, and Yü serve as our models, but in regard to the [Japanese] throne, Yao, Shun, and Yü express an ideal born from the unique political conditions of China. Therefore, they cannot be accepted in our country."[57] The spiritual concept on which Confucianism was based was the universal toward which all should strive; China's application, however, was inappropriate.

The historical idea that made Chinese Confucianism especially ill-suited to Japan was the Mandate of Heaven. The Chinese emperor was the Son of Heaven, not a manifestation of heaven itself. He ruled only as long as he received the Mandate of Heaven, and if he ceased to rule benevolently, he should be replaced. According to Shiratori, the idea that a poor farmer could become emperor had its origins in this concept of *heiminshugi*, but the process whereby such a thing could occur—abdication by a ruling emperor—was a historical phenomenon unique to China. In other words, while Confucius based his writings on a universal idea, important changes were made in its application: he omitted religiosity—the belief in heaven—and later Confucianists added the revolutionary idea of succession.

Shiratori found this lack of religiosity to be the key to explaining Chinese society. The Chinese, he argued, value the human being; there are no gods (or God) above man, and even the sages represent the ideal, virtuous man. While he considered the *Analects* a masterpiece in detailing human relations, he also argued that the lack of a god and the emphasis on human interaction led to a shift away from loyalty to the state toward adherence to form and ritual. In contrast to the strong regionalism and authoritarian rule of the Spring and Autumn period, Confucianism shifted basic political authority from the states (*kokka*) to the realm (*tenka*) of the emperor. The spirit of the *Analects* was no longer practiced in China, for the natural passion that should accompany ritual had been lost; ritual itself had become an empty form—increasingly elaborate, rigidly defined, conservative, and meaningless.[58] Thus, according to Shiratori, the absence of loyalty and the emphasis on human relations led to a unique aspect of Chinese society: a horizontal social structure.

From such an institutionalization of ritual, time is frozen and the acceptance of new and uncertain ideas that might improve one's society

---

57. Shiratori, "Kokutai to jukyō," in *SKZ* 10:282.
58. Ibid., 284.

becomes more difficult, if not impossible. Shiratori pointed out that from this conservatism, China did not decay; it just did not change: "Because the Chinese were often subjugated by other countries, they feared, unless they tenaciously preserved their own manners and customs, a loss of their national character [*kokuminsei*]. Thus, they did not modify existing morals; but the absence of change became the cause of moral decay."[59] Here Shiratori raised an important point regarding one's relation to the external: uncertainty and chaos can lead to the solidification of an idealized past that "corrects" contemporary problems.

The placement of *shina* in the North-South dualism—reflecting China's constant struggle with the Northern people—explained the separation of spirit from history. Because the Chinese, from before the Han through the Ch'ing period, managed either to repel or to assimilate barbarians, a self-centered view of the world, or Chinese "universalism" (*tenkashugi*), evolved. "Since the ancient period, Chinese people [*kanminzoku*] have continuously lived adjacent to culturally inferior barbarians. But it absolutely does not mean that they had such a [conservative] nature since their beginnings. I believe that if Chinese [*kanzoku*] existed next to a civilized country like Greece or Rome, their condition and nature would certainly be different than it is today. For this reason, I have concluded that Chinese conservatism is an effect of the barbarians."[60] He identified this tension as the reason that Chinese considered themselves to be the center of the world: they were the civilized inner confronted by the uncivilized outer.

Yet the very success of this China-centered worldview negated any sense of nationalism or allegiance to a geopolitical entity and led to the demise of *shina*. Because of the efficacy of culture as the main defense against others, Chinese idealized their past and lost any sense of loyalty to their ruler, who was often a Northern barbarian. After all, any person, as long as he possessed the proper virtue, could rule China.[61] Shiratori stated, "Because the family was the basis of social order, and familial ethics were the rules for individual interaction with the state, it goes without saying that military matters [*bu*], especially weaponry, were ominous. It therefore became inevitable to speak of wars—the killing of people—as irrational acts. Thus, in the Chinese ideal the use

59. Ibid., 286–87.

60. Shiratori, "Jūteki wa kanminzoku no ue ni oyoboshita eikyō," in *SKZ* 8:11.

61. Shiratori, "Waga kuni no kyōsei to narishi shiteki genin ni tsuite," in *SKZ* 9:161–64; and idem, "Shina rekidai no jinshu mondai o ronjite konkai no daikakumei no shinin ni oyobu," *Chūō kōron* 26 (December 1911), in *SKZ* 10:136–42.

of military force is the result of ineptitude, and the power of virtue in one's home can tame even lawless bandits."[62] Ironically, this pacifistic, democratic (*heiminshugi*), and China-centered way of thinking, the very basis of China's *kokutai*, is similar to Spencer's civil society, which has outgrown the need for military force. But to Shiratori such pacifism had emerged from specific historical circumstances over two thousand years before and were anachronistic in the twentieth century, where one must maintain a proper balance between universalism and nationalism, peace and war (i.e., defense), and self-interest and loyalty.

This analysis that showed why *shina* had declined also provided data to prescribe policy. Shiratori's ideal society was one that understood its own unique nature, maintained a balance between civilization and militarism, and accepted from others in order to improve itself. To Shiratori, societies decline not because of any inherent inferiority or incapacity, but because of a failure to adapt and maintain that balance. The decline of the Mongols occurred because they failed to maintain their own uniqueness (military skills) as they assimilated into Chinese culture and even incorporated aspects of the Southern cultures into their homeland.[63] He also predicted that Russia would not become a greater power because of the very strong impact the North had on its culture. Moreover, balance alone was not sufficient for success. A proper understanding of historical trends was also crucial. Despite his praise for Germany, a nation strongly influenced by both North and South and militarily possessing both a strong army and navy, he considered its World War I strategy suicidal. It was, he said, contrary to the dualism to fight both England and Russia—South and North—simultaneously. Here we find a corollary to the necessity for change. Change could not be effected haphazardly or merely for its own sake; one first had to understand the historical trends before correct decisions could be made. Needless to say, Shiratori was touting the practical value of historical scholarship in the highly conflictual international arena.

In China, the Han dynasty best exemplified this balance: their "emperor, who was the center of political power, was able to win the hearts of the people as a Confucian Son of Heaven." It was also during this period that the Chinese national essence (*kokutai*) took form.[64] The 1911 Revolution represented the culmination of the steady decline of

62. Shiratori, "Shina ni okeru gendai no kakumei," in *SKZ* 10:305.
63. See, for example, "Sekai ni okeru mōko no chii," in *SKZ* 8:89; and "Mōko minzoku no kako o ronjite," in *SKZ* 8:48–50.
64. Shiratori, "Jukyō no genryū," in *SKZ* 9:66.

shina. Shiratori did not see the uprising as merely another change in the dynastic cycle, despite the popularity of anti-Manchu slogans. Popular views that the revolution was a racial struggle between the Manchus and the Chinese, he argued, did not take into account more fundamental problems that are evident in China's past. Shiratori's prescription for achieving the goals of the revolution was to create a greater sense of nationalism and self-sacrifice.

Because they generally think of *minshushugi* as the ancient Confucian conception, they believe that, when *minshushugi* is implemented and a republican government formed, taxes will be lightened, military service will disappear, and all people will be happy. But if such beliefs are numerous and if they establish a republican government in this way, [such *minshushugi*] undoubtedly does not conform with today's trends. Is not a strong centralized government that establishes a nationalism responsive to these trends necessary for a country of China's stage [of development]? One must state that a vague universalism failed in the ancient Warring States period. In today's Warring States era, a resolute nationalism is essential, and it is extremely difficult to build a republican government based on a vague notion of *heiminshugi* from the past.[65]

Even though Shiratori and other Japanese believed that they understood the problems in China, he also recognized that "four thousand years of inertia" was difficult to change. He acknowledged that the old China-centered arrogance was firmly implanted; it was not until 1905, when Japan defeated Russia, a European nation, that some Chinese recognized the superiority and value of Japan's adaptation of Western culture. Even then, however, the number of Chinese leaders seeking change was small, and arguments that government programs such as taxation were necessary to build industry and an army were firmly countered by the Confucian distaste for government exactions from the people. Nevertheless, during the early 1910s Shiratori remained optimistic. An increasing number of Chinese students was coming to Japan to learn modern concepts and techniques, and this "new" thought was gradually spreading throughout China. He believed that although chaos would continue for a while, when history had run its course a stronger, unified China would emerge.[66]

Shiratori's aforementioned protestations that he was saving Confucianism were only half true. In several ways his analysis paralleled the debate on Confucianism in revolutionary China (though he would have vehemently denied this). Like the *chin-wen* revolutionaries such as

65. Ibid., 69.
66. Shiratori, "Shinkoku kakumei no zento to waga kuni no taido," *Tōyō keizai shinpō*, November 25, 1911, 746–48; and idem, "Shina rekidai no jinshu mondai," in *SKZ* 10:142–45.

K'ang Yu-wei, and *ku-wen* traditionalists such as Chang Ping-lin, Shira-tori, too, found in Confucianism a historical doctrine that still had value and might be used to preserve a sense of Asian culture—or difference—to offset Western influence. But while his interpretation of Confucianism gave China history, it was a history of China's decline. Indeed, his interpretation was perhaps closer to that of later Chinese revolutionaries such as Ku Chieh-kang, who could find only a negative value in Confucianism; Ku denied any suprahistorical truth in the classics, which, he said, were merely "contrived by controversialists to express their own ideas, religious and political, and not to render honestly the actual history of ancient China."[67] Shiratori, too, denied the existence of such truths in contemporary China, but unlike Ku, he did find merit in Confucianism: it provided examples of past errors, which people of *tōyō* must avoid lest they fall into the same predicament. In Japan, Confucianism would develop into the basis of a progressive national character.

Confucianism as Essence: Traditionalization of an Ethical Norm

As in China, Confucianism during Meiji Japan meant different things to different people. To the *kangaku* scholars who still revered the ancient classics as truth, Confucianism in Japan was essentially a continuation of the Mitogaku synthesis that emphasized ethical relations, especially filiality, as a source for establishing loyalty to the emperor. As this notion suggests, ethics were tied to political legitimacy and proposed a particular social order. The combination of loyalty, sovereignty, and the imperial system, moreover, differed according to one's vision of society. Matsumoto Sannosuke has shown that Confucianism was also used by early-Meiji natural rights theorists, such as Nakae Chōmin and Ueki Emori.[68] For these intellectuals the Confucian Will of Heaven represented the principle that "man should live out his life." Representatives of the state, in contrast, turned the emperor

---

67. Even though K'ang and Chang represented opposing schools, there was much similarity in their quest to reinterpret or preserve Confucianism at the end of the Ch'ing period; see Levenson, *Confucian China*, bk. I, 86–94 (quote at 93–94).

68. Matsumoto Sannosuke, "The Idea of Heaven: A Tokugawa Foundation for Natural Rights Theory," in Najita and Scheiner (eds.), *Japanese Thought in the Tokugawa Period*, 181–99.

into a political figurehead to facilitate their rule. Hozumi Yatsuka (1860–1912), a conservative legal scholar at Tokyo Imperial University, advocated a theory that would elevate the emperor from the position of an absolute ethical person to that of absolute political ruler. Although Hozumi stated that "the sovereign is for the welfare of the people [*jinmin*]," he located sovereignty in the emperor.

Those who opposed this last interpretation attempted to separate the emperor from governmental affairs, utilizing a concept of "medieval constitutionalism" to prevent arbitrary use of political power in the emperor's name. For example, Kuga Katsunan, the publicist known for his criticism of Japanese adulation of Western culture, distinguished between national authority and sovereignty to argue that the emperor, although sovereign, did not possess absolute political power. Rather, sovereignty was the final force for harmonizing the three branches of government with the rights of the people; the emperor possessed sovereignty to ensure the welfare of the nation as a cooperative body. Minobe Tatsukichi (1873–1948), professor of law at Tokyo University, also incorporated this concept in his "organ theory," for he, too, tried to connect the emperor to the people and envisioned a cooperative government between the people and emperor without bureaucratic mediation.[69]

During the Taishō period, Japanese specialists on ancient China sought to reconcile these issues by reintegrating the concept of individual fulfillment with heaven as an ethical concept. Ancient China provided the data for understanding Japan's past. Shiratori stated:

> We cannot discover the true nature of Japan's national essence [*kokutai*] by looking only at today's Japan, which has absorbed numerous civilizations and become a complex country; also, it is difficult to know the purity of China's national essence and Chinese national character by observing only present-day China. Instead, I believe that when one investigates the ancient age, the very beginning of Japan and of China as well, when there were few foreign influences, numerous moments present themselves through which we can understand the national character of Japan and China.[70]

In his "discovery" of Japan's national essence, Shiratori endowed Japan with the universal characteristics of heaven and simultaneously delin-

69. Sakai Yūkichi, "Meiji kenpō to dentōteki kokakan," in *Nihon kindai hōshi kōgi*, ed. Ishii Shirō (Tokyo: Seirin Shoin, 1973), 61–93. In addition to Kuga and Minobe, Sakai also included Konoe Atsumaro and Kita Ikki among those advocating positions in accordance with "medieval constitutionalism."

70. Shiratori, "Nihon ni okeru jukyō no junnōsei," in *SKZ* 10:235.

eated Japan's difference from the parts of *tōyō*. The end result was the elevation of an idealistic understanding of Confucianism into a tradition as value, and *shina* became a living reminder to Japanese of what would happen if they did not follow the proper path prescribed by history.

Shiratori's heaven was the universal that connected the present to ancient history as well as being the spiritual belief common to Europeans, Ural Altai, Chinese, and Japanese. But as we saw in the above discussion of *minponshugi*, the idea of democracy differed in each culture. Shiratori's research on ancient China established the historical authority to support his contention that the *spirit* of democracy differed from the *form*. He stated, "The position of the ruler is given by the law of heaven; the law of heaven appears through the will of the people. This connection to heaven is a characteristic of Chinese democracy, and it is a little different from people's rights in the West. But this is a form of thought, and actually the fundamental spirit is that the leader always obeys the people [*min*]."[71] The importance of this statement lies not in the apparent disavowal of dictatorship, but in the characterization of the "fundamental spirit of democracy" as a heavenly element. The form of democratic thought (*shisō no keishiki*) differed because of historical development. In the West, this concept had developed into one of people's rights, whereas in Asia it had developed into one in which the people had to protect themselves from bad rulers. The connection of the heavenly order to the people's will is characteristic of both Chinese and Japanese democracy. Western individualism played no part in the Japanese version of democracy.

While the spirit by which heaven ruled in Japan and China was similar, the employment of that spirit differed; thus the manifestation of heaven became the principal reason for both the political and the spiritual differences between Japan and China. While the Chinese heaven was a formless idea from which the emperor, the Son of Heaven, received his right to rule, in Japan the concept evolved differently. There, heaven was not an abstract phenomenon, but was manifested in the emperor himself. Japan, Shiratori asserted, has a spirit that is tied to the imperial institution:

In our country, heaven was turned into the imperial court, but in China, heaven existed as heaven and a representative reigned as emperor (Son of Heaven). Furthermore, in our country heaven was expressed as the imperial

71. Shiratori, "Jukyō no genryū," in *SKZ* 9:54.

household of Amaterasu and her grandson Ninigi, who as gods [*kami*] were human figures, but in China, heaven appeared as the open sky. . . . In other words, the form is slightly different, but in the fundamental spirit in which heaven itself rules the people, there is no difference between China and Japan.[72]

This historical divergence of the Will of Heaven was the basis for Shiratori's differentiation of the national essences of Japan and China. In contrast to China's horizontal society, Japan, like all other nations of the world, had evolved into a vertical society, held together by a belief in a religious figure, the emperor.

By pointing to this democratic ideal in the Chinese and Japanese traditions, Shiratori sought to redefine the Western notion of democracy, even to preclude its utility for Japan and China. When seen in the context of the political questions of the Taishō period, his difficulty in naming this concept becomes clearer. His conscious denial of the term *minshushugi* reflects the constitutional debate between Minobe and Hozumi's protegé, Uesugi Shinkichi, who charged that Minobe's use of the term *minshu* was in direct contradiction to the Meiji constitution and Japan's national essence.[73] Like Minobe, Shiratori relied heavily on concepts and ideas from the West; throughout his writings, Shiratori turned to, compared, and competed with Western scholars. Yet he did not feel compelled to follow those concepts as they had been formulated and, indeed, as a rule attempted to rewrite them. Just as *tōyōshi* as he helped formulate it differed from European Oriental studies, so did his discussion of Confucianism redefine the concept of democracy so that it fit Japan and China, unconstrained by definitions from the West.

Scholars like Shiratori, Minobe, Inoue, Yoshino Sakuzō, a political scientist at Tokyo Imperial University, and Hattori Unokichi, a leading Confucian scholar, did not limit their inquiry to the legalistic question of sovereignty and the continued preeminence of the emperor. Instead they were attempting to synthesize the various and often conflicting interests of their time into a harmonious whole.[74] Inoue, for example, tried to show that his family system incorporated the best of both socialism and individualism. And in 1918 Hattori, Inoue's successor, argued that the democratic concepts of the West in fact inhered within Confucianism. Hattori defined democracy as a constantly changing

72. Shiratori, "Nihon ni okeru jukyō no junnōsei," in *SKZ* 10:246.
73. See F. Miller, *Minobe Tatsukichi*, 30–31, 300. For the different nuances of *minshu, minpon, heimin,* see n. 53.
74. For a discussion of the perceived fragmentation of society and need to manage conflict, see the Introduction.

concept similar to *minponshugi* and Confucianism, whereby each person can demonstrate his or her abilities and contribute to a cooperative society. He even went so far as to argue that the last two parts of Abraham Lincoln's famous phrase "Government of the people, by the people, and for the people" existed in Japan and questioned whether the first part existed anywhere, even in England or the United States.[75] His reading of Lincoln's phrase as, in essence, "government based on the people, government for the sake of the people, and government of the people" certainly recentered the locus of government on the institution, not the people. Yoshino, though more supportive of the parliamentary order, also privileged the whole. Tetsuo Najita describes the role of Yoshino's political man: "It was primarily the 'right' and moral commitment of each individual to serve the nation by helping to determine what was ideally best for the entire country."[76]

Through his reinterpretation of Confucianism, Shiratori drew upon various positions regarding the emperor. He included Inoue's union of filiality and loyalty, and, rather than ignoring the Mandate of Heaven, the revolutionary concept of heaven's will, he eliminated the possibility of overthrowing the Japanese emperor by separating spirit—heaven—from form—Japan's peculiar religious government. Thus he could assert in 1915, "The national essence of Japan and China is completely different; consequently, even if China becomes a democratic polity [*seitai*], there will be no influence on Japan."[77] The influence many feared was the spread of social conflict and the revolutionary activity from China. But the potential for absolute power residing with the emperor was limited by ideas found in medieval constitutionalism. Like Kuga and Minobe, Shiratori saw the emperor as the embodiment of an ethical ideal that had existed in the past, and he also indirectly advocated the direct rule of the emperor without the mediating structures of government.[78]

75. Hattori Unokichi, "Jukyō to demokurashii," *Shibun* 1 (1919): 327–35.
76. Tetsuo Najita, "Some Reflections on Idealism in the Political Thought of Yoshino Sakuzō," in Silberman and Harootunian (eds.), *Japan in Crisis*, 47. There were occasions when Yoshino argued that the individual took precedence over the group, but this argument was based on historical, not theoretical or "natural," conditions.
77. Shiratori, "Nihon ni okeru jukyō no junnōsei," in *SKZ* 10:240.
78. Sakai, "Meiji kenpō to dentōteki kokakan," 61–93. Shiratori did not discuss the role of the bureaucracy, Privy Council, or Diet here, but in a later article on the Meiji Restoration he asserted that in times of international contact the emperor should rule directly; see "Tōyōshijō yori mitaru Meiji ishin," *Meiji ishinshi kenkyū* (1929), in *SKZ* 9:215–24.

Shiratori, however, also went beyond the concept of medieval constitutionalism, which removed the emperor from political responsibility, for he bestowed on the imperial system both religious and political importance. One governmental concern at the end of the Meiji period was the establishment of some form of religion to cultivate a national morality. Tokonami Takejirō, home minister under the second Saionji cabinet, for example, proposed to "bring together the three religions" (Shintō, Buddhism, and Christianity).[79] But in contrast to Tokonami, who was satisfied to unify the three religions, Shiratori privileged Shintō and deemphasized Christianity and, to a lesser extent, Buddhism. Here Shiratori argued that the spiritual unification which the rulers of the Han dynasty instituted, only to be subsequently lost in China, had always existed in Japan. Even though he did not use terms such as ancestor worship and family state, by elevating the emperor to the human embodiment of heaven, Shiratori's concept resembled Hozumi's, in which sovereignty was placed in the realm of the divine.[80]

Again, one must be careful not to draw facile conclusions. Shiratori was not interested merely in elevating the emperor, as Hozumi and Uesugi were attempting to do for different reasons. Nor was his project anti-Western. Instead, just as Ranke saw the Protestant God as the progressive spirit that separated the Protestant (especially German) people—the dynamic—from the Catholics—the mundane—Shiratori found in heaven a universal spirit common to the West, China, and Japan, but one that unfolded quite differently; in China it turned into a conservative doctrine, while in Japan and the West it became the source of a progressive spirit. Also like Ranke, Shiratori placed this spirit at the very foundation of his philosophy of history. It is here that the study of history as a social science merged with the "idea of the nation" as a value. This spirit was both real and unreal, timeful and timeless. The emperor was the historical manifestation of a timeless spirit; the imperial institution was an idea with an unbroken lineage that would exist as long as the Japanese nation. Just as the Western ontology rooted in God is rarely questioned, this spirit was not questioned. This spirit, however, also authorized the history of the Japanese nation-state. Shiratori argued that because this spirit served as a stabilizing yet

79. Oka, "Generational Conflict," 217–18.
80. Sakai, "Meiji kenpō to dentōteki kokakan," 87.

progressive force, the Japanese incorporated only those aspects of different cultures that did not conflict with it; for this reason, he pointed out, Islam, Hinduism, and Christianity were not accepted.[81] But while he recognized the debilitating effect that the traditionalization of Confucianism had had on Chinese society, he did not recognize that his identification of Japan's essence might have a similarly detrimental impact on Japan. The distinction between this essence as a progressive force that accepted difference and its traditionalization as a negation of alterity was a very fine one. In the end, his interpretation of Confucianism would be adapted by others.

Whether Shiratori's "preservation" of Confucianism played any role or not, the rebirth of organized Confucianism in Japan in 1918 was signaled by the reorganization of the Shibun Gakkai and other Confucian or moralistic organizations into the Shibunkai. This new organization enjoyed the broad support of both the government and major businessmen and commercial families, such as Shibusawa Eiichi and the Iwasaki and Mitsui families.[82] The goals of the Shibunkai were clearly stated at the outset:

As transportation between the East and the West has fully opened up and European power has proceeded eastward, of the various Asiatic nations there is only one which has avoided either having its independence threatened or having its territory seized. This lone one, Japan, has excelled majestically among these nations, being led by its eternally changeless imperial family. . . .

Considering matters, the great war of the world today is without parallel in history, and it goes without saying that it will bring great changes in every sphere. And especially in its influence on the intellectual world, it will demand deep consideration anew from men of intelligence. At this juncture, this association, with the approval and help of many talented men in the government and among the people, has taken the Confucian way for spreading our nation's characteristic morality and for endeavouring to arouse spiritual culture in order to attain [in this area] progress corresponding to that of the utility and well being of the people connected with materialistic culture. And by carrying this out

81. Shiratori, "Nihon ni okeru jukyō no junnōsei," in *SKZ* 10:237; and idem, "Kōdō no konpongi ni tsuite," *(Kōdō)* 344 (November 1920): 2–17. In the latter article on Japan's imperial way *(kōdō)*, Shiratori argued that the *kokugakusha* who proposed to end the use of foreign culture did not understand Japan's *kokutai*.

82. Shibusawa, Iwasaki, and Mitsui are names tied to three of the largest prewar *zaibatsu*, Shibusawa, Mitsubishi, and Mitsui. Shiratori was also a member of this new organization, though he did not publish in its journal, *Shibun*. For the formation of this organization, see Smith, *Confucianism in Modern Japan*, 100–102.

and achieving these [ends], for ages it will further the flourishing of the destiny of the nation and not fail to elevate the brilliancy of our national polity that excels among the ten thousand nations of the post-war world.[83]

This proclamation hints at changes that had occurred in the decade since the debate between Hayashi and Shiratori. Throughout this text, China was not mentioned at all, and instead Confucianism—or, more accurately, the Confucian way—became a tool for elevating *tōyō* morality to counter the evils of materialistic culture. Moreover, Confucianism was now not only completely identified with Japan, but also seen as the moral source of Japan's future.[84]

Hattori was a leading and perhaps the most influential Confucian scholar of this period. In contrast to Hayashi's effort to defend Chinese culture, Hattori displayed an aloofness toward China similar to that of Shiratori. Like his contemporaries, and despite his interest in Confucianism, he did not envision a return to pre-Meiji days; indeed, as early as 1900 he advocated both the necessity of knowledge to determine the future and Japan's responsibility to instruct China. For example, in reaction to the Boxer Rebellion he stated, "Parading an antiforeign thought [in China] is dangerous to the overall situation of East Asia. Japan must instruct the Chinese so that they do not mistake their future."[85]

This statement is indicative of the considerable change in Confucianism from an ethical worldview to its incorporation into positivistic history. In his article in the first issue of *Shibun,* Hattori stated: "Today, there are frequently those who, while recognizing the major impact Confucianism has had on our culture, national thought, and so on, also think that it is no longer useful. Unless we recognize that the causes of the past become today's effects, and today's effects become future causes, we will cease [to exist]; since it is undeniable that there is a deep relationship between the past, present, and future, one cannot say that

83. Quoted in ibid., 269–71.

84. Smith described Shiratori's preoccupation with morals in Japan but could not reconcile his reputation as an objective scholar with his concern for national unity. He commented (ibid., 256) on Shiratori's 1917 article "Kokutai to jukyō": "Since Shiratori was a scholar, ethnologist, and linguist of standing, it is surprising to find him writing here what seems like a nationalist tract. In this period, nationalism was not the intimidating force it was to become twenty years later in Japan; yet Shiratori associates Japan's national polity with a superior spiritual force which he claims gives Confucianism greater strength and permanence in Japan than China."

85. Ono Kazuko, "Shimoda Utako to Hattori Unokichi," in *Kindai nihon to chūgoku, jō,* ed. Takeuchi Yoshimi and Hashikawa Bunsō (Tokyo: Asahi Sensho, 1974), 214.

Confucianism is completely useless."[86] Such a notion of causality demonstrates that the fixed metaphysical realm of Confucianism—of which the ideals of Yao, Shun, and Yü were a part—had now been incorporated into a scientific theory of knowledge. Although superficially Hattori emphasized morals, his brand of Confucianism now became a higher authority, a political ideology to counteract self-interest and materialism, and also an idealistic vision for the future.

Hattori's analysis was based on a distinction between Confucianism and the teachings of Confucius, and on his division of the Will of Heaven into two forms. He adapted Shiratori's separation of spirit from history, or idea from form, to argue that Confucianism was an ethnic doctrine (*minzokuteki kyōgi*), not a universal one; it was unique to China and could not affect other peoples who had different customs, feelings, and history. Confucius, however, had compiled the Way of ancient sages and changed the ethnic doctrine into a world doctrine.[87]

Hattori argued that there were basically two forms of Will of Heaven: one passive and the other active. The former, that of Confucianism, involved doing "everything that is humanly possible and leaving the rest to fate." The latter, that of the teachings of Confucius, was an instruction to serve, actively and thoroughly, to "perform one's duty as it is received from heaven. But in performing one's duties, it is not merely enough for each person to fulfill his duties. Beyond this, with the self-confidence of a frontrunner one must lead the stragglers. Only then can the Will of Heaven be completely served."[88] There is little doubt that the former characterized China and the latter, Japan. The teachings of Confucius contained not only benevolence and justice, but also a progressive spirit. Such an interpretation is reminiscent of Shiratori's use of Confucianism to separate Japan from China. But unlike Shiratori, Hattori virtually eliminated individual autonomy from his ideal. With no mention of the question of *minponshugi* that so concerned Shiratori, he continued: "I believe that in each country there is a Will of Heaven for that country, and for each person there is also a Will of Heaven. . . . In Japan, the Will of Heaven is in the belief of the Japanese people. If the people do not possess a strong self-confidence in this Will of Heaven and then serve it, the progress and development

86. Hattori Unokichi, "Gendai ni okeru jukyō no igi," *Shibun* 1 (1919): 19.

87. This interpretation resembles Shiratori's argument that Confucianism developed out of the metaphysical thought of the Chinese people. Shiratori, of course, did not distinguish between Confucianism and the teachings of Confucius, but between ethics as a political philosophy and religion.

88. Nomura, "Kindai nihon ni okeru jukyō no shisō," 257.

[*shinpo hattatsu*] of Japanese society will not stand on a sufficiently strong base."[89] In this rewriting of Confucianism, as Nomura Kōichi has pointed out, Hattori tied the teachings of Confucius to Japan's destiny—which was equivalent to the destiny of the imperial court.[90] Hattori, too, eliminated the revolutionary doctrine of Confucian thought from Japanese Confucianism; the Mandate of Heaven was not part of the teachings of Confucius, but emerged later as Confucianists in China changed the original doctrine.

By the late 1910s *kangaku*, which had appeared to be approaching extinction, had found a way back to the center of sociopolitical discourse. Despite their similarities, Hattori, by focusing on Japan and by building on the separation of Confucianism from China, clearly removed the balances that Shiratori had established. While Shiratori used heaven as a universalistic spirit, Hattori turned the Will of Heaven into a tautology for Japan's superiority: he eliminated the ethical controls placed on the emperor by Shiratori's interpretation of *minponshugi*; and the imperial system, which served Shiratori's explanation of change and progress, became under Hattori the object of loyalty. Thus Hattori's theory turned this newly revived ethical doctrine into an ideal that beseeched Japan to lead the world. Moreover, his theory also allowed for the reappropriation of Confucianism as an ethical control mechanism for government—in this case the emperor—to correct trends that Shibunkai members considered subversive to the nation.[91] The traditionalization of Confucianism in Japan was now complete.

In 1915 Shiratori stated, "The Imperial Rescript on Education lives as a great moral precept that will hereafter control us as well as our grandchildren. The considerable influence Confucianism has had on our country is clear even here."[92] The confidence with which Shiratori was able to make such a statement belies the intellectual turmoil he had experienced over the preceding five years. By 1915, the domestic political

89. Ibid.
90. Ibid., 254–57.
91. The membership of the Shibunkai included many prominent members of society and government. These members, such as Shibusawa Eiichi and Mizuno Rentarō, often presented speeches on various contemporary social topics. Articles by scholars on proper labor management relations (stating, that is, that both sides should accept their role) and on moral and ethical education were not uncommon. For the connection of Confucianism to such social issues and government, see Smith, *Confucianism in Modern Japan*, esp. 122–45.
92. Shiratori, "Nihon ni okeru jukyō no junnōsei," in *SKZ* 10:238.

commotion surrounding the imperial system and the questions raised by the 1911 Revolution in China had passed. More important, Confucianism had undergone a transition in which it became further entrenched as a Japanese tradition.

It became evident during this period that such "traditional" concepts as loyalty were double-edged. This problem, of course, was not new; the revolutionaries of the Bakumatsu period justified their protest by asserting that they were acting out of loyalty to a higher authority. Shiratori separated the emperor from the possibility of revolution as had occurred in China by adapting Confucianism as another body of data, albeit a well-respected and venerable one, to fit Japan's perceived needs. In spite of their differences, the arguments of Hayashi, Inoue, and Hattori were remarkably similar to those of Shiratori: Confucianism was both the means for separating Japan from China and an ideal form of morals and ethics. Each of these men developed a strategy to show differences between Japan and China—Inoue's totalistic and individual families, Shiratori's heaven, and Hattori's teachings of Confucius and Confucianism—and to omit or eliminate the revolutionary potential from Japanese Confucianism. This separation of Confucianism from China and the use of Confucianism as merely another source for the study of Chinese history was also echoed by Naitō, who, although he may not have stated that Confucianism had shifted to Japan (this aspect of Naitō has yet to be studied), in his writings on the subject demonstrates that he, too, could easily have fallen into this discourse. By using Confucianism to distinguish between China's decadence or lack of progress and Japan's development, these scholars showed *shina* to be a historical territory that was one part of a broader geocultural realm, *tōyō*. Once the preeminent unit, *shina* had fallen into decay because of historical circumstances and had been surpassed by Japan, the new possessor and authority of the spirit or essence of *tōyō*.

The intellectual and political outcome of this view was the traditionalization of certain idealized aspects of society that emphasized cohesion. Here tradition and history were merged. As mentioned at the outset of this chapter, this emphasis on "traditional" ideas and institutions entails a choice; tradition, too, was a modern creation and supported by a historical framework that was also recently constructed. Both progress—that is, change—and the people were defined in relation to the imperial system, not vice versa. While Shiratori realized that neither the old nor the new (i.e., the West) was solely applicable to twentieth-century Japan, his effort to synthesize the two took an unexpected turn. Masao Miyoshi states, "If Maruyama Masao is right . . . in diagnosing the conspicuous absence of the speculative habit [*shisō*] in the whole Japanese tradition, it is a price the culture has been willing to pay. It has chosen to forgo universalistic knowledge, skeptical observation, and individual reflection in order to sustain a close and coherent community inherited from the long past."[93] This passage is interesting for two reasons. First, one has but to remember the complaint of Riess that Japanese historians considered only abstract ideas to realize that, although the allegation of a lack of speculative habit has become so common that it is often accepted as fact, the tradition here was "chosen."

The search for a history for Japan, which began with *bunmeishi*, inevitably led to such retrospection. Against universalistic knowledge and individual autonomy, Japanese elites chose, instead, to emphasize the organic community. Here, one is reminded of Tagore's 1917 description of Japan quoted at the beginning of Part Two. Tagore sees the submission of all Japanese into one uniform mass according to the governmental recipe. He attributes this acceptance of a predefined homogeneity to modernity, the "desire to turn themselves into a machine of power . . . and emulate other machines in their collective worldliness."[94] The discovery of an idealized communal past affirmed a monological system (bounded as the nation-state) that turned history from the idealistic goal of description to the prescription of what ought to be. As his insightful analysis of China suggests, Shiratori was not blind to this possibility. But while Shiratori unearthed the role of traditionalization in turning *shina* into a culturally insular place, he did not recognize that there was a only a very fine difference between his identification of the essence of Japan, as the source and stabilizing entity for progressiveness, and its traditionalization. Shiratori would undoubtedly be shocked to see Japan described in this way; but when intellectuals such as Hattori altered his interpretation to minimize the balances he carefully developed, it was but a small step further to change tradition from a value to a structure.

93. Masao Miyoshi, *As We Saw Them: The First Japanese Embassy to the United States (1860)* (Berkeley and Los Angeles: University of California Press, 1979), 124.

94. Rabindranath Tagore, *Nationalism* (1917; Madras: Macmillan India, 1985), 15–16.

CHAPTER FOUR

Shina: The Narration of Japan's Emergence

In his second article rebutting Hayashi's defense of Confucianism, Shiratori ended suggestively, in what seemed almost like an afterthought: "Thus, this form of yin-and-yang thought has reached our country and has had a sizable influence on the composition of the history of the age of the gods."[1] This statement, otherwise out of place in such a detailed, positivistic study of the Chinese classics, sums up one of the principal goals of Shiratori's studies of Asia: the establishment of a certain understanding of Japan.

The studies on Confucianism showed how universalistic forces, the spirit and North-South dualism, combined to explain the origin, or what Novick calls the "founding myth," a sacred reality that describes past accomplishments. But for Japan, the potential for alienness was still present.[2] Yet in their description of Japan as the possessor of the essence of Confucian thought, and therefore as a part of *tōyō*, these studies in effect were only removing the alienness of historical Chinese thought, that of *shina*. As Foucault reminds us, the more one searches the past for a singular identity, the more likely it is that one will find "something altogether different."[3] Despite the differentiation between a Chinese and Japanese version of Confucianism, the rediscovery of that ethical doctrine suggested that the "altogether

1. Shiratori, " 'Shōsho' no kōtō hihan," in *SKZ* 8:398.
2. Novick, *That Noble Dream*, 3.
3. Foucault, "Nietzsche, Genealogy, History," 142.

153

different" was in fact a Japan heavily indebted to China, a mere variation of Chinese culture.

To prove Japan's distinctiveness, it was therefore also necessary to
create a narrative of its emergence, establishing the historical nature of
its origin. The beginning of this historical narrative was protohistoric
Japan: therein lay the historical "reality" from which a narrative of Japanese development could be created. But this narrative was not about
political or structural institutions discovered in archeological digs;
rather, it encompassed ideology, broadly defined, the pure character of
Japan before its culture was altered or covered. As Foucault puts it,
"The historian's history finds its support outside of time and pretends
to base its judgments on an apocalyptic objectivity."[4] This evidence
"outside of time" was found in the ancient chronologies: the *Kojiki*, *Nihon shoki*, and Chinese compendia.

For Shiratori, the mythological and historical segments of Japan's
ancient past were the key to unlocking Japan's connection to *tōyō* and
the rest of the world, especially Europe. Speculation on the origins of
legends and folk tales, such as the *wani* (sea serpent or crocodile), the
ancient kingdom of Fuyo, Momotarō (Peach Boy), and especially
Himiko and Yamatai, the female ruler and kingdom in the land of Wa
recorded in the *Wei chih*, clarified historical truth. But more important,
it gave an aura of objectivity to research on the beginnings of Japan. In
other words, scientific research of ancient myths and legends created a
new myth, one that was "the recital of a creation; [that new myth] tells
how something was accomplished, began to *be*. It . . . speaks only of realities, of what *really* happened, of what was fully manifested."[5] Archeological evidence was secondary. (Even today, archeological findings,
when excavations are permitted, are often interpreted in ways that do
not upset this founding myth.)

Objectivity—or the pretense of objectivity—appeared in the discussion of such historiographic issues as the location of Yamatai. Through
detailed studies of textual sources, scholars attempted to verify and interpret the location, organization, and nature of this ancient kingdom.
Their conviction in this task is indicated by the tenacity of their various
historical positions: at least one of the academic debates between Naitō
and Shiratori continues still today—though in an arguably much less

4. Ibid., 152.
5. Mircea Eliade, *The Sacred and the Profane*, quoted in Peter Novick, *That Noble
Dream*, 3.

political manner.[6] The differences in this debate concern historical facts, not ideology. The similarities between the two sides, in fact, are striking. The various specialists on Asia, mostly associated with the Imperial Universities at Tokyo or Kyoto, either as professors or as students, worked within a common historical discourse. Thus, both Shiratori and Naitō believed that knowing the past was essential both for understanding the present and for predicting the future; both considered positivistic history the only means by which societies could scientifically understand the trends of the times; and both sought to understand the essence of a Japanese culture centered on the imperial institution. Even though they offered different interpretations of Japan's early formation, the supremacy of the latter institution was never questioned. They did not criticize the assumption of a Japanese unity put forth in the Japanese classics (although they did expand Japan's geographic boundaries); rather, they based their studies on this organic whole but redefined history in such a way that the ancient legends and myths could both coexist and be supported by the authority of science.

The history that emerged, then, proved historical continuity of the progressive spirit of all Japanese, a spirit that itself enabled the construction of the historical narrative. By placing certain aspects of Japan's past within the framework of his North-South dualism (though it is perhaps more accurate to say that he created the North-South dualism to bring Eurasia into the context of Japan), Shiratori constructed an objectivistic and seamless narrative that explained Japan's essential orientalness. His attempt to bring the Kōtaiō monument (a stone obelisk on the bank of the Yalu River near Tunghwa, erected in A.D. 414 to commemorate the deeds of King Kwanggaet'o [r. 391–413] of Koguryŏ) back to Japan is a somewhat comic example of his desire to find and possess evidence that suggests continuity.[7] This narrative also explained Japan's unique development. In his view, each region or culture acted according to its own temporality: China developed rapidly and then slowly declined; Europe developed next and is now or was just at its apex; and Japan, which has combined the best of *tōyō* and Europe, is

---

6. The question over the location of Yamatai continues to this day. Generally, those connected with the University of Kyoto argue for Yamato, while those from the University of Tokyo tend to support a location in Kyushu. See discussion below.

7. For information on the Kōtaiō monument, see Boleslaw Szczesniak, "The Kōtaiō Monument," *Monumenta Nipponica* 7 (January 1951): 242–68.

still developing. This vision of Japan as a unique and superior politico-cultural entity was authorized by science, not by historicism.

Yamatai: The Search for Japan's Origins

Any inquiry into Japan's origins and ancient history leads inevitably to the problem of the location of Yamatai (either in Yamato [Kinki] or on Kyushu) and the identification of Himiko. This perhaps irresolvable issue has troubled Japanese historians at least since the compilation of the *Nihon shoki* (720). It has, moreover, generated countless studies covering virtually every conceivable angle, and has stretched the meaning of historical research as well as the imaginations of not a few participants. My purpose is not to judge which is the correct interpretation; both sides, after all, have used only the evidence that supports their own interpretation. I do, however, wish to show the relation of various strategies to the broader task of creating a historical narrative of Japan.

One source of ambiguity is found in the conflicting records, primarily the *Wei chih* and the *Hou Han shu* on the one hand, and the *Kojiki* and the *Nihon shoki* on the other. Yamatai was first mentioned in the *Wei chih*, especially the *Wo-jen ch'uan* (Stories on the People of Wa, the Chinese term for ancient Japan), which is based mainly on the records of two Chinese emissaries who traveled to Wa via Korea.[8] These records present a rather detailed account of a kingdom called Yamatai that was ruled by a queen, Himiko. Reliance on these records, the single most accepted source, tends to give greater weight to the interpretation that Yamatai was in Kyushu. However, in that case the recorded distances and directions are inaccurate; if followed without adjustment, they put Yamatai in the Pacific Ocean. Furthermore, this account is controversial, for the struggle between Himiko and the king of Kunu implies that Japan was not always unified, the dispatch of an emissary to China in 247 requesting aid suggests Yamatai's political subservience to China, and the primitive living conditions described by the emissaries conveys cultural inferiority. The *Wei chih* recorded, "The land of Wa is warm and mild. In winter as in summer the people live on raw

8. Although the history of a later dynasty, the *Wei chih*, part of the *San Kuo chih*, was compiled in 297. Where discrepancies occur, the *Wei chih* has generally been given priority over the *Hou Han shu*, which was compiled in 445.

vegetables and go about barefooted." And also, "When they go on voyages across the sea to visit China, they always select a man who does not comb his hair, does not rid himself of fleas, lets his clothing get dirty as it will, does not eat meat, and does not lie with women."[9]

The *Kojiki* and the *Nihon shoki* have also been valuable sources of information, but are considered less reliable than the *Wei chih*. These texts were written centuries after the events in question and, as the official history of the imperial court, suggest that Yamatai was located in Yamato. Tsuda, for example, pointed to problems with the information itself—the same deeds are occasionally repeated in different situations and are often contradictory—and concluded that these chronicles were written to provide historical authority for the unification of Japan.[10] Archeological evidence, moreover, though suggestive, remains inconclusive owing largely to the reluctance to unearth the contents of the major tombs in the Kansai area.[11]

Another, and perhaps the most important, reason for the longevity of the issue of Yamatai's location is its centrality to an understanding of the political and cultural nature of the Japanese past. Yamatai constitutes Japan's historical beginning, the earliest society in the archipelago that is verified in non-Japanese sources. John Young sums up this historiographical and political issue: "The way in which Japanese historians approached the problem throws light on wider aspects of Japanese history. What the Japanese historians had to say on the problem also reveals a good deal about the thinking of the Japanese historians themselves."[12] One should add that such a revelation is not limited to historians. The centrality and sensitivity of this issue to how Japanese conceived of their nation-state were painfully evident in 1939, when Tsuda was accused of treason and later convicted because his interpretation of the matter did not abide by dogma.[13]

9. Quoted from Ryusaku Tsunoda, Wm. Theodore de Bary, and Donald Keene, eds., *Sources of Japanese Tradition*, vol. 1 (New York: Columbia University Press, 1958), 4–5.

10. The *Kojiki* was compiled in 712 by Yasumaro, who also participated in the compilation of the *Nihon shoki*, completed in 720. For a recent translation of the *Kojiki*, see Philippi (trans.), *Kojiki*; for the *Nihon shoki*, see Aston (trans.), *Nihongi*. For Tsuda's interpretation, see his *Jindaishi no atarashii kenkyū* (Tokyo 1913), in *Tsuda Sōkichi zenshū* (Tokyo: Iwanami Shoten, 1961), supp. vol. 1, 15–16 (hereafter cited as *TSZ*).

11. For a discussion on the relation and problems of archeological evidence in this debate, see Young, *Location of Yamatai*, 115–43.

12. Ibid., 24.

13. Formal charges that Tsuda had violated the Publication Law were brought in 1940. His trial lasted from November 1941 to January 1942; he was found guilty

Despite continued interest even today in this rather equally divided debate, the issue of the location of Yamatai did not preoccupy historians before the eighteenth century. One reason is that few questioned the veracity of the *Kojiki* and the *Nihon shoki*, the latter of which, written "to justify and strengthen the emperors' rule as a permanent one, as initiated in the time of the Gods and lasting without end," provided the initial grounds for locating Yamatai in Yamato.[14] The first major challenge to this idea came from Motoori Norinaga, the famous eighteenth-century nativist scholar, as a part of his attempt to reassert Japan's essence and distinguish Japanese culture from that of China. His interpretation that Yamatai was located in Tsukushi (Kyushu), not Yamato, became the common view through the early Meiji period. In the 1890s the question was again revived, but now most historians debated Yamatai's specific location on Kyushu, not whether it was on Kyushu or in Yamato.[15]

NAITŌ'S REVISION

The debate over the location of Yamatai reemerged in 1910 among a new generation of historians. In May and June of that year, Naitō published three articles that sparked a debate with Shiratori—or, more accurately, between *shinagaku* (Sinology) scholars of Kyoto Imperial University and *tōyōshi* advocates of Tokyo Imperial University.[16] It is still unclear exactly why Naitō took up the question of Yamatai. According to one biographer, his intent was pragmatic: he used the question to gain recognition for the newly established history department at Kyoto Imperial University.[17] But one should not overlook his conservative position; he defended the Japanese legends

on one of nine counts and sentenced to three months imprisonment. See Yun-tai Tam, "Rationalism Versus Nationalism: Tsuda Sōkichi," in Brownlee (ed.), *History in the Service of the Japanese Nation,* 165–88.

14. Young (*Location of Yamatai,* 50–51; quote at 51) cites the code of seventeen articles as evidence that Prince Shōtoku wanted to establish the authority of the emperor over the people and local governors.

15. For greater detail on the changes of interpretation up to this period and perhaps the most balanced overview of this historiographical issue, see ibid.; also Cornelius J. Kiley, "State and Dynasty in Archaic Yamato," *Journal of Asian Studies* 23 (November 1973): 25–49.

16. Naitō, "Himiko kō," *Geibun* 1 (May–July 1910), in *NKZ* 7:247–83.

17. Yue-him Tam, in his study of Naitō ("In Search of the Oriental Past," 230), pointed out that Kyoto University scholars gained recognition as well as respect through their debates with University of Tokyo scholars.

against those interpretations that, he felt, overemphasized China's role and downgraded the developmental character of the Japanese.[18] This debate also raises questions about the centrality of China in Naitō's history. He stated, "What is called Japanese culture is, to use a term common today, an extension of the culture of *tōyō* and *shina;* it is the continuity of Chinese culture. Thus one first has to know Chinese culture to know the foundations and origins of Japanese culture. . . . In other words, it is an utter mistake to consider the history of the orient [*tōyōshi*] as foreign [*igai*] to Japanese history."[19] Significantly, Naitō centered his research on China around Japan, not vice versa.

Naitō's study presented a thorough analysis (though essentially a philological one) of the names of places and people in an attempt to identify Yamatai with Yamato. No doubt it was a direct rebuttal of the advocates of the Kyushu theory, for example nativist scholars such as Motoori and Tsurumine Shigenobu, as well as the Meiji historians in Tokyo, including Suga Masatomo, Yoshida Tōgo, Naka, Kume, and Hoshino Hisashi. Like previous Yamato-theory advocates, Naitō relied more on ancient Japanese texts than on Chinese, a somewhat surprising selection given his reputation as a historian with great respect for Chinese culture and texts. To justify his decision Naitō chose to point out the difficulties of using the *Wei chih;* he found it useful, he said, only as a source for corroborating information in the *Nihon shoki.*[20]

Locating Yamatai in Yamato requires that the recorded distance be accepted over direction. Naitō—indeed, all historians who study this problem—had to second-guess not only the ancient travelers but also subsequent scribes. It was not uncommon, he argued, for ancient Chinese to interchange directions, such as east and south, west and north, and to lose their sense of direction. However, he found it inconceivable that these same travelers had not even heard of Yamato and that they could have been so easily duped into believing that a Kyushu tribe was the powerful Yamato people.[21]

18. Naitō, "Nihon bunka to wa nanzo ya?" in *Rekishi to shisō,* ed. Kuwabara Takeo, Gendai nihon shisō taikei, vol. 27 (Tokyo: Chikuma Shobō, 1965), 202–4. For a fine article that emphasizes the centrality of China in Naitō's research, see Masubuchi, "Nihon no kindaishi."

19. Naitō, "Nihon bunka to wa nanzo ya?" 211.

20. Naitō, "Himiko kō," in *NKZ* 7:251–52, 279. Throughout his analysis he referred to earlier proponents of the Kyushu theory; it was only after Shiratori's comments appeared in June that he confronted Shiratori. See also Young, *Location of Yamatai,* 93–95.

21. Naitō, "Himiko kō," in *NKZ* 7:261. Here Naitō assumes that Yamato was already a relatively powerful place, an assumption that Shiratori contests. Tsurumine's *gisen* theory, which appeared in 1820, further developed Motoori's proposal that Yamatai

Yet Naitō was also perceptive enough to note that a debate that relied solely on directions or distances could never be resolved. The main part of his argument, therefore, required matching as many as possible of the names, places, and events recorded in the Japanese chronicles with counterparts in the *Wei chih*. For example, he found that the story of Himiko's magic is similar to an account in the *Nihon shoki* in which Yamato-hime no mikoto is the servant of Amaterasu, the Sun Goddess; the names of the places mentioned in the *Wo-jen ch'uan*, he argued, correspond to names around Ise; and the *Wei chih* account of Himiko's brother assisting her probably concern Hime no mikoto's brother, Emperor Keikō (the twelfth emperor): "The rule of the land was in the hands of the emperor, and Hime no mikoto administered religious matters [*kamigoto*], but because of her power and influence they [the Wei emissaries] mistook her for a queen."[22] The identification of Himiko as Yamato-hime no mikoto, the sister of Emperor Keikō, suited his attempt to locate the actors and places in the *Wei chih* in Yamato. But because both positions necessitate a selection and elision of data, Naitō, like all who engaged in this debate, left himself vulnerable to criticism.

SHIRATORI'S DEFENSE OF KYUSHU

Shiratori responded quickly to Naitō's theory (which he referred to as that of a "younger historian"), publishing the first of his articles on Yamatai in June 1910, before Naitō's series was completed. Yet this essay was not hurried or careless, and very possibly had been in the works for quite some time.[23] According to Young, Shiratori's article was the best exposition of the Kyushu theory to date, a synthesis of all contributions of past Kyushu-theory historians. Unlike Naitō, Shiratori relied largely on the *Wei chih*, which, he believed, was closer to the actual events and based largely on the travels and first-hand ex-

---

lay in Kyushu. Tsurumine hypothesized that Yamatai was a falsified name used by Kumaso in imitation of Yamato; see Young, *Location of Yamatai*, 83–84.

22. Naitō, "Himiko kō," in *NKZ* 7:269–70, 271; for the account of Yamato-hime no mikoto in the *Nihon shoki*, see Aston (trans.), *Nihongi*, 175–76. Aston considered *hime* to be a suffix indicating a lady or princess, as in Mihakashi-hime and Ihoki no Iri-hime.

23. This thoroughness can be contrasted to other articles in which he reversed his position. His studies of the *kōgōishi* (stone foundations or walls in Kyushu and western Honshu), for example, came to opposite conclusions: "Iwayuru kōgōishi ni tsuite," *Rekishi chiri* 23 (January 1914); and "Iwayuru 'kōgōishi' ni tsuite," *Shigaku zasshi* 28 (August 1917), in *SKZ* 1:41–70.

perience of the Wei emissaries. The *Hou Han shu*, which was not compiled until 445, and the Japanese histories compiled in the eighth century he considered less reliable.[24]

By relying heavily on the *Wei chih*, Shiratori located Yamatai in Kyushu and, like previous Kyushu-theory advocates, found the directions recorded by the Wei emissaries to be more reliable than the distances, which are recorded using both spatial and temporal units. Like Naitō, he too used, manipulated, and discarded data to suit his interpretation. But even though he gave greater credence to the directions, he also pointed to "trifling" errors that "occurred often among ancient travelers"—and did not correspond with his views.[25] For example, the *Wei chih* reported that the total trip to Yamatai was twelve thousand *li*, a distance he used as a standard despite questioning the accuracy of recorded distances.[26] He then subtracted the sea travel from Tai-fang (Korea) to Funi (Kyushu) and found that only thirteen hundred *li* remained for the journey from Fumi to Yamatai, which was recorded as thirty days by land and one month by sea. This portion of the journey is subject to greatest disagreement. Because two months is an inconceivable amount of time for such a short distance, Shiratori accounted for this discrepancy by accepting Kume's interpretation that one month was mistakenly recorded (or later miscopied) for one day, suggesting that the emissaries most likely exaggerated the distance for two reasons: first, because the kingdoms on the archipelago were included in the power politics of the continent, if the emperor of Wei accepted the exaggerated distances, he would have deemed war "irrational";[27] second, it was a practice among the Chinese to record distance according to travel time when exact distance was unclear, and the emissaries sought to show their competence (or better, not show incompetence) and adjusted the duration to fall in line with the exaggerated distance.[28]

Another difficult problem is the passage in the *Wei chih* that describes a visit in 247 of an emissary from Yamatai requesting Chinese

24. Shiratori, "Wa joō himiko kō," *Tōa no hikari* 5 (June–July 1910), in *SKZ* 1:3–39. See also Young, *Location of Yamatai*, 105–6.

25. The lack of consistency is readily apparent and common among scholars attempting to "solve" this problem; Shiratori stated, for example, that the travel from Matsura to Fumi and then to Na was not to the southeast, as recorded, but to the northeast ("Wa joō himiko kō," in *SKZ* 1:6).

26. One ancient Chinese *li* is roughly equivalent to 346 meters.

27. Young (*Location of Yamatai*, 109) stated that Shiratori's international perspective was a "new and brilliant" contribution to this debate.

28. Shiratori, "Wa joō himiko kō," in *SKZ* 1:21–23.

aid in its conflict with Kunu. This tribe was described in the *Wei chih* as being to the south of Yamatai, and in the *Hou Han shu* as to the east. Shiratori criticized Naitō for overlooking this kingdom and used the *Wei chih* account to verify his thesis that Yamatai was located around Higo (present-day Kumamoto) in northwestern Kyushu, whereas Kunu (Kumaso in the *Nihon shoki*) was to the south. Naitō countered that Kunu was located around Higo; he read the location in the *Wei chih* as south of Na, not south of Yamatai.[29]

Although the debate of 1910 was considerably different from the earlier one concerning whether Yamatai was in Kyushu or Yamato, Naitō did succeed in reviving the Yamato thesis. He was so successful, in fact, that even today historians trained at the universities of Tokyo and Kyoto generally defend the respective positions of these prominent scholars, and bookstores devote whole sections to the "new," "final," or "valid" histories that are published every year.[30] But despite their opposing arguments, they in fact had much in common. By focusing the debate on China and Korea, for example, both had diverted Japan's origins away from Southeast Asia and suggested that the Japanese race is indigenous (see the following section). Also, both effected the separation of Himiko from political and secular power. That is, although they agreed that Himiko was the queen of Wa, both maintained that she was appointed for religious reasons. Shiratori acknowledged the *Wei chih* account of two consecutive women rulers (Himiko's death, this chronicle reported, was followed by internal disturbance, and only after the installation of Iyo, a thirteen-year-old girl, on the throne was peace restored), but he considered this occurrence unusual. At no time, he argued, had Japan been a matrilineal society, something that would suggest an affinity to the Malay-Polynesian peoples, as proposed by Inoue Tetsujirō.[31] Himiko was "a religious ruler, who, being confined to the depths of the palace and in devoting herself to religious [*shintō*] ceremonies [*saishi*], obeyed the divine will and won the hearts of the people."[32]

---

29. Ibid., 15–18. Shiratori was certainly not the first to locate Kunu to the south of Yamatai, but in reemphasizing this point he was criticizing a contemporary theory that located Yamatai in southern Kyushu and Kunu (or Kumaso) in Shikoku. See also Young, *Location of Yamatai*, 98–100, 104, 107; and Naitō, "Himiko kō," *NKZ* 7:279.

30. As an example of a study that relies heavily on the work of scholars from the Kansai area, see Barnes, *Protohistoric Yamato*. For a study that is more reliant on University of Tokyo scholars, but that does not ignore their opponents, see Kiley, "State and Dynasty in Archaic Yamato."

31. See discussion in Chapter 1.

32. Shiratori, "Wa joō himiko kō," in *SKZ* 1:32–33, 38.

This distinction had a similar purpose as the original Kyushu theory: to assert the prestige of the emperor and, indirectly, to separate Japan from China by eliminating any suggestion that the court was subservient to the Chinese emperor. While earlier studies could readily dismiss information, especially from the *Wei chih*, that did not fit, it was not possible to ignore obvious contradictions when early records and myths were being reexamined for their veracity. Interpretation—the separation of Himiko from political power—resolved those conflicts. In this task, both Shiratori and Naitō elevated the prestige of the emperor, removing any question that he had dispatched an emissary to Wei; reemphasized loyalty to the emperor (as a male position); and raised the level of his religious significance. The location of Yamatai no longer affected this prestige.[33] Because the subsequent debate on the location of Yamatai accepted this distinction between secular and religious rulers, it lost its political significance and became strictly a historiographical issue.

The Emergence of Japan: Debate over Chronology

The significance of this debate is not in the actual identity and location of Himiko and Yamatai. Rather, this debate was part of a broader issue, namely, which narrative of protohistoric Japan would become the norm. Himiko and Yamatai served as that objective proof from antiquity that supported different conceptions of the development of Japan—a Japan related to, but not fully dependent on or derivative of, continental culture.

Interestingly, both attempts to order Japan's past elided the issue of physiological origin.[34] Shiratori described the origin and emergence of Japanese culture as being a gradual, progressive movement. Like Hayashi's extrapolation of an ancient China, Shiratori created a primordial past: the original Japanese, he wrote, migrated to Japan "tens of thousands of years" ago. Discounting the theory that ancient Japanese migrated to Japan already possessing a relatively sophisticated

33. Young, *Location of Yamatai*, 110.
34. Shiratori summarily dismissed physiological research on Asians as too inconclusive. See his "Nihon jinshuron ni taisuru hihyō," *Tōa no hikari* 10 (August 1915), in *SKZ* 9:197–98.

culture, he stated: "In all countries, because society is not advanced at first, the level of culture is low and then gradually advances up to the present. In other words, progress is a special characteristic of Japan."[35]

"Proof" that the Japanese were indigenous lay in his careful and elaborate linguistic studies on the Ural-Altaic peoples. Here, positivistic analysis was utilized to establish an origin where one did not exist. His linguistic studies first proved the similarity between Japanese and Ural Altai, in particular Korean, then supported Japan's uniqueness. Evidence for each position depended on choice of evidence. His earlier work relied on cognates like the words for heaven, while in later work he used the Japanese numerals mentioned in the *Kojiki* to describe a Japanese society before continental influence (that is, he found evidence in the Japanese numerals to argue for uniqueness). The original Japanese numeric system, he suggested, was based on a reduplicative scheme that was in turn reflected in the counting system. Ancient Japanese used both hands to count: two (*puto*) was formed by adding one (*pito*) finger on one hand to the identical one on the other hand; three (*mi*) doubled to six (*mu*); four (*yo*) doubled to eight (*ya*); and five (*it*) doubled to ten (*to*). In each case the consonant remained the same while the vowel changed.[36]

Although he recognized some similarity between the ancient Japanese counting mode and the quinary system of Melanesia, it did not, in his mind, indicate any racial ties; it simply showed that both systems had evolved gradually from just one or two numbers. In other words, the people who migrated to the Japanese islands were extremely primitive and gradually developed a language system after their arrival. Also, unlike the Ural Altai, for whom odd numbers signify good fortune (Semites, seven; Turks, seven and nine; Khitans, seven), the Japanese favor even numbers, especially eight. Shiratori pointed out that eight, a number commonly found in the *Kojiki* (for instance, Ōyashima [the name for ancient Japan; lit., "eight great islands"]; the serpent with eight heads and tails that Susano-o killed, and the eighty deities who gathered outside the cave in which Amaterasu hid), is the largest

---

35. Shiratori, "Tōyōshijō yori mitaru nihon koku," *Kōdō* 254 (February 1913), in *SKZ* 9:177–88 (quote at 179). Shiratori used this speech on several occasions under different titles or as a basis for speeches given as late as 1939.

36. Shiratori, "The Japanese Numerals," *Memoirs of the Research Department of the Tōyō Bunko* 9 (1937): 1–78. Shiratori raised this issue in a 1905 speech, "Gengogakujō yori mitaru 'aino' jinshu," in *SKZ* 2:349–69. See also "Ni, Kan, Ainu sankokugo no sūji ni tsuite," *Shigaku zasshi* 20 (January–March 1909), in *SKZ* 2:417–57.

number between one and ten that can be divided twice into even numbers: eight, then four, then two.[37] By contrast, the use of seven and nine in the *Nihon shoki* was the result of Chinese influence. Such an "objective" interpretation of language served his purposes well. Shiratori managed to ignore the syntactic similarities of Japanese to Ural Altai and to prove, though using a tautological argument, that the Japanese are unique. Language became (and still is) the basis for Japan's uniqueness vis-à-vis the rest of the world.

Naitō, rather than positing theories about the origins of the Japanese, chose merely to assert their indigenous beginnings (something few disputed in the 1910s); he then started his narrative from China's late Warring States period, when, he stated, it is believed that the Chinese first learned of the land of Wa. Japan, or Wa, thus existed ipso facto. Proof was in the contact with China, which had already occurred in the early Han dynasty, when Chinese migrated as far as Korea and probably even entered or traded with Japan. Naitō argued, "It is unimaginable that this [expansionary] trend did not also reach Japan," which, he agreed with the Chinese records, was divided into "over one hundred countries."[38] While he accepted the *Wei chih*'s account of a fragmented Wa, he freely interchanged the words "Japan" and "Wa," thus suggesting that Wa was a subset of Japan.

For Naitō, the placement of Yamatai in Yamato was essential to his historical narrative of Japan. Just as Confucianism relied on the coevality of China's beginnings with the sage-kings, Naitō's narrative required coterminous beginnings for the imperial court and Yamatai. If Yamatai was in Kyushu, then Japan was not unified by the third century; indeed, one would have to ask whether a Japan even existed then. To remain faithful to the narrative presented in the *Nihon shoki*, therefore, Naitō had to argue that Japan was unified rather quickly around the reign of Wang Mang in China (A.D. 9–23). As proof, Naitō cited the Golden Seal, a medallion found in Kyushu, to corroborate that intercourse between Wa and China existed as early as A.D. 27 and that China respected the power of Yamato, whose control had already

---

37. Shiratori, "Hachi no kazu o mukabu koshū," *Gakushūin hōninkai zasshi* 79 (December 1909), in *SKZ* 2:459–61.

38. Naitō, "Nihon jōko no jōtai," in *NKZ* 9:25. Naitō found support for his Yamato theory from archeologists such as Tomioka Kenzō, who argued that the presence in Yamato of Chinese mirrors from the early Han and the Wang Mang periods and also of later mirrors is evidence that Yamatai was in Yamato. Naitō most likely based his periodization on this and similar evidence. For the position of archeologists in this debate, see Young, *Location of Yamatai*, 115–43.

reached Hakata (Kyushu) and possibly even southern Korea.[39] Furthermore, Naitō distinguished between ancient Japan's sociopolitical unification and its cultural maturity, which made the heavy importation of Chinese culture from the Later Han dynasty through the Six Dynasties period (222–589) credible. In short, Naitō's historical narrative depicted an autonomous Japan independent of the Chinese world order. Japan's unification and cultural borrowing were possible because of an initiative and spontaneity that, he implied, exists innately only among certain peoples. It was a matter of faith that Japanese had that progressive spirit. Korea, which, in contrast to Japan, failed to develop a sense of independent nationhood, provided a negative example, and consequently proof that Japan had this unique quality.[40]

Naitō's main purpose was to show the creative and dynamic potential of Japanese and, although his theory begs the question, to refute any suggestion that Japanese culture derived from the migration of advanced people from Korea or solely from Chinese culture. As a historian he tried to respect the ancient legends, which do not admit to a primitive past, while also adhering to the idea that Japan's development was due to indigenous characteristics. Such an argument, however, relies on the faith (or myth) that Japanese are unique and possess an innate creativity and dynamism. These qualities, the argument went, enabled ancient Japanese to learn from other cultures but still maintain their own sense of identity and autonomy relative to any other country or culture. Thus, even though Japan's cultural development lagged behind its sociopolitical growth, it was still young and, hence, able to learn and use its newfound knowledge energetically.[41] To maintain this position, however, Naitō trod dangerously close to the realm of cultural exceptionalism; he overlooked a considerable portion of the information in Chinese histories, defined Japan's unique spirit only very vaguely (to his credit he did not, as Shiratori did, go so far as to attribute such a singular trait directly to the emperor), and failed to extract himself from the narrow perspective he claimed to criticize but ended by defending.

39. Naitō, "Nihon jōko no jōtai," in *NKZ* 9:27. The Golden Seal refers to a gold seal that was found in northern Kyushu in 1784. Although there is much debate over its authenticity, initial interpretations suggested that the seal was given to the king of Ito (northern Kyushu) by Emperor Kuang-wu in A.D. 57. For background, see Young, *Location of Yamatai*, 81–85.

40. Naitō, "Nihon bunka to wa nanzo ya?" 206–7.

41. Naitō, "Nihon jōko no jōtai," in *NKZ* 9:28–29; and idem, "Nihon bunka to wa nanzo ya?" 204–7.

In a very different way, Shiratori, too, sought to show that the accounts in the Chinese records corresponded to the legends in the *Kojiki* and the *Nihon shoki*. Shiratori argued that the legends of the age of the gods provide valuable information as allegories of the ideals, not as history, of ancient Japanese. For example, he cited the story of the *tenson* (lit., heavenly descendant) people, whom the myth of Ame tsu no ninigi describes as coming to Japan, to show how misleading these legends can be as allegories of historical origin. Those people, he said, could only have been Chinese, because no other people in the area were advanced enough to perform such a feat (the idea that Koreans might ever have been more advanced than Japanese was inconceivable to Shiratori); linguistically, however, Japanese and Chinese have no similarity, therefore this story could not describe an actual event.[42] Here, Shiratori used positivistic evidence to refute a competing vision that relied heavily on the myths, but at the same time he relied on the simple fact of prehistory's antiquity to establish an origin that had to be accepted on faith. Assuming these legends to be allegories for the ideals of ancient Japanese, Shiratori argued, as in his interpretation of the Confucian legends as artificial constructs, that they were not necessarily contemporaneous accounts, but were recorded later, on the basis of both historical accounts and traditional ideals. Thus, just as he preserved a particular version of Confucianism, Shiratori was also able to preserve the ancient Japanese legends. For example, according to Shiratori, the conflict between Himiko and the king of Kunu, which was recorded in the *Wei chih*, was also recorded in the *Kojiki* and the *Nihon shoki* as the struggle between Ho no suseri no mikoto (Hoderi no mikoto) and his younger brother, Hiko hoho demi no mikoto (Ho Ori no mikoto).[43] In this "reflection of the political conditions" in Kyushu, Hiko hoho demi no mikoto represented northern Kyushu, while Ho no suseri no mikoto represented the Hayato people, an ancient tribe of southern Kyushu.

One reason Shiratori located Yamatai on Kyushu was to emphasize the gradual development of Japanese culture. Yamato was not yet a significant force, according to Shiratori's narrative. It was through Kyushu—the small "countries" of Wa and other relatively primitive

---

42. Shiratori, "Nihon jinshuron ni taisuru hihyō," in *SKZ* 9:191–92.

43. Shiratori, "Tōyōshijō yori mitaru nihon koku," in *SKZ* 9:254. In this legend, after losing his older brother's fish hook, which precipitated a conflict between the two, Hiko hoho demi no mikoto with the help of the sea deity subdued Ho no suseri no mikoto. See Philippi (trans.), *Kojiki*, 148–55; for a different version, see Aston (trans.), *Nihongi*, 91–103.

groups of people—that contact with China first occurred and Japanese culture subsequently developed. "This argument [that Japan's ancestors first settled in Kyushu]," he admitted, "will probably not be welcomed by scholars in Japan." But he reminded his readers, "This is not hypothesis, I am speaking from the findings of my research."[44] Yamato existed concurrently with Yamatai, but its power did not yet extend to Kyushu, and would not until the latter part of the third century. He stated, "If the Yamato court at that time had a close relationship with the Kyushu area, it would not have been ignored in the *Wei chih*'s *Wo-jen ch'uan*."[45] This is certainly a tautological argument, in that it requires a prior acceptance of Yamatai's location in Kyushu. In 1934, probably as a reflection of a more intense nationalism and in concession to archeological evidence, Shiratori suggested that the power of Yamato was somewhat more significant than he had previously allowed. But despite this change, he did not alter his description of ancient Japan: the separation of Kyushu from Yamato, the emphasis on gradual development, the fragmented political structure, and the importance of trade between Kyushu and China remained.[46]

A second, and more important, reason for locating Yamatai on Kyushu was to connect Japanese history to his North-South dualism. Evidence of the North-South dualism in both the Chinese histories and Japanese classics, Shiratori felt, provided historical weight for objective claims of Japan's uniqueness. According to him, the legends in the *Kojiki* and the *Nihon shoki* indicated the superiority of the imperial family, represented by Hiko hoho demi no mikoto (North), the grandfather of Emperor Jinmu, over the tribes of Kyushu (South).[47] While the existence of these typologies placed Japan within the same philosophy of history as the continent, this struggle between a militaristic spirit (*bu*) and civilization (*bun*) was markedly different from that of Japan's continental neighbors. The historical unfolding of Asia proper involved the struggle between North and South and the victory of one over the other, while the unfolding of Japan concerned the creation of a balance

44. Shiratori, "Tōyōshijō yori mitaru nihon koku," in *SKZ* 9:179.

45. Shiratori, "Wa joō himiko kō," in *SKZ* 1:28. The only mention in the *Wo-jen ch'uan* of people to the east of Yamatai was a vague reference of "over one thousand *li* to the east of the Queen's land (across the sea) there are more countries of the same race as the people of Wa" (Young, *Location of Yamatai*, 36).

46. Citing archeological evidence he acknowledged that it controlled the five Kinai districts (Yamato, Yamanashi, Kawauchi, Settsu, and Izumi) from around the beginning of the first century; see "Tōyōshijō yori mitaru nihon," in *SKZ* 9:254.

47. Shiratori, "Wa joō himiko kō," in *SKZ* 1:27; Philippi (trans.), *Kojiki*, 414.

between the North and South; this, clearly, set Japan apart from the other cultures. Even though the legend of Hiko hoho demi and Ho no suseri, the struggle between Himiko and Kumaso, and the supremacy of Yamato over Kyushu each represented Northern superiority, Shiratori seemed to ignore the possible contradiction in describing the imperial institution as deriving from a Northern (militaristic and despotic) people. Instead, Shiratori described all communities of the archipelago as comprising basically the same people; thus, unlike on the continent, where the typology converged with culture—that is, North/Mongol, South/Chinese—in Japan, both typologies existed within a single culture. Not only did Japan possess the characteristics of both North and South, but in most cases the dualism acted to enhance the best characteristics of both types. Since their early history, Shiratori said, Japanese possessed both the military skills and spirit of the North and the culture of the South.[48]

To illustrate the timelessness of Japan's unique combination of North and South Shiratori, in separate articles, described both General Nogi and Admiral Tōgō as quintessential modern Japanese who possessed both attributes. As soldiers, both men epitomized the militaristic skills and bravery that had led to the defeat of Russia during the Russo-Japanese War. Above all, their bravery was an exhibition of their loyalty to their country and the emperor. Yet at the same time, as presidents, respectively, of Gakushūin and the Academy of the Crown Prince (Tōgū Gakumon), both presided with the compassion and intelligence that only men of culture had.[49] These two articles suggest a convergence of past and present; the exemplary figures of Nogi and Tōgō, Shiratori observed, possessed the essence of the Japanese character, which can be traced back to Japan's formative years, should be emulated, and must be preserved.

According to Shiratori's narrative, once Yamato hegemony had been extended to Kyushu by the early fourth century, the dualism worked in a more typical fashion. In the unification of northern Japan, Shiratori pitted the Ainu (North) against a unified Yamato (South). Although he admitted that the origin of the Ainu remains obscure, he placed them within the Ural-Altaic family. The Ainu language, though monosyllabic

48. Shiratori, "Wa joō himiko kō," in SKZ 1:27.
49. Shiratori, "Tsuitōkai ni okeru Shiratori hakushi kōen," Gakushūin hōninkai zasshi 88 (December 1914): 33–43; "Waga kokuminsei no kenka Tōgō gensui," Kokuhon 17 (July 1934): 31–33.

like the languages of Southeast Asian cultures, provided, he said, objective proof of a Ural Altai affinity, for it exhibited agglutination like some Ural-Altaic languages, particularly Finn-Ugri and Samoyed, and also a similarity in the basic construction of some numbers, especially six through nine.[50] This evidence led Shiratori to speculate that the Ainu migration pattern was similar to that of other Northern peoples who moved to southern climates in search of more fertile land. Indeed, he pointed out, the Japanese classics are filled with accounts of attacks and battles with the Ainu.

One can find a number of problems with this categorization, but it did suit his purpose of explaining Japanese history within the North-South dualism. Recently unified Yamato now represented the Southern cultures, but, as was evident in the battles leading to the unification of Yamatai and Kunu and the Yamato conquest of the kingdoms in Kyushu, it was also quite proficient in militaristic matters (even Amaterasu appears as a warrior). The outcome of this North-South clash was contrary to the situation in the rest of Asia; there, "the Northern people leveled the Southern cultures, whereas in Japan the Ainu [North] were ultimately forced [by the Yamato] to withdraw, despite their very stubborn resistance."[51] In conquering the Ainu, who represented the North, Yamato overcame Northern militarism, thus reversing the historical tendency (as opposed to law) of the North conquering the South. The elimination of the Northern threat also relieved any foreign pressure that would foster a conservative ideology, as had occurred in China, or a loss of any Southern cultural attributes. The Yamato conquest of the Ainu, in short, only enhanced its already strong fighting ability, thus fostering a superior and unique militaristic spirit: "Through the wars with the Ainu, Japan was inspired to add the uniqueness of the Asiatic peoples to its militaristic spirit; they [the Japanese] crush and split the impossible. This is *bushidō* [the way of the warrior]. However, we should recognize that Japan has imported, assimilated, and absorbed from countries on the continent, India, China, and Korea; in particular, militarily it resembles someone, like a two-sword samurai, who does not lean solely toward either the army or the navy."[52] Japan, in other words, was unique among world cultures

50. For example, the Ainu word for eight (*tupesan*) is, literally, "ten without two," and nine (*shinepesan*) is "ten without one." See "Gengogakujō yori mitaru 'aino' jinshu," in *SKZ* 2:366–67.

51. Shiratori, "Tōyōshi yori mitaru nihon," in *SKZ* 9:235.

52. Shiratori, "Shijō yori mitaru ōa no taisei," in *SKZ* 8:36.

for it possessed the positive characteristics of both the North and the South.

The contemporary relevance of Shiratori's ancient Japan to post–Meiji Restoration society is clear. As he saw things, the emerging ancient Japan had existed within a microcosm of international power politics; Japan, that is, had not always been an isolated, inward-facing country. In contrast to Naitō's view, which emphasized political and social independence, Shiratori posited an early Japan that was fragmented, with certain parts even dependent on China for both political security and cultural development. In effect, he was showing that extensive, reciprocal foreign contact with the cultures of the continent, *not* isolationism, was a fundamental part of Japanese culture. Ancient Japan was not defined according to its geographical limits; territorial boundaries were not rigidly limited to the main islands of Japan. Instead, early Japanese recognized the importance of international relations, trade, and political ties with the continent. As an example of the early international balance of power politics, Shiratori cited Emperor Seimu's defeat of Yamatai in the early fourth century. He gave two reasons for Seimu's victory: first, the Yamatai were weakened following their victory over Kunu, and second, "the Chinese colonies of Lo-yang and Tai-fang, upon which the queen's country depended [*irai*]," had fallen at the end of the Western Tsin (265–317).[53] Moreover, Himiko's request to the Chinese court for aid in her fight with Kunu, as recorded in the *Wei chih,* offered evidence of Yamatai's close political ties with Wei. In other words, in describing the formation of a Japanese nation within the archipelago during the protohistorical period, Shiratori argued that the Japanese intellectual horizon was not limited to but extended well beyond those islands.

This interpretation also provided the route for the transmission of Confucianism and Buddhism to Japan through China, rather than Korea. Like Naitō, Shiratori was attempting with his Kyushu theory to remove any suggestion that Japan had ever been inferior to Korea. Japan did establish political relations with the kingdoms on the Korean peninsula: after Yamato had completely defeated Kunu (Kumaso) in southern Kyushu during the reigns of Chūai and Jingū, the Yamato court sent an expedition to Korea. But, Shiratori carefully pointed out, the Yamato government in Kaya, the establishment of Paekche as a protectorate, and the relation with Silla as a tributary state occurred at the

53. Shiratori, "Wa joō himiko kō," in *SKZ* 1:29.

request of these Korean kingdoms to help defend them against Koguryŏ. It was not an invasion by Japan!

This debate between Shiratori and Naitō indicates a convergence of interpretations in line with early defenders of the *Kojiki* and *Nihon shoki*. The difference between these historians was over the periodization of ancient Japan; that is, each interpreted the protohistoric period according to his own historical framework. As I will show in Chapter 5, Naitō required the particular periodization he postulated to support his theory of shifting cultural centers, though it still bore many similarities with Shiratori's view. In short, this debate was characterized by several shared assumptions: both scholars vaguely suggested that Japan's people and culture were indigenous; they denied any cultural debt to Korea; they considered Kyushu the region that had first maintained contact with China; they acknowledged Japan's debt to Chinese culture; they attacked the *kokugakusha*, those emphasizing a narrow Japanocentric view (Naitō, ironically, might have included Shiratori in this group); importantly, they sought to describe Japanese history as progressive, in which the driving force for development came from an innate spirit or character of the Japanese themselves; and finally, these histories established the Japanese archipelago as being coterminous with the Japanese nation.

But because Shiratori and Naitō were describing Japan's place in *tōyō*, the mere assertion of the Japanese people's uniqueness was not enough to erase the possibility that they in fact were not unique. To maintain both Japan's contiguity with *tōyō* and uniqueness, Shiratori and Naitō both traced the origin of Japan to an antiquity within the geocultural boundaries of the archipelago. Their vagueness on the roots of the Japanese people stemmed from a reluctance to accept evidence that the Japanese were not indigenous. The origin thus posited served as the beginning of the sort of internal history mentioned by Foucault, one that began with the first stone tool and continued through the development of the Yamato people to the present. To integrate "all differences, all dispersions, and all discontinuities," Shiratori turned to the *kami*, the gods of Japan's mythical past, to define the purity of the nation. In his hands, they became virtually historical figures that answered Japan's need for the origin that, in Foucault's words, would form that "single point of identity, the impalpable figure of the Same."[54] By discussing these affairs within the framework of

54. Foucault, *Order of Things*, 329–30.

modern history, Shiratori gave these myths an aura of veracity, with which he legitimized a narrative of Japan's uniqueness supported by objective research. Contestation over Japan's true origin shifted attention from what is mythological to what in the myths is historical. Thus the mythical past took on the character of historical reality. With that center, that point of identity, duly established, historians could turn to other pasts to give their narrative of Japan selective points of contact that describe a continuous history of *tōyō*.

Religiosity and Progress

During the 1910s Shiratori defended his concept of Japan's spirit fervently. That spirit, he said, was the principal reason for Japan's uniqueness, progress, and cultural independence; it was what propelled the Japanese to recognize the contribution that other cultures could make toward improving their own society, and it also maintained their identity and distinctiveness, even as they adapted from other cultures. In that decade Shiratori published several articles on the relation between ancient Japan and Confucianism, and his essays on the emperor system appeared in such popular journals as *Kōdō*, *Chūō kōron*, and *Taiyō*. This support of a religiosity in Japan was not necessarily a reactionary response, however; it was part of the formulation and preservation of Shiratori's totalistic historical vision of the world. Much of this vision was inspired by, not in confrontation with, a conviction that, as in the West, religiosity is an essential element in the development of a national culture; it was Shiratori's universal for writing a history of Japan on the same terms as that of the West. Without this universal which established a commonality among all peoples, his theory would result in a historicistic vision, one that in fact was taken up by scholars such as Hattori and gained increasing popularity during the early Shōwa period. But like some of the Western social scientific theories from which he borrowed, his framework was essentially a conservative one that emphasized progressive development only within an orderly social organism.

In 1915 Shiratori stated, "The classics [*Kojiki* and *Nihon shoki*] are similar to China's *Book of Documents*. They are not history but an elucidation of the esteem of the imperial institution and the unchanging difference between ruler and retainer; in other words, the belief in and ideals of the national essence."[55] Because the legends did not describe actual names, dates, or events, Shiratori could move freely from one age to the other in his search for the essential character of all Japanese. Such an ahistorical methodology was necessary to establish the source of a religious spirit: "By both worshiping and obeying the image of [Amaterasu] Ōmikami and revering a heightened virtue [*kōtoku*], we must feel the strongly rooted sun-worship ideology [*shisō*] of our people."[56] The coevality of the imperial line, from the Sun Goddess to the contemporary emperor, and the nation proved this spirit. It existed from the beginning; in other words, it is timeless. The "*Yamato dama-shii*," the spirit of the Japanese people, is rooted in this worship of the emperor, the leader of the state. History established a unity that was useful to the nation-state; it was a "recital of a creation" that turned the state into something as immanent as the spirit and essence of the Japanese. Shiratori called this government *matsurigoto* (magical government).

Taking legends as allegories for this spirit, Shiratori found ample evidence of a religious government, to show that all matters of the nation (*kokumin*) were determined by the gods (*kami*). For example, he stated: "As is expressed in these accounts, I believe that Himiko received the worship of one kingdom in Kyushu for exactly the same reason that Amaterasu Ōmikami reigned over the heavens and ruled all the gods through her deep reverence and filiality toward the heavenly ancestors." The difference was that "Himiko was merely a chief in the world below, while Ōmikami, as the supreme ruler of the gods who dwelled in heaven, became the imperial presence in the form of the sun and illuminated (ruled—*shōrin*) the land below for eternity."[57] A further parallel between Amaterasu and Himiko could be found in Amaterasu's fight with Susano-o. Shiratori compared Amaterasu's flight to the cave and the subsequent darkening of the land with the anger of Himiko over the king of Kunu's disrespect and the battle that followed. Amaterasu, after much urging by the gods, finally came out, and the light was restored to the land. Similarly, although Himiko died, the subsequent ruler, Iyo, restored order to that country. Jingū, too, the regent when Japan was unified, was not a militaristic ruler, but, "as the official who carried out and conveyed the will of the gods of heaven and earth,

55. Shiratori, "Nihon ni okeru jukyō no junnōsei," in *SKZ* 10:244–45.
56. Shiratori, "Wa joō himiko kō," in *SKZ* 1:36.
57. Ibid.

she won over the wishes of the people."⁵⁸ The power of these women was backed not by a political authority, but by their religious position. Shiratori believed that the relation between Himiko ruling as a queen and Jingū ruling as a regent is based on the same religious authority that incorporated the will of the gods. For Shiratori the similarity was understandable; "The editors of the *Nihon shoki* tacitly modeled Regent Jingū after Himiko."⁵⁹

Such an emphasis on the religious nature of the emperor and Japan's *matsurigoto* bore numerous similarities to the eclectic Mitogaku (Mito school) of the early nineteenth century. In his *Seimeiron* (The Rectification of Names), Fujita Yūkoku emphasized that the Japanese imperial system, the unbroken line of divinely born emperors, is Japan's great achievement and that which sets it apart from all other nations. That system is not only different from, but also superior to, all others, the Chinese in particular. In China, the emperor worships abstractions: heaven and ancestors. In Japan, by contrast, "heaven and the ancestors are manifest on earth in the person of the emperor himself." This version, Fujita noted, is better than that of the Chinese, for the worship of a human being provides a stronger model for relations between sovereign and subject, superior and inferior. In other words, the ideal hierarchical model for a proper political order is better manifested in the Japanese version. To these Mitogaku scholars the emperor also embodied selected Confucian ideals. Aizawa Seishisai wrote that the emperor represents the living incarnation of both Amaterasu Ōmikami and universal principle, and also certain values, namely, the twin virtues of loyalty and filial piety. The emperor, then, is the source of Japan as a sacred community. Aizawa turned the union of politics and religion into a political potential, " 'magical' government, according to which the example of ancestral rites carried out by the emperor radiates downward and outward through correctly aligned 'names and statuses,' stimulating imitation and infusing the polity with a spirit of reverence."⁶⁰

The similarities between Shiratori and these Mitogaku scholars are apparent. The following statement might easily have come from his predecessors: "Now, if we were to describe the history of the age of the gods, it is the principal story which elegantly and poetically depicts the beliefs, political system, government, customs, habits, and so on of

58. Ibid., 36, 37 (quote).
59. Ibid., 38.
60. Koschmann, *Mito Ideology*, 29–80 (quote at 76).

the ancient period of our country. The majesty of our national essence, the loyalty and bravery of the retainers, and the goodness and beauty of our customs all originate here. If we seek a comparable type in a foreign country, it is a code [*hōten*] that should be compared to China's *Book of Documents*."⁶¹ The age of the gods, he believed, provided the initial record of Japanese society, just as he considered the *Book of Documents* to be the first record of China. It was through these texts that he discovered the origin of society, a beginning before the culture of each changed. For both the Mitogaku scholars and Shiratori, the imperial system represented the "traditional" norm that was both timeless and dynamic; it was the essence of the Japanese nation. Both emphasized certain Confucian ethical norms, especially loyalty and filiality; and both considered the union of religiosity and politics as occurring in the Imperial institution.

Contemporary conditions also presented several parallels with those of the early 1800s. Both Shiratori and scholars of the Mito school were attempting to arrest a growing sense of domestic fragmentation and decay; both separated China and the Chinese emperor from Japan and the imperial institution; both used an "other"—China in the nineteenth century and the West in the twentieth—against which to compare themselves, identifying them as a principal cause of contemporary problems; and both turned to Japan's age of the gods for answers to contemporary problems. But here the similarity ends. The Mitogaku synthesis was an attempt to remove the corrosive effects of time from an idealized original state. Aizawa, for example, wished to erase the mediations of history from an original state grounded in a sacred community as a way of establishing order throughout the country.

Shiratori, in contrast, used a similar religious argument to establish progress as innate among the Japanese. His unbroken imperial line represented, as it did for the Mitogaku scholars, the discovery of an origin, a return to an antiquity before time obfuscated an understanding of the national essence. Shiratori's essence was, of course, timeless, a union of government and religiosity based on a universal spirit. "The national essence [*kokutai*] is different from a polity [*seitai*] as usually described," he explained. "It includes a deeper meaning, in other words, a conception like the fundamental spirit of a nation's existence. Here there is a religious meaning."⁶² But unlike the Mito school, Shiratori was at-

61. Shiratori, "Nihon jinshuron ni taisuru hihyō," in *SKZ* 9:192–93.
62. Shiratori, "Nihon ni okeru jukyō no junnōsei," in *SKZ* 10:239.

tempting neither to retain the *bakuhan* order, to return to an idealized agrarian society that romanticized the samurai, nor to transcend history in favor of an era still further removed in antiquity. He did not attempt to elide the past, but to arrange it into a history that accounts for orderly change. The religious ideal, the national essence, was timeless; the magical government (*matsurigoto*), however, was dynamic.

By the early Taishō period, Shiratori had at last offered Japan a history in the progressive sense that was also based on a universal spirit. While the Mito scholars described the magical government as timeless and proposed a return to a pure state, Shiratori positioned it as the source of Japan's progressive history. Like Ranke's Protestantism, the worship of the imperial institution was the source of Japan's progress. As the timeless norm and ancestral origins of the Japanese nation, the imperial system already embodied the universal spirit of the Japanese nation: it was the phenomenal and spiritual force that maintained the unity of the nation; contained the concept of *minponshugi*, that is, the spirit of Western democracy; and generated the progressive spirit of Japanese culture. Objective, scientific research on Japan's protohistoric past showed that its history was on a similar plane as that of the West. Because of a different manifestation, however, Shiratori elevated Japan's religiosity; "The reason that our way of the gods [*shintō*] is progressive and not conservative like other religions is because the imperial court, which appears as a god-figure [*arahitogami*], rules people benevolently and always follows those teachings." What sets Japanese religiosity apart from that of other nations is that whereas in the West God appeared as Jesus Christ, and in Buddhist countries god was Shakyamuni, in Japan god is living as the offspring of Amaterasu.[63] In other words, in Japan god lives, while other cultures worship a single figure who appeared in the past.

But, Shiratori continued, this spirit also gives Japan the unique, progressive ability to see excellence in other cultures and adapt those strengths to Japan. The uniqueness in this derives from the fact that the Japanese understand the centrality of the imperial institution and take in only those aspects that do not conflict with this spirit. As one example, he cited the trip of Ono Imoko, who was sent to China during the Sui dynasty by Shōtoku Taishi. The document that Ono presented to Emperor Yang (r. 605–17) was addressed to the "Son of Heaven of the land of the setting sun" from the "Son of Heaven of the land of the

---

63. Shiratori, "Nihon jinshuron ni taisuru hihyō," in *SKZ* 9:194–95 (quote at 195).

rising sun."[64] This recognition of the difference between the rising and setting suns, Shiratori believed, showed that Shōtoku fully understood the position of the imperial institution; there was thus no need to bow subserviently to the Chinese emperor. This ability to absorb from others to improve society without damaging, and in fact, enhancing, the prestige of the imperial court is what gives Japan its unique capacity to grow while maintaining its sense of nationhood.

NARRATIVE VARIATION

Debates like that over the location of Yamatai highlight the differences of contestants, but they also indicate points of commonality. Even though Naitō has been considered Shiratori's main academic foe, the disagreement between the two was not as great as it has been portrayed. I will discuss the similarity of their historical frameworks in the next chapter, but here let us examine their parity on the question of Japan's religiosity. For Naitō, like Shiratori, confirmed the importance of a belief that was closely tied to political rule.[65] Even though he sought to separate political, secular rule from religious rule, in his analysis the difference was so slim that the emissaries of Wei, who could not be duped into believing that Yamatai was Kumaso, had mistaken the religious rule of Hime no mikoto for that of the queen of Wa.[66]

Although Naitō did not call it a spirit, he recognized an innate Japanese characteristic that performed a similar function as Shiratori's spirit. This characteristic enabled Japanese both to assimilate Asian cultures and to prevent any form of cultural subservience. After Yamato unified Japan in the first century, Japanese used their initiative and spontaneity to extract the essence of Chinese culture in the development of the nation. Such cultural adaptation reached its height between the Later Han and the Six Dynasties period, when trade flourished and Japanese learned to produce metals, silk, and so forth. This adaptation was possible because, Naitō exclaimed, "from the formative period of the people, we can recognize that the character of Japanese was more talented than that of the Koreans."[67] Even though Japan was

64. Shiratori, "Kōdō no konpongi ni tsuite," 14.
65. Naitō's strong nationalist sentiment and the similarity with Shiratori's viewpoint are especially evident in his "Nihon bunka to wa nanzo ya?" 201–13.
66. Naitō, "Himiko kō," in *NKZ* 7:261.
67. Naitō, "Nihon no bunka nanzo ya?" 206.

culturally an adolescent (the implication of this metaphor of the human life course will become clear in Chapter 5), it was also, as viewed within Naitō's theory of Asia's shifting cultural centers, the center and possessor of the best of oriental culture (*tōyō bunka*).

Dissent came from an unlikely person, Shiratori's student, Tsuda Sōkichi. Tsuda argued in his *Jindaishi no atarashii kenkyū* (New Research on the History of the Age of the Gods) that "the stories of the age of the gods are not historical legends, but fabricated stories."[68] Tsuda distinguished between the political notion that the imperial institution was the family head of the *shizoku* (elite families), on the one hand, and the religious idea that the emperor was also *akitsukami* (Manifest Deity), on the other. These two concepts, he suggested, were not created simultaneously. The latter emerged only after the imperial family had established its political preeminence, its purpose being to merge the imperial family with the religious idea, thereby giving them spiritual as well as political legitimacy.[69]

Tsuda's interpretation has the potential to unravel Shiratori's unity, just as the latter unraveled the unity of Confucianism. But despite its revolutionary nature, it is important to realize that Tsuda was not taking aim at the imperial institution, nor did he deny that it is the focus of a religious spirit. Rather, by showing that the historical grounding of this spirit in the age of the gods was created by elites, he opened the possibility for a quite different narrative of Japan's development. Tsuda, that is, eliminated the universalistic idea that had allowed Shiratori to claim parts of Indian and Chinese culture and turn them into something Japanese. In other words, Tsuda saw through Shiratori's strategy of turning the alien into the same and sought to eliminate the contradictions involved.

These contradictions are apparent in both Shiratori's and Naitō's narratives, where they turned the negative implications of imitation and copying into the positive attributes of recognizing valuable aspects of other cultures. Japan, namely, relied heavily on China during the ancient period for the development of its culture. From the third century and even earlier, for example, Wa had considerable intercourse with China and absorbed the richness of that culture: its literature (Shiratori suggested that they already read Chinese), philosophy, art, and other

---

68. For Shiratori's description of their differences, see Shiratori, "Jo," in *TSZ*, supp. vol. 1, 3–4.

69. Tsuda, "Jindaishi no seishitsu oyobi sono seishin," in Kuwabara (ed.), *Rekishi no shisō*, 135.

cultural assets. The period of Japan's greatest intercourse corresponded with what Shiratori called China's renaissance, the T'ang dynasty. Japanese officials, students, and priests were exposed to and imported all aspects of Chinese culture at its height. From this contact, "One can say that since Japan imported the culture of the T'ang dynasty, Japan completely absorbed the purity [*seisui*] of China."[70]

According to Shiratori, Japanese virtually concluded their process of learning from significant cultures of *tōyō* during this same period, when they incorporated Buddhism from India. Even though Buddhism entered Japan from China, the sect that entered Japan was different from that which became most common in T'ang China. "Daijō Buddhism was based on Indian thought and included the ideas of the most progressive, civilized countries of the world at that time."[71] Shiratori explained that Daijō (Mahayana) derived from the Hinayana Buddhism and Brahmanism of the Punjab and Gandara regions along the Indus River, where people were heavily influenced by Western culture, that of Persia, Greece, and Rome. In contrast to Hinayana, Daijō has gods— Rojana, Shakyamuni, and Amida—and is active and positive: the state of nirvana is not eternal death as in Hinayana, but eternal life. "In other words, it was the rich Daijō Buddhism, the thought of India with that of western Asia (*seiiki*) appended, that came to our country."[72]

Having thus adapted the best of Indian and Chinese culture, Japan then turned to the West in the next great period of absorption, that of modern times. But rather than establishing subjective criteria to judge the worth of foreign ideas and objects, Shiratori reminded readers that it has been the nature of the Japanese to take in only that which matches Japan's national essence. In the past, for example, they did not import Hinduism, Islam, or those aspects of Confucianism that did not match this *kokutai*. Yet neither was Shiratori's interpretation a carefully cloaked argument for closing Japan off from the West, for he also criticized the "*kokugaku*" types, whom he considered too narrow minded. These people, he stated, hate foreign things and bombastically flaunt things Japanese.

No matter how much they fervently extol Shintō, this is not the imperial way, Japan's way. The imperial way is not that narrow; the imperial way gradually takes in the good things of the world. This is clear in each imperial proclama-

70. Shiratori, "Tōyōshijō yori mitaru nihon koku," in *SKZ* 9:180–83 (quote at 183).
71. Ibid., 183–84.
72. Shiratori, "Nihon kenkoku no seishin," *Shigaku kenkyū* 2 (July 1931), in *SKZ* 10:394–95 (quote at 395).

tion, recently the Charter Oath of the Meiji emperor, no matter which document one reads. Those things that benefit the country of Japan and do not conflict with the true nature of the imperial institution or of Japanese subjects are gradually taken in, regardless of whether they are Eastern or Western, are Japanicized, and are fashioned into magnificent things. This is Japan's true spirit [*yamato damashii*].[73]

Yet as soon as he created this narrative and thereby completed (to the extent that any history can be completed) a project that was started in the early Meiji period, he forfeited one of his major goals, that of finding a common basis and equivalence with Western nation-states. The Japanese quest for equivalence can, of course, be considered a reflection of the internal persuasiveness of the Western world vision and a hope for some form of dialogue between Japan and Europe, as equals. However, such an idealistic goal failed to materialize, because the new narrative was simply a monologue of Japan. Moreover, even though it was a monologue that sought to give Japan its own history, it was still one that, as Tsuda pointed out, was constructed from and dependent on the outside.

History as Sacred

By the Taishō period, Japan had succeeded in meeting most of the goals established during the Meiji period. It was a modern nation-state, with a strong industrial base, modern military force, and constitutional monarchy. It participated among the European powers in their imperialistic machinations on the continent, entered on the side of the Triple Entente in World War I (though belatedly), and subsequently joined the League of Nations. Yet modernity was the mechanically propelled Trojan horse of an alien civilization that "drastically disrupts and reorganizes the social fabric."[74] The international hierarchy of the West over Japan, international conflict, and social dislocation remained and even increased. Immigration problems in the United States, the rejection of Japan's attempt to include a statement on racial equality in the preamble to the covenant of the League of Nations, and the 5:5:3 ratio on battleships established at the Washington Conference (1921–22) indicated that Japan was still not equal—but

73. Shiratori, "Kōdō no konpongi ni tsuite," 16.
74. Dale, *Myth of Japanese Uniqueness*, 47.

not, Japanese believed, because of any lack of material or intellectual accomplishments.[75] While Shiratori at first attempted to downplay the issue of race by epistemologically and ontologically demonstrating the equivalence of Japan with the West and the Japanese with Caucasians, he did not pretend that such differences did not exist. In one of his articles on the Yellow Peril written in 1929, he stated: "The Caucasians of Europe and America have total contempt for Orientals, who, they believe, are completely inferior people and cannot possibly compare to themselves."[76] Indeed, the realization that the Western worldview was based on conditions other than knowledge and its rational formulation led him increasingly to emphasize Japan's uniqueness, though still within the framework of modern scientific methods.

To create a sense of equivalence, Japanese used Western tools and ideas to construct their own history and identity. But they were writing, after all, against a Western conception of development that was packaged as universal. By assuming that human society had to be studied scientifically and according to certain laws, these intellectuals had little choice but to create a different vision, though one just as monologic as that from which they were trying to escape. In this way, by combining the Rankean spirit with a different conception of world society, Shiratori elevated the imperial institution to an eternal "living" status. To be sure, Shiratori most likely believed that his formulation was dialogic; it functioned in a similar way as Ranke's Protestantism, and it conversed with other domestic issues of his day. But while Ranke's Protestantism was a "dominant tendency" of a specific era, Shiratori's was eternal. The difference was in the coevality of history and religiosity: "Because this god-figure appeared only once in the religions of foreign countries and only a lifeless canon remained, thereafter these religions gradually became ill suited to later generations. But in our country, because this god-figure is the emperor, whose descendants continue this lineage, and this gift of heaven is boundless, the virtue of Amaterasu Ōmikami lives eternally and expands in accordance with the changing times."[77] Japan's progress, then, was based on this *matsurigoto;* the emperor as both religious patriarch and ruler is the central sta-

75. The 5:5:3 ratio was the key provision of the Five-Power Treaty, signed in 1922, that placed limits on the most powerful weapon then in existence. The ratios, measured in tonnage, broke down as follows: Great Britain, 5; the United States, 5; Japan, 3; Italy, 1.67; and France, 1.67.

76. Shiratori, "Nihon minzokuron," *Shin kokugo dokuhon* 5 (1929), in *SKZ* 9:210; see also his article on the Yellow Peril, "Kōka to nihon kokuminsei," *Koko* 3 (May 1907): 29–32.

77. Shiratori, "Nihon jinshuron ni taisuru hihyō," in *SKZ* 9:194–95.

bilizing and progressive force throughout Japan's history. By returning to the age of the gods, Shiratori at last formulated a scientifically based history that unified culture and politics in the nation-state of Japan. But in Shiratori's interpretation, the imperial institution was no longer a manifestation of the universal; although contiguous to that universal, it had become a living spirit. As such, it was superior to any counterpart in the West. In addition, the North-South dualism, by operating in Japan differently than elsewhere, provided Japan with a balance that no other nation was able to develop. What had started as an attempt to conceptualize an equality in difference eventually led to a historical authorization of Japan's uniqueness and superiority. Like Naitō, however, Shiratori failed to recognize that his broader vision still considered Japan as the subject, while all others were objectified. (This, of course, was also a problem of European scholars against whom he was writing.) Ironically, while he criticized the *kokusui* scholars of the twentieth century, he moved much closer to the strategy of the eighteenth-century *kokugaku* scholars. Just as those nativists gradually pulled away from China, so did Japan shift away from the West.[78]

In combining religiosity and history, Shiratori left unaddressed a paradox between what was natural, or inherent, and the need for human intervention.[79] Even though people had to act on behalf of the emperor, Shiratori assumed (or envisioned) a natural, spiritual bond between the emperor and people. Truth was tied to this spiritual being, and historical laws, which were subject to this religiosity, were also seen as predestined. Intervention, if it can be called such, was through scientific knowledge: by understanding history and historical laws, one can understand the past and present and also predict the future. The problem with such a reliance on positivistic knowledge, or what George Lakoff and Mark Johnson call a "myth of objectivism," is that too much power is placed in the hands of those who define what is objective: "In a culture where the myth of objectivism is very much alive and truth is always absolute truth, the people who get to impose their metaphors on the culture get to define what we consider to be true—absolutely and objectively true."[80]

One of the ways that the history of other countries was used to establish an objective knowledge about what Japan should be was in

78. For a discussion of this function of China, see Harootunian, "Function of China in Tokugawa Thought," 9–36.

79. For a similar paradox among the Mitogaku scholars, see Koschmann, *Mito Ideology,* 130–31.

80. George Lakoff and Mark Johnson, *Metaphors We Live By* (Chicago: University of Chicago Press, 1980), 160.

metaphors of what the other countries were and how they compared to Japan. By the 1920s, Japanese commentators often used the external to define the internal—or, more specifically, the outside was described in terms of what Japan was not or should not become. By tying Japan's identity to a religiosity that allowed the incorporation of other cultures, Shiratori left vague the exact nature of the characteristics that make up that identity—who defines loyalty and its meaning, and who determines knowledge. To Shiratori and Naitō, these issues were evident in the objective historical past. But the past is not uniform, and a number of conflicting narratives can be constructed from that past. Both chose a conservative (but not ultranationalistic) position; they sought to arrest the fragmentation and conflict domestically and account for competition internationally.

The definition of the essence of Japanese society depended on two integrated components: the idealization of an oriental (tōyō) past to extract notions of what society should be, and the comparison of Japan to the outside world with all its ills. That external was the locus of a fragmentation that, Shiratori believed, resulted from individualism, self-interest, greed, conflict, competition, and imperialism—the problems of Western culture. These, however, were categorized as alien problems, and when he wrote about the essence of Japan, or what Japan should be, it was cast in terms opposite those ills: cohesion, cooperation, and loyalty centering on the imperial system. Antiquity, especially that of tōyō, provided the material for Japan's essence, indeed its very traditions, while the insufficiencies and failings of shina and the West were used to define what Japan was not. In the vagueness of this definition and the ready availability of scientific expertise, conflict over who determined such norms was perhaps bound to develop. Moreover, vagueness combined with objectivism to render Shiratori's ideas readily adaptable for more nationalistic ends. (This failure to recognize the particularity of objectivistic knowledge, needless to say, has not been limited to Shiratori and Japan.)

Naitō, too, wrote in the mid-1920s that Europe had begun to stagnate. One problem, he said, was rational society itself. The people failed to enjoy any freedom or culture in their daily lives: they were poisoned by wealth, the slaves of machines, dehumanized by mass production, and destructive of nature.[81] Yet Europeans were unable to see the

81. Naitō's criticism bears many similarities to Rabindranath Tagore's criticism of the nation; see Tagore, *Nationalism*.

positive attributes of other cultures or even their own problems; "The Occidentals," he wrote, "are overly indulgent and self-confident of their own culture." Only Japan (he used the word "orientals" [*tōyōjin*], but that he meant Japan is clear), which possesses the essence of Asian culture, has the character and youth to synthesize both Eastern and Western cultures and establish a more integrative world culture.[82]

Hattori Unokichi took this use of the past one step further to attempt a positive definition of Japan's role in the world, as opposed to defining Japan in terms of what other cultures were not. In this way, Hattori turned Confucianism into an alternative to Wilsonian internationalism. He asked rhetorically, "Will those who call for the League of Nations actually completely abolish the narrow-minded racial distinctions? Will the United States resolutely rescind its policy of excluding Asians as if throwing out a pair of old shoes? Are they not uneasy in trying to implement what is natural from [the perspective of] true justice and humanity? By all means, we should lead the world along the Great Way of justice and humanity."[83] Hattori argued that the major sources of world conflict lay in economic problems and self-interest— though he did not use the word "capitalism." To rid the world of these evils, a transcendent force based on the Confucian virtues of humanity and justice (*jingi*) was necessary. *Jin* was a virtue bestowed from heaven that allowed for the development of man's faculties, intelligence, compassion, and will. This was as close to individualism as Hattori would come; the individual could thereby reach his or her full potential, but such development occurred only within a superorganic body and did not include the unbridled self-interest of the Western concept. Justice (*gi*) was the ultimate form of reason that allowed man to recognize his responsibilities—in other words, loyalty and filial piety.[84]

Hattori was no pacifist, however. While he considered peace, based on Confucian ethics, to be the ultimate ideal, it was not attainable as long as Western materialism remained. In contrast to his metaphors of harmony to describe Japan, he used metaphors of conflict when discussing the alien. Confucius, he argued, also recognized the necessity of a military for the preservation of one's own culture: "Confucianism considers culture as the warp and the military as the woof." If there is

82. Naitō, "Nihon no bunka nanzo ya?" 212; Tam, "In Search of the Oriental Past," 312–13.

83. Hattori, "Gendai ni okeru jukyō no igi," 35.

84. Hattori argued that humans cannot exist outside of society, and thus they exist as a part of an organic entity, but because this entity has consciousness, he called it a metaorganism (*chōyūkitai*); see ibid., 29, 33.

a disturbance, internal or external, the military (that is, Japan's military) must restore order.[85] Under Hattori, Confucianism had again become a world doctrine; but now the "world" was much larger than *tōyō*. His Confucianism became a moralistic and idealistic universal that opposed both Wilsonian internationalism and Bolshevism, the two principal ideologies that organized the post–World War I world.[86] Hattori was certainly more specific than Shiratori. Although his writings were based on a very modern notion of society, he denied that the West had anything to offer Japan and focused instead on the materialism and self-interest of Western culture. But both shared a fundamental belief that Japan was neither bound nor inferior to Europe. Both emphasized an Asian sense of the whole (Japan being the only country that understood and possessed this organic concept), which was free of the problems inherent in Western concepts. Yet despite this spirit of justice and cooperation, both also forewarned of a need for military force. Words and ideals alone could not preserve independence. In both cases the emphasis was on defense, the locus of which was *tōyō*.

What is apparent in the writings of these men is a growing Japanese self-confidence and separation from the West, combined with a conviction that change was not necessary. Hattori argued that Western forms of thought were debilitating and that the Japanese version of Confucianism was inherently better. At the end of his career, Shiratori too argued, though not as arrogantly as Hattori, that the current system was basically sound. He did not condemn the systems of Europe, the United States, or the Soviet Union, but he did become more historicistic, emphasizing the historical conditions that gave rise to those cultures and, despite finding some superficially attractive features, endorsing none as being applicable to Japan. Instead, Shiratori exuded confidence in Japan and chose to emphasize its different historical development, pointing out that "our Japan has already reached such a level that even when compared with the countries of Europe and America it is unsurpassed."[87] Such positivistic—and, one might add, rational—thinking had at last affirmed Japan's independence and con-

85. Ibid., 25–26.

86. For a discussion on the competition between these conceptions of order, see N. Gordon Levin, Jr., *Woodrow Wilson and World Politics: America's Response to War and Revolution* (London: Oxford University Press, 1968); and Arno J. Mayer, *Political Origins of the New Diplomacy, 1917–1918* (New Haven: Yale University Press, 1959).

87. Shiratori, "Kigen nisenroppyaku nen o mukaete kan ari," *Tairiku shinpō*, February 11, 1940, in *SKZ* 10:437–41 (quote at 440).

tinuing success. By the 1920s, then, history had authorized the supremacy of both the imperial institution and Japan's development. But this understanding in a number of ways limited rather than enabled further growth. The lack of dialogue with the West evolved into satisfaction with existing conditions in Japan. Japan was now "unsurpassed." Even though Shiratori admitted to some attractive characteristics in other cultures, he concluded that while Japan might be a poor country, it should not imitate those cultures, especially in such things as baseball, which reflect the wealth of the United States, and communism, which is a result of centuries-old oppression in Russia. He did not deny that Japan in the early 1930s faced hardships, but corrections required merely minor reforms or adjustments, not major changes. Implicitly, Japan no longer needed to import anything from the Western nations.[88]

Nor did this narrative really free Japan from a dependence on Western history. While Japanese enlightenment historians struggled with the confines of a unilinear framework, this new history depended on Japan's ability to absorb from the outside. In an attempt to explain this problem, Shiratori stated: "Because Japan had placed Western culture one step ahead, it had to restrain its pride until it was ahead of China. When Japan adopted [*sesshu*] culture from other countries, it certainly did not imitate. The attitude was the same in the case of the culture of China and that of Europe and the United States. We must be mindful that culture was rectified."[89] Regardless whether Japan imitated or adopted—the difference involves a connotation of inferiority—the new narrative relied on outside cultures to support assertions of superiority and uniqueness.

88. Shiratori, "Tōyōshijō ni okeru mansen no ichi," in *SKZ* 9:379.
89. Shiratori, "Kigen nisenroppyaku nen o mukaete kan ari," in *SKZ* 10:441.

CHAPTER FIVE

Shina: The Authorization
of a Discourse

The debate on ancient Japan indicates that although substantial disagreement existed, and there was a belief that disputes were significant, in fact variation existed within a discourse of shared assumptions about Japan's origins. In the end these scholars, pushed by each other, prodded by current events, and obsessed with the ideal of objectivity, gradually developed a historical understanding that removed the constrictions imposed by notions of universality and at the same time authorized a new vision of Japan.

The seduction of this historical narrative is that it made sense to the Japanese nation-state: it explained the chaos on the continent, what Japan was, and what it should be in light of that conflict. Its power derived from the placement of various pasts into a coherent whole that rendered contemporary conditions understandable. The turmoil in Asia became comprehensible when the Chinese were seen to be acting as they had for centuries. There was comfort in knowing that the international conflict among the European powers, the United States, China, and Japan was a recent manifestation of balance-of-power politics and marked the reemergence of the North-South dualism. It did not make any difference that nobody really knew the past that rendered the present familiar. This "truth" was apparent throughout society.

The formation and power of this understanding of *shina* came from its ability to order Japan's world, but its longevity resulted from the ways that it was repeated at various levels of society. Edward Said describes the importance of the repetition of experience in historical understanding as follows:

Repetition connects reason with raw experience. First, on the level of meaning, experience accumulates meaning as the weight of past and similar experiences returns. . . . Second, repetition contains experience in a way; repetition is the frame within which man represents himself to himself and for others. . . . Finally, repetition restores the past to the scholar, illuminating his research by an inexhaustible constancy. . . . For Vico then, whether as the beginning of sense, as representation, as archeological reconstruction, repetition is a principle of economy, giving facts their historical factuality and reality its existential sense.[1]

These forms of repetition occurred on a number of levels in Taishō and early Shōwa Japan, fostered by the scientific methodologies of Shiratori, Naitō, and their students. These scholars who occupied important positions in the research and academic community not only possessed the "weight of the past," but their experience was endowed with an objective authority as the work of each confirmed, supported, and modified the findings of the others. Replicability is, after all, a central tenet of positivistic research.

The work of scholars reached popular audiences through a number of media. Michel de Certeau describes the relation between the historian, the popular media, and the historical field:

Scholarly discourse is no longer distinguishable from that prolix and fundamental narrativity that is our everyday historiography. Scholarship is an integral part of the system that organizes by means of "histories" all social communication and everything that makes the present habitable. The book or the professional article, on the one hand, and the magazine or the television news on the other, are distinguishable from one another only within the same historiographical field which is constituted by the innumerable narratives that recount and interpret events.[2]

As this quote suggests, various layers and voices intersect with the historian's tasks. The role of the historian is performative. During the early twentieth century, historians organized disparate material on *shina* into a unified totality that was congruent with everyday historiography: political cartoons, literature, elementary textbooks, popular writings, and the work of historians like Shiratori and Naitō are part of

1. Edward Said, *The World, the Text, and the Critic* (Cambridge, Mass.: Harvard University Press, 1983), 113–14.
2. Michel de Certeau, *Heterologies*, 205.

the "innumerable narratives" that constitute the historiographical field. Yamaji Aizan, who wrote for popular journals such as *Kokumin no tomo, Taiyō,* and *Chūō Kōron,* provides a fine example of the extent to which the terms that defined the discourse on *shina* had become common knowledge. Even though he criticized academics for not understanding China, his corrective version incorporated the same assumptions and historical framework that Shiratori and Naitō used. But one did not have to go to China or read widely for affirmation of China's backwardness; one had only to visit the Yokohama Chinatown to experience *shina* as that living past. By the turn of the century, that neighborhood reinforced the difference between a modern Japan and *shina;* it had become a collection of restaurants (Chinese culture) and craftsmen (reminders of the Chinese past), as well as the home of the often radical Chinese students (contemporary chaos).[3] The literate also encountered similar conceptions in novels such as Natsume Sōseki's *Botchan,* where, within a few pages, one encounters the old teacher of Chinese classics with a twisted and toothless mouth (the revered but now decrepit past), the Chinese devil (the guileful Chinaman), and celebration of the victory of modern Japan over China (the Sino-Japanese War).[4]

It is in the acceptance of this historical knowledge as common fact that it becomes discursive. I do not mean to suggest that history was the sole agent that created or "caused" a certain view of China and *tōyō.* My purpose is not to find firsts. Instead, I hope to suggest that historians interacted with social and political figures and ideas, and that each supported, differed with, and encouraged the other. History, here, provided a reassurance of understanding and certainty—regardless of accuracy—by showing precedence, trends, or continuity. As Peter Novick has demonstrated, this relation between history, nation, and mission also guided the American historical profession.[5]

But while they recognized difference in relation to the West, Japanese "interacted" with Asia only as an object of their own discourse—a relationship that would lead to tragic consequences. This history established the "rules of formation" for an understanding of *tōyō* that in-

3. Noriko Kamachi, "The Chinese in Meiji Japan: Their Interactions with the Japanese Before the Sino-Japanese War," in Iriye (ed.), *The Chinese and the Japanese,* 72–73.

4. Natsume Sōseki, *Botchan,* tran. Umeji Sasaki (Rutland, Vt.: Charles E. Tuttle, 1968), 148–52. For information on Sōseki's travels to China, see Joshua Fogel, "Japanese Literary Travelers in Prewar China," *Harvard Journal of Asiatic Studies* 49 (December 1989): 580–82.

5. Novick, *That Noble Dream.*

creasingly narrowed the range of alternatives for dialogue with other Asians. Japanese assumed that it was important to help, lead, or control *shina,* all of which required the assent of the Chinese.[6] With rising Chinese nationalism, unstable political conditions, and anti-Japanese sentiment, such assent became increasingly unlikely. Because the Japanese self-conception was closely tied to what they "knew" the continent was and should be, to change their understanding of China necessitated a reevaluation of their own recently reconstructed history. Many intellectuals, such as Ozaki Hotsumi and Tachibana Shiraki, were critical of the government and this discourse, but the nature of their criticism indicates that the breadth of *shina* was too well established by the late 1920s to be easily altered or eliminated.

Objectification of *Shina*

Shiratori's position at the University of Tokyo played a crucial role in his efforts to establish a cohesive field of study on Asia. As we saw in Chapter 1, scientific knowledge was a powerful tool for the new state, providing objective criteria that facilitated its claim to power and legitimacy. But the determination of what was to be considered objective and who had claims to that knowledge created much disagreement both within and outside of the bureaucracy.[7] Often these debates were conducted within the limits of a commonly accepted field of knowledge: the constitutional debate between Minobe and Uesugi, for example, did not challenge the privileged position of the emperor, but differed only on how he was to assert that position, with, of course, major implications for how others might use that institution. Also, the contest between the microbiologist Kitasato Shibasaburō and various government ministries over his Infectious Disease Center was not over its contribution to society, but over who would control it. At one time each debate was centered on the University of Tokyo.[8]

6. For examples of the relation of scholarly views and foreign policy, see Shumpei Okamoto, "Ishibashi Tanzan and the Twenty-one Demands," and Masaru Ikei, "Ugaki Kazushige's View of China and His China Policy, 1915–1930," in Iriye (ed.), *The Chinese and the Japanese,* 184–98 and 199–219, respectively.
7. See, for example, Marshall, "Growth and Conflict in Japanese Higher Education"; and Bartholomew, "Science, Bureaucracy, and Freedom."
8. Even though the Imperial University is the central force in Japanese academia, certainly not all contestations over knowledge revolve around the University of Tokyo; the

History, too, was important, for it defined what was to be objectively known and transmitted about Japan and the world. In the case of what was to be known about China, the pronouncements that emanated from the University of Tokyo usually set the parameters for the debates. The first generation of historians of Japan and China who took up positions at the major universities of Japan were often trained at the Imperial University in Tokyo, and more specifically, by Ludwig Riess. A selection of some of his students gives an idea of his influence. At the University of Tokyo were Shiratori; Ichimura Sanjirō, professor of Chinese history; and Murakami Naojirō, professor at the Historiographical Institute. At the University of Kyoto his students included Uchida Ginzō, professor of Japanese history; Miura Hiroyuki, professor of medieval Japanese history; and Kuwabara Jitsuzō and Yano Jinichi, professors of *tōyōshi*. And at Keio University, Kōda Shigetomo, professor of Japanese history, was also Riess's student.[9]

It is important to point out, however, that while the University of Tokyo can be considered the center of historical study in Japan, it does not necessarily follow that disagreement did not exist. Naitō's debate on Yamatai is but one example of differing interpretations. But although Naitō often disagreed with Shiratori, the topics he selected and questions he asked fell within the broad parameters of the framework used by his counterpart in Tokyo.[10] Because of the University of Tokyo's position as the most prestigious repository of knowledge, the very act of discussion gave focus and an aura of approval to certain notions that permeated society as a whole. What is especially important about these historical studies on *tōyō* is not whether Shiratori or Naitō was the "discoverer," but that together they authorized, through history, Japan's understanding of itself and the world.

Shiratori and Naitō shared similar temporal and spatial conceptions of world history. Shiratori's North-South dualism and Naitō's theory of shifting cultural centers both elaborated a common field of knowledge on *shina*. Not the nation, but the region, had formerly served as the locus of oriental culture; now it became part of a hierarchical order of

---

attribution of centrality is perhaps just as much the bias of modern-day historians who have chosen such topics.

9. Blussé, "Japanese Historiography and European Sources," 199–210.

10. For Naitō's efforts to use such debates to gain recognition for the newer Kyoto University, see Tam, "In Search of an Oriental Past," 230–33.

places—Japan, China, Korea, and Manchuria—within *tōyō*. History was now much more than a simple repository for analogies of past to present, for the world order and vision expressed by this framework were broadly assumed.

Surely Shiratori did not create this dynamic concept of the history of *tōyō*. Different aspects of such an overall scheme can be found in the writings of predecessors, such as Okakura Tenshin. The process of emergence was interactive; *tōyōshi* was based on a prescientific philosophy of history that incorporated previous images or notions about Asia as well as the West. But once established, the positivistic studies that Shiratori and his students conducted tested such a framework and, later, continued to affirm it. By the mid–Taishō period, basic temporal and spatial issues were rarely discussed within *tōyōshi*. Instead, scholars now generally sought to explicate various aspects of this framework and so affirm its validity.

The debates between scholars of the Imperial Universities at Tokyo and Kyoto aided this shift from questions of history to explication of parts of *tōyōshi*. Naitō's writings on China, for example, generally corresponded with this shift, falling securely within *tōyō;* they were simply more narrowly focused on China than were Shiratori's writings, which dealt more with other Asian peoples and countries. Naitō's *Shinaron* (Treatise on China) and *Shin shinaron* (A New Treatise on China) display well the points at which his conception of history in Asia and its relation to contemporary China intersect with those of Shiratori.[11]

Throughout his career, Naitō focused on discovering the "origins of modernity" in both China and Japan. Whereas Shiratori was concerned with the beginnings of civilization and the establishment of a modern history that incorporated Asia and allowed for "equality in difference" with the West, Naitō limited his studies to China, in particular the "modern" (*kinsei*) period. Through this work he made a considerable contribution to the field of Sinology. According to one biographer, his periodization of Chinese history has had a lasting effect on scholarship.[12]

Naitō was interested in explaining not Japan's difference and equivalence with the West, but China's relation to Japan; he merely assumed

11. While the gist of these two essays is similar, it is apparent in the latter essay that Naitō's confidence was shaken by China's continuing political chaos. By 1924 he condoned the use of violence and the greater involvement of Japan in China.

12. Fogel, *Politics and Sinology,* see esp. 163–210; also see Tam, "In Search of the Oriental Past," 261–82.

the equality with Europe embedded in *tōyō* that his predecessors had struggled to establish. In 1924 he stated,

Today, when there is little promise of cooperation with the [world] powers, when politicians in China conduct meaningless discussions on sovereignty because it's their job, when contempt toward Japanese and an increasing dislike of other foreigners lead more and more to violence and when Japan has endured beyond reasonable limits and is now taking a path that is on the verge, it seems, of exploding—how long Japan, which most painfully feels these interests, will continue relations with China without incident is beyond the wisdom of human beings.[13]

Beyond a sense that a certain equality existed with the European powers, there is an indignant tone in this passage, a sense that neither the West nor the Chinese truly understood Asia, especially the law of history. Japan, of course, Naitō assumed, did understand and should act, by itself if necessary, to ameliorate the tension.[14]

The central tenet of Naitō's philosophy of history was his theory of shifting cultural centers. According to this dynamic concept, the center of culture in *tōyō* constantly moved to new areas, which, being younger, surpassed the cultural level of previous centers. Most of the cultural centers had been in China. Until the Han dynasty, it was in the Yellow River Valley. Then it gradually moved to the southeast: until the T'ang dynasty it was in Shansi and Honan; through the Sung and Yuan dynasties it had shifted to Honan and Chihli; around the Ming dynasty it became located around Kiangsu and Chekiang; and more recently it had moved to Canton. The latter areas, he pointed out, even though within China, were once considered to be barbarian or foreign lands by the "pure"—that is, ancient—Chinese.[15]

Like Shiratori in his construction of *tōyō*, Naitō too used the notion of an oriental culture (*tōyō bunka*) as a geocultural entity that blurred the political boundaries of the countries of Asia. *Shina*, Naitō stated, was just one part—albeit until recently the central part—of that culture. He found much to praise, but respect was linked to antiquity when *shina* was the center of an oriental culture.

The increased Japanese influence against the Chinese revolution has not emerged from fleeting circumstances; one can say that [Japan's rise] is a natural [*tōzen*], historical outcome of the development of oriental culture [*tōyō bunka*].

13. Naitō, *Shinshinaron* (Tokyo: Hakubundō, 1924), *NKZ* 5:498.
14. For Naitō's conviction in his own and Japan's correctness, see ibid., 534–35; in English, see Tam, "In Search of the Oriental Past," 304–5.
15. Naitō, *Shinshinaron*, *NKZ* 5:509.

The existence of each nation [*kokumin*], China, Japan, Korea, and Annam, is rather important to each nation-state [*kokka*], but when viewed holistically [*zentai no mondai*], as the development of oriental culture, each [nation] is insignificant. The development of oriental culture ignores the distinction of nation [*kokumin*] and advances along a fixed path [*ittei no keiro*].[16]

Naitō assumed that an oriental culture existed; his task was to explicate its meaning—a historical narrative of the progress of the culture of *tōyō*, a fixed course that led straight to Japan.

But while the blurring of national boundaries enabled him to show development within *tōyō*, the movement of the cultural center also created a hierarchical order both synchronically (center/periphery) and diachronically. Since Japan had also received the culture of China, he wrote, and lies on the easterly path followed by the cultural center, Japan is becoming the center of the culture of *tōyō*.[17] Naitō's *shina* may have been more powerful in the past, but Japan was now assuming the lead. The other countries, such as Korea, Manchuria, and Southeast Asia remained on the periphery, both geographically and temporally. The end result for Japan was a history in which the past was described in terms of the progressive development of oriental culture. Praise for Chinese culture (that is, while it was the center of *tōyō*) was possible, for it now became part of Japan's past. Such respect—or, more accurately, nostalgia—could be realized both because of temporal continuity, which allowed for similarity, and because the present and past had been separated into two separate entities.

Although the historical narrative of Naitō's theory of shifting cultural centers is different from that of Shiratori's North-South dualism, the characteristics that emerge from these histories have several striking similarities. China's longevity, according to Naitō, was possible only because of the constant invasions of the Northern barbarians. Chinese culture, he speculated, would probably have declined after the Han; as cultures mature they become complacent and conservative, and problems such as bribery and corruption become prevalent. Even though the barbarians did not eliminate such problems, their presence did bring new vigor to the Chinese: "At any rate, while both the Mongols and Manchus controlled China, they also inherited both the corruption that infected the Chinese, such as bribery, and political abuses. But because they penetrated with a naive and straightforward attitude against a people that had become old and crafty, they were successful;

16. Ibid., 508.
17. Ibid., 509.

they rejuvenated the senile life of the Chinese before the latter realized it."[18] Like Shiratori, Naitō assumed conflict among societies outside of Japan; it is from the struggle (or lack thereof) to ameliorate such conflict that cultures progress (or decline). Yet while Shiratori attributed China's conservatism to the barbarians and its longevity to the strength of the culture, Naitō suggested that the conservatism was an inevitable result of nature and the barbarians were the major reason for China's long history. Thus the causes are reversed, but the end result is the same. Although both assumed the inevitability of international conflict and attributed China's longevity to this conflict, neither saw any salutary effects coming from conflict within a nation. In fact, both described the emergence of conservatism, pacifism, and stagnation as the locus of the Chinese failure to respond properly to this challenge.

To order and explicate the dynamic process established by his theory of shifting cultural centers, Naitō formulated a new periodization of Chinese history. He asserted rather boldly that history is not merely the separation of the past into convenient categories. Periodization has meaning; it reflects the changes of society according to certain historical laws. Naitō's periodization divided history into three developmental stages: the distant past (ancient), the middle period (medieval), and the recent period (modern—*kinsei*). The stages bear some similarity to Comte's three stages of human society. In fact, like Leibniz, who compared social development to human development and from whom Comte developed his sociology, Naitō too used stages of human development as metaphors for his historical stages. But unlike Comtean positivism, Naitō's philosophy of history eliminated the gradual linear progression that culminates in an ideal society. Naitō's stages have different characteristics. From infancy, the human being—or nation—advances to adolescence, and then to senescence. In his view, adolescence is the most vigorous and most productive period; this is when a country rapidly progresses, grows stronger, and expands. The final stage, senescence, is characterized by a more mature, reflective, and peaceful attitude; vigorous activities are shunned in favor of more sedate and conservative activities. As a senescent society, then, the Chinese became increasingly interested in cultural activities such as the arts and literature.

This framework corrected for what Naitō considered the overly simplistic history of his predecessors, which accepted the temporal inferiority of the orient. He wrote against a Western notion that Japanese (in

18. Ibid., 512–13.

fact, all non-Western cultures) could develop into a modern, progressive nation only after incorporating Western ideas and techniques. Like Shiratori, he sought to show that progress is not uniquely Western and to give Japan its own history. By revising the criteria for each stage, Naitō established Asia's and Japan's indigenous transition to a modern culture well before contact with the West (including the sixteenth century, when Jesuit activity in East Asia increased). According to Naitō, Japan's modern period began with the gradual transformation of society—the sudden rise of the militaristic class and the addition of the power of the masses (*heimin*)—as far back as the Kamakura period (1185–1333).[19] As for China, Naitō located the beginnings of the modern age there in the mid-T'ang and Sung dynasties.

This interpretation placed *shina* in an ambiguous position. On the one hand, it was the source of an oriental culture. China's most dynamic era, the medieval period, lasted from the Han dynasty, when the Chinese "synthesized name and practice," to the T'ang. During these dynasties, Naitō characterized the government as that of the "village bureaucrat," who administered the same locale from which he came. Government also was conducted from among the "families of high standing" (*zokubo*), an aristocratic elite. On the other hand, *shina* was a culture that had politically and socially passed its prime. The decline of this political and social vibrancy began to emerge during the Sui dynasty (589–618) and was quite apparent around the mid–T'ang dynasty through the era of the Five Dynasties (907–60): the government shifted to an absolute monarchy, the economy shifted from barter to commercial exchange, the people began to have greater say over their own affairs (here he identifies the origins of *heiminshugi*—populism), and the arts exhibited considerable creativity. The Sung dynasty, according to Naitō, was the beginning of China's modern period, which was characterized by the separation of government from the governed, the divorce of politics from culture, and the greater individuation of the people. This degeneracy (my term), he was careful to point out, was a universal phenomenon, not one limited to China.[20]

Naitō quite rightly indicated that modernity also brings social fragmentation. He identified the separation of ruler from the ruled as the root of the "national essence of China" (*shina no kokusui*) and the

19. Naitō, *Shinaron* (Tokyo: Bunkaidō Shoten, 1914), *NKZ* 5:308. Naitō's search for China's indigenous roots of modernity paralleled a search by Japanese specialists in Japanese history. Fogel (*Politics and Sinology,* 169) identified Uchida Ginzō or possibly Hara Katsurō as having a significant influence on Naitō.

20. Naitō, *Shinshinaron, NKZ* 5:533–35.

character of the people. The new elite class was characterized by its disinterest in politics: those who failed to pass the civil service exams and gain a position in the bureaucracy, Naitō suggested, became depressed at their failure and found solace in literature, academics(!), and the arts. The masses, too, were increasingly distanced from central authority—the distance and aloofness of the local administrators exacerbated their separation from the masses. The people, in turn, organized themselves around a system of village self-rule (*kyōdan jiji*), which coincided with and was also reinforced by the clan system. Naitō condescendingly used the metaphor of a worm to describe this fragmented social structure: Chinese society, he said, "has developed a form of low animal life, like an earthworm, where even if one part is severed the other part feels nothing and continues life as before."[21]

It is clear from his discussion that he saw the lack of both strong leaders and a concept of nation as a serious problem in the modern period. In his opinion, those politicians that there were, were just that: politicians, in the pejorative sense. Politics was like a game or contest for personal power and position, and national issues were not major concerns. Moreover, the people had little sense of any loyalty to any larger unit beyond their own village or clan. He argued that recent violence—the White Lotus Rebellion, the Long Hair Rebellion, and even the autonomous self-defense forces—grew out of this basic social structure inherent in village self-rule.[22]

Naitō's shifting cultural centers, then, presented a framework from which he could describe the evolution of the culture of *tōyō*. Unlike Shiratori's dualism, which focused on the Northern barbarians, Naitō's conception had *shina* at its center. But even though their narratives differed, the underlying outline of history was similar in both their theories. Both believed that Japan was equivalent to the West; both saw Japan as the modern pinnacle of the culture of *tōyō*; both worked within a dynamic framework that located *shina* in a category which suggested decay, senility, and lethargy, whereas Japan was young and vibrant; both assumed that international conflict was inevitable and could lead to progress (or decline); both depicted an increasingly conservative Chinese society incapable of generating its own forces for change; both used the Northern barbarians to explain this conservatism; both separated the horizontal society or masses organized around self-governing villages from the bureaucracy; and both disavowed any sense of nation-

21. Ibid., 499.
22. Ibid., 502.

alism among the Chinese. Finally, by recognizing Japan as the inheritor of the best of *shina*, both authorized Japan as the preeminent nation in this culture of *tōyō*. From this position as the cultural leader they envisioned Japan's taking on a leadership role (the victimized call it imperialism) in Asia.

In their histories, Naitō and Shiratori located what Foucault has called the emergence (*Entstehen*), the moments of arising, that establish the beginning or cause of present conditions. These moments are located in various points of the past where contention and conflict led to either degeneracy or resuscitation: "Emergence is thus the entry of forces; it is their eruption, the leap from the wings to the center stage, each in its youthful strength."[23] Such conflict is among unequals, not equals, and leads ultimately to the domination of one over the other; it is the victor who determines the course of history—not only the outcome, but also the narrative, of past events. In Naitō's and Shiratori's histories, international conflict was assumed, and was framed in a dualism of cultured versus militaristic or through a metaphor of the human body. The moments of this narrative were the failures of Chinese; both Naitō and Shiratori looked back into China's past for evidence of its decline and of Japan's oriental past. Armed with this material, they formulated a philosophy of history that praised *shina's* past and explained Japan's current superiority over its neighbor. The result was to describe China as a periphery of Japan.

At this point, the history of *shina*, the uncovering of the locations of emergence, returned to the contemporary period (one can argue that it never left). This totality was centered on China and Asia and disposed of any question of diversity and difference by incorporating variation within the total structure. Objective historical studies reinforced the placement of different pasts within this overall scheme. It was "a history that always encourages subjective recognitions and attributes a form of reconciliation to all the displacements of the past; a history whose perspective on all that precedes it implies the end of time, a completed development."[24] In this way Shiratori and Naitō could create different narratives but ultimately support the same framework. Thereafter, Japanese scholars and intellectuals could conduct research and write within the logic of that totality to describe relationships that affirmed Japan's dominance of Asia.

23. Foucault, "Nietzsche, Genealogy, History," 148–52 (quote at 149–50).
24. Ibid., 152.

Knowledge as Practice

The totality described through this historical perspective incorporated the separation of politics, or history, from a culture that was frozen in the past. Japanese could now praise ancient China as an early, glorious stage of an oriental culture (*tōyō bunka*) and at the same time view contemporary relations in the context of a progressive order led by Japan. In both cases *shina* bore static meanings. Foucault describes the implications of such history thus: "Once the historical sense is mastered by a suprahistorical perspective, metaphysics can bend it to its own purpose and, by aligning it to the demands of objective science, it can impose its own 'Egyptianism.' "[25] The hegemony of such Egyptianism, however, was obscured by what Renato Rosaldo calls imperialist nostalgia. The imperialist often goes to the colony seeking to understand and to help. Often, a nostalgia for the past—what his modern world has lost—coexists with a goal of assisting the colonial society. While such nostalgia leads the observer to sympathize with the object, usually he is also contributing to changes in the very parts of society for which he is longing. In *tōyō*, veneration for a past ideal and conviction of superiority toward the contemporary place coexisted. But because of the inclusion of both Japan and *shina* in *tōyō*, the objects of that nostalgia were part of *shina* as well as of Japan's past. Although veneration for a distant past remained active, China—or, more accurately, *shina*—was in the end an object within *tōyō* that Japan had to help.[26]

That "Egyptianism" allowed Japan to describe, teach, scold, and appropriate parts that it believed were necessary for China to survive. The questions that scholars asked within this field of knowledge, thus, were designed to refine its contents. While there was room to adjust the lines that bounded the temporal and spatial categories of the field, the general structure was largely fixed. Research unearthed the moment of emergence of a decentralized and decadent (or senescent) China, identified China's problems, and suggested criteria by which it could be reformed according to modern standards (defined by Japan). Scholars focused on pinpointing *shina*'s peak and the subsequent decline, stagnation, or rigidity; the causes of Chinese conservatism; why Chi-

25. Ibid., 152.
26. Renato Rosaldo, "Imperialist Nostalgia," *Representations* 26 (Spring 1989): 107–22.

nese social structure hindered the formation of a nation; and how Japan should lead China into the future.

The fruit of these scholars' labors was also served up to Japanese in their elementary school curriculum.[27] Because early-twentieth-century Japanese elementary school textbooks were the products of the Editorial Division of the Ministry of Education, they are a fair indication of the government's sense of what all Japanese citizens should know. The Editorial Division sought to prepare Japan's "future citizens" (after 1907, 97 percent of all Japanese students read these government textbooks) "for a more active role in China and inculcated in the minds of the young the view that Manchuria was a vital area for Japan."[28] The image of Asia presented in schoolbooks written between 1910 and 1923 echoed this notion of *shina:* Japan was indebted to ancient China, but contemporary China was helpless, antiquarian, arrogant, guileful, militarily incompetent, and misunderstanding of Japan's true aims; these texts "studiously" avoided calling China *chūgoku;* Taiwan, Korea, and Manchuria were inferior, and thus in need of instruction and assistance; and the Manchurian and Japanese economies were mutually beneficial. According to these books, it was Japan's duty to take an active role on the continent: "The God-given mission of peace in East Asia rests on the shoulders of such people as us. Japan has a heavy responsibility in advancing the civilization of the East"[29] (fig. 2).

Such "Egyptianism" also affirmed, under the guise of objectivity, Japan's actions ("help") on the continent and accounted for the perceived failure of the Chinese themselves to understand their own history and culture. Shiratori's interpretations of the 1911 and 1918 revolutions in China illustrate the relation between his historical totality and contemporary events. He knew what was going on; he stated: "An obscure universalism [*tenkashugi*] failed in the ancient Warring States period. We have to tell them [the Chinese] that today's period of warring states requires a firm nationalism and that it is extremely difficult

27. Harry Wray, "China in Japanese Textbooks," in *China and Japan: Search for Balance since World War I,* ed. Alvin D. Coox and Hilary Conroy (Santa Barbara: ABC-Clio, 1978), 115–31. For similarities of the Tōa Dōbunshoin (East Asia Common Culture Academy) to this discourse, see Douglas R. Reynolds, "Training Young China Hands: Tōa Dōbun Shoin and Its Precursors, 1886–1945," in *The Japanese Informal Empire in China, 1895–1937,* ed. Peter Duus, Ramon H. Myers, and Mark R. Peattie (Princeton: Princeton University Press, 1989), 210–71.
28. Wray, "China in Japanese Textbooks," 120, 116.
29. Ibid., 118.

Fig. 2. The Chinese is yelling, "Co—me, co—me," to the Japanese doves, while the Russian eagle lurks on the other side of Mongolia. The title is "Eagle in the Background." *Taiyō* 19, no. 12 (1913): 46.

to establish a republican government using the vague egalitarian [*heiminshugi*] ideology of the past."[30] The domestic and international conflict of twentieth-century China, he argued, was not merely the beginning of another dynastic cycle or the result of racial animosities against the Manchus. He did not believe that history is cyclical; the astute historian, he said, could find equivalences in the records of the past. Shiratori argued that the analogy to the present era of "warring states" was buried in the ancient Warring States period before China formed its national essence (*kokutai*). This earlier period was a "pure" era, prior to the formulation of Confucianism when the seeds of China's anachronistic thought, the "ideology of the past," were sown.

During the Warring States period the universalism and communalism of Confucianism emerged to counter historical conditions, particularly the regionalism and militarism of the princes. The combination of Confucian univeralism with a strong clan system led to an egalitarian, "horizontal" society that revered the past (that is, the ideals of Yao, Shun, and Yü), shunned change, and avoided conflict and war. Thus, while Confucianism was the central ideology that helped to end conflict and to unify China, a fragmented and non-nationalistic society evolved from this ethical ideology.[31] Although Shiratori did not at-

30. Shiratori, "Jukyō no genryū," in *SKZ* 9:69.
31. Ibid., 53–69; and "Shina ni okeru gendai no kakumei ni tsuite," in *SKZ* 10:295–302.

tribute negative values to Chinese universalism, he contended that it was no longer appropriate to modern "survival-of-the-fittest" conditions. China, in other words, had to change; it was necessary to adjust to new geopolitical realities, to join the hierarchy of nations, and, as one part of *tōyō*, to fall in behind Japan.

Shiratori then argued that a recognition of such changing conditions also required a similar reevaluation of China's Sinocentrism. The origin of this arrogance he located using his North-South dualism: despite constant successful invasions by Northern peoples throughout Chinese history, the more civilized Chinese culture had remained intact, with the conquerors adapting to it. Thus, the Chinese developed a sense of superiority; their world was the center of the universe (*chūka*, central fluorescence, or *chūgoku*). But, Shiratori pointed out, this status was possible only as long as China remained superior to all countries outside its realm. "Now that China is just one country within the universe," he said, "it has to compete with all world powers. In other words, a period of competition among powerful states that existed in the ancient Warring States period has reappeared. When this happens, a country will not survive with Confucian universalism. Now they must return to the ancient Warring States period and take up nationalism."[32] Nationalism here, of course, bore a particular meaning; it could be neither the assertion of Chinese superiority over Japan, for that betokened to the Japanese only China's old and outmoded arrogance, nor anti-Japanese activity and sentiment, which was little more than the misunderstanding of an unruly child.

In 1911, Shiratori offered a rather optimistic prognosis. Despite the small percentage of reformers in the Chinese population, he viewed the revolution of that year as evidence that a more modern consciousness was gradually spreading throughout China. Chaos and confusion were merely the "first step" toward the formation of a nation-state. As long as the Powers did not partition China and "if we entrust the course of events to China, we do not know whether as a passing phenomenon it will form a republican, constitutional, or federal system, but at any rate this country, China, for the first time will become a united and sound nation."[33]

By the 1918 revolution, however, that optimism had disappeared. The aborted monarchy of Yuan Shih-kai, the failure to achieve any

32. Shiratori, "Jukyō no genryū," in *SKZ* 9:68.
33. Shiratori, "Shina rekidai no jinshu mondai o ronjite," in *SKZ* 10:144–45. See also his "Shinkoku kakumei no zento."

Fig. 3. Japanese watching dark clouds of anti-Japanese sentiment moving in
from the continent—a "low pressure from the other side of the
sea"—lament, "After all, our hands are tied and we can only watch."
Taiyō 26, no. 14 (1920): 39. This image echoes a statement by Shiratori: "Our country's very close relationship with the peninsula is no
different now than in the past, and the dark clouds rumbling over
the peninsula have always started from the plains of Manchuria"
("Jo" to *Manshū rekishi chiri*, *SKZ* 10:449–50).

lasting reform, continued disorder, and the growing anti-Japanese
movements tempered his view. Shiratori saw little change: China still
needed to shed its anachronistic thought and unify the nation. The
state needed income; the educational system had to be reformed, industry developed, and the military unified. Yet Shiratori was now less certain about the means for accomplishing these goals. On the one hand,
the new modern consciousness could not be abandoned, but on the
other hand he questioned the ability of Chinese politicians and the extent of their popular support. In fact, he saw little alternative to continued chaos (fig. 3).

I believe that there is certainly a group of Chinese who have become aroused,
but it is an awakening that has no precedence on such a massive scale. Because
a major percentage of Chinese are anachronistic and still have no understanding of world affairs, the new ideas are not understood at all, and in particular
far beyond this group. A time will certainly come when both old and new
thought advance hand in hand, but since this cannot be accomplished quickly
or artificially, today's disorder will probably continue until that time arrives
naturally [*shizen*].[34]

From this conviction in his objective knowledge of what China needed,
Shiratori's understanding gradually diverged (if in fact there ever was a

34. Shiratori, "Shina ni okeru gendai no kakumei ni tsuite," in *SKZ* 10:309.

true understanding of actual conditions) from events there. For Shiratori, this eventually led to his declaration in 1940 that the Chinese
must eliminate their condescension toward Japan, recognize Japan's
superiority, and accept the value of Japan's syncretic culture over that
of Europe.[35]

This frustration reflects the limitation of his understanding of *shina*
and an emerging rift between Shiratori's *shina* and the real China. His
conviction of what China needed, who the enlightened leaders were,
and where China should go was not necessarily shared by many in
China, particularly after World War I. Ironically, the anti-Japanese
movements were a manifestation of the same new nationalism that
Shiratori claimed was essential. Even a liberal colonial administrator in
Korea like Yanaihara Tadao failed in his attempts to reform the colony;
this discourse hindered Japanese understanding of a nationalism that
was directed against Japan.[36]

NAITŌ'S *SHINA*

Despite differences with Shiratori, Naitō came to similar
conclusions on the needs of China. In fact, Naitō was much less reti-
cent in asserting Japan's role as leader and extended this discourse from
the level of knowing, informing, and assisting to that of guiding and,
to play on his metaphor, even scolding the Chinese when necessary.

Here we see Naitō's preoccupation with the origins of modernity.
The late T'ang and Sung periods served as a time of emergence, when
a narrative that described the nature and problems of contemporary
shina was begun. The main characteristics, or "essences," that Naitō
discovered here were the separation of the people from government, an
increase in self-sufficiency and self-government within the local units (a
trend that was complemented and strengthened by the family system),
a shift in government toward an absolute monarchy, and the rise of a
money-based economy. Society was characterized by a declining adherence to established norms and greater autonomy, something that Naitō
discerned even in the arts. The elites, the politicians, and the compradores (according to his shifting culture theory, shifts at the elite level
from powerful clans, to intellectuals, to merchants paralleled shifts in

35. Shiratori, "Kigen nisen roppyakunen o mukaete kan ari," in *SKZ* 10:440–41.
36. Yanaihara is considered a liberal who proposed greater self-government in Korea.
Despite his views, he failed to understand Korean nationalism. See Mark R. Peattie,
"Japanese Attitudes Toward Colonialism, 1895–1945," in *The Japanese Colonial Empire,
1895–1945*, ed. Ramon H. Myers and Mark R. Peattie (Princeton: Princeton University
Press, 1984), 80–127, esp. 114–18.

Fig. 4. Wearing traditional Chinese clothes, Yuan Shi-kai in *shina* is holding the prize and sending assassins to kill Sun Yat-sen, who has just arrived in Japan wearing modern attire. *Taiyō* 19, no. 12 (1913): 47.

the cultural center) were concerned only with their own power and wealth, not that of the people and nation (fig. 4).[37]

According to Naitō, the local, self-governing units had both a conservative and progressive potential. On the one hand, an immunological effect was embedded in this social structure. As his earthworm metaphor implies, Naitō believed that these local units served as a positive check; when evil spreads, "the best policy is to turn it into an antibody and spread it throughout the countryside." Such an antibody, he thought optimistically, would bring an end to the anti-Japanese movement, just as it had prevented the spread of "red propaganda."[38] Others might call this thinking conservative, but Naitō saw here the potential for leading China on a more productive path. Naitō's argument is little different from that of other imperialists. He believed that if China was to change, it would have to tap the energies of its people and export its natural resources. Growth would not be the result of large-scale industrial policy. Furthermore, the leadership and capital for this small-scale, though massive, mobilization should not come from the politicians and compradores, whose interests were often opposed to those of China,

37. Naitō, *Shinshinaron*, NKZ 5:517–24.
38. Ibid., 500–501.

nor from the Western powers; England was inappropriate because of its global ambitions, while the United States saw only the economic potential of China and would leave with the profits after exploiting its resources.[39]

For Naitō, as for Shiratori, the best leader for the reform of such a fragmented society was Japan. He disagreed with those Chinese who claimed that because Japan possessed nothing unique and was only a "translation of Western culture" China was better off going to the source of modernity rather than to a Japanese rendition. Japan, he argued, already had the necessary experience of building from its past. It only discarded the anachronistic institutions that hindered change and adapted what was suitable to oriental culture: "Over the past fifty to sixty years, Japan has been transforming Western culture to suit oriental culture, particularly through its accumulated experience in economic institutions. There is a tendency to transform large-scale Occidental things to a smaller scale and to give magnificent items a mundane appearance. But the new culture in the orient is not that which has completely cut away the trunk of oriental culture and grafted on Western culture."[40] The implication is that because Japan best understands *tōyō*, it alone can distinguish the outmoded past from relevant traditions and then know how to fit modern society to *shina*.

Naitō presented a specific outline for the reform of China that was fully compatible with his theory of shifting cultural centers. His theory showed that even though Japan had at one time been a peripheral country, the natural progression of the cultural center of *tōyō* was from Canton to Japan. Because older areas were constantly being rejuvenated by the younger center, it was fully consistent with *tōyō*'s long history that the new center, Japan, fulfill that same role. "We must recognize that to extend the life of the Chinese people, Japan's economic drives actually have a tremendous effect. If these movements are halted, the Chinese people will be inviting their own slow death."[41] The economic drives to which he referred revolved around the Japanese emigrants and entrepreneurs who went to northwestern China, opened new areas and enterprises, were replaced by capitalists, and then moved on to new frontiers. He acknowledged that such expansionism sparks conflict between the Japanese and Chinese, but he believed occasional force was a necessary expedient to accomplishing a larger goal. The

39. Ibid., 515.
40. Ibid., 510.
41. Ibid., 513.

process, he said, was like using dynamite to remove boulders when digging a drainage ditch.[42]

Naitō separated Chinese culture from politics and economics to show that Japan, the new core of oriental culture, had the responsibility to revitalize *shina*. Indeed, one of the new "rules" affirmed by this discourse was that, as the cultural center of *tōyō*, Japan was obliged, owing to its Confucian heritage, to use its modern knowledge—political, economic, and social—to lead those other less fortunate regions of *tōyō* such as *shina* out of their decrepit state.[43] The result was a teleology that, while professing to eliminate the sources of conflict, assumed the inevitability of conflict and authorized violence through its rational, scientific framework.

The transference of the histories of Naitō and Shiratori to politics can be seen in the actions and pronouncements of policymakers. Ugaki Kazushige, a general who became minister of war in 1929, argued that establishment of a hierarchical relation between Japan and China was the only possible means for achieving peace in the Far East. Thus, Ugaki considered Japan's Twenty-one Demands of 1915 as "proper" and "natural" (though he criticized the Foreign Ministry for bungling the policy); he supported investment initiatives that strengthened Japan's position in Manchuria; and he lamented Japan's troop withdrawal from Siberia in 1922.[44] Even in 1948, Ugaki remained convinced that the means to effecting this hierarchical relationship, not Japan's historical understanding of the situation, was at fault in recent events. He still believed that the war was not one of aggression, but one "based on the imperatives of self-preservation and self-defense, defense of Japan's vested interests, and the [attempt to] recover for the weak peoples of East Asia that which had been stolen from them by the Europeans and Americans."[45] Other leaders, especially colonial administrators, looked to a policy of assimilation (*dōka*)—but assimilation as defined by Japan. Mark Peattie has identified four assumptions underlying this policy: (1) a belief in cultural and racial affinity (*dōbun dōshu*), (2) a Confucian notion of benevolence implicitly tied to the imperial will, (3) the emperor as head of Japan's imperial "family," and (4) a conviction in Japan's unique experience, talents, and knowledge.[46]

42. Ibid., 514.
43. Ibid., 510.
44. Ikei, "Ugaki Kazushige's View of China."
45. Quoted in ibid., 219.
46. Peattie, "Japanese Attitudes Toward Colonialism," 96–104.

There was no doubt in Japanese minds that the Asian masses would, or more accurately should, follow Japan, for not only was leadership on the continent—including China—in disarray, but also, and more important, Japan's recent experience had shown that it is possible to emerge from the pasts of *tōyō* and move up the ladder of modernity. One can dismiss Ugaki for his activist and militaristic extremes, but Naitō too complained that the leaders of the May Fourth Movement did not understand their own culture and were misleading the masses. Ozaki Hotsumi, a member of the Shōwa Research Assocation who was convicted of treason in the Sorge spying incident, interpreted Chiang Kai-shek's unification efforts as merely a tool of English ambitions— that is, monopoly capitalism—in China.[47] Japan's self-appointed position as leader of *tōyō* was rarely contested within the country, for history had established it as fact. While each differed on how to effect change, all fell within this field of knowledge that defined the relations between Japan and *shina* as that between center and periphery, present and past. Knowledge was the authority that established Japan as the center, and its possession enabled the government, intellectuals, and activists to advocate programs for change.

A POPULAR VERSION: YAMAJI AIZAN

The breadth of this historical understanding is difficult if not impossible to measure. Each historian was writing against what he considered to be an oversimplistic or plainly wrong idea. Others were accused of not knowing the facts, of not understanding. The arguments and disagreements were real, but usually they were a matter of interpretation, not basic philosophy. In fact, although fine distinctions obscured commonalities, the debate brought writers closer together, for by its very nature it required a common ground.

The extent of this field of knowledge and its ability to incorporate even a critic are evident in the case of the newspaper columnist and historian Yamaji Aizan. In his *Shinaron* (Treatise on China), written one year after Naitō's own *Shinaron,* Yamaji criticized Japanese scholars for their misunderstanding of China: "They did not even know about Chinese history and had not even touched Chinese thought; they merely carried their lecture notes to Chinese schools and opened a branch of

47. James B. Crowley, "Intellectuals as Visionaries of the New Asian Order," in *Dilemmas of Growth in Prewar Japan,* ed. James W. Morley (Princeton: Princeton University Press, 1971), 340–42.

the Imperial University." As an example of this ignorance, he said that Japanese were teaching about a form of nationalism that, while appropriate to Europe and modern Japan, did not fit China. The conviction that the nation is equivalent to the ethnic group (*minzoku*) and that race (anti-Manchu) is the cause of revolutionary activity was a "creation of Japanese academia."[48]

Yet despite this criticism, which seemed to be pointed indirectly at Shiratori and Naitō, Yamaji's writings can be seen as a synthesis of their histories. In his description of basic Chinese characteristics, for example, Yamaji employed a framework similar to Shiratori's North-South dualism. His description of the people on Asia's periphery—the Ural Altai (he called them Finno-Turanian), the Min yüeh, and the Japanese—remind one of Shiratori's Northern people. They were not very cultured, did not like debates, were slow-witted (*chidon*—that is, without philosophical ability like that of Confucius, Wang Yang-ming, and Lao Tzu), loved order (*chitsujō*), possessed a strong sense of loyalty, were skilled soldiers, ruled over other people, and built empires. Spiritually, they worshiped heaven, and because their leaders were descendants of heaven (thus no thief could become the ruler, as in China) they maintained a high degree of loyalty toward their leader, rules, and the group. Although they were militarily skillful, that prowess was only a land-based ability. In fact, Yamaji argued, had the Ming been more experienced in naval warfare, they could have defeated the Manchus. Finally, he was impressed that the Northern people were quick to absorb Chinese culture, especially because they controlled China.[49]

This connection between the Japanese and Ural Altai allowed Yamaji to posit Japan's Asiatic heritage and to ascribe to Japan those characteristics that were necessary to the twentieth century. Yet like Shiratori, while Yamaji argued for an affinity, he was also careful to distinguish the Japanese from the Ural Altai and Min yüeh. Historical and ethnological evidence, he said, indicated that the ancestors of the Ural Altai and the Min yüeh came together on the Japanese archipelago during some prehistoric era and probably intermarried to form the Japanese race.[50] Thus, Japanese had distant racial affinities to Asia and

48. Yamaji Aizan, *Shinaron* (Tokyo: Minyūsha, 1916), 96, 101.
49. Ibid., 151–56. See also Yamaji, "Teiseikoron," in his *Shinaron*, 230–49. Shiratori ignored the Min yüeh, but Yamaji ascribed to them similar characteristics as the Ural Altai: they worked in groups, were proud and patriotic, valued prestige, and upheld a code of honor.
50. Yamaji, "Teiseikoron," in *Shinaron*, 257–58.

possessed the characteristics that embodied the best of *tōyō;* yet the combination was unique.

China, in contrast, was the opposite, what the Japanese should not become lest they invite their own decline. Yamaji described the Chinese as cultured people and compared China to ancient Greece: "One can say that their everyday life is that of civilized men: they both possess philosophy; both possess literature (songs and poems); both are skilled debaters; and their literature elegantly adorns the literary history of the world. However, both lack cohesiveness as a nation [*kokumin*]."[51] His assertion that the Chinese could not form a nation was not proven but simply stated as fact. The debate among intellectuals and publicists did not question whether this assertion was true, but whether specific examples held up to scrutiny.[52] Yamaji argued that the Chinese had little tendency to stick together; were effeminate (as proven by the withering of Manchu military skills); were self-centered; only mouthed loyalty, filiality, and honor; and, because they believed that China and the world were synonymous, were rather narrow-minded. For evidence he pointed to the end of the Ming period, when officials were more concerned with their position, money, and self-preservation than with the problems of the dynasty. Even Cheng Ch'eng-kung, the half-Japanese, half-Chinese pirate, revolted against the Ch'ing for his own gain, not out of loyalty to the Ming.[53]

Yamaji's debt to Naitō is less clearcut than that to Shiratori. The principal similarity is in the way Yamaji separated the Chinese people from the government. He argued that the principal characteristic governing their behavior was their egoism (*kojinshugi*) and a weak public spirit (*kōkyōshin*). This self-centeredness hindered a spirit of unity; they "have become people who are strongly tied to interests of their home.... [They] are not people who do not feel compassion and bitterness [*onen*] or do not understand humanity and justice [*jingi*]. However, self-preservation is the first rule that controls all their behavior."[54] In an argument reminiscent of Naitō, Yamaji asserted that these characteristics emerged after the transition of the political structure from feudalism to the district (*gunken*) system some three thousand years earlier. This decentralized system fostered a reliance on knowledge,

51. Yamaji, *Shinaron,* 154–55.

52. See also Yamaji, "Teiseikoron," in ibid., 233, 234, 240.

53. For Yamaji's account of Cheng's problems, see esp. ibid., 266–80.

54. Yamaji, *Shinaron,* 14–18 (quotes at 14 and 16). See also Masui Tsuneo, "Naitō Kōnan to Yamaji Aizan," in *Kindai nihon to chūgoku, jō,* ed. Takeuchi Yoshimi and Hashikawa Bunsō (Tokyo: Asahi Shinbunsha, 1974), 283–98.

212 Creating Difference

courage, speech, power, and money, what he called mammonism (figs. 5 and 6). Such egoism had not yet developed in Japan because it had only recently abolished the feudal system and still possessed a form of communalism.[55] In other words, Japan was younger.

Although Yamaji did not demonstrate the progression of culture from China to Japan, he too assumed that Japanese have much to teach Chinese, and felt that the latter should listen. (Of course, there would have been strong disagreement among Yamaji, Naitō, and Shiratori on which Japanese the Chinese should listen *to*.) Yamaji, though, used the allegory of a Confucian family to describe this ideal relationship. In one case *shina* lacked trust: "It is a neighboring family [*ie*] that is separated only by a single fence. Nevertheless, we cannot touch their hearts with ours. Chinese jealousy is the disease." In another, China was an ungrateful wife: although dependent on others, it turns around and acts superior. "It has to be said that the position of China, while pitiful, resembles the position of a miserable wife who says, 'One hundred years of suffering and happiness, depending on others.'" It was also infelicitous: "China is not only a powerless country like a single woman, it is an infelicitous country like a prostitute."[56] As in these Confucian relationships, Yamaji was placing China as the inferior in an ethical hierarchy (even when they were called our "second brethren" [*daini no dōhō*]), the one to be guided, taught, and occasionally scolded. The problem with *shina* was that it no longer understood and adhered to these ethical, oriental relationships.

Yamaji found lessons for China in the past. While the story of Cheng Ch'eng-kung illustrated the difference between Japanese and Chinese, Cheng's failure was to succumb to the principal weakness, the "disease of the Chinese," the absence of cohesiveness.[57] The implication is that had he remained loyal and filial—that is, followed those traits of his Japanese half—he would have succeeded. On a different level, using the Ming relationship with Taiwan as a historical allegory

55. The estimate of three thousand years is Yamaji's (*Shinaron*, 17); see also Masubuchi Tatsuo, "Rekishi ninshiki ni okeru shōkoshugi to genjitsu hihan," in *Rekishika no dōjidai shiteki kōsatsu ni tsuite* (Tokyo: Iwanami Shoten, 1983), 171–224. I am indebted to Gotō Gimpei for bringing Masubuchi's article on the role of feudalism in Yamaji's writings to my attention.

56. Yamaji, *Shinaron*, 124, 110, 112. These images are similar to the concept behind a popular film, *Shina no yoru* (The Night of China), in which a Japanese boat captain saves a Chinese, marries her, and shows great patience in his attempt to civilize her despite frequent betrayals.

57. Here he used the character for Han Chinese to imply the innateness of this troubling characteristic; Yamaji, "Teiseikoron," in *Shinaron*, 266–80.

Fig. 5. Using U.S. dollars to attract the Chinese masses,
Yuan Shi-kai discovers, "I've run out of bait!"
Taiyō 19, no. 12 (1913): 47.

Fig. 6. The supporter of the provisional government in Nanking (Sun Yat-sen), on the right, states, "It is best to win," while his other half, who supports Yuan, states, "It is even better to have money." *Taiyō* 19, no. 12 (1913): 46.

for contemporary relations between China and Japan, Yamaji raised four principal points supporting Japan's closer ties with the continent: (1) that Taiwan (Japan) must not lose its rights to the sea, (2) that trade is an island's lifeline, (3) that a base on the continent is important to maintain trade and one's rights, and (4) that the Ming (Chinese) probably could not unify into a nation.[58] Yamaji, in sum, offered historical reasons for the inability of Chinese to form a nation, emphasized the importance of Japan's maintaining its position on the continent, and saw it as natural for Japan to take the leadership role in *tōyō,* culturally and militarily.

DISAGREEMENT WITHIN THE WHOLE

The differences among Shiratori, Naitō, and Yamaji were ones of degree, but those differences blinded them to their fundamental similarities. Ironically, the more they studied China, the farther they

58. Ibid.

moved Japan away from Asia. This separation is perhaps best illustrated by Naitō's frustrated complaint that the Chinese did not understand their own culture:

Because of a lack of historical understanding the new men of China do not know the abuses and strong points of the past. There are many who think that the most progressive view is simply to eradicate all of China's culture and graft on Western culture regardless of good or bad. If implemented, the result would be either failure or even worse abuses than those of the past. Since the first revolution up through today, the above ideas have been circulated in the debates on reform in China. But contrary to expectations, foreigners who have researched China's long history possess a more accurate opinion.[59]

The foreigner who knew best was, of course, Naitō. He understood the overall trends of the culture of *tōyō,* and when others, especially the Chinese, understood those trends they would realize that Japan's actions were for the good of China. A recent biographer described well, though inadvertently, the monologic manner in which Naitō took possession of this object, *shina:*

Here was a man who had devoted his life to the exposition of the greatness of Chinese culture, who was deeply and personally concerned with the state of affairs in contemporary China, and who assumed that Japan would play a part in Chinese reform, even if only as a model. Now the Chinese had turned on him not only as a Japanese, but on *his* Chinese culture, too; they seemed to be rejecting any place for Japan in Chinese reform and to be blaming their own cultural tradition for China's present sorry state. In short, they both condemned Naitō's politics and disregarded the fruits of his Sinological studies.[60]

Here, history gave Naitō possession of *shina.* The revolutionaries who rejected Naitō's China, or "*his* Chinese culture," understood better than Naitō that his politics and "fruits" of research benefited China only as long as it accepted and remained in its historical place, as defined by Japan.

The result of such a narrative is evident. Now that the foundation, the philosophy of history, had been established, objective research could be used and manipulated to authorize present conditions, but within a rather narrow scope. The Japanese could now manipulate historical knowledge for their own purpose and, to use Foucault's term, impose their own "Egyptianism."[61] The extent to which China had

59. Naitō, *Shinshinaron,* 542–43.
60. Fogel, *Politics and Sinology,* 273; italics in the original.
61. Foucault, "Nietzsche, Genealogy, History," 152.

become wrapped up within Japan's world was summed up in Shiratori's prescription for the revival of Chinese culture:

We believe that there is no other way; above all, Sino-Japanese mutual cooperation is the shortest route. For this reason, through cooperation with Japan they can combine and absorb both the culture of the world that is concentrated here and Japan's unique culture. They do not have to go to Europe and America for Occidental culture; everything is abundant in present-day Japan. It is most convenient and economical to seek it in Japan. Sino-Japanese mutual cooperation yearns for the following way of thinking from both peoples. At this time, Japanese citizens should not look down on contemporary Chinese culture. They must sufficiently recognize and heartfully appreciate the positive contributions of Chinese culture in nurturing that of Japan in the past. At the same time, the Chinese people must recognize and respect the creative power of a superior culture and the possessors of the power of understanding. . . . Chinese intellectuals must eliminate their condescension that what they might call *chūgoku* is the teacher and Japan the student because ancient Japan used Chinese culture as a model. They must moderate their unwillingness to admit that Japan, which is one step ahead in adapting Occidental culture, is ahead of *chūgoku*. It is certainly not imitation when Japan absorbs the culture of other countries. This same attitude exists in the case of China, Europe, and America. We certainly have to direct attention to rectifying this [attitude].[62]

This statement suggests, however, that the prescriptions for China's revival were intricately tied to Japan's own identity. This relationship was not merely one of the colonizer extracting from the colonized, for the history, rules, and rituals that emerged defined the rights and obligations of both. In allowing this understanding of Japan, *shina* served as an integral part of that knowledge, a part that deserved—and rightfully so—significant respect. But the praise was for antiquity—a Chinese culture no later than the Sung period from which Japan had borrowed considerably. The culture that Japan adapted was the best that China had to offer, but after that high point of Chinese civilization, that history, according to these Japanese historians, virtually stopped. Even though Shiratori and Naitō differed in their narrative of this history, the centripetal tendencies of language discussed by Bakhtin were certainly at work among these eminent Sinologists;[63] China as the revered culture of Asia existed only in the past. The use of the word *chūgoku* in the above quote is important, for Shiratori (and Naitō) clearly rejected any notion of Chinese centrality. The Chinese must first

62. Shiratori, "Kigen nisenroppyaku nen o mukaete kan ari," in *SKZ* 10:440–41.
63. For a discussion of the way that language organizes diverse and contradictory pasts, see the Introduction.

admit, before change could occur, that *shina* had been superseded by other cultures (fig. 7). From this distinction between the China of past and present, the term *shina* derived its meaning. After the beginnings and philosophical underpinnings of theories and symbols that supported an argument for harmony, loyalty, and cohesiveness had been extracted, China became the opposite of these qualities. Metaphors of harmony were now applicable only to Japan, while those of conflict, dissension, individualism, and self-interest were used to describe cultures outside Japan.

Boundaries of the Discourse

In his study of this discourse on China, Nomura Kōichi commented on its increasing restrictiveness: "The activities of those who were aroused by the so-called 'China problem' and tried to understand it as substantively related to problems in Japan moved abreast with the Meiji, Taishō, and Shōwa periods, when such differences [between the two countries] were rendered abstract. And while the parameters for action were contracting, the arena of activity rose higher and higher, beyond the power structure."[64] Nomura was describing the increasing gravitation of activists such as Miyazaki Tōten, Kita Ikki, and Ozaki beyond the center of government. Even writers such as Yamaji, not known for radical writing or activism, saw the government as the central actor that had erred. In 1916 he wrote that the China problem, especially the increasing Chinese distrust of Japan, was becoming worse because of inept government policy: "We cannot but deplore the directionless and incompetent foreign policy of imperial Japan."[65] These intellectuals believed that others did not properly understand the true conditions in China and that only he had the answer. This dissatisfaction reflects the way the separation of knowledge from contemporary *shina* had restricted the arena for activity.

The problem, however, was not a lack of proper understanding, but the nature of what understanding there was. As Nomura's perceptive comment suggests, *tōyōshi*, which established an understanding of the different parts of Asia, both facilitated action (no matter how

64. Nomura Kōichi, *Kindai nihon no chūgoku ninshiki* (Tokyo: Kenbun Shuppan, 1981), 205.
65. Yamaji, *Shinaron*, 124.

Fig. 7. The young Japanese with a modern airplane is confronted by an old Chinese with a biplane built from plans. The Chinese proudly exclaims, "What do you think, aren't you envious?" *Taiyō* 27, no. 7 (1921): 141.

misguided) and restricted the range of alternatives. As *shina* became an object of study that explained what the problems were and how Japan must correct them, contemporary conditions and events became increasingly separated from "objective" interpretations. Because this discourse on *shina* functioned as that which unified Japan's rather disparate pasts, it would have been difficult to alter "objectivity" without changing Japan's self-understanding. One might say that Japan was beholden to *shina* for providing its past, but at the same time, as the leader of a *tōyō* that integrated *shina* and Japan, Japan needed *shina* to affirm its modern identity as well.

In the 1930s, numerous intellectuals concerned with Japan's relations with China seemed to recognize that such contradictions of history had brought Japan's understanding of contemporary Asia to a standstill. For example, Tachibana Shiraki (1881–1945) stated, "It [Japan] is already troubled over the limits [*ikizumari*] [of modernity] and is struggling to open some kind of new society."[66] Both Tachibana's and Ozaki's search for answers took them to Marxism, on quests for more objective data, and to employment with organizations that fostered Japan's imperialist policies, such as the Research Bureau of the South Manchurian Railway Company (SMR). As Ozaki put it, "Grasping the China problem from the position of a leftist has completely fascinated me. But Marxist research did not arouse my interest in the China problem; contrarily, recent changes in the China problem deepened my interest in Marxist theory."[67] Yet while Ozaki looked to Marxism to close the gap between knowledge and actual conditions, Tachibana discerned a similar problem in the application of Marxist scholarship. Tachibana acknowledged a considerable debt to Marxism, but he was also critical of that theory when applied to Asia:

While observing social movements in a wide-ranging area, Peking, Shanghai, Hong Kong, and Canton, I gradually noticed that there was something missing in Marxist theory and methodology. In other words, is the character [*shitsu*] of society in both the Occident and the orient not different? Therefore, while we must of course plan both the reform and development of oriental [*tōyō*] society, I have become uneasy that, fundamentally, contemporary Marxist method and theory have been created from European history and social organization. Is it not impossible to shoehorn both this theory and methodology into the orient?[68]

66. Quoted in Ozaki Hotsumi, *Gendai shinaron* (Tokyo: Keisō Shobō, 1964), 218.
67. Nomura, *Kindai nihon no chūgoku ninshiki*, 177–206 (quote at 177).
68. Quoted in Ozaki, *Gendai shinaron*, 216–17.

The writings of Ozaki and Tachibana also indicate the difficulty of extracting themselves from the rigid and predefined categories of *tōyō*; they sought different frameworks that eliminated the hierarchy of progress or dialectic materialism to remove Japan from the confines of its past, *shina*, and to establish new grounds for understanding the complexity of contemporary China.

Both scholars identified the linear structure of *tōyō* as a principal problem and sought ways to overturn that structure. For Ozaki, a major problem in Japan's understanding of Asia lay in the fact that Asia was always depicted in terms of the past. China, he exclaimed, is diverse and to understand it one has to grasp everything; it is a living entity, not merely the remains of a once-great civilization. China should not be reduced to an area that was carved up, spatially, intellectually, or temporally, and studied. He stated, "It is essential that [knowledge on China] be scientific. However, experimentation is not limited to a microscope and is not the dissection of a corpse. Vivisections are more important than other methods."[69]

Tachibana replaced the unilinearity of the Orient/Occident dichotomy by a different construct that did not predetermine cultural characteristics. He turned to Toennies's *Gemeinschaft* and *Gesellschaft*, which he rendered as the split between a communal society (*kyōdō shakai*) and an assembled society (*shūgō shakai*). Neither was better than the other, nor did one inevitably develop into the other. They were merely different. This distinguishing of societies shifted the difference between the West and Japan from a superior/inferior relationship to one of coeval types. This mode allowed for the rehistoricization of cultures according to different geocultural conditions, not a universalistic temporal framework:

In essence, using the diverse and fluid [peoples] near the Mediterranean Sea as the stage, Occidental culture responded to and developed according to various complex natural and social conditions in both periods of rapid development—the genesis, during ancient Greece and Rome, and the early modern period, during the Renaissance. Occidentals have turned this arbitrary point into the foundation of all that is normal, and that which differs is considered to be on a lower level. But from the position of an oriental [*tōyōjin*], this is certainly not the case; values of better or worse aside, the communal society, a characteristic of oriental society, should be considered as the basis of oriental culture.[70]

69. Quoted in Nomura, *Kindai nihon no chūgoku ninshiki*, 184.
70. Quoted in Ozaki, *Gendai shinaron*, 221–22.

The efficacy of Tachibana's construct was to reconstitute a past in which Japan was restricted neither to a limited vision of time nor to the categories through which history assigned meaning. Removing *shina* from Japan's past would, of course, unravel the historical narrative of Japan as the cultural pinnacle of *tōyō*. He agreed that early Japan had maintained close relations with China and fit into the Chinese orbit, and that until the nineteenth century both were primarily communal societies.[71] The major change in Japan occurred after the Meiji Restoration. "In short, this communal characteristic survives in all the people of the orient, beginning with China, and oppresses their development. It has largely been eliminated in Japan through great effort over several decades and has been replaced by a Western-style assembled society. Are the differences rather than the similarities between Japanese and Chinese society today not stronger?"[72] Japan, in other words, had changed and was no longer beholden to its past.

But Ozaki and Tachibana were still delimited by this discourse on *shina*. To extract China, they turned to the present, but they were unable to eliminate Japan's temporal superiority over *shina*. Their dilemma was that they sought to move beyond the power structure by using objective knowledge about *shina*—the same foundation that supported that structure. Ozaki was limited by his conviction in the scientific objectivity of Marxist theory. By the 1930s, the framework established in *tōyōshi* was so widespread that even a person such as Ozaki, who had spent five years in Shanghai and had witnessed and "lived" the revolution, believed in the objectivity of the material produced by the SMR. As Ozaki sought to go beyond government, therefore, he worked within it, used it, and tried to change it from the inside. He stated, "Especially because it was information obtained by the SMR, I believed that it could be trusted completely; in fact, of the information obtained from the SMR, there was nothing off the mark."[73]

The irony of this endeavor, of course, was that although he perceived the need to change the historical framework that gave Japan its understanding, Ozaki turned to the same source that gave that structure its power. In prewar Japan, knowledge had held a preeminent

71. Tachibana located the change of Chinese society toward a despotic bureaucratic system—the beginning of the stagnation of Chinese society—in the Sung period, while Hirano Yoshitarō placed it in the Sui dynasty. See ibid., 227–30.
72. Ibid., 218–19.
73. Quoted in Miyanishi Yoshio, *Mantetsu chōsabu to Ozaki Hotsumi* (Tokyo: Aki Shobō, 1983), 5.

position ever since the establishment of the bureaucratic state; it was the objective standard by which the possessor could lay claim to power, but in the same regard, because it was objective, those against established power could also obtain and use it.[74] Objective information was considered neutral; it was also necessary for exposing the "deficiencies of scientific methodology" and formulating a different construct that, with Marxist theory, could provide alternate temporal distinctions within East Asia.

Thus, while Ozaki saw the need to consider China as a diverse, living entity, this sense of difference existed only in conditions within China. China was still an object from which information could be obtained to create better policies. Although Ozaki had attempted to eliminate the temporal hierarchy that set parameters for Japan's relations with China, he assumed the sameness of China and Japan, that they were part of a single politico-economic unit against the West. Hence, he could not eliminate the hierarchy altogether. China was still an object to be acted upon.

Tachibana recognized that this subject-object relation hindered Japan's understanding and relations with China. He argued that a main problem of Japanese intellectuals was that they always considered the people of Asia objectively—that is, from the position of knower. But like Ozaki, he also assumed that some type of Asian entity was necessary to resist Western imperialism. To resolve this quandary, Tachibana proposed that Asians be treated as equals; then they would realize the advantages of following Japan.[75] In other words, it was not only important to take *shina* out of Japan's past, but it was also important not to place it in a fixed category in which the knower, Japan, defined the known, *shina*. Nevertheless, the possibilities open to create an understanding that was not subject to the same limitations of Marxism and positivism proved more elusive. Tachibana's strategy was to argue for a society that could accommodate diverse characteristics, primarily by freeing past and present from the invidious connotations of archaic and modern, bad and good.

Their resolution to free Japan from the confines of a history of *tōyō* was through a union of East Asian countries that emphasized the po-

---

74. Silberman, "Bureaucratic State in Japan."
75. In the 1920s Yanaihara Tadao proposed a policy of home rule in Taiwan and Korea. This, he believed, would reduce pressure for independence and increase recognition of the benefits of membership in the Japanese empire. See Peattie, "Japanese Attitudes Toward Colonialism," 114–18.

litical rather than the cultural. Ozaki saw these changes as a means for unleashing the potential for reform in Japan as well as abroad. China was now necessary to help Japan because its own revolutionary impetus was weak. "In order for Japan to reach this point of transition, I first aimed at establishing a people's cooperative [*minzoku kyōdōtai*] among the East Asian people [*tōa minzoku*] because close mutual support of the three peoples—in the form of a *shina* that is completely under the hegemony of a Japan that has broken from the Soviet Union and capitalist structures and of the Chinese Communist party—is the necessary nucleus."[76] *Shina*, then, or the people of China, provided the means for Ozaki to correct Japan's domestic troubles, expunge harmful Western ideas from Asia, and reform Asia into an integral whole. The new space he proposed would be characterized by a political-economic union (*tōa*—East Asia) rather than a cultural one (*tōyō*).

Tachibana proposed a more flexible system in which Western concepts and the notion of a *kyōdōtai* (communal body) could coexist. His total system was described as a pyramid, with the emperor at the pinnacle and the huge middle comprising both *kyōdō* and *shūgō* forms. It was in this middle area that Tachibana's ideal society allowed for a variety of new organizations, such as the military (through the draft), consumer organizations, and cultural organizations. The point of his system was to avoid the extremes and allow for diversity within a whole. He emphasized three points: (1) a suitable distribution between the progressive and flowing elements of *Gesellschaft* was needed to ensure that the conservative and preservationist tendency of *Gemeinschaft* did not lead to stagnation; (2) it was necessary to eliminate the tendency of *Gemeinschaft* to revert to the old-fashioned; and (3) positive value inhered in a society that accepted contradictions and variety, including a respect for the elements of *Gesellschaft* (though not all parts), as long as unity and harmony were not broken.[77]

Although Tachibana separated Japan's past from that of China, he also envisioned the possibility of reuniting Japan and China within a slightly different *kyōdōtai*. Tachibana used different ideographs to distinguish the two types of *kyōdōtai* as to precise meaning. The symbol for *kyōdō* within Japan uses the *kyō* for *tomo* (sameness, togetherness), while that for the international level, symbolizing a cooperative body of different peoples (*minzoku*), incorporated the character used in *kyōryoku* (cooperate). The difference in nuance, according to Tachibana,

76. Quoted in Nomura, *Kindai nihon no chūgoku ninshiki*, 200.
77. Ozaki, *Gendai shinaron*, 235–36.

is that the former "ignores the individual" while the latter "thinks first of the individual and signifies the cooperation of fellow individuals."[78] This separation of the domestic from the international *kyōdōtai* corresponds with the metaphors that Shiratori used to distinguish international society from Japan. Whereas domestic Japan was still depicted in terms of harmony, loyalty, and communality, the international scene remained tied to individualism and competition. Tachibana's concept of relations among peoples of East Asia, however, was conceived as political need rather than cultural affinity: "I believe that to emancipate oriental people [*tōyō minzoku*] and to satiate ethnic demands [*minzoku-shugiteki yōken*] there is no other way than to combine all the people of *tōyō*. The problem is the formula for union, but one body of people is a relatively versatile and malleable body."[79]

As the character *kyō* in the international *kyōdō* suggests, the nation-state took priority in Tachibana's new cooperative entity. Here, he attempted to accommodate both the perceived needs of Japan's growth and expansion and the demands of other Asian countries for equality in a union that would stand up to Western exploitation. Tachibana did call for a reappraisal of Japanese policy toward the continent, the goal being recognition of each nation-state on its own terms rather than through predefined categories; in that way, he hoped, Japan would avoid emulating Germany's mistaken invasion of Belgium, Holland, and Poland. "Today for the first time we have the sincerity and ability to achieve respect for nationalistic demands. I feel that politically there is absolutely no other way than to establish a position of equality [*byōdō*] [with Asia]. If Japan returns to an equal position, then I believe that all countries, like it or not, will recognize Japan's leadership as objective fact."[80] Despite his realization that the objectification of Asian countries was a result of the monologic language of *tōyō*, Tachibana could not relinquish Japan's preeminent position in Asia. He argued, as did most other Japanese at the time, that the adoption of a policy that depended not on force but on persuasion would sway other countries to accept the geocultural order that most Japanese had declared as fact.

In hindsight, Ozaki's and Tachibana's approaches seem like little more than intellectual exercises in coercing East Asian countries to join with Japan. Both had shifted to a political union, *tōa*, from the natural, time-

78. Ibid., 238–39.
79. Ibid., 240.
80. Ibid., 240.

less cultural entity, *tōyō*. Ozaki's union consisted strictly of China and Japan (by now, Japan also included Korea and Manchuria), whereas Tachibana hoped that China, Java, India, and Annam would join his union. Both extended the political venue that Naitō opened within the geocultural unit beyond the political structure to a regional political system. But while they were right to alter the nature of the relation from cultural to political, they still relied on components of *tōyō*. Tachibana used a social typology reminiscent of *tōyō* that exposed the limitations of his acceptance of difference: "Those to whom we feel the greatest kindredness and who can reassuredly bring this [union] about have to be those who are part of the same social structure, of the same social ideology [*rinen*] and culture. In short, it is the union into a co-operative society of like-minded people."[81] Ozaki, for his part, argued that a revolution in Japan was necessary to remove *shina* from Japan's past. The extremeness of Ozaki's formulation indicates the narrow realm of possibilities: Japan—and its understanding of *tōyō*—could not change unless *shina* did.

Clearly, by 1940 the perceived alternatives available to the Japanese were severely constricted. The historians and activists discussed in this chapter did not question the integrity of a *tōyō*; it was an objective fact that Japan was the only country of *tōyō* that had successfully combined Eastern values and Western techniques. Japan was the leader of this realm, and regardless whether the union was a natural cultural union or political act of need, there was little room for dissent (fig. 8).

Japan's self-defined obligation to *tōyō* was captured in Satō Haruo's "Song of the Dawn in Asia":

> Singapore, the celebrated
> Showcase of modern weapons,
> The bastion of infamy, has fallen.
> The heads of the hobgoblins have dropped
> Under the keen Japanese swords.
> Ah, the calamity of Asia
> Surely now will be extirpated.[82]

Satō's hobgoblins represent the imperialism of the West, modernity, and the root of Asia's ills. By the twentieth century, the West served as an increasingly negative ideal against which intellectuals argued for the protection, reform, or development of both Japan and the continent.

81. Ibid., 246.
82. Donald Keene, *Dawn to the West: Japanese Literature of the Modern Era* (New York: Holt, Rinehart & Winston, 1984), 934.

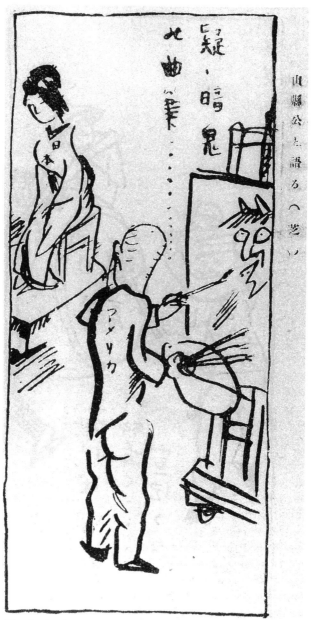

Fig. 8. An American painter's depiction of the beautiful
Japanese model as devil is indicative of American
misunderstanding of Japan's true self. The title is
"The Distorted Brush of the Devil of Suspicion."
Taiyō 27, no. 7 (1921): 140.

But because of the conviction in the objectivity of this history, blame for misunderstanding Asia was placed on the West, not on Japan itself. Shiratori and Naitō argued that it was the meddling of the West in East Asia that upset Japan's rightful role, whereas Ozaki believed that Japan's acceptance of Western capitalist and imperialist structures had prevented further progress. The presence of the West, in short, reinforced the need for an Asian union, whether it be cultural or politico-economic. The West also accounted for the absence of fixed boundaries delineating that which was *tōyō;* it was a spirit and innateness that was somehow different. The novelist Tanizaki Jun'ichirō captured this sense of orientalism (*tōyōshugi*):

First of all, what is meant by the term? This is not entirely clear even to me, but briefly stated, it refers to oriental aesthetic preferences, ways of thinking, physical build, character. I am not sure just how to describe it, but I can sense in the Orient something special and different from the Occident, not only in literature and art but in everything, from politics, religion, and philosophy down to the happenings of ordinary daily life and the small details of clothing, food, and shelter.[83]

This "sense" makes *tōyō* wonderfully malleable; as events and goals changed, explanations for problems were attributed to the West, while *tōyō* provided the historical data for corrective measures. But because prognoses were filtered through an idealized West and a romanticized past, alternatives were limited and knowledge did not necessarily match contemporary problems—though they could be made to fit. Because of the belief in objectivity, that is, it was much more difficult to change that knowledge, for it required a different conception of Japan itself. Thus it was necessary for Japan to convince, through persuasion or force, other Asian countries to understand their orientalness and Japan's preeminence—when this occurred, those other countries would accept Japan's leadership as well.

83. Ibid., 756.

CHAPTER SIX

Archeology: The Institutionalization of *Shina*

The image of antiquity had been recovered but at the same time it ceased to speak directly to the modern world. History was becoming academic. What it discovered might be archeologically true but it was irrelevant to the concerns of a later age.

Myron Gilmore, *Humanists and Jurists*

During the late 1920s and throughout the 1930s more and more observers, including Yamaji, Tachibana, and Ozaki, complained that the Japanese government, intellectuals, military, businessmen, and public did not understand China. One potential resolution to this problem was the further research and the establishment of new research institutions, but paradoxically, with the rise in research activity misunderstanding only increased. Criticism was generally directed at others, but as we saw with Shiratori, Naitō, Yamaji, Ozaki, and Tachibana, debate always revolved around a single instrumental question: How could Japan make the rest of Asia understand? As a whole, the chorus was in harmony. Why, then, were some of the most knowledgeable and intelligent figures in Japan unable to extract themselves from this dilemma?

Science, of course, unified the various members of the chorus. Scientific research depends on replicability, allowing events and objects to be objectively and neutrally studied, tested, and verified. Numerous scholars, government officials, businessmen, China adventurers, imperialists, and Marxists were actively engaged in seeking a better understanding of China. But with most, contrary to their goals, their separation from China widened. As historical knowledge became institutionalized, certain norms were created by which truth was judged, and those norms, whether accurate at any point or not, did not change as quickly as current events demanded.

An overemphasis on rationality and objectivity prevented many Japanese from fully grasping these changes. Understanding had less to do with sympathy or political ideology (in a particularistic sense) than with one's relation to the overall discourse. In his criticism of positivistic, or what he called "documentary," history, Dominick LaCapra points out that there is often little difference between the historian who is sympathetic to the object of study and one who approaches it objectively; the problem is the nature of the historian's conversation with the past. History is often written as a revision of other histories. Yet in fact, that dialogue occurs among historians, not with the past or pasts. As LaCapra put it, "This restricted view obscures the strangeness of a dialogue with the dead who are reconstructed through their 'textualized' remainders, and it resists any broader reconceptualization of the nature of historical understanding in terms of the interaction between 'documentary' knowledge and 'rhetorical' exchange."[1]

The existence of this separation among prewar Japanese specialists on China was acknowledged in the 1960s debate over the Asia and Ford Foundations.[2] A number of former employees of the South Manchurian Railway's Research Bureau criticized the role of that institution's researchers—including themselves—for their lack of self-criticism and reflection. A particularly strong statement was issued by Noma Kiyoshi, who attempted to explain the contradiction between researchers' sympathy toward China and their participation in the research projects of this imperialistic institution:

Were we clearly and keenly conscious that we are Japanese and were members of the Research Bureau of the SMR? We were not. We thought that we "are doing nothing wrong" and subjectively that "we feel sympathy and especially

1. Dominick LaCapra, *History and Criticism* (Ithaca, N.Y.: Cornell University Press, 1985), 36.
2. Just after Japan renewed the security treaty with the United States, the Asia and Ford Foundations offered grants for research on Asia. Although the treaty and grants were not explicitly connected, this proposal rekindled memories of the connection between government, funding, and research direction, and sparked considerable debate on whether Japanese researchers should accept such funds.

compassion for the Chinese farmer." The self-awareness that we were one wing of Japanese imperialism was, at the very least, obscure and poorly understood. The ambiguous awareness of our position rendered our understanding of the Chinese people's resistance and movements obscure and placed them outside our field of vision. Therefore, while verbally criticizing Japan's colonial control over China, we could not entertain serious doubts over its continuation because we clearly were unaware. Consequently, we did not question this research that turned the Chinese rural village into an object and was not conducted in Japan. Instead, we took the position of "self-confident researchers."[3]

The culprit here, according to Noma, was objectivity. Had they themselves only been more self-reflective, their research might have been different. One problem was the transparency of Japan's "position," its temporal and political superiority over China. Also, while Noma correctly pointed to overreliance on objectivity, the problem extended to the far-ranging structure that grew as research became increasingly specialized. This structure was reproduced in several ways; the students of Shiratori, for example, were attempting to produce objective and accurately detailed studies of increasingly delimited regions and topics, whereas other researchers sought ever more accurate knowledge to understand better the socioeconomic conditions of the occupied territories. Despite disagreement over details, different views, and conflicting ideologies (in a particularistic sense), these researchers shared a common view in a totality that "integrates the present with the past."[4] This totality was acceptable to both Marxists and imperialists; it was repeated through personal experience, in the writings of scholars and publicists, and in government policy, and it was refracted through events on the continent.[5]

In this chapter I will focus on the research institutions most closely related to Shiratori and other academics, in particular the Research Bureau of the SMR. Although numerous other organizations (the Tōa Dōbun Kai, for instance), the China experts in the Foreign Ministry, and the cultural policies of the Foreign Ministry could easily be included in this chapter,[6] my purpose is not a comprehensive treatment. Instead I hope to suggest that these research efforts were all part of an

3. Noma, "Chūgoku nōson kankō chōsa," 14.
4. Quoted in LaCapra, *History and Criticism*, 24–25.
5. For two essays that discuss Japan's China policy, see Gordon M. Berger, "The Three-dimensional Empire: Japanese Attitudes and the New Order in Asia, 1937–1945," *Japan Interpreter* 12 (Summer 1979): 355–83; and Peattie, "Japanese Attitudes Toward Colonialism."
6. See, for example, Reynolds, "Training Young China Hands"; and Sophia Lee, "The Foreign Ministry's Cultural Agenda for China: The Boxer Indemnity," in Duus, Myers, and Peattie (eds.), *Japanese Informal Empire in China*, 272–306.

institutional structure that relied on objective knowledge for which the discourse on *shina* set the norms for an understanding that encompassed both those who believed themselves to be sympathetic toward China and those who sought to control it. Much debate, disagreement, and criticism of various methodologies existed, but although China was the object, it was largely left out of that debate or included only as a data source.

Constructing a Research Network

In spite of his reputation for detailed and objective historical research, Shiratori's concept of the role of the historian cannot be compared to the gap between historians and the public in the United States today.[7] Shiratori published numerous articles using history to explain contemporary events in popular publications such as *Sekai, Chūō kōron*, and *Tōa no hikari*, ones that are often used to unearth popular Japanese attitudes.[8] Just as important, Shiratori argued that the work of historians is crucial to politicians as well as intellectuals.

Nevertheless, he separated knowledge into two types: pure research of the academic realm and practical research suited to political and economic needs. Pure research involved objective knowledge of Asian cultures—accurate descriptions of historical events and characteristics of peoples—which he compared to the academic research of European Orientalists. Practical research, in contrast, was necessary to understand accurately and to create policies related to the continent, especially Manchuria and Korea. Through this division, Shiratori's history merged with politics on an institutional level. It was no accident that his organizational efforts began after the Russo-Japanese War, when historical and contemporary information was needed for the administration of southern Manchuria and for the protection and development of Korea.

Just as the notion of *tōyō* was developed in opposition to the West, Western research institutions also supplied the rationale for an institutional structure to support that idea. In a short reminiscence about Gotō Shinpei, Shiratori recalled that he first recognized the need for

7. For a discussion of this separation, see Theodore S. Hamerow, "The Bureaucratization of History," *American Historical Review* 94 (June 1989): 654–60.
8. See, for example, the list of publications in volume ten of his collected works. He also published articles in *Bunshō sekai, Shin kokumin, Mainichi denpō, Osaka mainichi shinbun, Yomiuri shinbun, Yamato shinbun, Kōdō, Yūshū, Taiyō, Kokuhon, Shien*, and *Akarui ie*.

collective research on Asia after visiting the various Orientalist institutions in Europe just before the Russo-Japanese War. He stated with admiration and admonition, "Oriental studies in Europe was already fairly advanced, and the research findings that exert influence [ken'i] bring out the irony of what is continuously published in the world. To prevent the Japanese, the very same orientals, from succumbing to this research by European and American scholars, I advocated the necessity of establishing a major association for the research of oriental history by forming a union of scholars, industrialists, and politicians and conducting fundamental research on the orient."[9] To Shiratori, the connection between the historical knowledge generated by these Oriental institutes and empire was clear: England had its Royal Asiatic Society with branches in India, China, and Korea; France had the Ecole des Langues Orientales Vivantes, Société Asiatique, and also the Ecole Française d'Extrême Orient in Hanoi; Germany had the Seminar für Orientalische Sprachen at the University of Berlin; and Russia had an Oriental Institute in St. Petersburg and also one in Vladivostok. In his mind, it was no coincidence that the region about which each country knew most corresponded to its own growing sphere of influence in Asia. In fact, he used the metaphor of war to urge all Japanese to support such research. After the Russo-Japanese War Shiratori wrote,

Our country's interests in the Far East certainly do not compare to those of each Occidental country. However, we still have no academic association devoted to the research of this region; there is no library to collect the numerous books written by Westerners; and consequently, there are few useful publications written by our countrymen. It is natural that our countrymen are in the dark about conditions in the Far East. But along with this surprising oversight among our countrymen, we fear that the power, which we gained through considerable effort in this victorious war, will disappear in a peaceful competition. Nevertheless, we intend to compete with Westerners over our interests here. It is for this reason that we cry out for research on Asia and hope to arouse the attention of the world.[10]

Such language, employing metaphors of war to describe future relations between Japan and the West, was not unusual after the Russo-Japanese War. Kenneth B. Pyle, for example, cited a civil servant who argued for national unity, self-sacrifice, increased taxes, and greater in-

9. Shiratori, "Mansenshi kenkyū no sanjūnen," *Kokuhon* 14 (August 1934), in *SKZ* 10:403.
10. Shiratori, "Ajia kenkyū wa sengo no ichidai jigyō nari," *Gakushūin hōninkai zasshi*, special issue (March 1910), in *SKZ* 10:55–56.

vestment to prepare for the "coming 'peaceful war' in which every country would be Japan's enemy."[11]

The significance of Shiratori's statement is that he used his position to identify the importance of research to contemporary affairs and to promote the founding of research institutions focused on *tōyō*. In retrospect, we see that this statement virtually sets out his agenda for correcting the errors of European Oriental studies. One of the purposes of the establishment of research institutions was to encourage knowledge and understanding of Asia. But it is evident here, as well as in quotes cited in previous chapters, that countering the research of the Orient by Europeans was important not as friendly scholarly competition, but as knowledge related to imperialism. While Shiratori believed that Japanese should be educated in the history and contemporary affairs of the continent, such learning was necessary not merely "for the sake of knowing China," but for the protection, and even defense, of Japan's interests in Asia.[12] He probably wrote on the possibility of losing the peaceful competition with the indignation of the Triple Intervention (1895) in mind;[13] but on a broader level, knowledge was important to solidify what was believed to be Japan's rightful position on the continent, in *tōyō*.[14]

Even though Shiratori distinguished between pure and practical research, the rationale for fostering pure research, which he viewed through the prism of contemporary affairs, was based on national interest. Whether the agenda was conscious or not, "pure" research, for example on the Mongols, folklore, language, the Chou dynasty, and Korean mythology, privileged a position that benefited one's own view, either as a scholar or as a nation, within the justifying framework of

11. Kenneth B. Pyle, "The Technology of Japanese Nationalism: The Local Improvement Movement, 1900–1918," *Journal of Asian Studies* 33 (1973): 57.

12. Takeuchi Yoshimi used this phrase in *Chūgoku o shiru tame ni*, which criticized the study of *shina* as an object for Japan's own ends and advocated the study of China as *chūgoku*, that is, apart from the narrow framework to which it had been restricted.

13. Soon after the signing of the Treaty of Shimonoseki, which ceded the Pescadores, Formosa, and Liaotung Peninsula to Japan, Germany, France, and Russia "asked" the Japanese government to renounce possession of the Liaotung Peninsula "in the interests of peace." The government complied. For many Japanese this intervention served as a reminder that Japan must acquire even more power if it was to compete with Western nations.

14. The vision of Japan as the leader of *tōyō* and its defender against Western imperialism was not created by Shiratori and this discourse. One can identify numerous "first instances": in 1884, for example, when Japanese were debating the nature of Japan's connection to Asia, Sugita Teiichi warned that the yellow race was about to be devoured by the white race. See Hashikawa, "Japanese Perspectives on Asia," 331–32.

positivistic methodology. The discovery of the "source of what others know" established one's own view—the historical laws and parameters established through *tōyō*—as historically prior to all others. Even those who criticized academic historical research for being detached from reality used the same belief in objectivity when asserting the superiority of *their* understanding of the conditions and events that gave rise to contemporary conditions.

Certainly there was a difference in subject matter; the objects of "pure" *tōyōshi* were from the past, whereas practical research focused on contemporary events and issues. But whether pure or practical, to understand China researchers conducted scientific, objective, and detailed studies that were constrained by precisely the same epistemology and philosophy of history. An important difference in Shiratori's two forms of knowledge was the locus of research: pure research was to occur in university settings or affiliated institutions; practical research was to occur in centers tied to policymaking institutions.

ORGANIZING PURE SCHOLARS

One of Shiratori's goals was to organize a comprehensive academic organization that "promoted oriental studies [*tōyōshi*] by bringing together research on all of *tōyō* and scholars from throughout the world." His first attempt to organize specialists on Asia came just after the Russo-Japanese War, when, along with Torii Ryūzō, he undertook to form the Ajia Gakkai (Asia Society) in 1905. He stated retrospectively, "Because scholars assumed an independent posture, such research had little effect. Scholars from all fields must come together and cooperate. From this conviction, at the beginning of 1905—during the Portsmouth Conference—I emphasized that we had to unite those with even a small interest in research on Asia, form a major academic association of scholars in Japan, and conduct research using this power of cooperation."[15] Even though these efforts met with general apathy, in 1907 Shiratori convinced Katsura Tarō, president of the Tōyō Kyōkai (Oriental Society, formerly the Taiwan Kyōkai, founded by Katsura in 1898), to merge with his Ajia Gakkai. As an extension of this association they formed a research group that in 1909 began to publish the *Tōyō kyōkai chōsabu gakujutsu hōkoku*, which two years later

15. Shiratori, "Gotō haku no gakumon no kōseki," in *Warera no Gotō Shinpei haku* (1929), *SKZ* 10:387.

became the *Tōyō gakuhō* (Reports of the Oriental Society). Gotō assisted in the founding and funding of this publication.[16]
One reason that the creation of a scholarly society got off to a slow start was the small number of specialists. This lack is not surprising, for at the turn of the century research on China and Asia was in transition from the exegetical study of Chinese texts to the historical study of Asia. In 1896, the same year that Naka Michiyo was appointed to lecture on Chinese history and language at Tokyo Imperial University, Hayashi Taisuke was appointed to teach Chinese literature and philosophy. When Hayashi was forced to resign after students accused him of being old-fashioned (*furukusai*), he was replaced by Ichimura Sanjirō. Shiratori succeeded Naka in 1904. The systematic training of specialists on *tōyō* began under Ichimura and Shiratori, who held these positions until 1925.[17]

The list of scholars trained by Shiratori is impressive, and his legacy survives still today, his influence still acknowledged in the memoirs of many a Japanese orientalist. For example, in a series of interviews with Asian specialists, the sociologist Nakane Chie referred to the "tradition of Professor Shiratori Kurakichi."[18] A grand, and not inaccurate, claim in the centennial history of the University of Tokyo also acknowledged Shiratori, though not by name; "It is no exaggeration to say that almost all the faculty [of the University of Tokyo and other prestigious schools such as the Universities of Kyoto, Waseda, and Keio] were initially graduates of the Faculty of Letters of the University of Tokyo, in particular the Department of Oriental History."[19] Those trained up to 1916 included Hamada Kōsaku, Haneda Tōru, Harada Yoshito, Hashimoto Masukichi, Hori Kentoku, Ikeuchi Hiroshi, Imanishi Ryū, Inaba Iwakichi, Ishida Mikinosuke, Fujita Toyohachi, Katō Shigeru, Kuwabara Jitsuzō, Matsui Hitoshi, Nakayama (formerly Nakamura) Kyūshirō, Shimizu Taiji, Wada Sei, and Yanai Watari. Of these historians, Harada, Ikeuchi, Fujita, Katō, Nakayama, Wada, and Yanai

16. Goi, *Kindai nihon to tōyōshigaku*, 67; and Shiratori, "Gotō haku no gakumon no kōseki," in *SKZ* 10:389.

17. Yoshikawa, *Tōyōgaku no sōshishatachi*, 238. *Tōkyō teikokudaigaku gakujutsu daikan, sōsetsu-bungakubu* (Tokyo: Tōkyō Teikoku Daigaku, 1942), 286–308, lists all the scholars who held positions in the department. A later history (*Tōkyō daigaku hyakunenshi*, 628–29), in contrast, has narrowed the narrative to the most influential scholars, attributing the beginning to Naka, a lecturer between 1898 and 1904, followed by Ichimura and Shiratori.

18. Nakane Chie, "Shakai kōzōronteki ajiakan," *Ajia*, September 1976, 270.

19. *Tōkyō daigaku hyakunenshi*, 628–69.

eventually took up positions at the University of Tokyo. Fujita left his professorship for the newly established University of Taipei in 1928, and Nakayama took a position at the University of Hiroshima. Hamada, Haneda, Imanishi, and Kuwabara were instrumental in the development of Sinology at the University of Kyoto. Shiratori also took some of his students with him in 1908 when he formed the Center for Historical and Geographic Research on Manchuria and Korea of the South Manchurian Railway. This, too, was a rather illustrious group: Yanai, Ikeuchi, and Wada would succeed him as professors at the University of Tokyo; Matsui went to work at Kokugakuin University, and Tsuda at Waseda University. Inaba and Seno were employed by the Government General of Korea to oversee the historical materials on Korea.

The role of this training program was to produce those who could fill the narrative gaps of history. Each student specialized in a different region and period of *tōyō*, filling in one more piece of the puzzle of the workings of that "inevitable mechanism" that, Shiratori believed, governs all societies. To return to his metaphor of a carpenter, his students were providing the different materials that go into the construction of a house. There was much diversity in the types of materials, but everything fit together according to the broader totality that their narratives were meant to help construct.[20]

Those familiar with the university system in Japan will not be surprised by the genealogy of *tōyōshigaku* at the University of Tokyo. After Shiratori and Ichimura retired in 1925, they were followed by Yanai and Ikeuchi, who had been associate professors there since 1918 and 1916, respectively. Yanai specialized in China and Mongolia during the Yuan dynasty, and Ikeuchi held the initial lectureship on Korean history. Upon Yanai's death in 1926, Fujita, a specialist on the Six Dynasties and the Western region, took over until he left for Taipei in 1928. Fujita was replaced by Wada Sei, a specialist on post–Yuan dynasty Mongols, Manchuria, and China.

A characteristic of the second generation of scholars is their greater degree of specialization. In contrast to Ichimura, who wrote general histories of China and *tōyō*, and to Shiratori, whose work crossed numerous boundaries, the next generation concentrated on specific periods, but still within the framework set by their mentor. For example, complementing Shiratori's study of pre–Yuan dynasty relations be-

20. For a discussion of Shiratori's concept of history see Chapter 1. His use of the metaphor of the carpenter can be found in Shiratori, "Shihitsu no kyokuchi."

tween the Northern people and China (the North-South dualism), Yanai focused on those relations during the Yuan dynasty, Fujita mainly studied the Six Dynasties and the Western region, and Wada conducted much of his work on post–Yuan relations between China and the Mongols.

In organizing research while at the South Manchurian Railway, Shiratori assigned topics to his students that allowed each to conduct a thorough, detailed, and accurate investigation: Matsui specialized in the Tatar dynasties, the Liao (907–1125) and Chin (1115–1234); Yanai worked on the period from the Yuan dynasty to the early Ming; Inaba worked on the late Ming through the Ch'ing dynasties; and Ikeuchi and Tsuda were responsible for materials up through the T'ang dynasty. Ikeuchi was also responsible for tribes in Manchuria and the Korean peninsula, such as the Jürchin, Hsien-pei, and Wu-huang, during the Yi dynasty, and Tsuda conducted research on other tribes that appeared on China's northern borders up through the Koryŏ dynasty, such as the Khitan, Hsiung-nu, and T'o-pa.[21]

The postwar generation of specialists should also be placed within this genealogy. Maejima Shinji, a student of Fujita and Ikeuchi, assumed a position at Keio University; Egami Namio, who has become known for his horseriders theory, was a student of Ikeuchi; Hatada Takashi, who worked in the Research Bureau of the South Manchurian Railway, was a student of Ikeuchi with a specialty on Korea; Mikami Jirō, a student of Ikeuchi and another Korea specialist, was Ikeuchi's successor; Yamamoto Tatsurō, trained by Ikeuchi and Wada, was the first to specialize in Southeast Asian history; Nakane Chie, the well-known University of Tokyo sociologist, was a student of Yamamoto, Wada, and Egami; and Enoki Kazuo, who became director of the Tōyō Bunko, studied under Ikeuchi.

A JAPANESE RESEARCH INSTITUTE FOR ORIENTAL STUDIES: TŌYŌ BUNKO

Without the proper research facilities for his students and other researchers it would have been difficult for Shiratori to accumulate sufficient data to solidify his historical framework. In 1924 he moved a step closer to his goal of a research structure comparable to that of the great European Oriental institutes with the founding of the

21. Hara Kakuten, *Gendai ajia kenkyū seiritsu shiron* (Tokyo: Keisō Shobō, 1984), 502.

Tōyō Bunko, an independent research library that proved a critical re-
source in Japan's competition with other nations. Finally, more than
twenty years after publishing his first articles in Europe, Shiratori felt
enough confidence in the level of research in Japan that he could display the achievements of Japanese specialists to European Orientalists
through the library's Western-language series *Memoirs of the Research
Department of the Tōyō Bunko*.[22] But more important, while the level of
this research was equal to that of Europe, it was also research that was
completely formulated and conducted by Japanese; it was not a reiter-
ation or imitation of Western Oriental studies. The "research themes"
and methodology belonged to Japan's own, original (*dokuji*) brand of
oriental studies, and thus were free from the ethnocentrism of the
Western Orientalists. In other words, this objective research was suited
to Japan's version of itself. The library provided the research facilities
for each succeeding generation of scholars to produce the monographs
that would affirm the premises of Japan's understanding of *tōyō*.

The Tōyō Bunko was based on the acquisition of the considerable
Far Eastern library (twenty-four thousand volumes) of Dr. George
Earnest Morrison, the Peking correspondent for the *London Times* (and
also Yuan Shih-kai's adviser during his ill-fated attempt to reestablish a
monarchy). This library was purchased in 1917 by Iwasaki Hisaya, the
eldest son of Iwasaki Yatarō, founder of Mitsubishi, through the mediation of Inoue Junnosuke and Odagiri Masunosuke of the Yokohama
Specie Bank. (Both companies had strong interests on the continent.)
The collection included publications, journals, and pamphlets on the
Far East in both Western and Asian languages, and although there
were few rare books, the library was highly regarded for its breadth.
After Iwasaki outbid his competitors, which included some of the more
prestigious American universities, the collection was temporarily
housed in a Mitsubishi building until 1923, when a permanent building at the present location in Komagome was completed.[23] When the
Tōyō Bunko was opened the following year, Shiratori, who had been
occasionally consulted about the potential and value of the library since
its initial availability, became the director of the research and library
departments.

22. Tsuda recalled, "What was shown to the world through these [English] publications was that in both quantity and quality our *tōyōshigaku* has been raised to the level
of that of Europe and is completely different from what it was twenty years ago. In both
research themes and methodology, *tōyōshi* took shape independently in our country over
those years and can now contribute to Oriental studies of the world" ("Shiratori hakushi
shōden," 56–57).

23. Tōyō Bunko, *Tōyō bunko jūgonen shi* (Tokyo: Tōyō Bunko, 1939), 1–11.

Upon his retirement from the University of Tokyo, Shiratori devoted his full attention to his duties as research director and to the promotion of research on Asia. Tsuda, who also served as a research associate of the library, summed up the activities of this center thus:

Since our country is concerned about its subordinate position in *tōyō* relative to Europeans and Americans with their grand designs, and about Chinese condescension toward us, a wide range of important individuals proposed that a major research institution under the auspices of the nation-state [*kokka*] be established to conduct documentary research, dispatch expeditions and investigators, train researchers, collect library materials, and publish the results of research throughout the world.[24]

Under Shiratori's leadership, the research division accomplished most of these goals: it accepted and trained young researchers from the major universities, sponsored conferences, collected materials, and issued three publications, the *Tōyō bunko ronso*, *Memoirs of the Research Department of the Tōyō Bunko*, and *Monographs in European Language Edited by the Tōyō Bunko*.

Shiratori's position as research director ensured a close connection between the library and the University of Tokyo, a connection that was perhaps most succinctly described in the history of that institution: "There was no direct relation with Tokyo Imperial University, but the faculty and students of the Department of Oriental History have received considerable assistance, and the staff of the research department of the Tōyō Bunko has maintained a very close relationship with the graduates and faculty of that department."[25] Administrative directors Ishida and then Enoki were students of Shiratori. The initial research staff consisted of many names by now familiar to the reader—Ikeuchi, Katō, Tsuda, Haneda, Harada, and Wada.[26]

Practical Study: Research Bureau of the South Manchurian Railway

In addition to pointing to the need to acquire greater expertise—"pure knowledge"—about the continent, Shiratori's division

24. Tsuda, "Shiratori hakushi shōden," 52.
25. *Tōkyō daigaku hyakunenshi*, 630.
26. Tōyō Bunko, *Tōyō bunkō jūgonen shi*, 38.

of pure and practical knowledge indicated a realization that information was needed for the economic administration of southern Manchuria and for the protection and development of Korea. Shiratori's opportunity to foster an institutional setting to encourage and channel research in this direction came through a meeting with Sawayanagi Masatarō (1865–1927), vice minister of education, who introduced Shiratori to Gotō, president of the newly formed South Manchurian Railway Company.

The SMR was formed in November 1906, just after the signing of the Portsmouth Treaty that ended the Russo-Japanese War.[27] The ostensible purpose of the SMR was to administer the railroad and land ceded to Japan under this treaty. Japan received Russia's leasehold in the Liaotung Peninsula, the seventy kilometers of Chinese Eastern Railway between Dairen and Changchun, as well as five spur lines, the right-of-way along this track, and rights and property of the Fushun and Yentai coal mines. In essence, the SMR controlled the major transportation, industrial, and urban centers of southern Manchuria.[28]

Under the leadership of Gotō, the SMR would become an aggressive arm of Japan's expansion onto the continent. Gotō set the tone for the next thirty years of activity. He brought with him his experience in the colonial administration of Taiwan, where he was well known for his use of research findings on local Taiwanese customs and society to develop administrative policy.[29] Matsuoka Kinpei, director of the East Asia Economic Research Center (Tōa Keizai Chōsakyoku) between 1911 and 1921, described the importance of science and objectivity in Gotō's planning of the Research Bureau: "He was a man who, above all, respected academics. He had a deep understanding of science and natural science. . . . Even in the management of operations, these fundamentals did not mix with feelings and had to originate from objective [reisei] plans and investigations . . . Both old and new materials were collected and classified scientifically."[30]

27. As a semipublic company, over half of its capital came from the issuance of 100,000 shares of stock, far from the 16,643,418 shares requested by 11,467 people. See Yamada Gōichi, Mantetsu chōsabu (Tokyo: Nikkei Shinsho, 1977), 29.

28. For a description of the South Manchurian Railway, see Ramon H. Myers, "Japanese Imperialism in Manchuria and the South Manchurian Railway Company, 1906–1933," in Duus, Myers, and Peattie (eds.), The Japanese Informal Empire in China, 101–32.

29. See E. Patricia Tsurumi, Japanese Colonial Education in Taiwan, 1895–1945 (Cambridge, Mass.: Harvard University Press, 1977).

30. Hara, Gendai ajia kenkyū seiritsu shiron, 345.

The Research Bureau, which was formed in April 1907, less than one year after the founding of the SMR, was to supply the objective knowledge for this policy of a "culturally attired military preparedness" (*bunsō bubi*).[31] Okamatsu Santarō (1871–1921), professor of law at the University of Kyoto and previously a member of Gotō's Taiwan colonial administration, was appointed managing director of the SMR and the initial director of the Research Bureau. The presence, indeed necessity, of the military on the continent was assumed, but practical research was not defined solely in terms of contemporary events. Gotō also sought historical and anthropological knowledge to explicate the social and economic customs of the Chinese. He had effectively used such knowledge in his colonial administration of Taiwan. For example, information uncovered through the Special Taiwan Customs Research Association (Zanji Taiwan Kyūkan Chōsakai) facilitated the reorganization of the police along the lines of the old *pao-chia* system (mutual aid and protection society). Such studies also facilitated the reform of land holdings and taxation so that producers had greater incentives to increase production.[32]

Research on Manchuria and Korea was carried out in three major divisions and divided into historical studies and contemporary research, which "scientifically analyzes political and economic movements from a global perspective."[33] The first division was located at the main office in Dairen and housed three subdivisions: the old customs research group (*kyūkan chōsahan*), the economic research group (*keizai chōsahan*), and the Russia research group (*roshia chōsahan*). The second division, the Center for Historical and Geographic Research on Manchuria and Korea (Mansen Rekishi Chiri Chōsabu), formed in January 1908 and housed in the Azabu district of Tokyo, was proposed and headed by Shiratori. The third division, the East Asia Economic Research Center (Tōa Keizai Chōsakyoku), was formed in November 1908. Its charge was to "collect and catalog all materials on the world economy, and in particular the East Asian economy, and, based on this information, be fully informed of the economic position of Japan as well as Manchuria and Mongolia."[34]

31. Yamada, *Mantetsu chōsabu*, 28.
32. See Han-yu Chang and Ramon H. Myers, "Japanese Colonial Development Policy in Taiwan, 1895–1906: A Case of Bureaucratic Entrepreneurship," *Journal of Asian Studies* 22 (1963): 433–49, esp. 439–43; for a description of the educational policy, see Tsurumi, *Japanese Colonial Education in Taiwan*.
33. Hara, *Gendai ajia kenkyū seiritsu shiron*, 344.
34. Itō Takeo, *Mantetsu ni ikite*, rev. ed. (Tokyo: Chikuma Shobō, 1982), 28.

At this early stage, historical, anthropological, and geographic research was given greater emphasis than "practical," especially economic, research. The most important of these research divisions was the old customs research group, headed by Okamatsu himself. Even though the stated purpose was very broad—to "investigate the civil and commercial customs" of China—research was limited to landholding and land usage customs in northern China. Gotō considered "research on the land and customs as the essential precondition for administering the continent. Knowing especially the legal and economic habits of the people [*minzoku*] is the fundamental secret to a successful colonial policy."[35]

The connection between such research on customs and imperial policy is clear. Early research focused on the landholding practices and laws in Manchuria, with the geographic area of inquiry limited first to that around Mukden, then incorporating Kirin province, which extended to the Amur region, and eventually including Mongolia. Researchers paid particular attention to matters concerning land for the railroad, the purchase of adjacent land, and land connected to company operations. These early studies, surprisingly, rarely involved any fieldwork, interviews, or data collection in the actual region of study. Researchers were preoccupied instead with collecting important documents, records, contracts, and descriptions of legal customs of China. Furthermore, the work was heavily historical, centering on land use and the formation of landholdings during the Ch'ing dynasty. The three basic focuses were real estate rights—mortgages, pawning, and rental; land categories—private, government, and bannerland—especially around Mukden, Kirin, and the Amur River; and comparatively new land categories introduced by the Ch'ing. The results of this research were published in nine reports between 1912 and 1915: *Lands of the People (Ippan minchi*, 3 vols.); *Official Villages Under the Imperial Household Department (Naimufu kansō)*; [Manchu] *Imperial Properties (Kōsan)*; *Lands of the Mongols (Mōchi)*; and three volumes on real estate rights: *Mortgage Customs (Tenken)*, *Pawning Customs (Ōken)*, and *Rental Rights (Soken)*.[36]

In addition to the larger research project on customs, researchers also conducted more specific studies. In 1909, at the request of the governor-general's office of Kwantung, the customs research group

35. Hara, *Gendai ajia kenkyū seiritsu shiron*, 478.
36. The compilers of these volumes were Kamefuchi Tatsunaga, Amagai Kensaburō, Miyauchi Toshiko, and Sugata Kumaemon.

submitted the "Outline of Old Land Customs of Kwantung" (*Kantōshū tochi kyūkan ippan*). This investigation, conducted by Amagai Kensaburō (1884–1962) and Kamefuchi Tatsunaga, was one of the few projects at that time in which researchers actually conducted fieldwork. This and other reports, such as the "Outline of Old Land Customs Along the Right of Way between Antung and Dairen" (*An-hō ensen tochi kyūkan ippan*) by Amagai and Miyauchi Toshiko, were no doubt helpful in effectuating the territorial expansion of the SMR.

Such information was useful in facilitating the resolution of an early land issue faced by the management of the SMR involving the settlement of land taken or used by the army during the war and the acquisition of additional land. The study of the land along the right-of-way included land classification and recognition of rights; it was useful in determining how much the land was worth, whom to pay, what rights the landlords and tenants held, the compensation due for water rights, and even how much to compensate for gravesites.[37] This information certainly strengthened the SMR position against Chinese and often resulted in settlement prior to litigation. The efficacy of this research to the SMR is evidenced by the increase of its holdings, from 14,672 to 18,800 hectares between 1906 (the company's first year) and 1908.[38]

Given this emphasis on customs, it is not surprising that Gotō "immediately approved" Shiratori's proposal for a research department to study the history and geography of Manchuria and Korea. Like Shiratori, Gotō believed in the necessity of accurate information, both historical and contemporary, on which to base policy decisions. Gotō stated, "In order to make Japan's unique destiny in *tōyō* known and to clarify the fundamental activity in the orient of orientals, the investigation of historical customs is extremely important to colonial policy."[39] Shiratori, too, believed that unless Japanese possessed accurate geographic and historical facts, it would be impossible to gain any understanding of the character of the people, to know the potential for development, and to administer the region properly.[40] Through this research, Shiratori attempted to bring his work directly in touch with policymaking.

The geographic and historical research conducted in this office was rather conventional, with an emphasis on ancient history. The center's

37. Hara, *Gendai ajia kenkyū seiritsu shiron*, 489.
38. Yamada, *Mantetsu chōsabu*, 33–36.
39. Hara, *Gendai ajia kenkyū seiritsu shiron*, 496.
40. Shiratori, "Jo" to *Manshū rekishi chiri* (1913), in *SKZ* 10:451.

three major studies were published between 1913 and 1914: *The History and Geography of Manchuria* (*Manshū rekishi chiri*, 2 vols.), *The History and Geography of Korea* (*Chōsen rekishi chiri*), and *War of the Late Sengoku Period* (*Bunroku keicho no eki*). The volumes on Manchuria—the collaborative work of Shiratori, Inaba, Matsui, and Yanai—covered the period from the Han dynasty to the early Ch'ing; the volume on Korea, written by Tsuda, went up to the Koryŏ dynasty; and the *Bunroku keicho no eki*, written by Ikeuchi, focused on Toyotomi Hideyoshi's invasion of Korea. An example of the way Shiratori envisioned these studies as "practical" history is evident in Ikeuchi's volume. Shiratori wrote in the preface:

The quest for the truth and clarification of the causes of his [Toyotomi's] failure is not only an interesting historiographical issue. It also provides excellent information to understand well both the international relations of the East Asian powers and the national character of the Koreans. In particular, now that the peninsula has become our territory, we need a compassionate policy toward these newly annexed people, practical management of this land, and full intercourse with the continent; all this must be learned from these vestiges of the past.[41]

The research on Korea provides an example of how a "proper" understanding of the past corrected mistaken interpretations of relations with continental regions and, consequently, facilitated administration. According to Shiratori, Japan's activities were not imperialistic, for the past shows that Korea "has returned [*kaeru*] to our protection."[42] The use of the verb *kaeru* suggests that one is returning home, as children return to their parents. History provided the precedent for this return: protohistoric Japan, after all, had been asked for aid by the ancient Korean kingdoms of Paekche, Kaya, and Silla in their fight against Koguryŏ. It was only because of this request, Shiratori continued, that Japan established its rule in Kaya, turned Paekche into a protectorate, and made a tributary state of Silla. Moreover, he left no doubt that he considered the Sei-Kan movement of the early Meiji period to "open Korea" and impose Japanese "aid" during the twentieth century in a similar vein.[43] Thus, pure and practical historical knowledge were in

41. Shiratori, "Jo" to *Bunroku keicho no eki*, by Ikeuchi Hiroshi, in *SKZ* 10:456.
42. Shiratori, "Jo" to *Manshū rekishi chiri*, in *SKZ* 10:452. In the introduction to Tsuda's volume on Korea, *Chōsen rekishi chiri*, Shiratori asserted that the southern part of the peninsula had been Japan's dependency (*waga zokuryō*) in the ancient period; see "Jo" to *Chōsen rekishi chiri*, in *SKZ* 10:453.
43. Shiratori, "Tōyōshijō yori mitaru nihon," in *SKZ* 9:259.

fact quite similar: in the former, objective research was necessary to correct mistaken views, especially among Westerners, and foster a historical understanding suitable to modern Japan; in the latter, objective research was the means for understanding proper relations and creating suitable policy.

Reaction to the studies produced by the Center for Historical and Geographic Research on Manchuria and Korea was mixed. From the position of the academic scholar trying to further research and understanding, this early research was certainly successful. In pointing to those prewar publications that made the greatest contribution to the development of *tōyōshi*, Enoki listed the following: *Research Reports on the History and Geography of Manchuria and Korea* (*Mansen chiri rekishi kenkyū hōkoku*), *Reports on Investigations into the Old Customs of Manchuria* (*Manshū kyūkan chōsa hōkokusho*), *Private Law in Taiwan* (*Taiwan shihō*), *Adminstrative Laws of the Ch'ing Dynasty* (*Shinkoku gyōseihō*), and *Investigation of Rural Practices in China* (*Chūgoku nōson kankō chōsa*).[44] The first two are the initial studies of the Research Bureau, the third and fourth are products of Gotō's administration in Taiwan; the last, which was compiled by the Research Bureau in the 1940s, will be discussed below.

A different evaluation was recently offered by the historian Yamada Gōichi. Yamada argued that the "pure" academic research of Shiratori's research division had little practical value, making it clearly different from other research sections. Its only utility, according to Yamada, was in giving the Research Bureau an academic aura, and its only politicality was the favorable public relations image it (as represented by the division's publications) gave to academia: "It had the desired effect of enlightened [*keimō*] public relations consistent with [Gotō's] policy of 'culturally attired military preparedness.' The purpose of the Center for Historical and Geographic Research on Manchuria and Korea was academic, and in this way it had a political purpose."[45]

44. *Mansen chiri rekishi kenkyū hōkoku* was prepared by the research team led by Shiratori at the South Manchurian Railway and finished at the University of Tokyo; *Taiwan shihō* and *Shinkoku gyōseihō* were compiled by the Zanji Taiwan Kyūkan Chōsakai; *Manshū kyūkan chōsa hōkokusho* was published by the Research Bureau of the SMR; and the *Chūgoku nōson kankō chōsa* was a joint research project of the Tōa Kenkyūjo, University of Tokyo, and the SMR. See Enoki, *Tōyō bunko no rokujūnen* (Tokyo: Tōyō Bunko, 1977), 265.

45. Yamada, *Mantetsu chōsabu*, 36; see also Andō Hikotaro, *Nihonjin no chūgokukan* (Tokyo: Keisō Shobō, 1971), 87–111; and Andō and Yamada, "Kindai chūgoku kenkyū to mantetsu chōsabu," 36–43. The latter is a criticism of Marxist thought during the

Yamada is a bit harsh in his assessment. Shiratori's center was not mere window dressing, and there were many similarities between it and the Research Bureau: both argued that history must be scientific— that is, objective; both emphasized the historical and cultural basis of socioeconomic conditions; and both focused on rural society as the key to understanding China. The difference was one of disagreement over which past was most efficacious. For Shiratori, the lessons of the past as well as the understanding of positivistic trends in historical research constituted sufficient reason to justify the attention and support of the public and political spheres. Shiratori, and Naitō as well, criticized the oversimplistic attitudes that, relying on impressionistic data, failed to understand the historical laws that governed society and were reflected in popular opinions and even government policy. SMR administrators, in contrast, looked to a more recent past of those Chinese institutions and customs that would facilitate administration of their possessions.

Shiratori's conviction that historical knowledge was fully relevant to current events was evident in his reaction to the closing of his center in January 1914.[46] The new SMR president, Nomura Ryūtarō, argued that research at the Azabu office was not practical enough. Shiratori lamented, "I was completely perplexed. Even though we had produced [many] volumes over the past seven years, it was only a foundation and the first step toward our goal. We first investigated geography to establish a basis for our goal of researching the history of Manchuria and Korea. But as we were about to start on that history, the center was abolished. We could not attain our original aim."[47] The center's failing, Shiratori seemed to feel, was that they had begun to emphasize history too late; the relevance of history did not enter into the matter. Had he begun his historical research sooner, he was convinced, politicians and the directors of the SMR would have understood the importance and connection of such historical and geographic research to policy.

Shiratori was probably wrong in his assessment. By the 1910s it was not that more history was needed; indeed, much of the history that he believed was essential background had already been accepted. A prin-

---

1930s; see, for example, Hirano Yoshitarō, "Shina kenkyū ni taisuru futatsu no michi," *Yuibutsuron kenkyū* 20 (June 1934): 6–7.

46. The group was able to continue its research at the College of Letters at the University of Tokyo until 1934 with partial funding from the SMR.

47. Shiratori, "Gotō haku no gakumon no kōseki," in *SKZ* 10:388.

cipal assumption common to the various studies produced by the center was that Manchuria and Korea are regions, not countries or nations. This assumption is part of the historical hierarchy embedded in *tōyōshi* as a field of knowledge: *shina*, though of deflated standing, was still the central object of attention, while Korea and Manchuria held an even lower position on the periphery. In the case of *shina*, both Shiratori and Naitō envisioned some form of nation emerging from the chaos, but Korea and Manchuria were little more than geographic regions that had been and could be used in various ways to further Japan's growth, accommodate its excess population, and serve as a defensive barrier. In fact, this region was generally referred to as *mansen*, a contraction of the Japanese names *manshū* (Manchuria) and *chōsen* (Korea) that in itself suggests the combination of these two countries into one domain.

This status of Manchuria and Korea as virtual nonentities was supported by history—or, more accurately, by the pure and practical narratives written by Japanese specialists on *tōyō*. For example, Shiratori used the Korean creation myths to show that Korea was not a unified country until the fifth century, well after the unification of Japan. (Naitō, too, took pains to describe Japan as the prior of the two.) He did not deny all connections between Japan and Korea alluded to in the ancient myths, or similarities between Korean and Japanese artifacts found in recent archeological excavations. But he carefully described the Korean peninsula as an area that was often subject to the dominant power of the continent, either China or the various Northern barbarians. Rarely, according to Shiratori, was Korea able to maintain an independent government. Manchuria, for its part, was described as the staging ground for the Northern barbarian tribes preparing for their forays into China. It was sparsely populated and had no real semblance of being a nation-state; it was simply a "neutral zone" for the conflicting forces of his dualism.[48]

Such a narrative provided historical proof for the centrality of *mansen* in Japan's defense perimeter. The reason that Japan was never invaded, continued Shiratori, was not only because it is an island country, but also because the people of *mansen*, while acting in their own defense, also served as a barrier against any would-be attackers. Although he was careful to acknowledge the prestige of the court and the bravery of the Japanese in the effort of self-defense, he emphasized that

48. Shiratori, "Mansen shiron," *Taihō*, April 1921, 57–64; and idem, "Nikan kōshō kaishi ni kansuru kodensetsu" (speech, ca. 1914), in *SKZ* 2:29–45.

Korea and Manchuria had played a major role in protecting Japan from the Mongols in the thirteenth century, and in the twentieth century this region must again protect Japan, this time from Russia.[49] But in the twentieth century Shiratori saw a weak and disorganized region: the Chinese could no longer be relied upon, the Koreans were a failure at self-administration, and the Manchurians were helpless to defend themselves. Thus, Japan must assume the leadership role for the defense of *mansen:* a "fireproof door [which, of course, led to Russia] has to be built with the power of our Japan."[50]

Both Shiratori and Naitō found historical precedence for the annexation of Korea. Shiratori cited Jingū's assistance at the request of Korean kingdoms fighting against Koguryŏ and, more recently, the Yi dynasty's "elated" acceptance of annexation for their mutual interest.[51] Naitō, too, argued that Korea was stagnant, impoverished, and incapable of developing on its own for at least a century: "The kindest thing the Japanese can do for Koreans is implement an austere government and remake their human natures, which have fallen into decay over the past few centuries. . . . [A child] must first submit to disciplined training. Even if you provoke the child's resentment for a time, such treatment will bring true happiness in its future growth."[52] This conviction that Japan knew what was best for Korea is strikingly similar to comments of colonial administrators and policymakers. Nitobe Inazō, for example, stated in 1919:

I count myself among the best and truest friends of Koreans. I like them. . . . I think they are a capable people who can be trained to a large measure of self-government, for which the present is a period of tutelage. Let them study what we are doing in Korea, and this I say not to justify the many mistakes committed by our militaristic administration, nor to boast of some of our achievements. In all humility, but with a firm conviction that Japan is a steward on whom devolves the gigantic task of the uplifting of the Far East, I cannot think that the young Korea is yet capable of governing itself.[53]

The second step in rebuilding this barrier was to maintain the now-historic position of Manchuria as a neutral zone, that "fireproof door." Shiratori first presented his neutral-zone theory in 1904, just after the

49. Shiratori, "Tōyōshijō yori mitaru nihon," in *SKZ* 9:264–65.
50. Ibid.
51. Ibid., 265.
52. Fogel, *Politics and Sinology,* 238.
53. Inazo Nitobe, "Japanese Colonization," *Asiatic Review* 16 (January 1920): 118. See also Peattie, "Japanese Attitudes Toward Colonialism."

outbreak of the Russo-Japanese War. In an indirect way, it seemed to be a reply to John Hay's Open Door notes, or in any case an adaptation of this concept to Manchuria. In 1904, Naitō too addressed the issue of the neutrality of China, and by 1910 he had become an advocate of Manchuria's neutrality.[54] Shiratori described this region as largely uninhabited despite its fertility because it was the locus of conflict among competing powers: at the end of the Ch'in dynasty, conflict occurred between the Northern peoples (Mo and Wei), inhabitants of the Korean peninsula, and Chinese; the T'ang dynasty saw contention among the P'o-hai (Tungus), Silla, and China; and during the Ch'ing period Russia, Korea, and China waged a new competition for the region.[55] A balance-of-power analysis is malleable enough to explain shifting conditions and power relations; not only does it draw on historical precedence, but it also adjusts to a wide variety of contemporary situations. And Shiratori proved to be adroit in applying this model to twentieth-century international politics in East Asia.[56]

At the outbreak of the Russo-Japanese War, Shiratori identified the three contesting powers as Russia, China, and Japan (Japan had already replaced Korea). He proposed that it would be best for Japan not to acquire Manchuria, but instead to ensure that it remained a neutral zone. If Japan did become actively involved, it would have to confront both a Northern power (Russia) and a Southern power (England; it was, he said, a transition period in which the declining power of China was being replaced by England). Rather than face the virtually suicidal situation of confronting both powers and becoming embroiled in the "rough seas" of continental politics, he proposed that Japan negotiate a settlement with Russia and China to ensure that Manchuria remain neutral. Thus the balance in Asia would be retained, Japan would remain independent, its prestige would be enhanced, and Russia's expansionary drive would be diverted.[57] Indeed, on July 30, 1907, Japan and

54. Shiratori first presented this theory in his "Waga kuni no kyōsei to narishi shiteki gen'in ni tsuite," *Sekai* (July 1904), in *SKZ* 9:161–75; see also Goi, *Kindai nihon to tōyōshigaku*, 72. Naitō's initial statements on his neutral-zone theory are "Mantetsu chūritsu mondai" (lecture, January 1910), in *NKZ* 4:459–73; and "Minami manshū mondai," *Bu no sekai* 2 (July 1913), in *NKZ* 4:495–99.

55. Shiratori, "Manshū mondai to shina no shōrai," in *SKZ* 10:147–54.

56. Some scholars have seen these shifts as evidence of Shiratori's manipulation of historical material to match and connect to policy; see Goi, *Kindai nihon to tōyōshigaku*, 72–77.

57. Shiratori, "Manshū no kako oyobi shōrai," in *SKZ* 8:21–23.

Russia signed a treaty in which Japan recognized Russia's interests in Outer Mongolia, Russia acknowledged Japan's control over Korea, and both recognized each other's spheres of influence in Manchuria. Four years later, however, conditions in the Far East had altered considerably. Probably the most important change was the election of William Howard Taft as president of the United States. During his administration, what support and sympathy Japan had enjoyed under Theodore Roosevelt was shifted toward China. Under Taft, the Open Door notes took on new meaning as his secretary of state, Philander C. Knox, interpreted the policy more aggressively and used it to limit Japan's position and expand U.S. markets on the continent.[58] Yet as the U.S. Open Door policy changed, so did Shiratori's neutral zone. In 1912, Shiratori again described the three contesting powers in the region as Russia, China, and Japan. But because of China's chaotic state, Japan gained a more prominent position (England was dropped) and now confronted Russia directly. Unlike his discussion seven years earlier, Shiratori did not mention the need for negotiations, guarantees, or dependence on other countries to maintain this neutral zone. Instead, Japan was now firmly involved: "The current division of the territory of Manchuria between Japan and Russia using Changchun as the border is not new; it was the same during the age of Koguryŏ twelve hundred years ago. If both Japan and Russia violate each other's spheres [Russia in northern Manchuria and Japan in the southern part] . . . this balance of power will most likely be broken and have grave consequences. This, I believe, is the reason that today's status quo will prolong peace in the region."[59] Now, Japan was representative of both the South and *tōyō*. Whereas Shiratori had distinguished between Manchuria and Korea in 1904, by the beginning of Taishō both were considered as *mansen*, an essential territory for the defense of Japan.

By the 1930s Japan's position in all of Manchuria was even more crucial, not only to peace in Asia but also to Japan's defense. Shiratori consistently maintained that this neutral zone must be preserved through compromise by the Soviet Union, China, and Japan. But compromise now meant unilateral action: how should China and Japan respond to the Soviet Union's growing power? Japan and China were now joined (under Japan's leadership) against the Soviet Union. Shiratori rationalized Japan's leadership in the following way. China pos-

58. Raymond A. Esthus, "The Changing Concept of the Open Door, 1899–1910," *Mississippi Valley Historical Review* 46 (1959): 435–54.
59. Shiratori, "Manshū mondai to shina no shōrai," in *SKZ* 10:154.

sessed considerable territory, but "Japan has no room to develop out-side of Manchuria. Thus if Japan returns [Manchuria], the existence of Japan would be severely threatened." By the 1930s, even though *mansen* remained a "neutral zone" between these powers, it was now considered an integral part of Japan, necessary not only for its defense, but also for its development.[60]

Similar views were expressed by Naitō during the Taishō period as well. The role of the center in Naitō's theory of shifting cultural centers complemented Japanese activity of developing and settling the conti-nent. Naitō's belief that the center (Japan) must return its vigor to the periphery could certainly be considered by Gotō as historical justifica-tion for expansion of the SMR holdings along the rail right-of-way and development of key cities such as Changchun. No doubt Gotō would also welcome the frontier spirit of Naitō's small Japanese entrepre-neurs, the pioneers of this expansion and development. Moreover, "ob-jective" arguments could be (and continue to be) made that Japan did improve conditions in the colonies.[61] Of course, Naitō was not neces-sarily in agreement with all the activities of the SMR, but he and Shira-tori were working from the same assumptions: that the continent was essential to Japan's defense, that Japan was a part of *tōyō*, and that it was Japan's duty to provide leadership for the development of the continent.

The limitation of Shiratori's version of practical, historical research is that it could provide only suggestions and directions, rather than detailed plans for the formulation and implementation of policy.[62] All he could offer was objective historical monographs that pointed to broad, general trends and suggested how to interpret and even pre-dict events. In a sense, Shiratori was a victim of his own success. Be-cause historical research was not specific enough for policymaking, the

60. Shiratori, "Tōyōshijō ni okeru mansen no ichi" (lecture presented to the Nari-tasan summer university lectures, 1931), in *Gendai nihon no kenkyū* (February 1932), *SKZ* 9:369–71.

61. See, for example, Samuel Pao-San Ho, "Colonialism and Development: Korea, Taiwan, and Kwantung," in Myers and Peattie (eds.), *Japanese Colonial Empire*, 347–86. Ho does attempt to show negative effects, but his caveat indicates the problem of such rationalistic analyses: "Finally, colonialism burdened the native populations with many intangible costs that we have so far neglected: the humiliation of being second-class cit-izens, the loss of political and often personal freedom, and the lost opportunity to de-velop their own type of society. These intangibles cannot be measured, and if a general assessment of the colonial period is to be made, they must *somehow* be taken into account" (386; italics mine).

62. John Young, *The Research Activity of the South Manchurian Railway Company, 1907–1945* (New York: Columbia University Press, 1966).

research direction of the SMR turned toward contemporary issues that contributed directly to the development and exploitation of this comparatively undeveloped region.

History remained an integral part of the investigation of contemporary conditions. But its role shifted from that of a positivistic aid in understanding historical trends and current events to just another scientific data source. Nonetheless, the discourse on *shina* had set the parameters within which more practical investigation took place. Research topics were now compartmentalized into discrete units within that history. In describing activities at the Research Bureau, Noma Kiyoshi stated, "We expected that we had not only to grasp all historical change that supports and gives rise to tenant issues, but also to clarify the social and economic conditions that support current tenant issues."[63] Hence, the issue for researchers in the 1930s was to ensure that research topics were not separated from the historical, social, and economic conditions that defined those objects of research.

Noma's statement indicates a different conception of the importance of history to social understanding. History, in his view, was important as a narrative structure, the foundation for a better understanding of contemporary conditions. But because the method thereby becomes particularistic and retrospective, researchers did not inquire into the suitability of the prevailing framework but merely accepted it. Study of the old landholding customs, for example, was grounded in an assumption that the central government had little power in local affairs and that any negotiation would occur directly with the local people. Further, the more basic assumption was that both Korea and Manchuria were part of the same region, a region to be acted upon.

In many ways Shiratori was correct in his assessment that he had provided a basis for further research. The early work of the Research Bureau on the evolution of the customs and lives of the people led to the next level, study of the modern people and their everyday lives: everything that one could know about how and under what conditions the people lived, what customs and laws governed their behavior, and how such variables could be put to better use. This research on the land, its productivity, climate, and the people brought Shiratori's research full circle. From Buckle's geography and climate, the point of

---

63. Noma, "Chūgoku nōson kankō chōsa," 12–13.

departure for his historical narrative, research now returned to geoclimatic conditions—but now as a data set for the scientific management of *mansen*. Perhaps the only difference between practical and pure research was one of perception: because Japanese researchers worked within the same field of knowledge, institutional, methodological, and emphatic distinctions appeared greater than they actually were.

Scientific Research

By the 1930s one sees an interesting turn of events. The earlier advocates of scientific and positivistic research, those of the 1910s and 1920s, were closely tied to Japan's China policy; thus they became the foils for the new advocates, armed with Marxist formulas, of scientific research on China. Debate was now over whose information was more objective and more scientific. This argument in fact suggests that the range of difference had narrowed: after all, both Marxist and imperialist researchers (a problematic division at best, as indicated by the discussion on Ozaki and Tachibana in Chapter 5), though differing in particularities, worked within the same discursive frame. What little dialogue did exist occurred among intellectuals and elites in Japan, not between researchers and China.

In a 1934 article, Hirano Yoshitarō (1897–1980), a proponent of the *kōza* (lecture) faction of Japanese Marxism, divided research on China into two basic categories: scientific and imperialistic.[64] Those of the latter school, he asserted, used research merely as an embellishment of policy; they were blatantly interventionist, seeking the reform of China through *dismemberment* (*kaitai*).[65] Hirano included both pure and practical researchers in the imperialistic category. He cited two of Shiratori's students, Matsui and Nakayama, as examples, and

64. Marxism had a profound impact on Japanese intellectual life during the 1920s and 1930s, with two interpretations emerging in the 1930s to counter the developmental view of history. The *kōza ha* (lecture faction) described the Meiji Restoration as an incomplete revolution in Japan's transition from feudal to industrial. The collusion of feudal forces with industrialists, they said, led to the absolutism of the twentieth century. The other faction, the *rōnō ha* (laborer-farmer faction), argued that the Meiji Restoration was a bourgeois revolution.

65. Hara, *Gendai ajia kenkyū seiritsu shiron*, 775–77.

was probably pointing his finger at Shiratori, his disciples, and other Sinologists, such as Naitō, as well. In condemning these researchers' studies on China, Hirano stated that "even though he [Nakayama] conducts academic research, current methods—the positivistic exegesis of ancient texts—have separated national, religious, and Chinese philosophical, in short all ideological, phenomena from the social and economic structure of China; are immersed in the illusion of the 'brilliance from the east' [*hikari wa tōhō yori*], the theory of benevolent government and the kingly way; and have left scientific research impoverished."[66] He also included in this group the *rōnō* (laborer-farmer) faction of Marxist scholarship, which he accused of being feudalistic, agrarian, and bourgeois. Their failure was that they did not clarify the inevitable laws of the development of Chinese society and the modes of production.

Hirano was correct to take issue with the increasing separation of research from its object. He pointed to the danger of assuming the sameness of the ideological construct and the social structure of China, charging exegetical and positivistic studies with blinding the researcher to a critical perspective that would prevent the confluence of research and imperialism. His criticism of the *rōnō* faction suggested that the problem was the identification of the proper ideology (narrowly construed) that informs research. In other words, a proper scientific—that is, critical—perspective would ensure that researchers detached themselves from those parts of the social structure that had been developed to control the people. But despite Hirano's conviction that Marxist research would lead to a more accurate understanding of China, like positivistic researchers he, too, believed that one can understand past conditions objectively. His approach entailed the omission of political structures and an emphasis on the obverse of the politico-economic system, rural society; it was deemed more scientific because it was based on the "correct" perspective, but this approach just altered the criteria that Japanese used to determine the problems of China. China remained an object to be manipulated.

Hirano's dialogue was with other Japanese researchers, not with China.[67] Here one recalls the lament of Tai Chi-t'ao, the Kuomintang leader, that *shina* was constantly cut up and placed in test tubes, or the

66. Hirano, "Shina kenkyū ni taisuru futatsu no michi."
67. On the tendency of historians in a "scientific" or objectivistic mode to engage in conversation with other historians, see LaCapra, *History and Criticism*, 15–44, esp. 36–43.

criticism of Hatada or Noma, themselves former employees of the Research Bureau, that research was excessively objective to the point of atheoreticalness.[68] Hirano's ideas were not atheoretical. But he was concerned with the relation between data and theory, especially how theory should be modified to account for different conditions in China and Japan. "The fundamental duty of contemporary scientific research on China," he repeats from a Soviet encyclopedia, "is an analysis of the special Oriental characteristics—the unique 'centralized' and 'bureaucratized' feudal system—in the feudal development of China."[69] In other words, the whole Chinese system could be understood by explaining where Oriental characteristics emerged and where China deviated from the universal path of development as described in Marxist theory. There was little discussion about China itself, except as a source of data. He concluded, "We should value, deepen, and critically advance research that is related to the materialistic and social foundation of a despotism tied to special Asiatic characteristics."[70] It was the interpretation of events and conditions in China that were important to a scholarly framework. China, ipso facto, was not significant.

Because the debate occurred among scholars, Hirano took far more from the discourse on *shina* than he realized. He, Shiratori, and Naitō, that is, were still working within a Western framework, and on two levels. Marxism was an attractive alternative to orthodox historiography on China because it provided a critical framework addressing many of the ills overlooked by orthodoxy. Even though Shiratori helped shift history from kings and dynasties to peoples, the unit of analysis was still a nation, a region, or a group. Shiratori's positivistic history centered attention on people, but only in general terms, as parts of an organic unit, the nation-state. Marxism corrected some of this bias by problematizing the various tensions within that unit. But it was still a modern, Western concept, formulated to interpret Western ills. Hirano, as well as other Marxist scholars, was working within a linear and hierarchical framework in which the modern West was at the top, followed by a Japan that should help China. In discussing the suitability of the Asiatic mode of production to Japan and China, for example, Hirano argued that China, in sharp contrast to Japan, did not develop feudalism: "In terms of world history it [Japan] was late, but it fully

68. Tai, *Nihonron*, 6; Hatada, "Nihon ni okeru tōyōshigaku no dentō"; and Noma, "Chūgoku nōson kankō chōsa."
69. Hirano, "Shina kenkyū ni taisuru futatsu no michi," 14–15.
70. Ibid., 18.

and systematically followed the proper stages."[71] In other words, Japan was more like the West because its history fit the universalistic characteristics of Marxist development. The developmental categories were different, but he did not question the ontological status of the Orient as unique and backward, and indeed, he sought to find the reasons for this peculiarity.

There were, to be sure, important differences between Marxist and imperialist historians in Taishō and early Shōwa Japan. Yet the two categories were not polar opposites.[72] My intent here is not to blur differences, but to point out some important similarities. The disagreement over universalistic frameworks, for instance, only obscured an agreement concerning the data and the objects of research—the landlord system, the socioeconomic conditions of agriculture, and the bureaucracy. This agreement was part of a national predilection for objectivistic research—with objectivity being defined in terms of a Japanese vision of Asia. This common discourse helps to explain why imperialists and Marxists could work side by side in the Research Bureau, and how they could both experience the growing separation of their research from the object of that study, China.

Although scholars such as Hirano were critical of imperialistic research, they too were afflicted with a blindness to their own complicity with Japanese imperialism. And not only Marxist scholars suffered from this blindness. Many whom Marxists identified as being within the positivistic/imperialist school were critical of Japan's imperialist policy as well. In 1939, for example, Ikeuchi criticized Japan's invasion of China, and later, near the end of the war, he was detained for one week by the *kenpeitai* (secret police). Similarly, Tsuda was tried for treason between November 1941 and January 1942, and Wada spoke out in his defense.[73] One reason for this myopia was that denunciation of opponents as imperialist freed the critic to believe that he was sympathetic to China and that his research—studies that would lift the oppressive politico-economic system from the backs of the peasants—was for the good of the Chinese. But just as important, such a belief covered over the acceptance by both groups of Japan's role as a leader of Asia against a greater evil, the West. Hirano stated, "The locus of the true problem is in the semicolonization of China, bourgeois development of the landlords (!), and the denial of a feudalistic, exploitative

71. Quoted in Ozaki, *Gendai shinaron*, 226.
72. For a discussion on the ways that Marxism and nationalism coincide, see Anderson, *Imagined Communities*.
73. *Tōkyō daigaku hyakunenshi*, 631.

system in agriculture."[74] By semicolonization he referred to Western imperialism, not that of Japan. Like earlier scholars of whom he was critical, Hirano accepted the notion of a *tōyō*, which he called a "metanational greater regionalism" (*chōminzokuteki daichiikishugi*). The use of a term suggesting the existence of people in a space more inclusive than a nation-state differentiated his concept from imperialism, in which "the mother country is pitted against the colony." Hirano's regionalism, like that of Tachibana and Ozaki, was a political, not a cultural, union. It "is a new political principle that places the national defense [*kokubō*], financial affairs [*zaisei*], and diplomacy in this regional unit, and at the same time preserves self-independence in the internal government, economics, culture, and tradition of each people [*minzoku*] on a high plateau."[75] Yet he too, as his colleagues had done, restated, but did not eliminate, the hierarchical, geocultural region, *tōyō*.

Scientific, objective research was the means to achieving this regional system. The connection between these points was made clear in a roundtable discussion held in October 1941 on Japan's southern advance.[76] Three items were debated: first, the need for research that is scientific; second, the urgency of developing trade in commodities in the Greater East Asia Co-Prosperity Sphere; and third, the status of ethnographic information on that region. Hirano's support for imperialism (or his blindness to his connection with it) was evident in his advocacy of "pure" research on Southeast Asia. He stated, "Isn't [research needed] for [knowing] the living conditions when we Japanese go to the tropical region? In tropical living, what does one eat? In what type of house does one live? And what does one wear?"[77] Despite Hirano's professions of being objective and not imperialistic, the above comments indicate that his scientific research was in fact quite compatible with imperialistic policy. The range of research had narrowed. Marxist researchers could coexist quite peaceably within the Research Bureau of the SMR because they, too, accepted a notion of *tōyō* and were equally obsessed with maintaining scientific objectivity, as opposed to those whom they considered imperialistic.

The complicity of Marxist and imperialist researchers is evident in one of the major large-scale projects conducted by the Research Bureau and published after the war as the six-volume *Chūgoku nōson kankō*

74. Hirano, "Shina kenkyū ni taisuru futatsu no michi," 14.

75. Quoted in Ozaki, *Gendai shinaron*, 237.

76. The participants of this meeting were Sakatani Yoichi, Ozaki Hotsumi, Onishi Chiifuru, Fukuda Shōzō, and Hirano. See Hara, *Gendai ajia kenkyū seiritsu shiron*, 57.

77. Ibid., 58–59.

(Chinese Agricultural Practices). In his study of the Research Bureau, Hara Kakuten stated: "There was a particularly high interest in problems concerning Chinese agriculture and rural society in research during this period [1930s]. It was considered the basis and prerequisite for all research on China."[78] Marxists such as Hirano identified rural society—that is, feudal or semifeudal Chinese agriculture—as the key to understanding Chinese development. Hirano believed that by uncovering the emergence and thus relations of this system one could understand the system of land tenure, household manufacture, handicraft production, malformation of manufacture, and the characteristics of Asiatic cities. Unlike Shiratori and Naitō, who identified the main hindrance to further Chinese development as governmental incompetence, a culture of passivity, and a self-governing, atomized village structure, Hirano found the main impediment to progress in the socioeconomic system that exploited the people.[79] In the end, however, what is significant is that each group turned to a Chinese village society in need of leadership as the key to understanding, reforming, and developing China.

In the early 1930s, Hirano worked at the Research Institute on East Asia (Tōa Kenkyūjō, or Tōken) and participated in the planning for the project on Chinese agriculture. The Research Bureau finally started research in 1940 and continued through 1942. The delay was caused mainly by negotiations between Tōken and the Research Bureau over purpose and applicability. What is interesting about these negotiations is the desire of both institutions to be scientific and neutral, despite the public statement that indicated a relation to policy: "Unless we understand how Chinese everyday society [*shina minzoku shakai*] is structured and how people live, it is difficult to expect harmony and competence in our country's policies toward China."[80] At the meeting between the Research Bureau and Tōken planners, Suehiro Izutarō pointed out the conflict between the insistence that research and survey methods be scientific, on the one hand, and the design and purpose of the SMR, on the other. He asked, "Why are you conducting this investigation for policy? Isn't this supposed to be scientific [*gakujutsu*] research?"[81]

78. Ibid., 764. Hara also pointed out that Westerners, such as J. L. Buck, W. L. Thorp, and A.H.C. Wagner, also emphasized Chinese rural society in their research.
79. Hirano, "Shina kenkyū ni taisuru futatsu no michi," 15, 17–18.
80. Hara, *Gendai ajia kenkyū seiritsu shiron*, 762; see also Noma, "Chūgoku nōson kankō chōsa," 6–7.
81. Ibid., 7.

These criticisms, however, did not lead to a reevaluation of the project. One reason was that the cooperation of the Kwantung Army was necessary for the investigators to gain access to and receive protection in the research area and also for the securing of supplemental funds necessary to conduct the research.[82] Further, despite shortcomings, this project was seen as a corrective to the 1913–15 study *Manshū kyūkan chōsa hōkokusho*. The change in the title from "old customs" (*kyūkan*) to "practices" (*kankō*) reflected criticisms of the earlier study, including some by the researchers themselves. The earlier study was faulted for being unscientific and for relying too heavily on texts rather than current conditions.[83] In the new survey, field research was a major component; all participants were confident that data collected in interviews and observation would yield accurate information that would not be tainted by ideological filters or imperial policy. With these corrections and cautions, scholars of the Research Bureau and Tōken believed it would be possible to keep their work and the colonial administration distinct.

Despite their faith in objectivity and science, however, these researchers were unable to avoid many of the problems inherent in ethnographic research. The survey conditions both forced a physical and cultural distance between the researchers and their object of study and tied the investigators directly to the symbols of power. Even though they were attempting to avoid the construction of a "survey of the authorities" (*kenryoku chōsa*), that power was always present. For example, on entering a new area researchers first consulted with the provincial bureaucracy and business association, they lodged at official facilities, and they received armed protection for the journey between their lodgings and the research site.[84] The interview process itself had problems as well. Interviews were usually conducted in public places and were of questionable quality. Amagai himself stated that most of the interviewers were amateurs, who often used Japanese expressions in their questions; "therefore, even when they interviewed farmers, they asked things that were commonsensical and seemed meaningless."[85] It would

82. Ibid.
83. In criticizing the older study, Noma wrote, "They went no further than a simple enumeration of historical facts and did not have a scientific theoretical structure. Moreover, this was a survey that tried to respond to 'practical affairs' [*jitsumu*], and it was really a survey for Japan's colonial control of the Chinese northeast" (quoted in Hara, *Gendai ajia kenkyū seiritsu shiron*, 771).
84. Noma, "Chūgoku nōson kankō chōsa," 10.
85. Hara, *Gendai ajia kenkyū seiritsu shiron*, 794.

be improper to fault these researchers for not having our hindsight; many of the problems of their investigation—interviewer bias, class/hierarchical differences between interviewer and interviewee, the very nature of the questions, expectations of certain answers, and so on—have only recently begun to receive attention.[86] In the end, however, even good faith could not have overcome the bounds within which the survey researchers worked, whatever their commitment to objectivity.

Suehiro, a principal researcher on this project, summarized the group's work as follows: "We investigated to what extent the system of old China [*kyū shina*] has been preserved, to what extent both old and new coexist, and furthermore, in which direction it is moving."[87] The emphasis here is on the fact that China and its people were not static objects, but constantly changing, and that it was important to investigate the people rather than books. Yet the limits of this research are evident in the assumption that the conditions were a "historical product" (*rekishiteki shosan*). Noma wrote, "In this survey, we did not consider all customs, the social norms that were used in old Chinese rural society, simply as independent phenomena, but expected an organically related social and economic base that was historically situated. We believed that customs as social phenomena are not isolated and do not materialize through individual will; they materialize from specific social and economic conditions. They are historical products."[88] Noma belies here an important characteristic of the group's "practical" research: they were examining contemporary conditions that had a known historical base. The survey was not designed to inquire into the veracity of those historical conditions, but to understand contemporary social and economic conditions *through* that known history.

The questions the researchers asked presupposed that the Chinese were behind, that an old system existed that had already been defined, that change toward the modern (as defined by the Japanese) was desirable, and that although it was not quite certain in which direction China was going, with further study Japan might be able to help it along the right path. This does not mean that all researchers consciously supported Japan's imperialism. But most did believe that re-

---

86. For recent discussions of issues in survey research methodology, see, for example, Seymour Sudman and Norman M. Bradburn, *Asking Questions* (San Francisco: Jossey-Bass, 1982); and in anthropology, see Fabian, *Time and the Other;* and James Clifford and George Marcus, eds., *Writing Cultures: The Poetics and Politics of Ethnography* (Berkeley and Los Angeles: University of California Press, 1986).

87. Hara, *Gendai ajia kenkyū seiritsu shiron,* 772.

88. Noma, "Chūgoku nōson kankō chōsa," 12.

search could be objective and unbiased, and as the numerous comments from the 1960s debates over the Asia and Ford Foundations indicate, they did not adequately consider the much broader historical and discursive framework within which they were conducting their investigations.

These "practical" studies parallel Shiratori's and Naitō's "pure" descriptions of the history of China and Asia. Both approaches relied on a separation of the people from the nation-state and, in their appraisals of the revolutionary upheavals, concluded on the basis of historical evidence that any remedy had to come from the Chinese themselves, but under Japan's leadership. It was in furtherance of this interest that "practical" researchers—adherents of science in its various manifestations—and historians of *tōyō*, such as Shiratori and Naitō, both worked. The geocultural unit of *tōyō* explained Japan's similarities with and responsibilities toward other Asian countries, as well as how Japan was able to progress beyond the others. Japan's ties to the continent were not questioned. But more important, few questioned the narrative of Japan's history. Criticism was certainly directed at contemporary conditions, but proposed resolutions were aimed at reaching the next step along the continuum, not at altering the continuum altogether. Whether one considered Japan to be a colonial power or the center of oriental culture, both views necessitated the political and economic leadership of Japan over Asia.

This belief, that Japan as a nation-state had already undergone the same process along which it was now seeking to help China, ultimately blinded these Japanese scholars—Marxists and non-Marxists alike—to China's own needs. The process—proven by Japan's successes—was assumed. Science empowered social research to criticize policy and propose alternatives, with the instrumental question being how to help *shina*. A political, regional alliance seemed to offer China greater voice, but it was a voice within Japan's system, not an autonomous one. Even those who considered themselves friends of China, such as Naitō, and Marxists who criticized Japanese imperialism fell within this structure. The following defense of the "old liberalism" of the academic professors at the University of Tokyo and their complicity with imperialism can be applied equally to the Marxist scholars: "In the end, whether they hid deep thoughts in shallow, related themes aloof from the times, whether they confirmed national policy as a result of direct grappling with the state of affairs of *tōyō*, or whether they were in an awkward position because they publicly criticized national policy, because they faced this dilemma, they were no different from other intellectuals of this period."[89] These scholars knew their object and the path that their knowledge ordained. They did not see or hear those Chinese voices that fell outside their categories, and they were not going to allow *shina* to deviate from that proper path.

89. *Tōkyō daigaku hyakunenshi*, 631.

Epilogue:
The Renovation of the Past

"This was a narrow, but not an unreasonable, way of creating a usable past, and at the same time of giving the citizens of each nation a sense of pride in their national heritage and, it was hoped, a feeling of loyalty toward the current establishment. This was roughly the state of affairs in the late 1930s when I first became aware of history."[1] This statement could easily have come from an apologist for Shiratori, his colleagues at the Imperial University at Tokyo, or other prewar China specialists. What makes this quote so interesting is that it was written by Lawrence Stone in 1987 in defense of the history profession in the United States, one not much different from that which Shiratori helped to establish.

Stone has raised one of the central problems of history: the contradiction between its role in national affairs and the obsession of historians to deny that role by claiming objectivity and neutrality. This contradiction is one that confronted Shiratori and his colleagues in the formulation of a historical field in Japan. Their endeavor to overcome the limitations of the Western version of world history indicates an awareness of the problem, but at the same time, they reproduced this contradiction in their effort to build an objective field, one that was applicable to the new Japanese nation-state. To explain issues such as political development, military and cultural expansion, and political ideals, Japanese historians had to turn to the past for authority and precedence, that is, to create a historical foundation that clarified mod-

1. Lawrence Stone, review of Gertrude Himmelfarb, *The New History and the Old*, in the *New York Review of Books*, December 17, 1987, 59–62, quote from 60.

ern Japan's actions and ideals. In this effort, the various pasts became an archive from which they could unearth the necessary evidence to construct a historical narrative. Recently, several studies—such as ones by Benedict Anderson and Eric Hobsbawm focusing on the role of language, education, the press, and symbols in the formation of the modern nation-state—have suggested that the notion of nation is a creation or "invention."[2] An equally potent agent in the invention of nations is history. History orders and explains the significance of the different pasts that gave and give meaning to the nation-state. Such diachronic narrative authorizes which past is to be transmitted by means of various symbols, media, schools, and dialogues. In modern Japan, those historic symbols might suggest the ideal modern man, a blend of old and new as embodied in Admiral Nogi and General Tōgō, or an ideal of the people as is found in the folk tale "Momotarō," symbolizing the belief of ancient Japanese in the yin and yang, Izanagi and Izanami, and bad and good.[3] The meanings embedded in these heroic figures and myths were authorized through the history of tōyō.

It is no accident that a particularly active period in the formulation of national cultures described by Anderson and Hobsbawm coincided with the time when great historians, such as Ranke, Michelet, and Macauley, were writing their national histories. History validates what is and who decides the usable past, what is the national heritage, and to whom or what one's loyalty should be directed. In Japan, this heritage was disseminated in numerous ways. Previous scholars have noted the important role of various organizations and institutions in the Meiji, Taishō, and Shōwa periods in establishing a sense of common purpose: the educational system taught a common language and propagated objective knowledge of a modern and successful Japan; conscription instilled a sense of nation in young farmboys; the press contributed to the unification of language and of the body of Japan; and institutions such as the local improvement associations sought to mold the people. There were many other similar institutions, but all represented an effort to instill in the people a common identity that transcended their village, region, or domain. I do not mean to suggest that humble people thereby became pawns of the state or the central powers. One needs

2. Anderson, *Imagined Communities*; Hobsbawm and Ranger (eds.), *Invention of Tradition*; and Lowenthal, *The Past Is a Foreign Country*.
3. Shiratori, "Tsuitōkai ni okeru Shiratori hakushi kōen," 33–43; idem, "Waga kokuminsei no kenka Tōgō gensui," 31–33; and idem, "Momotarō no hanashi," *Shigaku zasshi* 34 (April 1923) in *SKZ* 2:123–25.

to read only a part of the histories of these periods to realize that endeavors to homogenize the culture were highly contested issues. Traditions and memory can be equally potent weapons against centralization. But history, as I have described it, is also important—in fact, it is indispensable—to the centralization of the nation-state. Without history, the elite could not have created the new Japan.[4]

The profession of history that developed in Japan at the turn of the century was similar in many ways to its counterparts in the United States and Europe.[5] It was a professional discipline, grounded in archival research, and concerned with the nation-state, political development, and military and cultural expansion (their own as well as others'). It was concerned with relations between the individual and the state, but instead of seeking limitations of the state (if indeed this is a valid characterization of Western discourse and not an ideal type), history imposed limitations on the people by using traditions unearthed from *tōyō*. Also, like its Western counterparts, the Japanese historical profession constructed a history that secularized relations between the state and religion, equated the activities and interests of the elite class (which had in the meantime legitimized itself) with those of the nation, and ignored other civilizations not directly related to its own genealogy.

Yet this history was not dictatorial; it was not imposed by a small band of politicians or scholars on the mass public. History, as David Lowenthal points out, is consensual, though not necessarily willingly or consciously so; it occurs on various levels, from that of everyday life to that of the professional historian. In this sense, it is discursive. Using Carl Becker's "Everyman His Own Historian," Lowenthal writes:

Our sense of history goes beyond knowledge to empathetic involvement. In constructing his own history, Everyman "works with something of the freedom of a creative artist; the history which he imaginatively re-creates . . . will inevitably be an engaging blend of fact and fancy", dominated by data "that seem best suited to his interests or promise most in the way of emotional satisfaction". Professionals' insights come in much the same way, through "a sudden perception which gradually makes sense of a whole large area of the past".[6]

The history that was created in prewar Japan organized the past in such a way that it could encompass the shared experience of many people.

4. For the relation between the state and ideology, see Gluck, *Japan's Modern Myths*.
5. See, for example, Novick, *That Noble Dream*.
6. Lowenthal, *The Past Is a Foreign Country*, 212.

One way that Japanese historians made that shared national experience a part of the individual's everyday life was through metaphors of the family—one frequently employed to explain the past. Lowenthal has shown how the European and American rendering of the past is often drawn in terms of the relation between the parent (past) and the child (present):

Since classical times the parent-child analogy has repeatedly been invoked to underscore the rival claims of past and present. To follow blindly the footsteps of past masters was to remain forever a child; one should aim to rival and finally to displace them. Inherited wisdom was a source of guidance and a fount of inspiration, but it should be assimilated and transformed, not simply revered and repeated. Only by manipulating the past to one's own purposes could one truly achieve autonomy. . . .
Nations and communities confront analogous dilemmas. They must draw sustenance from their past, yet to be fully themselves must also put it away from them. Societies, like individuals, imitate the ancients and pay homage to precursors, but also need to act for themselves, to innovate and create—hence to break with tradition and reject inherited patterns. Whether avowedly traditional or defiantly iconoclastic, every generation must reach a *modus vivendi* that simultaneously embraces and abandons precedence.[7]

Like a parent, a past helps us understand who we are. The past not only gives us identity, but in doing so also renders the unfamiliar into an understandable order, reaffirms and preserves certain parts of ourselves, and provides guidance. Yet as Lowenthal points out, it is important to learn from the past, to assimilate and transform prior experience, but not to follow it blindly. For the nation-state—as well as for the individual—there is a need for autonomy.

The limitation of this parental metaphor is that the past is not singular; there are multiple "voices" from which one can construct a history. *Tōyōshigaku* (and *shinagaku*) ordered those different Asiatic pasts to show not only Japan's indebtedness to *tōyō* but also its autonomy from it. But unlike Western nations that deal primarily with their own past, in the modern world non-Western nation-states must confront another issue: the same relation of past and present, parent and child, exists also between the West and non-West. Even as non-Western countries must deal with their own past—their "parent"—they must also grapple with the West, another "parent." The problem is that although the West is also a parent, it has a quite different past and, moreover, one that has relegated its own non-Western past to antiquity.[8]

---

7. Ibid., 72.
8. The dilemma in intercultural relations is compounded by national perspective. To

The existence of this dilemma, of course, depends on the acceptance of the superiority of Western weapons, technology, political and economic systems, and ideas. It is well known that the Japanese endorsed the epistemology and many of the methodologies of Western historiography and imbibed the writings of Western historians such as Guizot, Buckle, Spencer, and Ranke. But in attempting to adapt these histories, Japanese historians discovered that Japan was among the ignored entities of history, those who were relegated to the past—the Orient. According to that Western historiographical framework, the Japanese past and present were synonymous. To merely plug Japan into the developmental model of Enlightenment would thus have meant the virtual denial of Japan's past and acceptance of a perpetual state of inferiority. Worse, Japan's own identity would have been merely an incomplete variation or anomaly of that of Europe. In fact, early historians such as Taguchi plainly stated that Japan had no history.

The efforts of Japanese intellectuals beginning in the 1890s either to rework Japan's past so that it did have history, in a developmental sense, or to redefine the universal, making it less heavily biased toward Europe, was an attempt to resolve this dilemma. Early scholars who have been considered enlightenment (*bunmei*) historians, such as Miyake Yonekichi and Naka Michiyo, embarked on ambitious projects to write multivolume histories of Japan and China. They soon aborted these projects, however, in favor of detailed, positivistic research into Asia's—and consequently Japan's—past. Another group, consisting of intellectuals like Miyake Setsurei and Okakura Tenshin, proposed new norms for defining universality based on ethical, nonrational standards for human behavior and development, such as art, truth, beauty, and goodness.[9] Ōkawa Shūmei revived these standards during the 1930s in an attempt to escape the confines of rationalist discourse. But in each case, the purpose was to place an autonomous Japan within a modern perspective, not to divorce it from modernity. *Tōyōshi* was a part of this

---

the West, the non-West, having been relegated to antiquity, can be seen only in terms of the past (or backwards). Yet to the non-West, nations must come to terms with their own national past, that of the region (where applicable), as well as the hegemonic past of the West.

9. For a description of Miyake Setsurei's attempt to combine progress with the less Eurocentric norms of "Truth, Goodness, and Beauty," see Pyle, *The New Generation in Meiji Japan*, 148ff. There is a remarkable parallel between Miyake's concept and Japanese high school textbooks of the early 1980s, which state that "the search for . . . truth, goodness, and beauty . . . is the basis for progress" (Thomas P. Rohlen, *Japan's High Schools* [Stanford: Stanford University Press, 1983], 263).

endeavor; its purpose was to create a usable past through which Japan could remove the contradiction of forever being the "child" of both Asia and the West, which included extricating itself from the category of the Orient, the decrepit parent.

"The West" is, of course, a vague term, but as a reflection and refraction against which Japan measures itself (here it has both positive and negative connotations) it serves numerous positions. Shiratori recognized the relativity of East and West and throughout his career worked to clarify the difference between Japan and Europe. In 1938, for instance, he pointed out correctly that whereas Japanese consider the East and West as Asia and Europe, these identifications are relative and could just as easily indicate Japan and China or China and Inner Asia.[10] Although Shiratori himself accepted the identification of East and West as Asia and Europe, he did so only after he turned his North-South dualism into the basis for a philosophy of history that eliminated the linearity implicit in the Western distinction between Orient and Occident. In this dualism he clearly used Asia for his own means. *Tōyō* became the center of his new world vision; it existed not as an autonomous entity but as both the cultural past from which Japan had developed and a geographic and cultural area that Japan had to protect and guide. The formulation of this notion also enabled Japan to progress beyond its Eastern past; as *shina*'s successor it possessed all the attributes of *tōyō* (positive ones of course), but it had also transcended those to gain its own autonomy, one comparable to the West.

One cannot help but be impressed by these historians' breadth, creativity, and recognition of historical problematics. Nor can one easily fault Shiratori and other Japanese intellectuals for such manipulation; after all, the East had been similarly created and manipulated as long before as the Roman Empire. Raymond Schwab states the situation thus:

Sometimes qualified by "Near" or "Far," sometimes identified with Africa or Oceania, when not identified with Russia or Spain, the concept of "the East" has come full circle. As Sylvain Lévi put it, since the world is round, what can this word mean? . . .

The separation lasted less than eighteen centuries. The effect of oriental studies was to undermine the wall raised between the two cultures; such studies fulfilled their real purpose by transforming the exile into a companion. However, the partition was dismantled in accordance with special interests and controversies, intellectual, spiritual, or political, in the West itself. More and more

10. Shiratori, "Tōzai kōshōshi gairon," *SKZ* 8:111–36.

the concept of the Orient was drawn into polemics, pushed toward the right or the left, the top or the bottom of the map, depending on the disposition and the stakes of those who invoked it.[11]

Over the past two centuries these different orients have played important roles in the construction of modern nation-states.[12]

"The East" was important, in fact essential, to the understanding of national culture in Western Europe and Japan. The orients formulated in (European) Oriental studies and (Japanese) *tōyōshi* were necessary for self-comparison, for the extraction of resources (tangible and symbolic), and to offer help. In these orients both groups found a beginning from which they could create a narrative that demonstrated a connection to that which was universal and belonged to their own heritage: as primordial, it was the Origin; as primitive, it demonstrated ties to purity; and as a remote realm, it possessed the proper mystique, to which only certain people could gain access.

Both used the Orient or *tōyō* as the temporal and spatial location for a new beginning. It was from this beginning that the past "emerged" as if it had not yet existed. Eighteenth-century German Oriental scholars such as Friedrich Schlegel and Baron Ferdinand Eckstein, for example, discovered in the Orient (India) the universal, a "primitive revelation," which gave the world a new beginning—centered, of course, on Germany. As Schwab points out, "Germany's only question was whether it would become absorbed in the India revealed by England or whether it would, rather, transform India into a national interest."[13] For German Orientalists, India represented the origins of Germany's universal religion, from which a new philosophy of history emphasizing its future emerged. Japan's *tōyō* played a similar role. Shiratori found in China and Inner Asia the beginnings of Japan's universal spirit, which enabled him to claim equivalence with the West. In other words, using the territory of their own orient, each side sought to define the totality by which a larger world, one of difference, could be understood within

11. Schwab, *Oriental Renaissance*, 1.

12. Schwab describes the important role that the Orient played for Germany: "The period between 1780 and 1830 should be viewed as half a century of young people, all ready to give the world a new beginning: the past that was emerging could not be considered dead, for it advanced under the banner of the future. Fulfillment of the desires of artists and believers was anticipated from it. One of the principal reasons for India's success was that India was not regarded as something to look back on, but rather as something in which to seek the future" (ibid., 221). A similar role of the Orient in British and French thought has been described in Said, *Orientalism*.

13. Schwab, *Oriental Renaissance*, 203. See also Gossman, "History as Decipherment"; and Said, *Orientalism*.

their own present.[14] In this sense, Bakhtin's notion of an internally persuasive discourse is apparent in the way Japanese used many of the same
concepts and methods that Western scholars used to create an orient.
But to paraphrase Bakhtin, *tōyō* was made into Japan's own.

In this endeavor, however, the Japanese quest for equivalence con-
flicted with Western history: both East and West were contending over
the same region for the origin that gave authority to their own philosophy of history. By laying claim to the Asian spirit, Japanese intellectuals sought a new beginning, one which predated that of Europe. Just
as the German Orientalists and philosophers connected Germany to
the primordial beginnings they discovered in India, Japanese scholars
discovered in China and among the Northern barbarians the anonymous seeds of their civilization. This strategy served to equalize the
East and West and also to narrate positivistically the true emergence
of the Japanese present within a universal framework. This idea is, of
course, contradictory: one cannot establish one's own truth and at the
same time claim universality. But this is precisely the problematic that
these Japanese historians confronted. Asia became the object of both
Europe and Japan; the Orient and *tōyō* served as that primordial past
from which both had progressed and would continue to advance. Such
beginnings allowed for a prior existence to which one's own society
could be connected. By demonstrating a connection to the original
nature of man, the possessor of that beginning can create both a narrative that ties the origin to the present and a narrative that distinguishes past from present. The detailed and positivistic research of
what has become known as Orientalism and *tōyōshi* played an important
role in providing the authority for a certain point of view; in fact, it
provided a world vision.

Tōyōshi, then, was able to bring together contradictory ideas. It organized culturally and temporally different societies, the primordial,
primitive, feudal, and modern, into a totalistic framework. *Shina* (and
by extension Asia) and Japan, though culturally distinct and separated
by time, became part of a single cultural unit. As Japan's past, *shina* became part of the same *tōyō*, thus enabling the formulation of a historical
narrative of Japan's development into a modern nation. Yet *tōyōshi* also
provided the explanation for temporally unifying Japan and the West,

14. Sack (*Human Territoriality*, 19) defines the concept of territoriality as "the attempt by an individual or group to affect, influence, or control people, phenomena, and
relationships, by delimiting and asserting control over a geographic area."

however culturally different. The West and Japan had both achieved the state of modernity.

But while *tōyō* provided the vehicle for Japan's claims to equivalence, it also created the potential for sameness between Japan and China as well as the West. It then became necessary to find difference, or uniqueness. This was achieved with a history of Japanese assimilation and transformation of many pasts, and thus Japan's superiority.

Even though late-nineteenth-century Japan considered itself temporally separate from Asia, according to European definitions it was (and is) spatially a part of the Orient. The development of *tōyōshi* thus turned toward the fine distinction both of Japan from Asia and of Japan, as a part of Asia, from Europe. To paraphrase Lowenthal, it was important for Japan to mature from the child and to displace the parent and step-parent. This could be accomplished by using the parent's inspiration, assimilating and transforming that past but not revering and repeating it. Lowenthal concludes, "Only by manipulating the past to one's own purposes could one truly achieve autonomy."[15] The historical framework and the lessons of history that emerged within this discourse now unified those pasts into a history that showed how Japan surpassed the parents.

But the historical search for ties to Asia also revealed a contradiction in this strategy. In Japan, as well as in Europe, history—or what Foucault called genealogy—shows that there is really no definable origin or essence:

If the genealogist refuses to extend his faith in metaphysics, if he listens to history, he finds that there is "something altogether different" behind things: not a timeless and essential secret, but the secret that they have no essence or that their essence was fabricated in a piecemeal fashion from alien forms. . . . What is found at the historical beginning of things is not the inviolable identity of their origin; it is the dissension of other things. It is disparity.[16]

It was this disparity, that of multiple pasts, in the origins of the Japanese (a hopelessly obfuscated issue even today) that led to the mythification of its protohistoric past.

The connection to Asia was important precisely because of these historians' failure to find Japan's origins. Ancient Asia provided that remote past which allowed the Japanese to enshroud their own history in

15. Lowenthal, *The Past Is a Foreign Country,* 72.
16. Foucault, "Nietzsche, Genealogy, History," 142.

mysticism, yet it rang true to most people; it was a history that emphasized Japan's roots in *tōyō* and a uniqueness grounded in the imperial system. As Tsuda's research on the ancient texts shows, Japan's protohistory consisted of myths created by Japan's ancient clans for political purposes. But myths placed within positivistic history are powerful; during and after Tsuda's elaborate studies, these myths have remained. It is easier to reiterate common knowledge, regardless of accuracy, than to challenge it.

To establish these "truths" historians devised intricate and often convoluted theories, under the guise of objectivity, to explain Japan's origins. Inoue Tetsujirō argued that the Japanese came from the South Seas, while Shiratori used his linguistic and etymological research to claim Japan's uniqueness. It was perhaps because of this uncertainty that historians turned to Japan's ancient myths for its origins. The debate between Naitō and Shiratori (or the Universities of Kyoto and Tokyo) over the location of Yamatai became the center of an emerging narrative that facilitated the remythification of Japan's past. Despite important differences, however, the assumptions—the prestige of the imperial system, the continuous line of emperors, the importance of religious ritual, and the worship of this system by the people—showed that the debates were over historical facts that only filled in the gaps of the narrative. The major issues, in contrast, were tacitly agreed upon. In comparison to the pre-Meiji debate, then, the Taishō debate, though involving more participants and generating more paper, contested relatively minor issues. Nevertheless, the significance of these debates cannot be overemphasized, because they incorporated Japan's mythical religious past into the modern study of history.

The result was the objectification of certain notions of what Japan is not and should not become. Because they could not uncover a precise narrative of Japan's past, historians turned to vague notions, the "timeless and essential secrets": *bushidō*, Confucianism, *shintō*, and the *kokutai*, the national essence of Japan. All these provided the objects for a "faith in metaphysics." But because these essences were recently "discovered" or recreated, they had to be newly defined and in turn helped to define Japan increasingly in terms that neutralized problems found within both *tōyō* and the West.

To continue with the family metaphor, the Japanese had two parents who had to be surpassed. Many narratives that described why the Chinese became a stagnant culture depicted the separation of Chinese society from its Confucian ideals, or the Sinification of Confucianism.

Others showed why and how—fortunately for the Japanese—the essence of Confucian teachings was transformed in Japan. The outcome was the conversion of Confucian teachings into an oriental (*tōyō*) ideal. This new Confucianism was suitable to Japan because it fit a vague notion of the Japanese *kokutai*, providing historical proof why the Japanese must not act in certain ways (i.e., selfishly, individualistically, disloyally) lest they follow the wayward path that led the Chinese to stagnation. Here, Japan learned from one of its parents so well that it took possession of the essence of Confucianism, as its harmonious society demonstrated; and in the ultimate display of filiality, it would also protect and help that aged parent, *shina*.

This relation to *shina* was confirmed by Japan's other parent—or more accurately, stepparent—the West. Japanese historians used a developmental framework to prove that the combination of Japan's oriental past and its more recent Western education had enabled Japan to transform itself and surpass its stepparent. According to this narrative, even though Japan had been inferior, Japanese had learned only what was important to better themselves, but not the evils that provided examples of what not to become. Certain parts of their oriental past were thus selected to counter such debilitating Western characteristics as greed, individualism, and corruption.

By making these systems suitable to modern Japan and describing how people should act, these historians were inventing modern traditions. For example, Confucianism, shorn of its revolutionary potential, became the foundation of an ethical ideology that dictated how all Japanese should behave. The irony is that in this use of the past the common people were possibly more Japanese than the elites who defined "Japaneseness." One need only look at the few ethnographies and travelogues that describe Everyman to question the extent to which these "traditional" behaviors were common throughout Japanese society.[17] History authorized the validity of these "traditions" no matter how

17. A number of studies point to a much more varied and less traditionalistic mass Japanese society. Anne Walthall's study of peasant martyrs, for instance, shows how different groups over two centuries have manipulated the image of peasants into that which they believe mass society should be; see "Japanese *Gimin:* Peasant Martyrs in Popular Memory," *American Historical Review* 91 (December 1986), 1076–1102. Irokawa Daikichi, *The Culture of Meiji*, describes a grass-roots tradition in the late nineteenth and early twentieth centuries that was subjugated by the central government's emperor system ideology. The change in behavior of farm village inhabitants toward what is now considered traditional Japanese deportment can be found in Ella Wiswell and Robert J. Smith, *Women of Suyemura* (Chicago: University of Chicago Press, 1982).

different they were from Everyman's culture. What became tradition certainly existed in early Japan, in particular in elite society. The elements of Confucianism and *bushidō* that were incorporated into Japan's present were those aspects that encouraged and assured a passive and loyal population. This popularization of certain types of ideals is not unique to Japan; indeed, it was common in Europe during the nineteenth century as well.[18] But while traditions are not always or necessarily created by elites, by connecting the past and Japan's present history fixed these ideals as inherently Japanese and endowed them with a timeless character.

It would be a mistake, however, to claim that these Japanese intellectuals were interested merely in claiming Japan's uniqueness. Such a strategy differed little from that of the West; one can even see it as a parody of the Western vision of itself. Rather, these scholars accepted the Western division of Orient and Occident, but not the temporal hierarchy with its implications of superiority and inferiority. For them, Japanese difference was immanent. Japanese claims to uniqueness thus incorporated many elements used by Westerners to explain Oriental inferiority but turned them into positive characteristics that accounted for Japan's development.

This strategy raises questions about the role of history in people's efforts to understand other cultures. While most historical research pointed to the diversity of Japan's past and the absence of any one origin or essence, the methodology employed necessitated the elimination of such diversity. Strictly speaking, of course, diversity was not so much eliminated as relegated to predefined positions in order to create a facade of unity and, indeed, uniformity. *Shina* and *tōyō* evoked two complementary images: on the one hand, *shina* deserved praise and admiration as the past, but on the other, it was recognized that Japan had a duty to protect and assist the development of this past, now constituted as *tōyō*.

Tōyōshi has been widely considered an objective, even atheoretical, field of history. But this very belief in objectivity helped to create a framework for a self-serving understanding not only of Asia, but of the world. The order, meanings, and norms embedded within it became transparent. According to Emmanuel Levinas, "Objectivity is not what remains of an implement or a food when separated from the world in which their being comes into play. It is *posited* in a discourse, in a *con-*

18. Eric Hobsbawm, "Mass-producing Traditions: Europe, 1870–1914," in Hobsbawm and Ranger (eds.), *Invention of Tradition*, 263–307.

versation [*entre-tien*] which *proposes* the world."[19] Objectivity requires norms that decide what is and is not to be considered accurate. Such criteria were established in what I have called the discourse on *shina*. In essence, this discourse created a monologue on the history of the modern world, now Eurasia rather than Europe. But this narrative was powerful because it answered for Japan the questions of conflict without drawing any attention to itself: it included variations on social Darwinism that assumed the need for conflict in order to survive; it ordered the nations of the world; it created an ideology that privileged an Asian past based on social harmony; and it allowed for various contingencies. As Geertz writes, "It is . . . the attempt of ideologies to render otherwise incomprehensible social situations meaningful, to so construe them as to make it possible to act purposefully within them, that accounts both for the ideologies' highly figurative nature and for the intensity with which, once accepted, they are held."[20] This new narrative, then, not only explained domestic and international conditions; it also allowed Japanese intellectuals and elite to "act purposely" and gave Japan its modern identity.

Such transparency raises a question about the nature of critical inquiry among academic researchers relative to their own discourse. Because of the difficulty—or impossibility—of ascertaining intention, we can only speculate why these Japanese scholars were blind to the particularity of their work. For one thing, their ability to identify and criticize the weaknesses of Western scholarship prevented them from seeing similar problems in their own work. Their criticism of other histories, rather, implied not only that they would not fall into the same errors, but also that they wrote the correct story. This "correctness" was further supported by methodology, the belief in the possibility of objectivity using science. Lowenthal notes, "Only within the past century or two has describing the past as it actually was become some historians' major commitment. Purged of their predecessors' biases, successive generations have erroneously fancied themselves free of bias."[21] The belief in the scientific nature of history, then, helped to mystify the past. The need for ever more detailed information, in turn, encouraged the fragmentation of research into small units that further convinced scholars of their objectivity and further obscured the ideological structure of which they were a part. Large entities were carved up into

19. Levinas, *Totality and Infinity*, 95–96; italics in the original.
20. Geertz, *Interpretation of Cultures*, 220.
21. Lowenthal, *The Past Is a Foreign Country*, 235.

smaller geographic and temporal units so that one person could describe the contents with exactitude. This fragmentation was evident in the specialization of Shiratori's students, as well as in the proliferation of research organizations devoted to the study of China in the 1930s. Japanese orientalists objectified *tōyō* in the same way that European Orientalists objectified the Orient. And when reality did not correspond to historical "facts," the fault lay in *shina*, not in the research. Hence the attempt to understand a different culture was precluded by the totalization of *shina* within *tōyō*. That culture already was "understood," and the duties of research institutions such as the Tōyō Bunko and even the Research Bureau of the SMR thus became the positioning and affirming of subthemes within that overall framework.

By the 1930s other intellectuals recognized that this monologue obscured understanding and sought to challenge many of the predefined categories that merged *shina*, an other, into *tōyō*, the same. Indeed, many were aware by then of the growing separation between China and Japan's understanding of *shina* and sought to restore a sense of difference, of variability within and among cultures, events, and ideas. Moreover, they increasingly recognized that *shina* facilitated some of the contradictions between Japanese history and contemporary Japanese society.

As the writings of Ozaki and Tachibana indicate, numerous scholars and intellectuals, especially during the 1930s, identified the obstacles embedded within this discourse, pointed to the misunderstanding that the discourse created, and attempted to correct it or extract themselves from it. In a speech delivered in 1975, Takeuchi Yoshimi recalled an incident in 1936 when he and his colleagues sent the twelve-page inaugural issue of their magazine *Chūgoku bungaku geppō* (Chinese Literature Monthly) to their Chinese counterparts. They received in return an unsolicited, voluminous journal, in appreciation, recalled Takeuchi, for their use of the term *chūgoku* rather than the more common *shina*.[22] This recollection indicates well the complexity of the name *shina;* more than the Japanese pronunciation of China, it was a metaphor for a set of terms, a field of knowledge, that defined China. And for at least

22. Takeuchi Yoshimi, *Hōhō to shite no ajia* (Tokyo: Sōjusha, 1978), 28.

these Chinese intellectuals, it was not a definition to their liking. During the 1930s the quest for better relations with China led a few people to realize that the problem lay in the very name that was being used, *shina*. Takeuchi was one of the few who recognized the need for an understanding that did not relegate China to a fixed position defined by Japan. He was also one of the few people in Japan to be appropriately critical, I believe, of both the established scholarship on China and the left-wing traditions of Japanese history.

The problem with Japan's understanding of China, as he explained more thoroughly after the war, had to do with Japan's adaptation of modernity.[23] War came about not because of the incompleteness or failure of Japan's prewar modernization drive, nor because "traditional" or feudal forces upset that process, but because of the very success of modernization. His criticism of modernity led to his recognition of the way modern Japan's *shina* obscured difference and to his support of the Pacific War—not the Fifteen Year War—against the West. The problem, in short, lay in the monologic nature of knowledge in modern societies, both Japan and the West.

Takeuchi's discontent was shared by a number of intellectuals who participated in a 1942 symposium on "overcoming the modern." Kamei Katsuichirō, for example, complained about the specialization and compartmentalization that modernity, science, and the West had wrought on Japan. Because of this foreign thought, he argued, Japanese were now alienated from their own past. Kobayashi Hideo, while confirming that Japan was modern, complained that "conceptions of progressive history inevitably misled modern men and created false expectations by deluding them with a 'poetry of the future.'"[24] Instead, and like earlier Meiji intellectuals such as Okakura and Miyake Setsurei, he identified the ideal of beauty as a timeless norm not subject to the restrictions of history.

Many of the participants in this symposium suggested that the twentieth-century construction of history was a source of Japan's predicament. Historical knowledge, no matter what the intention of the

23. Maruyama Noboru, "Lu Xun in Japan," in *Lu Xun and His Legacy*, ed. Leo Oufan Lee (Berkeley and Los Angeles: University of California Press, 1985), 226–35.
24. H. D. Harootunian, "Visible Discourses/Invisible Ideologies," *South Atlantic Quarterly* 87 (1988): 450–52.

author, can easily misinform as well as inform, and often does more disservice than it contributes to our understanding of others and ourselves. This problem, experienced simultaneously in Europe, is described by Levinas:

> For there to be a separated being, for the totalization of history to not be the ultimate schema of being, it is necessary that death which for the survivor is an end be not only this end; it is necessary that there be in dying another direction than that which leads to the end as to a point of impact in the duration of survivors. Separation designates the possibility of an *existent* being set up and having its own destiny to itself, that is, being born and dying without the place of this birth and this death in the time of universal history being the measure of its reality. Interiority is the very possibility of a birth and a death that do not derive their meaning from history. Interiority institutes an order different from historical time in which totality is constituted, an order where everything is *pending*, where what is no longer possible historically remains always possible.[25]

Levinas, too, was searching for some timeless norm through which people could interact and know themselves outside of history. For him, the face-to-face encounter allows neither side to predetermine what the other is. It is an encounter in which one learns from, gives to, and looks upon one's opposite not as some defined object but as another human being.

One prewar historian who perhaps came closest to identifying the problems embedded in *tōyō* was Tsuda. In a general way, Tsuda's writing paralleled the historical strategies that Shiratori used to construct the notion of *tōyō*. But in his book *Shina shisō to nihon* (Chinese Thought and Japan) and an article, "Tōyō to wa nanka?" (What Is That Which We Call the Orient?), Tsuda properly identified the notion of *tōyō* as a Japanese, not universal, concept. To reconceive the spatial interactions of that realm, Tsuda used time differently, attributing virtually all development to history as a whole rather than assigning discrete characteristics to universalistic patterns, oriental characteristics, and historical circumstances. "Because history is the unfolding of life [*seikatsu no tenkai*], in one life there is one history, and two distinct peoples [*minzoku*] cannot have one history. And where there is no history, there is no culture. Therefore culture is formed through history and develops historically."[26] By emphasizing the historical development of a specific culture, Tsuda questioned both the narrative of *tōyō*

---

25. Levinas, *Totality and Infinity*, 55; italics in the original.
26. Tsuda, *Shina shisō to nihon*, 147.

and the mythification of Japan's origins, which, he believed, confined Japan to ill-suited categories. The concept of *tōyō*, he argued, always places Japan in an inferior position relative to both the West and China. To the West, Japan is Oriental; yet *tōyō* is similar enough to the Western Orient that it allows the placement of Japan within the latter category, again making Japan inferior to the West. To the Chinese, Japan's use of China's past allows them to see Japan as only a derivative of China with Western learning, thus eliminating the need for the Chinese to learn from Japan. This attitude, he stated in 1938, "fosters a misperception of Japan among Chinese and, furthermore, caters to the Sinocentrism [*chūka ishiki*] and Chinese arrogance toward Japanese that, even today, has not disappeared."[27]

To deny the notion of a common oriental culture and the idea that the Japanese and Chinese are the "same culture, same race" (*dōbun, dōshu*), Tsuda argued that Indian and Chinese cultures are completely different, geographically, culturally, and racially: Indian thought is religious and metaphysical, India has myths, and the lives of the people are sensuous (*kannōteki*), whereas Chinese thought is practical and political, China has chronicles, and the people are self-centered and present-oriented. This difference, he stated, is readily apparent to anyone who looks closely at living conditions in China.[28] He did not deny previous contact and transmission between the two cultures, but that contact, he said, was minimal; China accepted only the few parts of Buddhism that accorded with the beliefs of the people. The factual difference between Shiratori and Tsuda on this point is small; yet their interpretations differed considerably: while Shiratori interpreted China's acceptance of Buddhism as proof of a culture of *tōyō*, Tsuda used it as evidence to separate India and China.[29]

Tsuda's critique was part of an attempt to create a different historical narrative of the development of Japan, one dependent on neither China nor the West. He was seeking a narrative that would allow the child to break from its parents completely or, to paraphrase Lowenthal, to assimilate and transform on his own terms, not simply revere and repeat. His criticism was directed at the reverence and reification of both pasts, the West's and China's. He complained,

The appellation *tōyō bunka* [oriental culture] is used because of the opposition to Occidental culture, but in addition, because this opposition is placed in

27. Ibid., 7.
28. Ibid., 171–72.
29. Ibid., 120–49.

Japan, *tōyō bunka* is seen as that of Japan. Those who extol a *tōyō bunka* condemn praise for so-called Western culture. But because it is condemnation of foreign things that have not originated in Japan, we must likewise condemn those Chinese and Indian things that are revered. Since they are similarly foreign, is it not groundless to replace praise for the West with that for India and China? However, the reason for this is that they [i.e., Shiratori and most of his successors] see the cultures of China and India as if they are inherent [*naizai*] within Japan.[30]

In Tsuda's view, Japan did not set out to imitate other cultures in order to develop; rather, he stated, cultures develop from a variety of connections, which generally include contact with other cultures—such as, in Japan's case, China and the West. Thus, by releasing Japan from its dependence on China and the West, Tsuda altered the dichotomy between the Orient and Occident and the accompanying conceptual baggage—traditional/modern, spiritual/material, and backward/advanced.

The potential in Tsuda's deconstruction of *tōyō* was to free Japan from a rigid and fixed concept of itself and its future. His narrative did not attempt to place either the West or China in fixed positions, and he recognized that history is dialogic in that it is shaped by different forces. This he did largely by denying Japan's dependence on the two pasts of China and Europe. A country develops on its own and interacts with other cultures; it does not develop from others. Japanese society and its characteristics should not be conceived in terms of static, essentialistic principles derived from an oriental past. Nor was Japan's conception of the future necessarily related to that narrow path blazed by Western countries. Tsuda seemed to be trying to extract Japan from the dilemma created by his predecessors, for even though the historians of Asia wrote about change, the change that they described was fixed to a course of development based on the past. The irony was that within the concept of *tōyō*, the international change that was being described was informed by history, not necessarily by contemporary events. Tsuda's writings presented the potential that the past could be used in ways quite different from that to which it had been put during the previous thirty years, with important implications for social and foreign policy in Japan.

Although he created a different narrative of Japan's development, Tsuda was still not able to extract Japan from its dilemma vis-à-vis China and the West. He was not a "radical" and was constrained by several factors, most importantly the breadth of the discourse on *shina*,

30. Ibid., 184–85.

the political milieu of Japan, international conditions, and widespread faith in the utility of history. Although he argued that the ancient myths were created for political purposes, to give the emperors an ancient and divine ancestor, he nevertheless continued to maintain that the emperor in fact was divine. Even this questioning of the ancient myths opened him to attacks from nationalists who fervently believed in the mythical religious foundation of the emperor. His trial and imprisonment indicate the potency of mythology and the critical role the discourse played in reifying the imperial system. Moreover, despite his attempt to eliminate China as Japan's past, Tsuda's Japan remained more developed than China; and because modernization (*gendaika*) was widespread in Japan, but quite superficial and limited in China, Tsuda proposed a messianic policy toward China: "If Japan seeks to help develop the culture of China, it should aid that which spreads contemporary [*gendai*] and world culture there."[31] This statement is certainly less forceful than the causative construction used by some of his colleagues. But the main difference between Tsuda and predecessors such as Shiratori and Naitō was that the need to help China now emanated from the universal spread of modern culture, not because *shina* was also oriental. The spread of civilization, however, was the mission of Britain and the United States that Japanese intellectuals had sought to modify.

The end of the Pacific War brought renewed questions about the relation of history, the understanding of China, and Japanese policy. Indeed, much of the self-criticism of prewar and wartime historiography was quite harsh, and admissions are admirable. In the journal *Rekishigaku kenkyū*, for example, an anonymous member wrote the following critique of the journals *Shigaku zasshi* and *Tōyō gakuhō*, two of the major organs that supported Japan's prewar study of *tōyō*:

Tōyō gakuhō, along with *Shigaku zasshi*, is the quintessential official history [*kanfu shigaku*]. However, it is different from *Shigaku zasshi* in that during the war it could feign political transparency. Even all the scholars who were war criminals, such as Katō and Hashimoto, did not espouse ultranationalism through the journal. That is prudence. But these men joined with the militarists in the background and ridiculed the shallowness of public attitudes toward China. Thus, because of this duplicitous character they could not act constructively toward the latter and, conversely, even seemed to strengthen gradually that shallow view of China.[32]

31. Ibid., 199.
32. Quoted from Ogura, *Ware ryūmon ni ari*, 45–46.

What is important here is that during the postwar period several historians did raise questions about the relation of nation-state, historical knowledge, meaning, and objectivity. One can argue that such criticisms did not go far enough. The charge that prewar and wartime Japanese research on China was official and hollow in its claims to be objective, scientific, and nonpolitical does not interrogate the structure within which that research was conducted. This critique could have been the beginning of deeper inquiry into the practice of history in Japan, the meaning and role of objective knowledge, and Japan's identity in the post–World War II era; instead, the writers for *Rekishigaku kenkyū* revived an alternative, still unilinear chronology of Chinese history that had been proposed before the war, with Chinese history divided into two periods: the ancient period up through the T'ang dynasty and the feudal (post-T'ang) period. Regardless whether one agrees with the Marxist influence in this chronology, the very presence of this alternative did revive debate on the interrelation between knowledge and a philosophy of history. The proposed framework was a substitute for the geographical and temporal fragmentation of Chinese history into discrete units—that is, categories that existed in prewar Japan.

Up to approximately 1950 the debates on history, historical facts, and historical methodologies bore some promise that the new issues which were emerging during the 1930s would be seriously addressed. But by 1951, when a number of historical journals, especially those representing prewar positivistic history, began to be republished, much of the prewar historiographical tradition had been revived. In addition to *Tōyō gakuhō* and *Shigaku zasshi*, other comebacks during this period were the *Tōhōgaku*, *Chōsen gakuhō*, *Tōhō shūkyō*, and *Kōkotsugaku*. It is probably no accident that this reversion to earlier modes of discourse coincided with the outbreak of the Korean War, the signing of the San Francisco Peace Treaty and the U.S.-Japan Security Treaty, as well as various markedly conservative trends in Japanese society. A statement symbolizing this revival was written in 1952 in the *Shigaku zasshi* by Enoki, who called for the resuscitation of oriental studies (*tōyōshigaku*):

Historical theory [*riron*] and perspective are certainly essential in investigating historical facts and grasping historical development. However, facts are not born and history is not formed from theory. Theory is induced from historical facts, and theory is abstracted from history. Historical theory acquires the support of historical facts and then everybody pays attention to it. Facts are synthesized through the historical perspective of the investigator and then given structure. Certainly one area of growth and advancement of our postwar historical profession is the understanding and integration of such a commonsensical methodology and the recognition of the necessity of a "rich and fruitful" historiographical structure. In any event, 1951 was the fruitful year that our historical profession gradually regained composure and equanimity and inaugurated new advances.[33]

Here, "rich and fruitful" means that facts gained priority over theory. Enoki's statement indicates that the questioning of the meaning of history and of objectivity and the implications of the prescientific philosophy of history were again relegated to a position secondary to facts. In other words, the students of Shiratori who prioritized historical facts over questions of method and perspective regained preeminence in post–World War II Japanese oriental studies. The reemergence of historical objectivity overwhelmed issues of theory and understanding. But after all, it is much easier to apologize for the past and immerse oneself in a quest for true facts than to grapple with the meaning of history and Japan's self-representation.

33. Quoted from ibid., 48–49.

Works Cited

Anderson, Benedict. *Imagined Communities*. London: Verso, 1983.

Andō Hikotarō. *Nihonjin no chūgokukan*. Tokyo: Keisō Shobō, 1971.

Andō Hikotarō and Yamada Gōichi. "Kindai chūgoku kenkyū to mantetsu chōsabu." *Rekishigaku kenkyū* 270 (November 1962): 28–35.

Asad, Talal. *The Idea of an Anthropology of Islam*. Occasional Paper Series, Center for Contemporary Arab Studies, Georgetown University, Washington, D.C., 1987.

Aston, W. G., trans. *Nihongi*. New ed. Tokyo: Charles E. Tuttle, 1972.

Baker, Keith Michael. *Condorcet: From Natural Philosophy to Social Mathematics*. Chicago: University of Chicago Press, 1975.

Bakhtin, Mikhail M. *The Dialogical Imagination*. Edited by Michael Holquist; translated by Caryl Emerson and Michael Holquist. Austin: University of Texas Press, 1981.

Barnes, Gina. *Protohistoric Yamato: Archeology of the First Japanese State*. Ann Arbor: University of Michigan Center for Japanese Studies, 1988.

Bartholomew, James R. "Science, Bureaucracy, and Freedom in Meiji and Taishō Japan." In *Conflict in Modern Japanese History*, edited by Tetsuo Najita and J. Victor Koschmann, 295–341. Princeton: Princeton University Press, 1982.

Berger, Gordon M. "The Three-dimensional Empire: Japanese Attitudes and the New Order in Asia, 1937–1945." *Japan Interpreter* 12 (Summer 1979): 355–83.

Blussé, Leonard. "Japanese Historiography and European Sources." In *Reappraisals in Overseas History*, edited by P. C. Emmer and H. L. Wesseling, 193–222. Leiden, Neth.: Leiden University Press, 1979.

Bowen, Roger. *Rebellion and Democracy in Meiji Japan*. Berkeley and Los Angeles: University of California Press, 1980.

Bowler, Peter. *The Invention of Progress*. London: Basil Blackwell, 1989.

Brace, C. Loring. "Reflections on the Face of Japan: A Multivariate Craniofacial and Odontometric Perspective." *American Journal of Physical Anthropology* 78 (1989): 93–113.

Braisted, William, trans. *Meiroku Zasshi*. Cambridge, Mass.: Harvard University Press, 1976.

Bryce, James. "The Relations of History and Geography." *Contemporary Review* 49 (March 1886): 426–43.

Buckle, Henry Thomas. *History of Civilization in England*. Vol. 1. London: Longmans, Green, 1908.

Certeau, Michel de. *Heterologies: Discourse on the Other*. Translated by Michael Massumi. Minneapolis: University of Minnesota Press, 1986.

Chang, Han-yu, and Ramon H. Myers. "Japanese Colonial Development Policy in Taiwan, 1895–1906: A Case of Bureaucratic Entrepreneurship." *Journal of Asian Studies* 22 (1963): 433–49.

Chatterjee, Partha. *Nationalist Thought and the Colonial World: A Derivative Discourse*. London: Zed Books, 1986.

Clifford, James, and George Marcus, eds. *Writing Cultures: The Poetics and Politics of Ethnography*. Berkeley and Los Angeles: University of California Press, 1986.

Crowley, James B. "Intellectuals as Visionaries of the New Asian Order." In *Dilemmas of Growth in Prewar Japan*, edited by James W. Morley, 319–73. Princeton: Princeton University Press, 1971.

Dale, Peter. *The Myth of Japanese Uniqueness*. London: St. Martin's Press, 1986.

de Bary, Wm. Theodore, Wing-tsit Chan, and Chester Tan. *Sources of Chinese Tradition*. New York: Columbia University Press, 1960.

Duus, Peter. "Whig History, Japanese Style: The Min'yūsha Historians and the Meiji Restoration." *Journal of Asian Studies* 33 (May 1974): 415–36.

Egami Namio. *Kiba minzoku kokka: nihon kodaishi e no apurochi*. Tokyo: Chūō Kōronsha, 1967.

Enoki Kazuo. *Tōyō bunko no rokujūnen*. Tokyo: Tōyō Bunko, 1977.

———. *Yōroppa to ajia*. Tokyo: Daitō Shuppansha, 1983.

Esthus, Raymond A. "The Changing Concept of the Open Door, 1899–1910." *Mississippi Valley Historical Review* 46 (1959): 435–54.

Fabian, Johannes. *Time and the Other: How Anthropology Makes Its Object*. New York: Columbia University Press, 1983.

Fogel, Joshua. "Japanese Literary Travelers in Prewar China." *Harvard Journal of Asiatic Studies* 49 (December 1989): 575–602.

———. *Politics and Sinology: The Case of Naitō Kōnan (1866–1934)*. Cambridge, Mass.: Harvard University Press, 1984.

Foucault, Michel. *The Archeology of Knowledge*. Translated by A. M. Sheridan Smith. New York: Pantheon Books, 1972.

———. "Nietzsche, Genealogy, History." In *Language, Counter-Memory, Practice*, edited by Donald F. Bouchard, translated by Donald F. Bouchard and Sherry Simon, 139–64. Ithaca, N.Y.: Cornell University Press, 1977.

————. *The Order of Things: An Archeology of the Human Sciences*. Translated by Alan Sheridan. New York: Vintage Books, 1973.

Fukuzawa Yukichi. *An Outline of a Theory of Civilization*. Translated by David A. Dilworth and G. Cameron Hurst. Tokyo: Sophia University, 1973.

————. *Fukuzawa Yukichi zenshū*. 21 vols. Tokyo: Iwanami Shoten, 1958–63.

Fujita Shōzō. *Tennōsei kokka no shihai genri*. 2d ed. Tokyo: Miraisha, 1983.

Geertz, Clifford. *The Interpretation of Cultures*. New York: Basic Books, 1973.

Gluck, Carol. *Japan's Modern Myths: Ideology in the Late Meiji Period*. Princeton: Princeton University Press, 1985.

————. "The People in History: Recent Trends in Japanese Historiography." *Journal of Asian Studies* 38 (November 1978): 25–50.

Goi Naohiro. *Kindai nihon to tōyōshigaku*. Tokyo: Aoki Shoten, 1976.

Gossman, Lionel. "History as Decipherment: Romantic Historiography of the Discovery of the Other." *New Literary History* 18 (Autumn 1986): 23–58.

Guizot, François. *The History of Civilization from the Fall of the Roman Empire to the French Revolution*. Translated by William Hazitt. 3d U.S. ed. Vol. 1. New York: D. Appleton, 1874.

Habermas, Jürgen. *Knowledge and Human Interests*. Translated by Jeremy J. Shapiro. Boston: Beacon Press, 1971.

Hamerow, Theodore S. "The Bureaucratization of History." *American Historical Review* 94 (June 1989): 654–60.

Hara Kakuten. *Gendai ajia kenkyū seiritsu shiron*. Tokyo: Keisō Shobō, 1984.

Harootunian, H. D. "The Functions of China in Tokugawa Thought." In *The Chinese and the Japanese*, edited by Akira Iriye, 9–36. Princeton: Princeton University Press, 1980.

————. "Introduction: A Sense of an Ending and the Problem of Taishō." In *Japan in Crisis*, edited by Bernard S. Silberman and H. D. Harootunian, 3–28. Princeton: Princeton University Press, 1974.

————. "Visible Discourses/Invisible Ideologies." *South Atlantic Quarterly* 87 (1988): 445–474.

Hashikawa Bunsō. "Japanese Perspectives on Asia: From Dissociation to Coprosperity." In *The Chinese and the Japanese*, edited by Akira Iriye, 328–55. Princeton: Princeton University Press, 1980.

Hatada Takashi. "Nihon ni okeru tōyōshigaku no dentō." *Rekishigaku kenkyū* 270 (November 1962): 28–35.

————. *Nihonjin no chōsenkan*. Tokyo: Chikuma Shobō, 1969.

Hattori Unokichi. "Gendai ni okeru jukyō no igi." *Shibun* 1 (1919): 19–36.

————. "Jukyō to demokurashii." *Shibun* 1 (1919): 327–35.

Hayashi Taisuke. "Futatabi Gyō, Shun, Wu no massatsuron ni tsuite." *Tōa kenkyū* 2 (1912): 22–26.

————. "Gyō, Shun, Wu no massatsuron ni tsuite." *Kangaku* 2 (1911): 863–74; *Tōa kenkyū* 1 (1911): 20–25 and 30–34. [*Kangaku* was renamed *Tōa kenkyū* in 1911.]

——. "Tōyōgaku ni okeru kinji no shinsetsu ni tsuite." *Tōyō tetsugaku* 17 (January 1910): 28–35.

Hegel, Georg Wilhelm Friedrich. *The Philosophy of History*. Translated by J. Sibree. New York: Dover, 1956.

Hirano Yoshitarō. "Shina kenkyū ni taisuru futatsu no michi." *Yuibutsuron kenkyū* 20 (June 1934): 5–27.

Ho, Samuel Pao-San. "Colonialism and Development: Korea, Taiwan, and Kwantung." In *The Japanese Colonial Empire, 1895–1945*, edited by Ramon H. Myers and Mark R. Peattie, 347–86. Princeton: Princeton University Press, 1983.

Hobsbawm, Eric. "Mass-producing Traditions: Europe, 1870–1914." In *The Invention of Tradition*, edited by Eric Hobsbawm and Terence Ranger, 263–307. Cambridge: Cambridge University Press, 1983.

Hobsbawm, Eric, and Terence Ranger, eds. *The Invention of Tradition*. Cambridge: Cambridge University Press, 1983.

Hulsewe, A.F.P. *China in Central Asia: The Early Stage—125 B.C.–A.D. 23*. Leiden, Neth.: E. J. Brill, 1979.

Ienaga Saburō. *Nihon no kindai shigaku*. Tokyo: Nihon Hyōron Shinsha, 1957.

Ikei, Masaru. "Japan's Response to the Chinese Revolution of 1911." *Journal of Asian Studies* 25 (February 1966): 213–27.

——. "Ugaki Kazushige's View of China and His China Policy, 1915–1930." In *The Chinese and the Japanese*, edited by Akira Iriye, 199–219. Princeton: Princeton University Press, 1980.

Ilyon. *Samguk Yusa: Legends and History of the Three Kingdoms of Ancient Korea*. Translated by Tae-Hung Ha and Grafton K. Mintz. Seoul: Yonsei University Press, 1972.

Inoue Tetsujirō. "Jinshu, gengo oyobi shūkyō nado no hikaku ni yori, nihonjin no ichi o ronsu." *Tōhō kyōkai hōkoku* 20 (December 1892): 27–53.

——. *Tetsugaku to shūkyō*. Tokyo: Kōdōkan, 1915.

——. "Tōyōshigaku no kachi." *Shigakkai zasshi* 2 (November 1891): 704–17; (December 1891): 788–98; (January 1892): 1–14.

——. "Waga kokutai to kazoku no seido." *Tōa no hikari* 6 (1911): 1–19.

Iriye, Akira. *Power and Culture: The Japanese-American War, 1941–1945*. Cambridge, Mass.: Harvard University Press, 1981.

Irokawa Daikichi. *The Culture of Meiji*. Edited by Marius Jansen. Princeton: Princeton University Press, 1985.

Itō Takeo. *Mantetsu ni ikite*. Rev. ed. Tokyo: Chikuma Shobō, 1982.

Jansen, Marius B. *Japan and China: From War to Peace, 1894–1972*. Chicago: Rand McNally, 1975.

Kamachi, Noriko. "The Chinese in Meiji Japan: Their Interactions with the Japanese Before the Sino-Japanese War." In *The Chinese and the Japanese*, edited by Akira Iriye, 58–73. Princeton: Princeton University Press, 1980.

Katō Shūzō. *Kikō zuisō: tōyō no kindai*. Tokyo: Asahi Sensho, 1977.

Keene, Donald. *Dawn to the West: Japanese Literature of the Modern Era*. New York: Holt, Rinehart & Winston, 1984.

Keightley, David N. *Sources of Shang History.* Berkeley and Los Angeles: University of California Press, 1978.

———. "The Late Shang State: When, Where, What?" In *The Origins of Chinese Civilization,* edited by David N. Keightley, 523–64. Berkeley and Los Angeles: University of California Press, 1983.

Kiley, Cornelius J. "State and Dynasty in Archaic Yamato." *Journal of Asian Studies* 23 (November 1973): 25–49.

Koschmann, J. Victor. *The Mito Ideology: Discourse, Reform, and Insurrection in Late Tokugawa Japan, 1790–1864.* Berkeley and Los Angeles: University of California Press, 1987.

Krieger, Leonard. *Ranke: The Meaning of History.* Chicago: University of Chicago Press, 1977.

Kume Kunitake. "Nihon fukuin no enkaku." *Shigakkai zasshi* 1 (December 1889–February 1890): no. 1, 15–20; no. 2, 10–17; no. 3, 9–17.

Kuwabara Takeo, ed. *Nihon no meicho.* Tokyo: Chūkō Shinsho, 1962.

———. *Rekishi no shisō.* Gendai nihon shisō taikei, vol. 27. Chikuma Shobō, 1965.

LaCapra, Dominick. *History and Criticism.* Ithaca, N.Y.: Cornell University Press, 1985.

Lacouperie, Terrien de. *Western Origin of the Early Chinese Civilization: From 2300 B.C. to 200 A.D.* 1894; repr. Osnabrück: Otto Zeller, 1966.

Lakoff, George. *Women, Fire, and Dangerous Things: What Categories Reveal About the Mind.* Chicago: University of Chicago Press, 1987.

Lakoff, George, and Mark Johnson. *Metaphors We Live By.* Chicago: University of Chicago Press, 1980.

Laroui, Abdallah. *The Crisis of the Arab Intellectual: Traditionalism or Historicism.* Translated by Diarmid Cammell. Berkeley and Los Angeles: University of California Press, 1976.

Lattimore, Owen. *Inner Asian Frontiers of China.* New York: American Geographical Society, 1940.

Ledyard, Gary. "Galloping Along with the Horseriders: Looking for the Founders of Japan." *Journal of Japanese Studies* 1 (1975): 217–54.

Lee, Sophia. "The Foreign Ministry's Cultural Agenda for China: The Boxer Indemnity." In *The Japanese Informal Empire in China, 1895–1937,* edited by Peter Duus, Ramon H. Myers, and Mark R. Peattie, 272–306. Princeton: Princeton University Press, 1989.

Levenson, Joseph R. *Confucian China and Its Modern Fate: A Trilogy.* Berkeley and Los Angeles: University of California Press, 1958.

Levenson, Joseph R., and Franz Schurmann. *China: An Interpretive History.* Berkeley and Los Angeles: University of California Press, 1967.

Levin, N. Gordon, Jr. *Woodrow Wilson and World Politics: America's Response to War and Revolution.* London: Oxford University Press, 1968.

Levinas, Emmanuel. *Totality and Infinity: An Essay on Exteriority.* Translated by Alphonso Lingis. Pittsburgh: Duquesne University Press, 1969.

Lowenthal, David. *The Past Is a Foreign Country.* Cambridge: Cambridge University Press, 1985.

Manuel, Frank E. "From Equality to Organicism." *Journal of the History of Ideas* 17 (January 1956): 54–69.

Marshall, Byron K. "Growth and Conflict in Japanese Higher Education, 1905–1930." In *Conflict in Modern Japanese History,* edited by Tetsuo Najita and J. Victor Koschmann, 276–94. Princeton: Princeton University Press, 1982.

———. "Professors and Politics: The Meiji Academic Elite." *Journal of Japanese Studies* 3 (Winter 1977): 71–97.

Maruyama Noboru. "Lu Xun in Japan." In *Lu Xun and His Legacy,* edited by Leo Ou-fan Lee, 226–35. Berkeley and Los Angeles: University of California Press, 1985.

Masubuchi Tatsuo. "Nihon no kindaishi ni okeru chūgoku to nihon." *Shisō* 462 (1963): 1–18; 468 (1963): 863–76.

———. "Rekishi ninshiki ni okeru shōkoshugi to genjitsu hihan." In *Rekishika no dōjidai shiteki kōsatsu ni tsuite,* 171–224. Tokyo: Iwanami Shoten, 1983.

Masui Tsuneo. "Naitō Kōnan to Yamaji Aizan." In *Kindai nihon to chugoku, jō,* edited by Takeuchi Yoshimi and Hashikawa Bunsō, 283–98. Tokyo: Asahi Shinbunsha, 1974.

Matsumoto Sannosuke. "The Idea of Heaven: A Tokugawa Foundation for Natural Rights Theory." In *Japanese Thought in the Tokugawa Period, 1600–1868,* edited by Tetsuo Najita and Irwin Scheiner, 181–99. Chicago: University of Chicago Press, 1978.

Mayer, Arno J. *Political Origins of the New Diplomacy, 1917–1918.* New Haven: Yale University Press, 1959.

Miller, Frank O. *Minobe Tatsukichi: Interpreter of Constitutionalism in Japan.* Berkeley and Los Angeles: University of California Press, 1965.

Miller, Roy Andrew. *Origins of the Japanese Language.* Seattle: University of Washington Press, 1980.

Miyanishi Yoshio. *Mantetsu chōsabu to Ozaki Hotsumi.* Tokyo: Aki Shobō, 1983.

Miyazaki Ichisada. "Chūgoku jōdai no toshikokka to sono bochi." *Tōyōshi kenkyū* 28 (December 1969): 265–82; 29 (December 1970): 147–52.

Miyoshi, Masao. *As We Saw Them: The First Japanese Embassy to the United States (1860).* Berkeley and Los Angeles: University of California Press, 1979.

Myers, Ramon H. "Japanese Imperialism in Manchuria and the South Manchurian Railway Company, 1906–1933." In *Japanese Informal Empire in China, 1895–1937,* edited by Peter Duus, Ramon H. Myers, and Mark R. Peattie, 101–32. Princeton: Princeton University Press, 1989.

Naitō Kōnan. *Naitō Kōnan zenshū.* 14 vols. Tokyo: Chikuma Shobō, 1969–76.

———. "Tōyō bunka to wa nanzo ya?" In *Rekishi no shisō,* edited by Kuwabara Takeo, Gendai nihon shisō taikei, 27:201–13. Tokyo: Chikuma Shobō, 1965.

Najita, Tetsuo. "Intellectual Change in Early Eighteenth-Century Tokugawa Japan." *Journal of Asian Studies* 34 (August 1975): 931–44.

———. "Introduction: A Synchronous Approach to the Study of Conflict in Modern Japanese History." In *Conflict in Modern Japanese History,* edited by Tetsuo Najita and J. Victor Koschmann, 3–21. Princeton: Princeton University Press, 1983.

———. "Some Reflections on Idealism in the Political Thought of Yoshino Sakuzo." In *Japan in Crisis,* edited by Bernard S. Silberman and H. D. Harootunian, 29–66. Princeton: Princeton University Press, 1974.

Najita, Tetsuo, and J. Victor Koschmann, eds. *Conflict in Modern Japanese History.* Princeton: Princeton University Press, 1983.

Najita, Tetsuo, and Irwin Scheiner, eds. *Japanese Thought in the Tokugawa Period.* Chicago: University of Chicago Press, 1978.

Naka Michiyo isho. Tokyo: Dai Nihon Tosho, 1915.

Nakae Chomin. *A Discourse by Three Drunkards on Government.* Translated by Nobuko Tsukui. New York: Weatherhill, 1984.

Nakane Chie. *Japanese Society.* Berkeley and Los Angeles: University of California Press, 1970.

———. "Shakai kōzōronteki ajiakan." *Ajia,* September 1976, 268–88.

Nakayama Kyūshirō. *Shigaku oyobi tōyōshi no kenkyū.* Tokyo: Kenbunkan, 1935.

Nisbet, Robert A. "Conservatism and Sociology." *American Journal of Sociology* 58 (1952): 167–75.

———. "The French Revolution and the Rise of Sociology in France." *American Journal of Sociology* 49 (1943): 156–64.

Nitobe, Inazo. "Japanese Colonialization." *Asiatic Review* 16 (January 1920): 113–21.

Noma Kiyoshi. "Chūgoku nōson kankō chōsa no kikaku to jisseki." *Rekishi hyōron* 170 (October 1964): 1–15.

Nomura Kōichi. "Kindai nihon ni okeru jukyō no shisō no hensen ni tsuite no oboegaki." In *Kindai chūgoku kenkyū,* edited by Kindai chūgoku kenkyū iinkai, 3:233–70. Tokyo: Tokyo Daigaku Shuppansha, 1959.

———. *Kindai nihon no chūgoku ninshiki.* Tokyo: Kenbun Shuppan, 1981.

Notehelfer, Frederick G. *Kōtoku Shūsui: Portrait of a Japanese Radical.* Cambridge: Cambridge University Press, 1971.

Novick, Peter. *That Noble Dream.* Cambridge: Cambridge University Press, 1988.

Numata Jiro. "Shigeno Yasutsugu and the Modern Tokyo Tradition." In *Historians of China and Japan,* edited by W. G. Beasley and E. G. Pulleyblank, 264–87. London: Oxford University Press, 1961.

Ogura Yoshihiko. *Ware ryūmon ni ari.* Tokyo: Rōkei Shoten, 1974.

Oka Yoshitake. "Generational Conflict After the Russo-Japanese War." In *Conflict in Modern Japanese History,* edited by Tetsuo Najita and J. Victor Koschmann, 197–225. Princeton: Princeton University Press, 1982.

Okamoto, Shumpei. "Ishibashi Tanzan and the Twenty-one Demands." In *The Chinese and the Japanese,* edited by Akira Iriye, 184–98. Princeton: Princeton University Press, 1980.

Okakura Tenshin. *The Ideals of the East.* 1904; Rutland, Vt.: Charles E. Tuttle, 1970.

Ono Kazuko. "Shimoda Utako to Hattori Unokichi." In *Kindai nihon to chūgoku,* edited by Takeuchi Yoshimi and Hashikawa Bunsō, 201–21. Tokyo: Asahi Shinbunsha, 1974.

Ozaki Hotsumi. *Gendai shinaron.* Tokyo: Keisō Shobō, 1964

Ozawa Eiichi. *Kindai nihon shigakushi no kenkyū: Meiji hen.* Tokyo: Yoshikawa Kōbunkan, 1968.

———. "Meiji keimōshugi rekishi to Miyake Yonekichi." *Shichō* 70 (November 1959): 1–28.

Peattie, Mark R. "Japanese Attitudes Toward Colonialism, 1895–1945." In *The Japanese Colonial Empire, 1895–1945,* edited by Ramon H. Myers and Mark R. Peattie, 80–127. Princeton: Princeton University Press, 1984.

Peel, J.D.Y., ed. *Herbert Spencer: On Social Evolution.* Chicago: University of Chicago Press, 1972.

Philippi, Donald L., trans. *Kojiki.* Tokyo: University of Tokyo Press, 1968.

Polanyi, Karl. *The Great Transformation.* 1944; Boston: Beacon Press, 1957.

Pollack, David. *The Fracture of Meaning.* Princeton: Princeton University Press, 1986.

Pulleyblank, E. G. "The Chinese and Their Neighbors in Prehistoric and Early Historic Times." In *The Origins of Chinese Civilization,* edited by David N. Keightley, 413–66. Berkeley and Los Angeles: University of California Press, 1983.

Pyle, Kenneth B. *The New Generation in Meiji Japan.* Stanford: Stanford University Press, 1970.

———. "The Technology of Japanese Nationalism: The Local Improvement Movement, 1900–1918." *Journal of Asian Studies* 33 (1973): 51–65.

Reynolds, Douglas. "Training Young China Hands: Tōa Dōbun Shōin and Its Precursors, 1886–1945." In *The Japanese Informal Empire in China, 1895–1937,* edited by Peter Duus, Ramon H. Myers, and Mark R. Peattie, 210–71. Princeton: Princeton University Press, 1989.

Riisu Rudōhi. "*Shigakkai zasshi* ni tsuite iken." Translated by Ogawa Kinjirō. *Shigakkai zasshi* 1 (April 1890): 1–14.

Rohlen, Thomas P. *Japan's High Schools.* Stanford: Stanford University Press, 1983.

Rosaldo, Renato. "Imperialist Nostalgia." *Representations* 26 (Spring 1989): 107–22.

Sack, Robert David. *Human Territoriality: Its Theory and History.* Cambridge: Cambridge University Press, 1986.

Said, Edward. *Orientalism.* New York: Pantheon Books, 1978.

———. *The World, the Text, and the Critic.* Cambridge, Mass.: Harvard University Press, 1983.

Sakai Yūkichi. "Meiji kenpō to dentōteki kokakan." In *Nihon kindai hōshi kōgi,* edited by Ishii Shirō, 61–93. Tokyo: Seirin Shoin, 1973.

Schmidt, Nathaniel. "Early Oriental Studies in Europe and the Work of the American Oriental Society, 1842–1922." *Journal of the American Oriental Society* 43 (1922): 1–14.

Schwab, Raymond. *The Oriental Renaissance.* Translated by Gene Patterson-Black and Victor Reinking. New York: Columbia University Press, 1984.

Shigeno Yasutsugu. "Shigaku ni jūji suru mono wa sono kokoro shikō shihei narazarubekarazu." *Shigakkai zasshi* 1 (December 1889): 1–5.

Shiratori Kurakichi. "The Japanese Numerals." *Memoirs of the Research Department of the Tōyō Bunko* 9 (1937): 1–78.

———. "Kōdō no konpongi ni tsuite." *Kōdō* 344 (November 1920): 2–17.

———. "Kōka to nihon kokuminsei." *Kōko* 3 (May 1907): 29–32.

———. "The Legend of the King Tung-ming, the Founder of Fu-yu-kuo." *Memoirs of the Research Department of the Tōyō Bunko* 10 (1938): 31–39.

———. "Mansen shiron." *Taihō*, April 1921, 57–64.

———. "The Queue Among the Peoples of North Asia." *Memoirs of the Research Department of the Tōyō Bunko* 4 (1929): 1–69.

———. "Rekishi to chishi no kankei." *Shigakkai zasshi* 1 (December 1889): 56–64.

———. "Rekishi to jinketsu." *Shigakkai zasshi* 2 (January 1890): 5–9.

———. "Shihitsu no kyokuchi." *Bunshō sekai* 3 (January 1908): 64–69.

———. "Shinkoku kakumei no zento to waga kuni no taido." *Tōyō keizai shinpō*, November 25, 1911, 746–48.

———. *Shiratori Kurakichi zenshū*. 10 vols. Tokyo: Iwanami Shoten, 1969–71.

———. "Taisei no gakusha ga indo jimanshu de aru to shōsuru hokuteki seii no shurui ni tsuite." *Shigaku zasshi* 11 (December 1900): 117–21.

———. "Tsuitōkai ni okeru Shiratori hakushi kōen." *Gakushūin hōninkai zasshi* 88 (December 1914): 33–43.

———. "Waga kokuminsei no kenka Tōgō gensui." *Kokuhon* 17 (July 1934): 31–33.

Silberman, Bernard. "The Bureaucratic State in Japan: The Problem of Authority and Legitimacy." In *Conflict in Modern Japanese History*, edited by Tetsuo Najita and J. Victor Koschmann, 226–57. Princeton: Princeton University Press, 1982.

Smith, Warren W. *Confucianism in Modern Japan*. Tokyo: Hokuseido Press, 1959.

Sōseki Natsume. *Botchan*. Translated by Umeji Sasaki. Rutland, Vt.: Charles E. Tuttle, 1968.

Stone, Lawrence. Review of *The New History and the Old*, by Gertrude Himmelfarb. *New York Review of Books*, December 17, 1987, 59–62.

Sudman, Seymour, and Norman M. Bradburn. *Asking Questions*. San Francisco: Jossey-Bass, 1982.

Sugimoto Naojirō. "Honpō ni okeru tōyōshigaku no seiritsu ni tsuite." *Rekishi to chiri* 21 (April 1928): 413–42.

Szczesniak, Boleslaw. "The Kōtaiō Monument." *Monumenta Nipponica* 7 (January 1951): 242–68.

Tagore, Rabindranath. *Nationalism*. 1917; Madras: Macmillan India, 1985.

Tai Chi-t'ao. *Nihonron*. Translated by Ichikawa Hiroshi. Tokyo: Shakai Shisōsha, 1970.

Takada Shinji. *Nihon jukyōshi*. Tokyo: Chijin Shokan, 1941.

Takeuchi Yoshimi. *Chūgoku o shiru tame ni*. 3 vols. Tokyo: Chikuma Shobō, 1967.

———. *Hōhō to shite no ajia.* Tokyo: Sōjusha, 1978.

Tam, Yue-him. "In Search of the Oriental Past: The Life and Thought of Naitō Kōnan (1866–1934)." Ph.D. diss., Princeton University, 1975.

Tam, Yun-tai. "Rationalism Versus Nationalism: Tsuda Sōkichi." In *History in the Service of the Japanese Nation,* edited by John S. Brownlee, 165–88. Toronto: Joint Centre on Modern East Asia, 1983.

Todorov, Tzvetan. *The Conquest of America.* Translated by Richard Howard. New York: Harper Colophon, 1984.

———. *Mikhail Bakhtin: The Dialogical Principle.* Translated by Wlad Godzich. Minneapolis: University of Minnesota Press, 1984.

Tōkyō daigaku hyakunenshi, bukyokushi. Vol 1. Tokyo: Tōkyō Daigaku Shuppankai, 1986.

Tōkyō teikoku daigaku gakujutsu daikan, sōsetsu-bungakubu. Tokyo: Tōkyō Teikoku Daigaku, 1942.

Tōyō Bunko. *Tōyō bunko jūgonen shi.* Tokyo: Tōyō Bunko, 1939.

Tsuda Sōkichi. *Shina shisō to nihon.* Tokyo: Iwanami Shinsho, 1938.

———. "Shiratori hakushi shōden." *Tōyōgakuhō* 29 (January 1944): 325–87.

———. *Tsuda Sōkichi zenshū.* Tokyo: Iwanami Shoten, 1961.

Tsunoda, Ryusaku, W. Theodore deBary, and Donald Keene, eds. *Sources of Japanese Tradition.* New York: Columbia University Press, 1958.

Tsurumi, E. Patricia. *Japanese Colonial Education in Taiwan, 1895–1945.* Cambridge, Mass.: Harvard University Press, 1977.

Uyenaka, Shuzo. "The Textbook Controversy of 1911: National Needs and Historical Truth." In *History in the Service of the Japanese Nation,* edited by John S. Brownlee, 94–120. Toronto: Joint Centre on Modern East Asia, 1983.

Vološinov, V. N. *Marxism and the Philosophy of Language.* Translated by Ladislav Matejka and I. R. Titunik. New York: Seminar Press, 1973.

Walthall, Anne. "Japanese *Gimin:* Peasant Martyrs in Popular Memory." *American Historical Review* 91 (December 1986): 1076–1102.

Ward, Robert, and Sakamoto Yoshikazu, eds. *Democratizing Japan: The Allied Occupation.* Honolulu: University of Hawaii Press, 1987.

White, Hayden. *The Content and the Form.* Baltimore: Johns Hopkins Press, 1987.

———. *Metahistory: The Historical Imagination in Nineteenth-Century Europe.* Baltimore: Johns Hopkins University Press, 1973.

Wiswell, Ella, and Robert J. Smith. *Women of Suyemura.* Chicago: University of Chicago Press, 1982.

Wolf, Eric R. *Europe and the People Without History.* Berkeley and Los Angeles: University of California Press, 1982.

Wray, Harry. "China in Japanese Textbooks." In *China and Japan: Search for Balance Since World War I,* edited by Alvin D. Coox and Hilary Conroy, 115–31. Santa Barbara, Calif.: ABC-Clio, 1978.

Yamada Gōichi. *Mantetsu chōsabu.* Tokyo: Nikkei Shinsho, 1977.

Yamaji Aizan. *Shinaron.* Tokyo: Minyūsha, 1916.

Yoshikawa Kōjirō, ed. *Tōyōgaku no sōshishatachi.* Tokyo: Kōdansha, 1976.

Young, John. *The Location of Yamatai: A Case Study in Japanese Historiography, 720–1945*. Baltimore: Johns Hopkins University Press, 1958.

―――. *The Research Activity of the South Manchurian Railway Company, 1907–1945*. New York: Columbia University Press, 1966.

Yü, Ying-shih. *Trade and Expansion in Han China*. Berkeley and Los Angeles: University of California Press, 1967.

Index

Compositor:	BookMasters
Text:	Galliard 10/13
Display	Galliard
Printer:	Maple-Vail Book Mfg. Group
Binder:	Maple-Vail Book Mfg. Group